SB

Shojo Beat

yona of the Dawn

29

Story & Art by
Mizuho Kusanagi

YONA OF THE DAWN

Story Thus Far

Hak

One of the greatest heroes in the nation, known as the "Thunder Beast." He'd obeyed King Il's orders and became bodyguard to his childhood friend, Yona. He walks away from his position as general in order to protect his tribe.

Yona

While on the run, this princess of Kohka comes to the realization that she's spent her life being protected by other people. She sets out to locate the Four Dragons in order to protect herself and the people who are most important to her.

Su-won

A young scion of the royal bloodline and king of Kohka. To keep Kohka safe from invasion by the Kai Empire to the north or the nations of Xing and Sei to the south, he is trying to create a powerful nation by uniting and ruling over the Five Tribes.

Keishuk

Having helped Su-won take the throne, he's now the king's advisor. When he learns that Yona is still alive and that the Four Dragon Warriors really exist, he fears they will threaten Kohka's status quo.

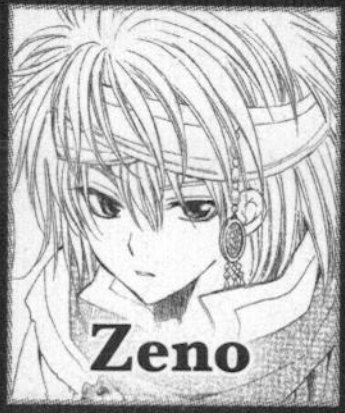
Zeno

The Yellow Dragon of the Four Dragon Warriors. He has the power of a dragon in his body—the power of immortality! He is one of the first Dragons who served the Crimson Dragon King, and he finally met Yona after many years of waiting.

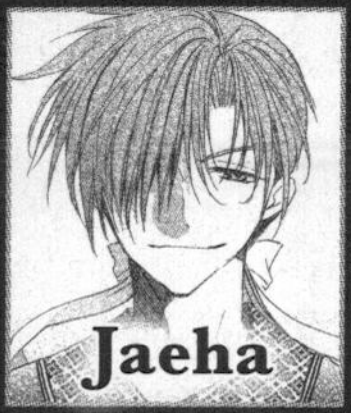
Jaeha

The Green Dragon of the Four Dragon Warriors. With the power of a dragon in his right leg, he can leap to tremendous heights. He loves freedom and hates the idea of being tied down to duty as one of the Four Legendary Dragons.

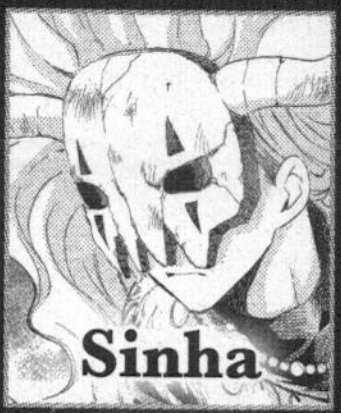
Sinha

The Blue Dragon of the Four Dragon Warriors. With the power of a dragon in his eyes, he can paralyze anyone he looks at. He grew up being hated and feared for his incredible power.

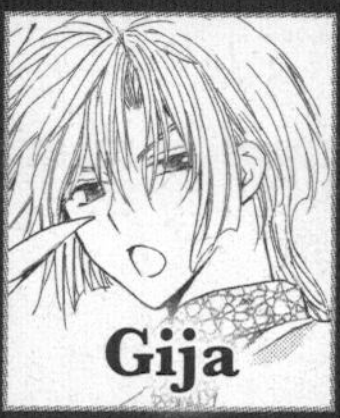
Gija

The White Dragon, one of the Four Dragon Warriors. His right hand contains a dragon's might and is more powerful than ten men. He adores Yona and finds fulfillment in his role as one of the Four Legendary Dragons.

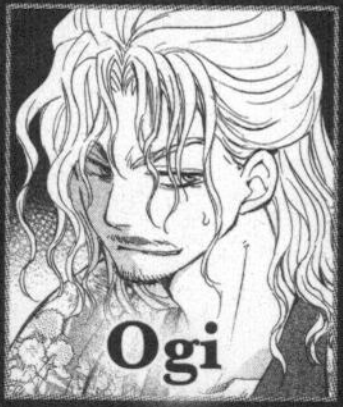
Ogi

An informant from Kohka. He traveled with Yona to confirm the rumors about the Four Dragon Warriors. He also knew Yona and Hak when they were children.

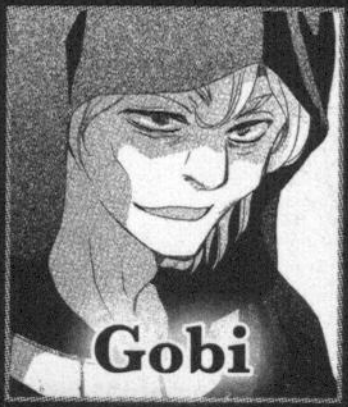
Gobi

A priest from Xing. He went to the Kai Empire after being driven out of Xing. He's trying to gain control of Yona and the Four Dragon Warriors.

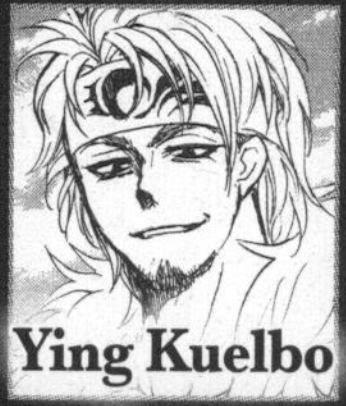
Ying Kuelbo

The ambitious king of the Tuuli Tribe in North Kai. He controls Sen Province in the Kai Empire.

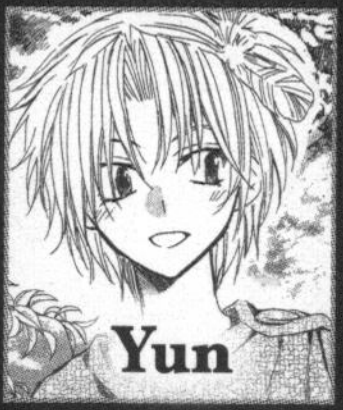
Yun

A mouthy pretty boy, he has a lot of practical knowledge and takes good care of others. He is like a mother to Yona and her friends.

The Four Dragon Warriors… In the Age of Myths, a dragon god took on human form and founded a nation. As the Crimson Dragon King, he was the first ruler of the Kingdom of Kohka. Four other dragons shared their blood with humans so that they could protect him. Those warriors became known as the Four Legendary Dragons, or the Four Dragon Warriors, and their power has been passed down for generations.

STORY

Yona, the princess of the Kingdom of Kohka, was raised by her kind, loving father, King Il. She has deep feelings for her cousin Su-won, a companion since childhood. On her 16th birthday, she sees her father being stabbed to death—by Su-won!

Driven from the palace, Yona and Hak meet a priest named Ik-su who tells Yona a prophecy that leads her to gather the Four Dragon Warriors together. Yona then decides to take up arms and defend her nation with the Four Dragon Warriors at her side.

War between Xing and Kohka is narrowly averted thanks to Yona and her friends. After this tension lifts, Hak tells Yona the truth about his feelings for her.

The Fire Tribe, devout followers of the Crimson Dragon King, learn about Yona and the Legendary Dragons thanks to their assistance against the Kai Empire attack. When Keishuk, Su-won's right-hand man, arrives in Saika Palace, he has Fire Tribe Chief Kyo-ga ask the Four Dragons and Hak to assist them in battle. Although he feels conflicted, Hak agrees to help. Later, while Hak is elsewhere, Ogi arrives in search of Yona and her friends.

*The Kingdom of Kohka is a coalition of five tribes: Fire, Water, Wind, Earth and Sky. The throne is held by the tribe with the greatest influence, so the current royal family are of the Sky Tribe. The royal capital is Kuuto. Each tribe's chief also holds the rank of general, and the Meeting of the Five Tribes is the nation's most powerful decision-making body.

Yona of the Dawn
Volume 29

CONTENTS

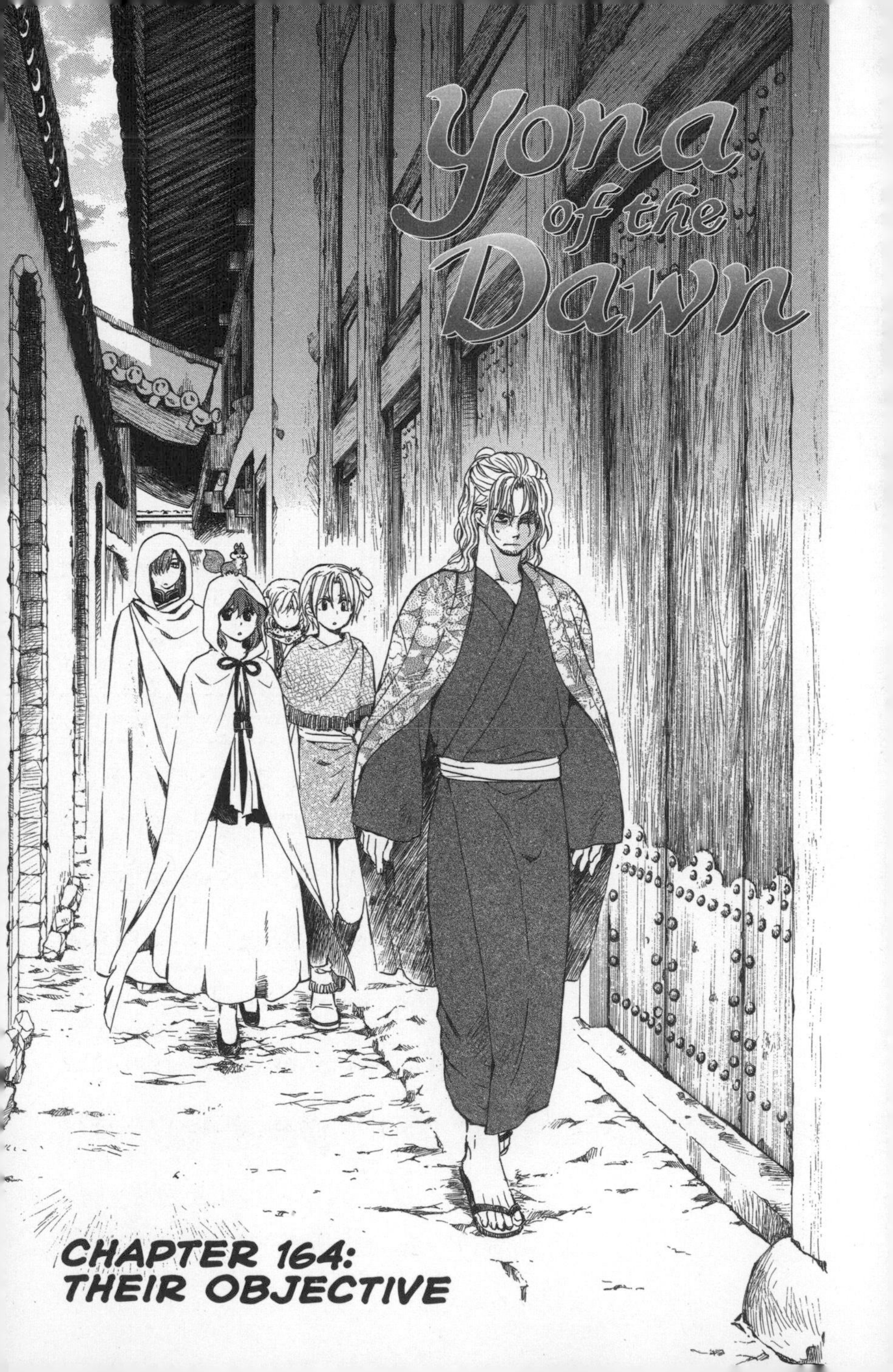
Yona of the Dawn
CHAPTER 164:
THEIR OBJECTIVE

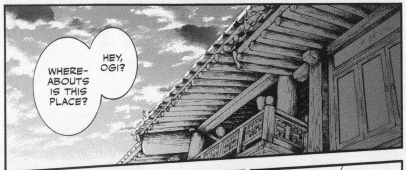

HEY, OGI?
WHERE-ABOUTS IS THIS PLACE?
WE SHOULDN'T GO TOO FAR.
AH... WE'RE ALMOST THERE.
"WE KNOW YOU'VE BEEN WORKING WITH THAT GIRL."
THTHUMP

Yona of the Dawn

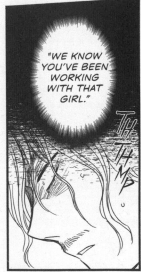

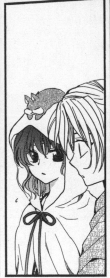

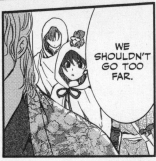

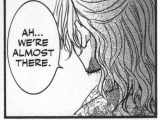

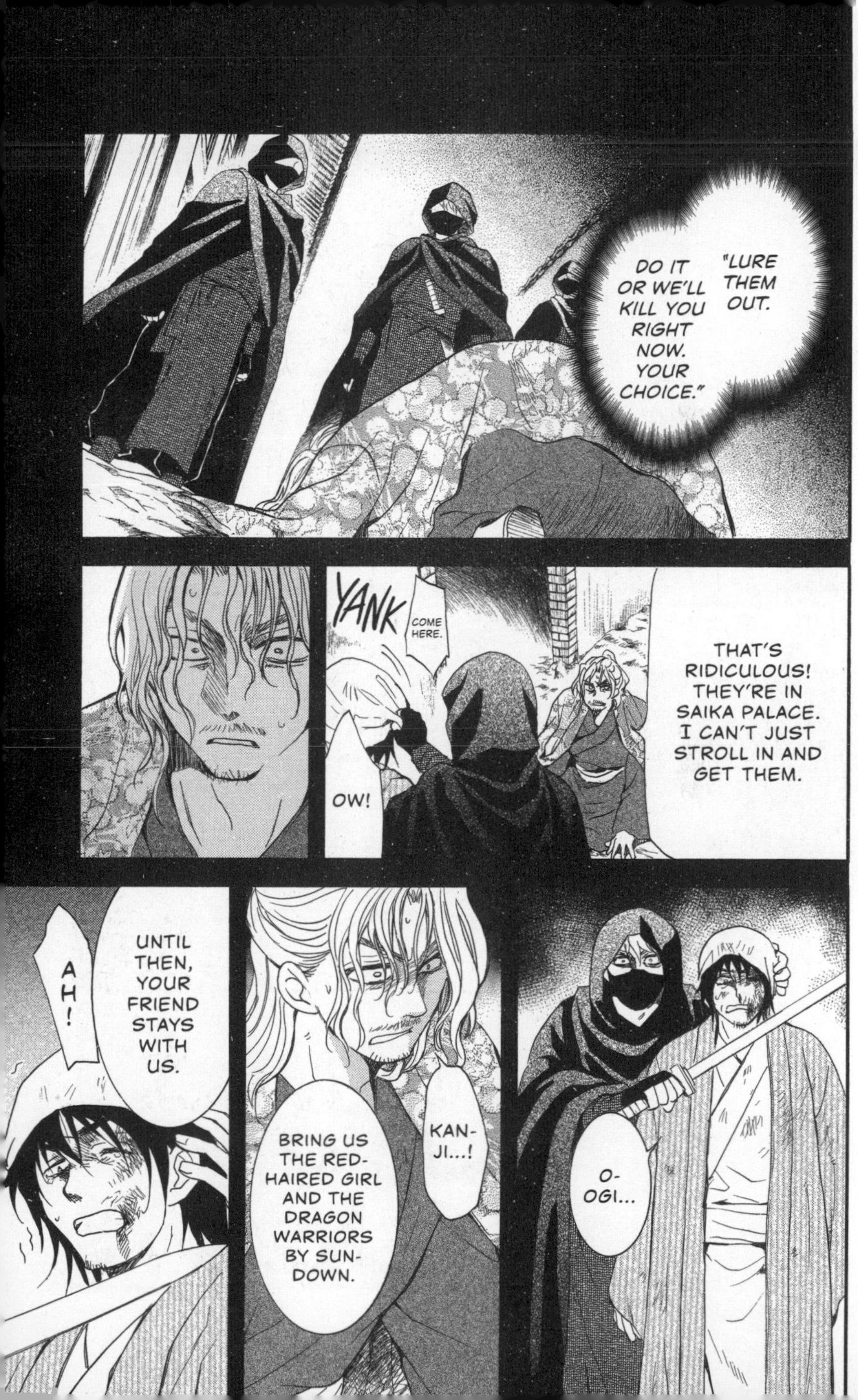
"LURE THEM OUT.
DO IT OR WE'LL KILL YOU RIGHT NOW. YOUR CHOICE."
THAT'S RIDICULOUS! THEY'RE IN SAIKA PALACE. I CAN'T JUST STROLL IN AND GET THEM.
YANK
COME HERE.
OW!
O-OGI...
KAN-JI...!
BRING US THE RED-HAIRED GIRL AND THE DRAGON WARRIORS BY SUN-DOWN.
UNTIL THEN, YOUR FRIEND STAYS WITH US.
AH!

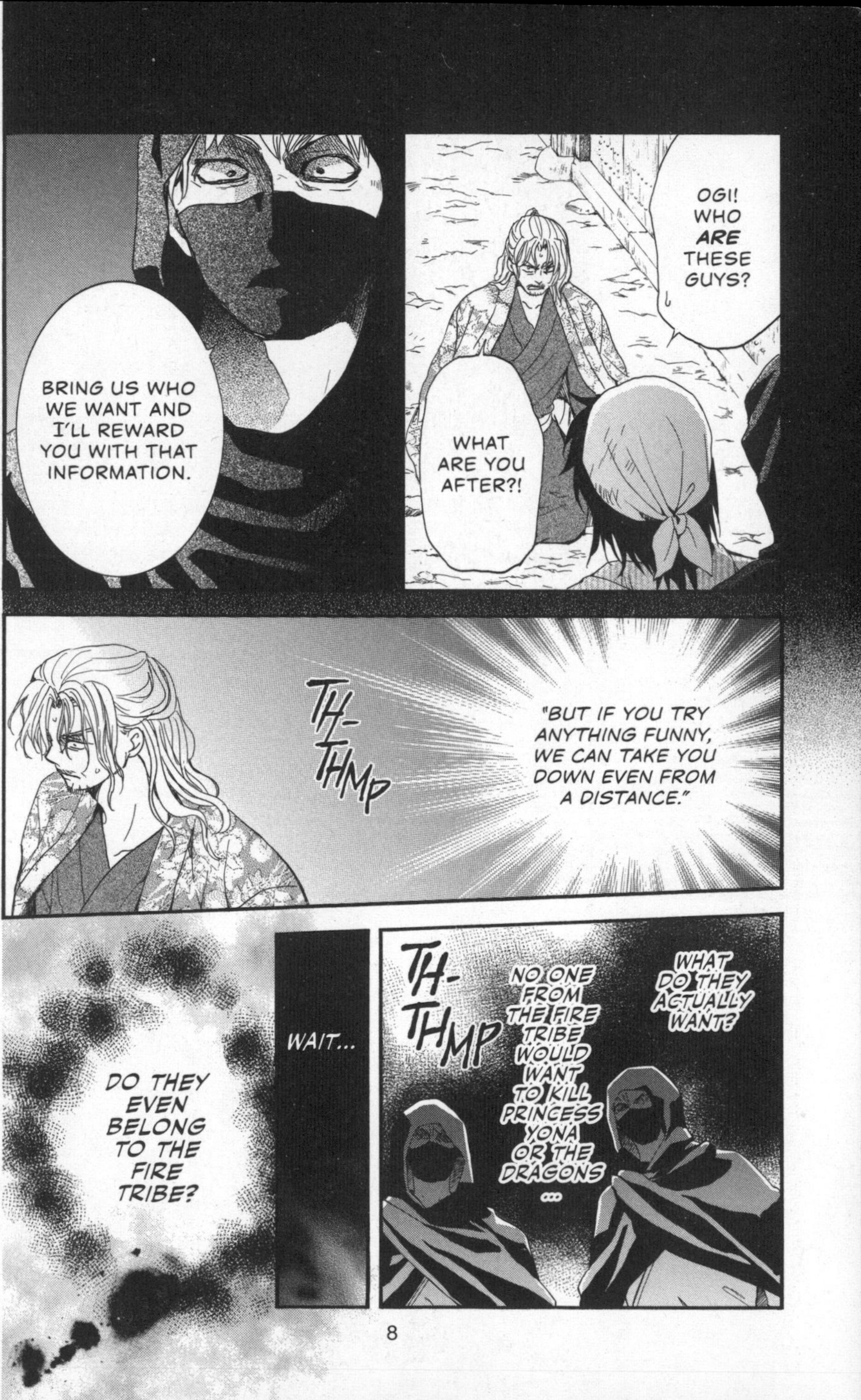

OGI! WHO ARE THESE GUYS?
WHAT ARE YOU AFTER?!
BRING US WHO WE WANT AND I'LL REWARD YOU WITH THAT INFORMATION.
"BUT IF YOU TRY ANYTHING FUNNY, WE CAN TAKE YOU DOWN EVEN FROM A DISTANCE."
TH-THMP
WHAT DO THEY ACTUALLY WANT?
NO ONE FROM THE FIRE TRIBE WOULD WANT TO KILL PRINCESS YONA OR THE DRAGONS...
TH-THMP
WAIT...
DO THEY EVEN BELONG TO THE FIRE TRIBE?

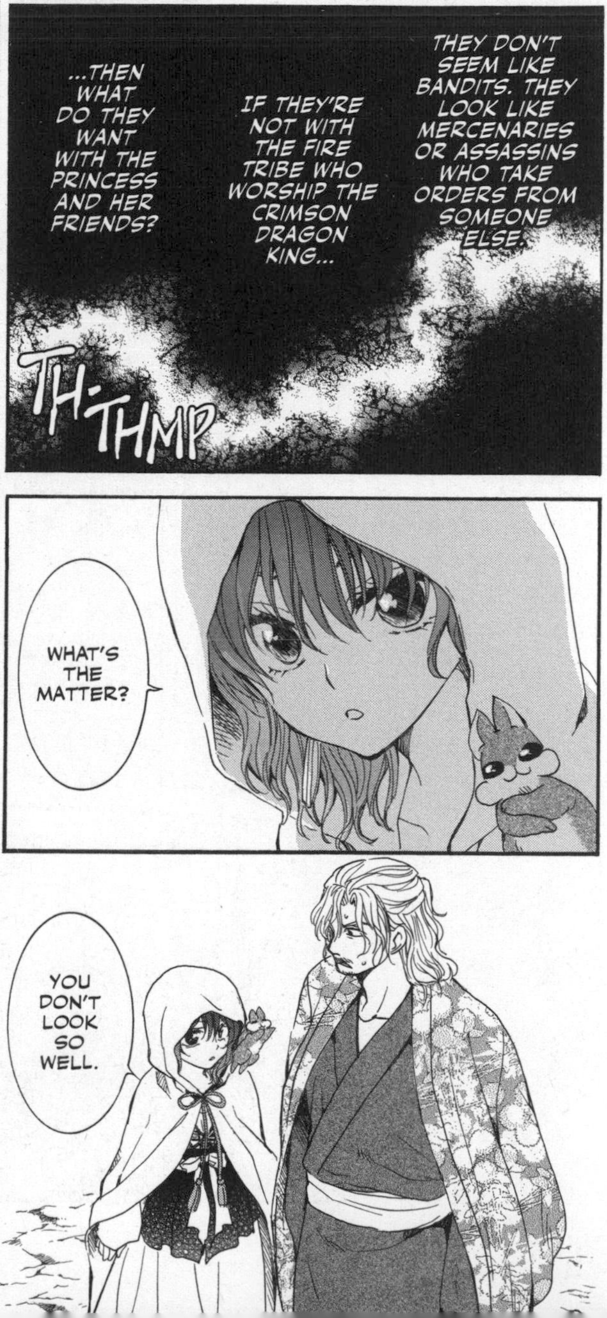
THEY DON'T SEEM LIKE BANDITS. THEY LOOK LIKE MERCENARIES OR ASSASSINS WHO TAKE ORDERS FROM SOMEONE ELSE.
IF THEY'RE NOT WITH THE FIRE TRIBE WHO WORSHIP THE CRIMSON DRAGON KING...
...THEN WHAT DO THEY WANT WITH THE PRINCESS AND HER FRIENDS?
TH-THMP
WHAT'S THE MATTER?
YOU DON'T LOOK SO WELL.

Hello! Thank you very much for picking up Yona volume 29.

I'm so glad my readers liked the fan book I put out last year!

I've heard from some people who've only recently started reading Yona. Please check out the fan book! It's got sketches, comics and illustrations.

In the fan book Q&A, I said that I was hooked on flavored nori seaweed, but now I'm hooked on toasted nori. The nori my assistant got from Ariake Sea in Saga was especially tasty. I've bought a ton of it and snack on it during work.

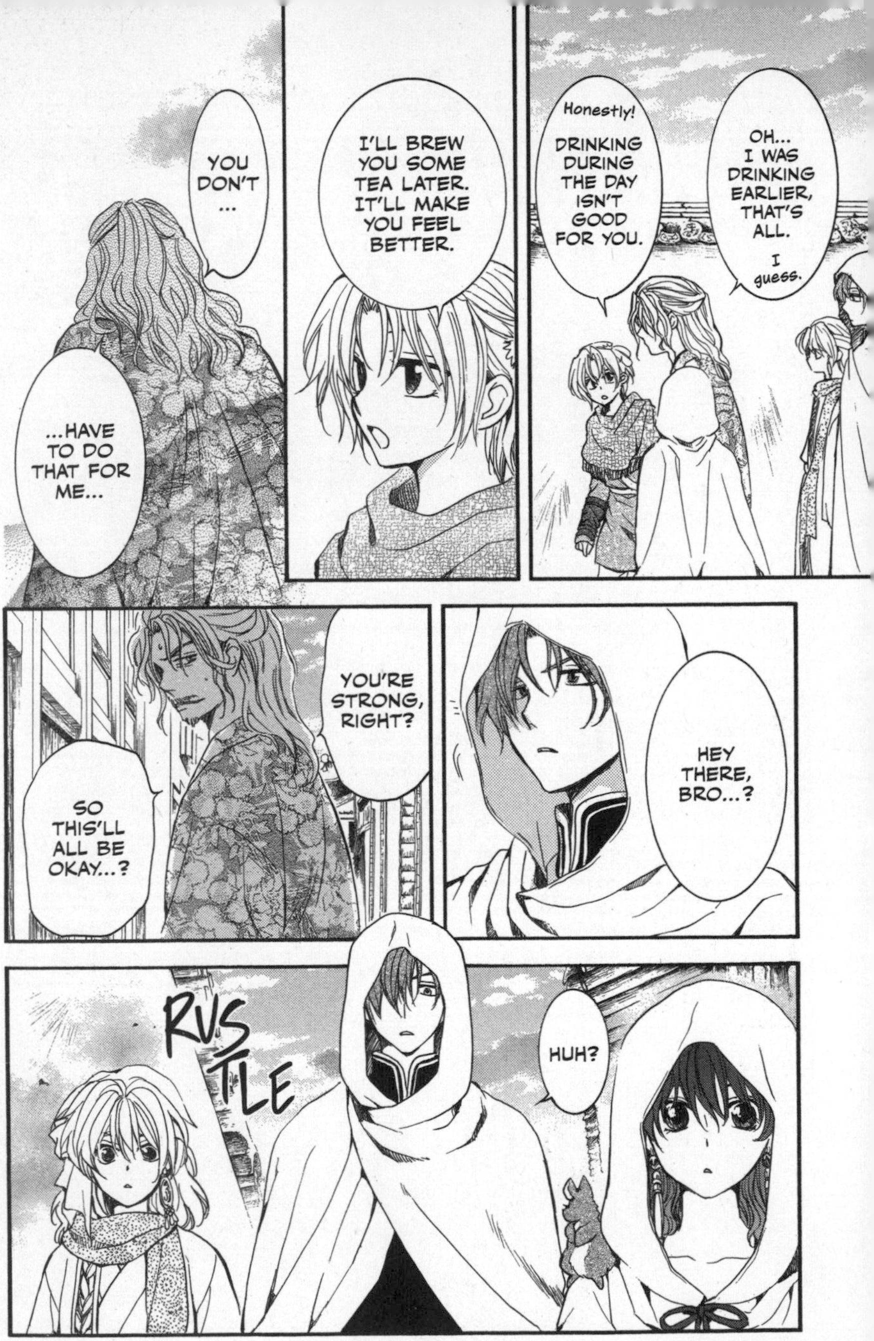
OH... I WAS DRINKING EARLIER, THAT'S ALL.
I guess.
Honestly!
DRINKING DURING THE DAY ISN'T GOOD FOR YOU.
I'LL BREW YOU SOME TEA LATER. IT'LL MAKE YOU FEEL BETTER.
YOU DON'T ...
...HAVE TO DO THAT FOR ME...
HEY THERE, BRO...?
YOU'RE STRONG, RIGHT?
SO THIS'LL ALL BE OKAY...?
HUH?
RUSTLE

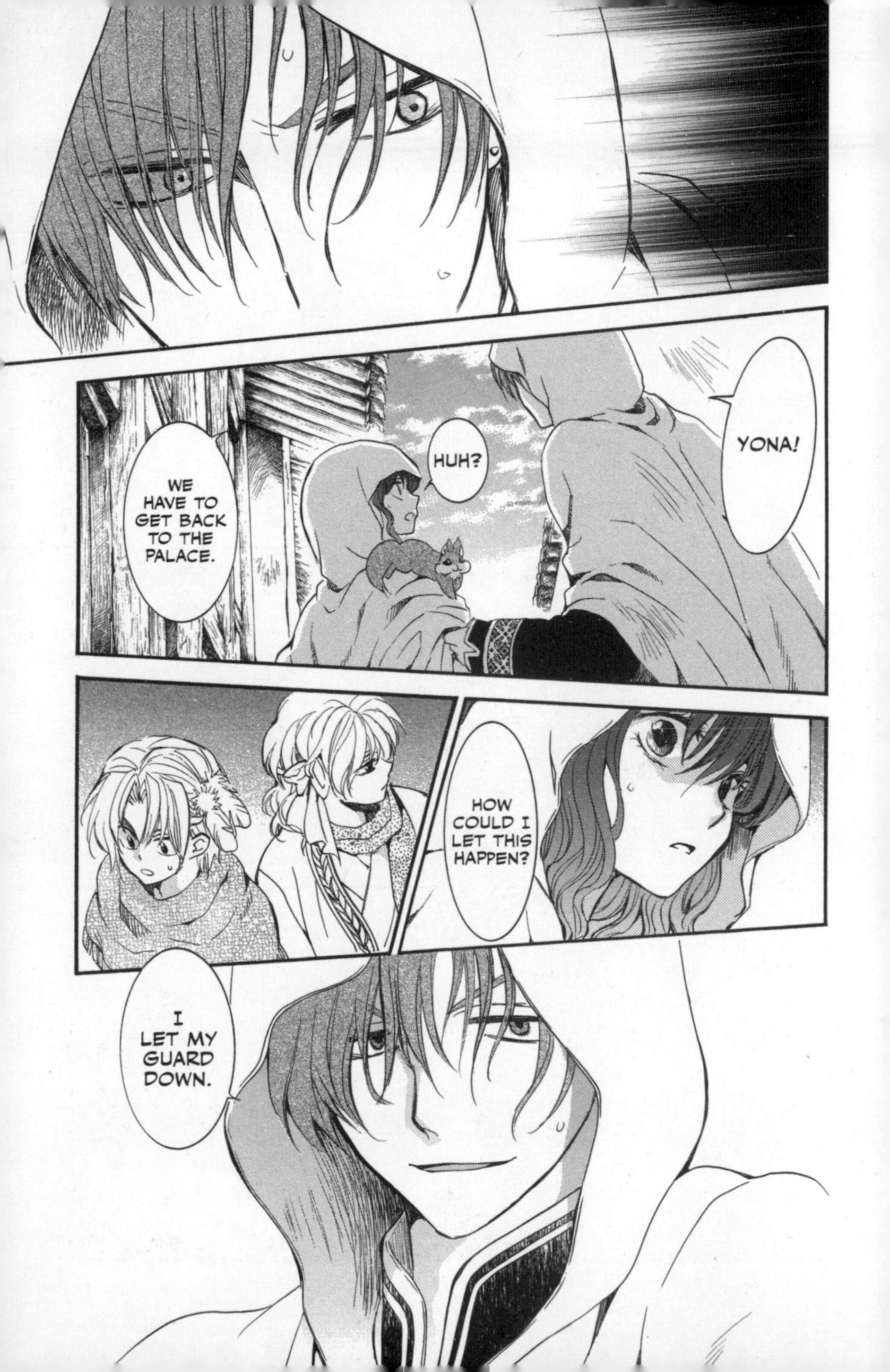
YONA!
HUH?
WE HAVE TO GET BACK TO THE PALACE.
HOW COULD I LET THIS HAPPEN?
I LET MY GUARD DOWN.

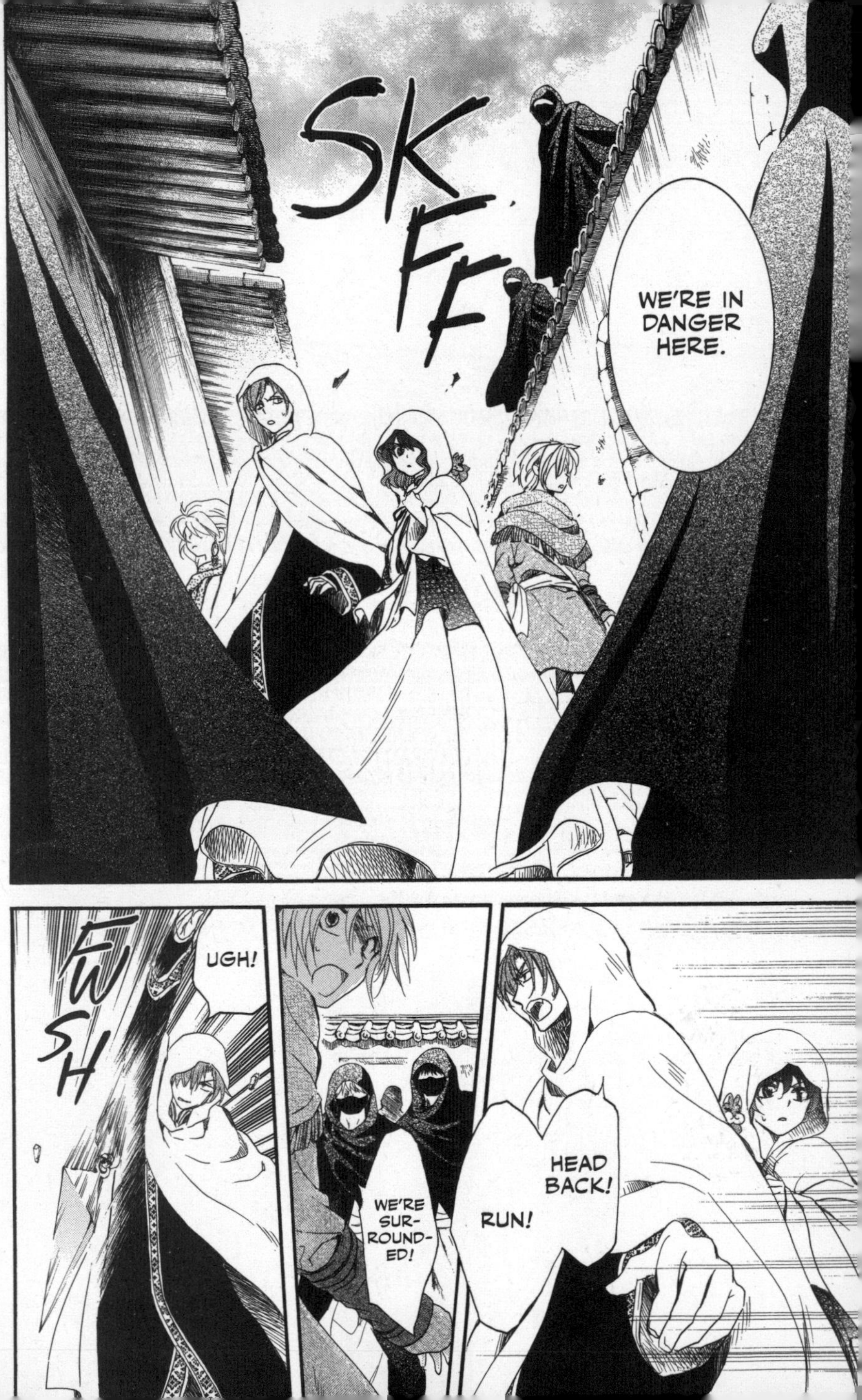
SKFF
WE'RE IN DANGER HERE.
HEAD BACK!
RUN!
WE'RE SUR-ROUND-ED!
UGH!
FWSH

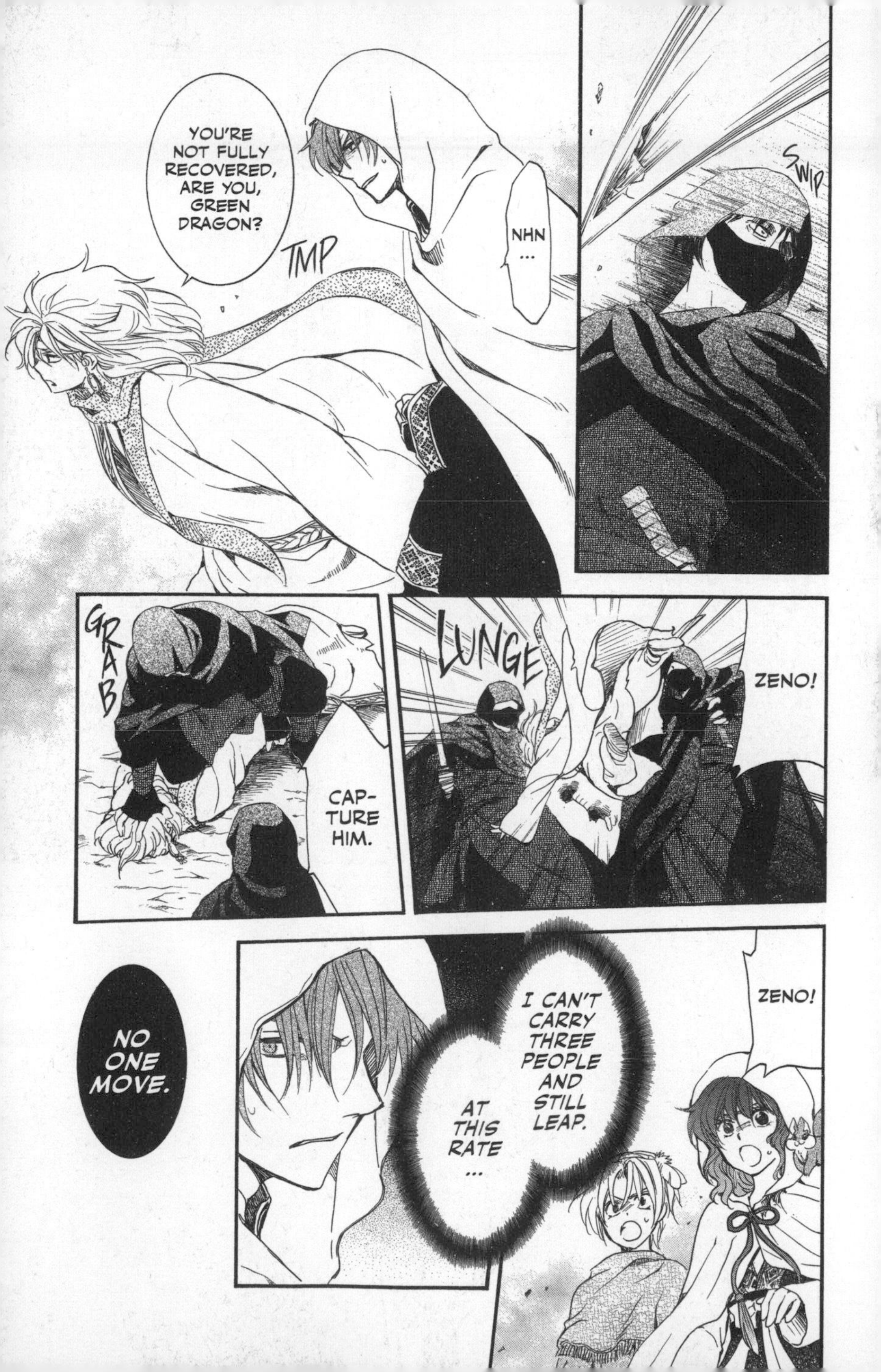
SWIP
NHN ...
YOU'RE NOT FULLY RECOVERED, ARE YOU, GREEN DRAGON?
TMP
ZENO!
LUNGE
GRAB
CAP-TURE HIM.
ZENO!
I CAN'T CARRY THREE PEOPLE AND STILL LEAP.
AT THIS RATE ...
NO ONE MOVE.

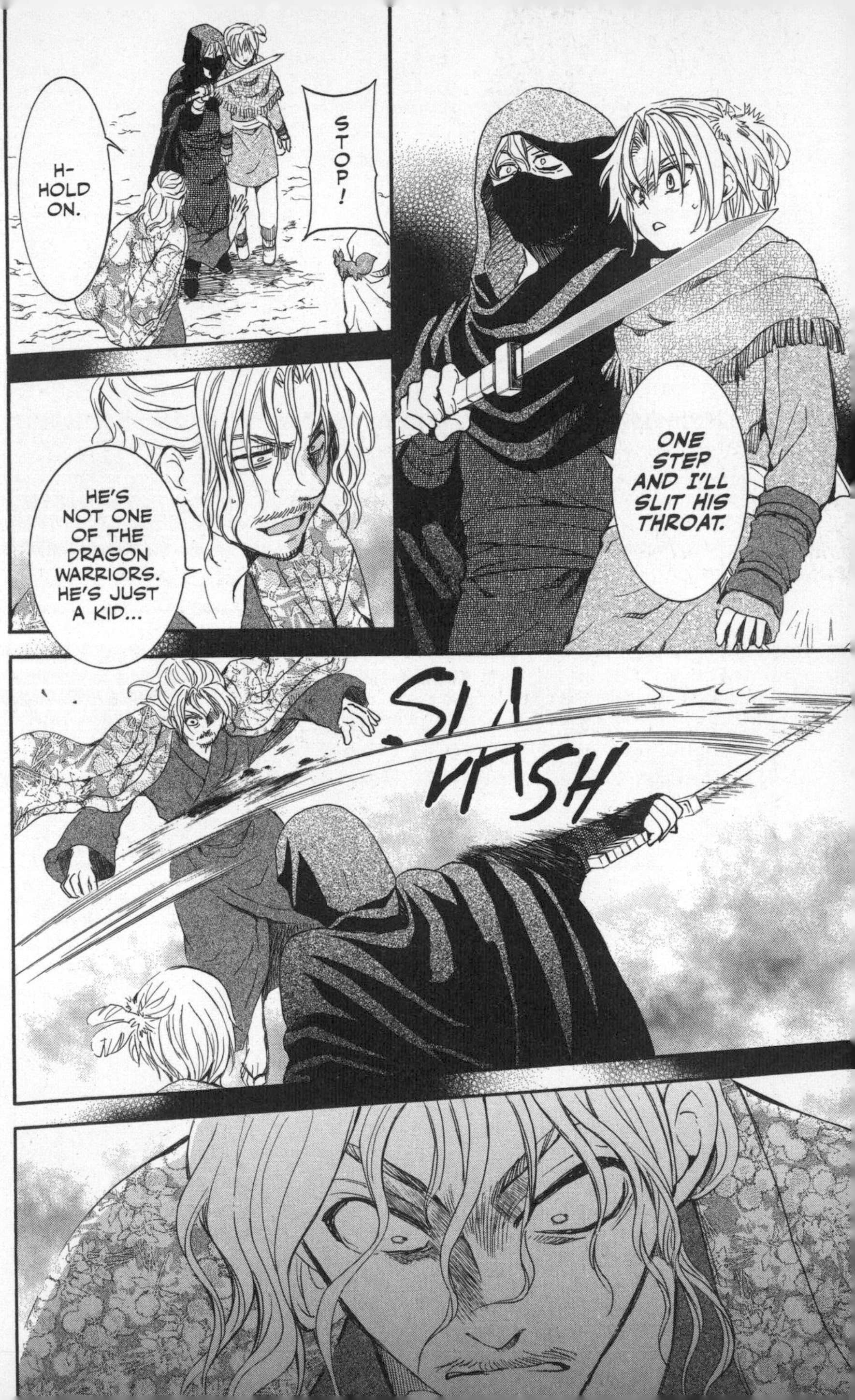
ONE STEP AND I'LL SLIT HIS THROAT.
STOP!
H-HOLD ON.
HE'S NOT ONE OF THE DRAGON WARRIORS. HE'S JUST A KID...
SLASH

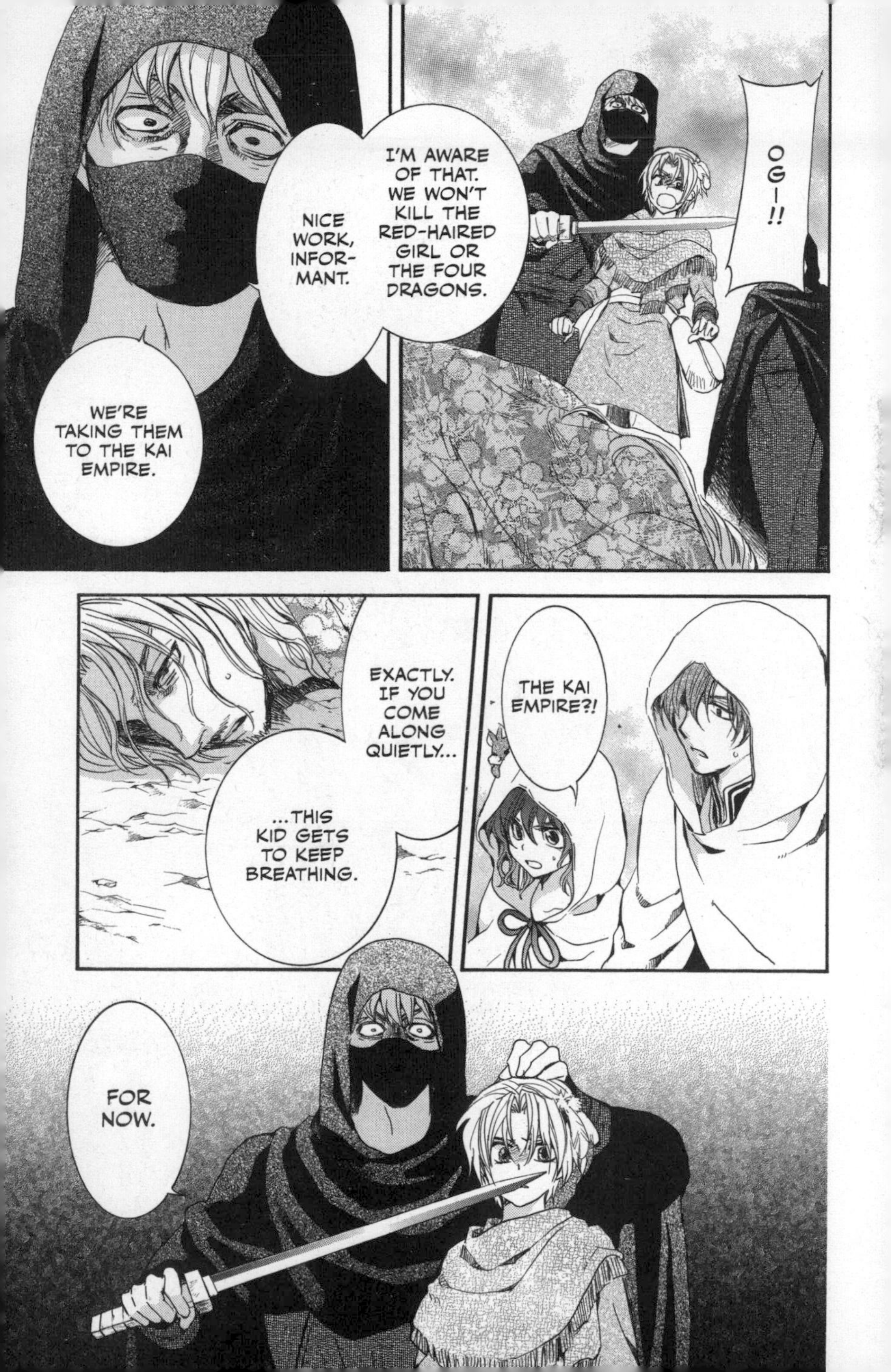
OG—!!
I'M AWARE OF THAT. WE WON'T KILL THE RED-HAIRED GIRL OR THE FOUR DRAGONS.
NICE WORK, INFORMANT.
WE'RE TAKING THEM TO THE KAI EMPIRE.
THE KAI EMPIRE?!
EXACTLY. IF YOU COME ALONG QUIETLY...
...THIS KID GETS TO KEEP BREATHING.
FOR NOW.

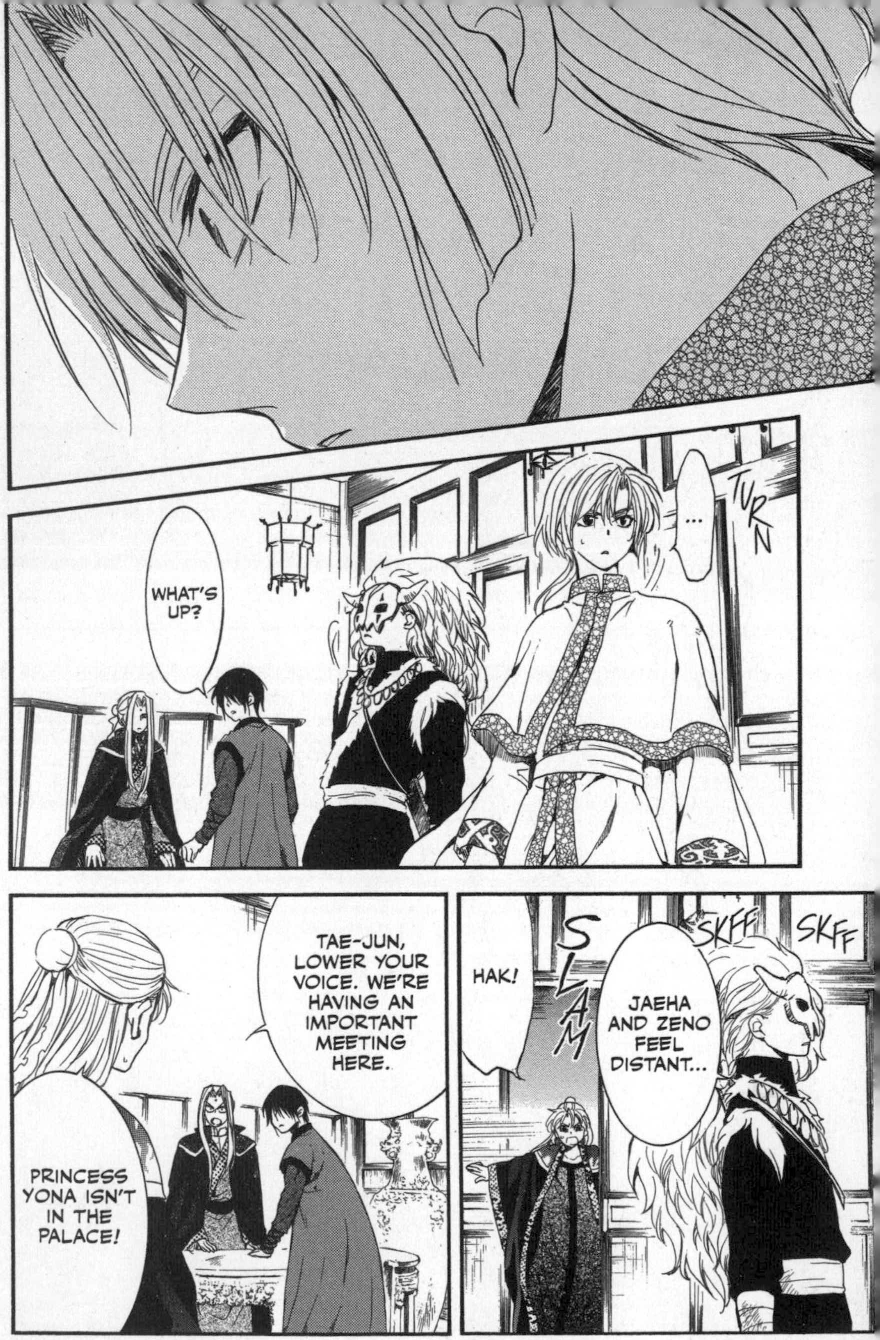
...
TURN
WHAT'S UP?
SKFF SKFF
JAEHA AND ZENO FEEL DISTANT...
SLAM
HAK!
TAE-JUN, LOWER YOUR VOICE. WE'RE HAVING AN IMPORTANT MEETING HERE.
PRINCESS YONA ISN'T IN THE PALACE!

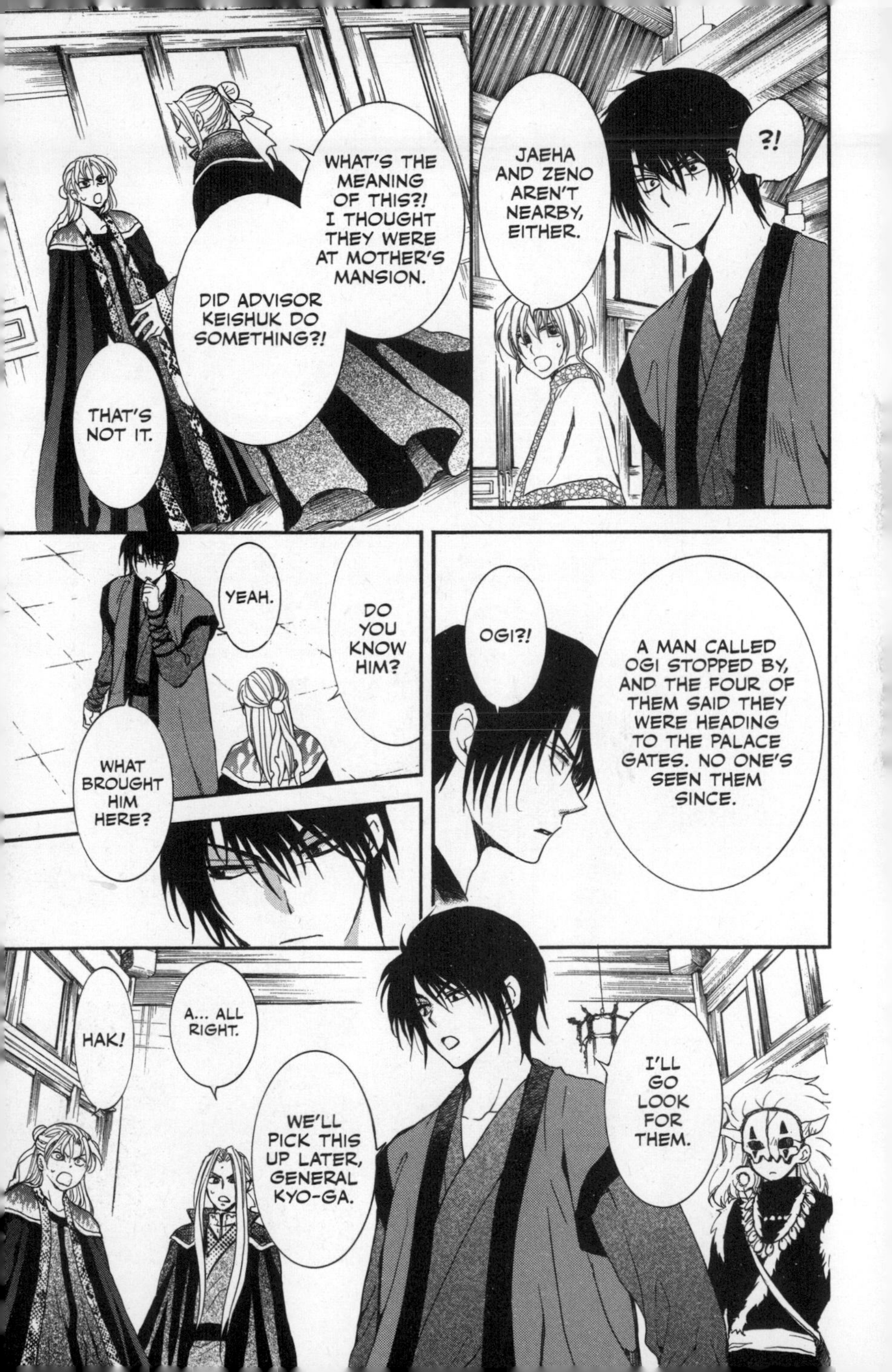
?!
JAEHA AND ZENO AREN'T NEARBY, EITHER.
WHAT'S THE MEANING OF THIS?! I THOUGHT THEY WERE AT MOTHER'S MANSION.
DID ADVISOR KEISHUK DO SOMETHING?!
THAT'S NOT IT.
A MAN CALLED OGI STOPPED BY, AND THE FOUR OF THEM SAID THEY WERE HEADING TO THE PALACE GATES. NO ONE'S SEEN THEM SINCE.
OGI?!
DO YOU KNOW HIM?
YEAH.
WHAT BROUGHT HIM HERE?
I'LL GO LOOK FOR THEM.
WE'LL PICK THIS UP LATER, GENERAL KYO-GA.
A... ALL RIGHT.
HAK!

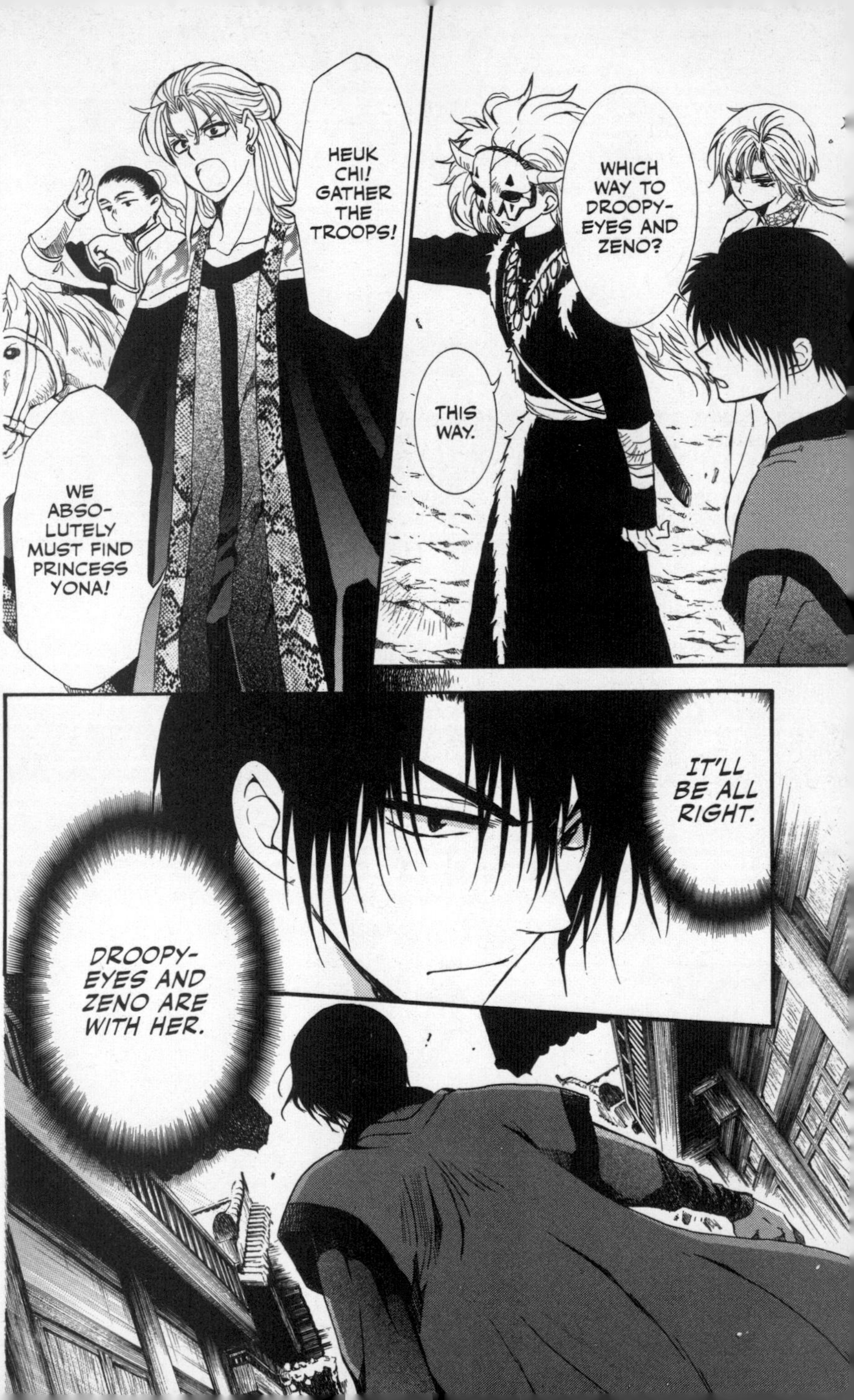
WHICH WAY TO DROOPY-EYES AND ZENO?
THIS WAY.
HEUK CHI! GATHER THE TROOPS!
WE ABSOLUTELY MUST FIND PRINCESS YONA!
IT'LL BE ALL RIGHT.
DROOPY-EYES AND ZENO ARE WITH HER.

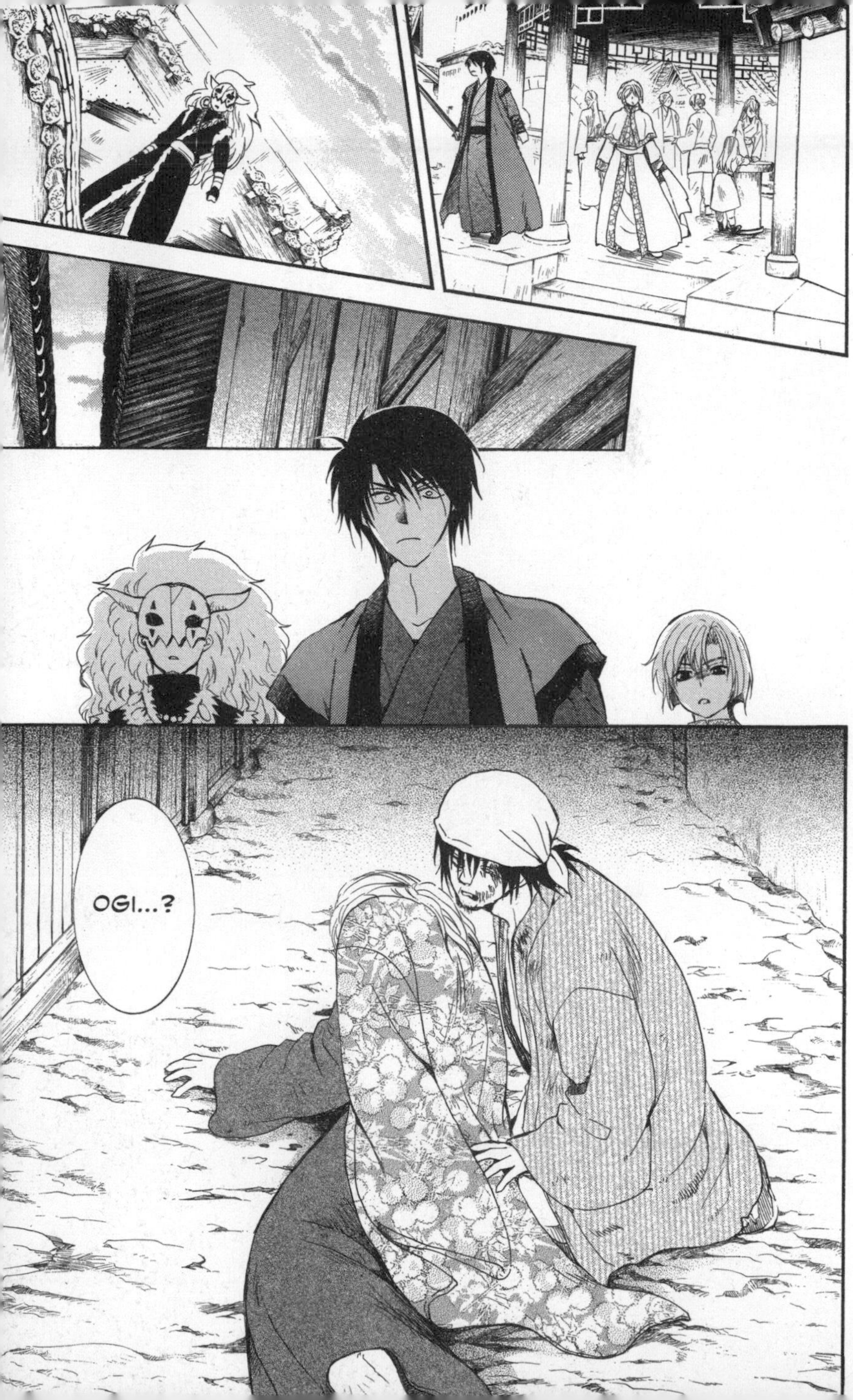
OGI...?

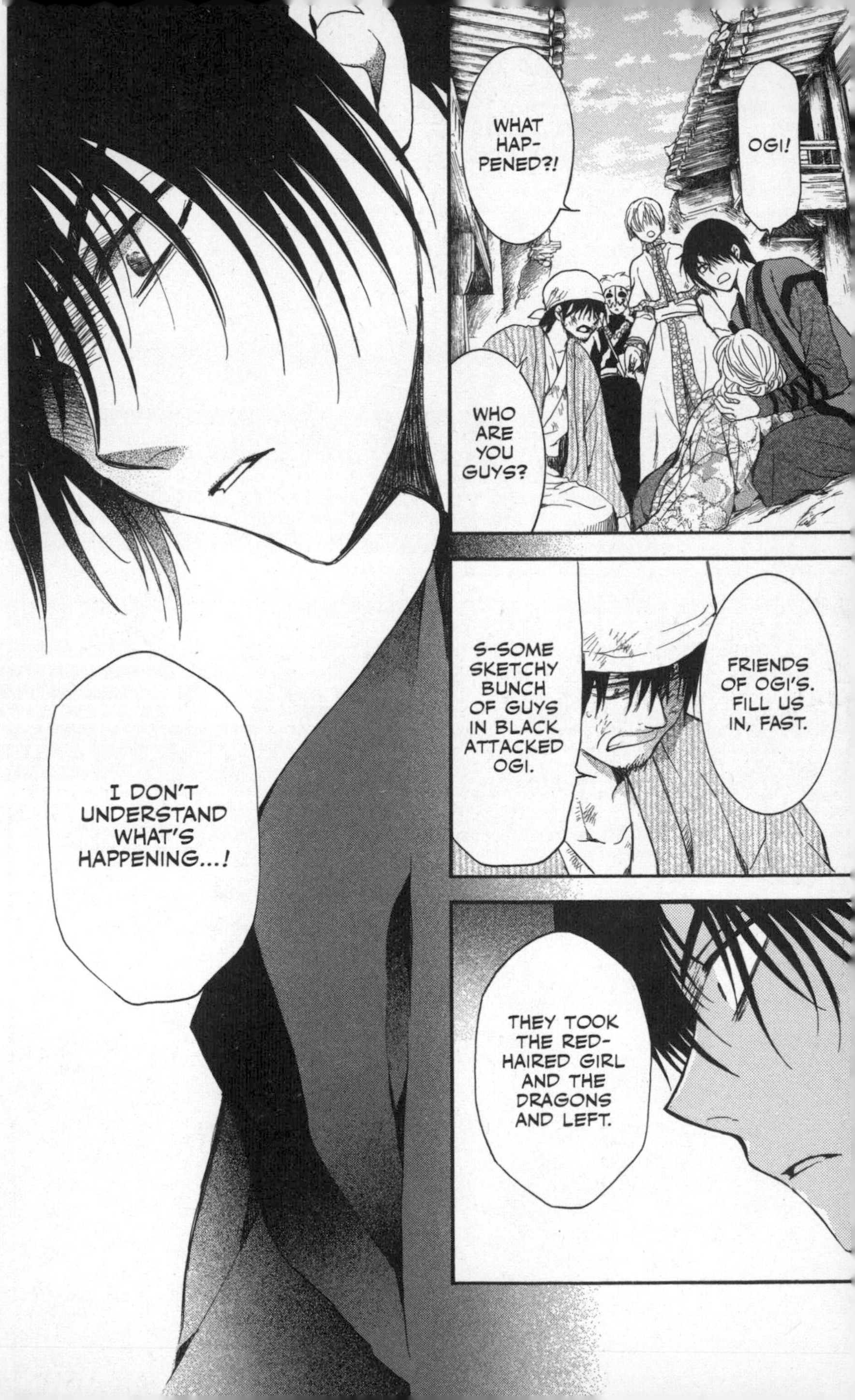
OGI!
WHAT HAPPENED?!
WHO ARE YOU GUYS?
FRIENDS OF OGI'S. FILL US IN, FAST.
S-SOME SKETCHY BUNCH OF GUYS IN BLACK ATTACKED OGI.
THEY TOOK THE RED-HAIRED GIRL AND THE DRAGONS AND LEFT.
I DON'T UNDERSTAND WHAT'S HAPPENING...!

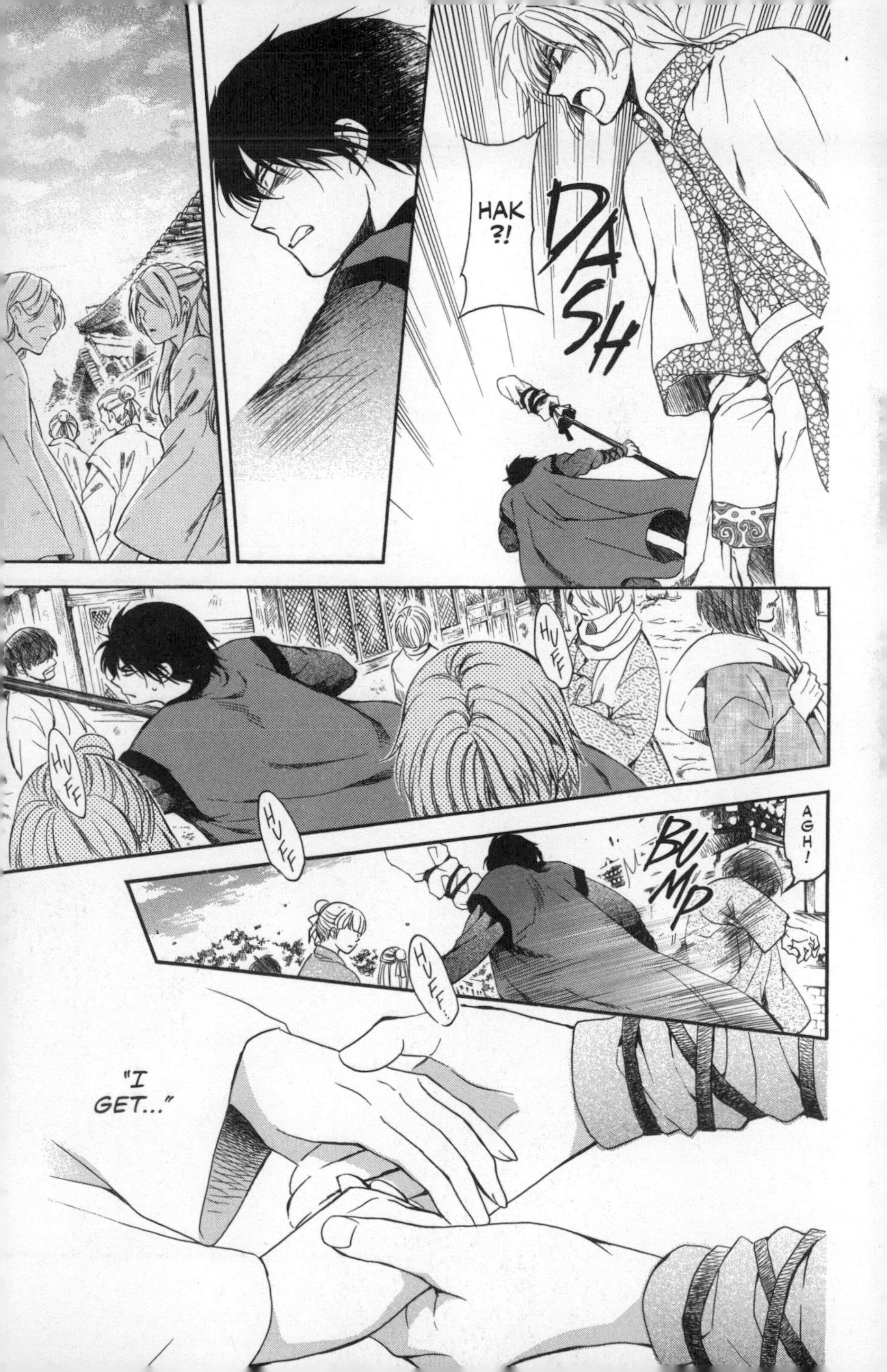
HAK ?!
DASH
HUFF
HUFF
HUFF
AGH!
BUMP
HUFF...
"I GET..."

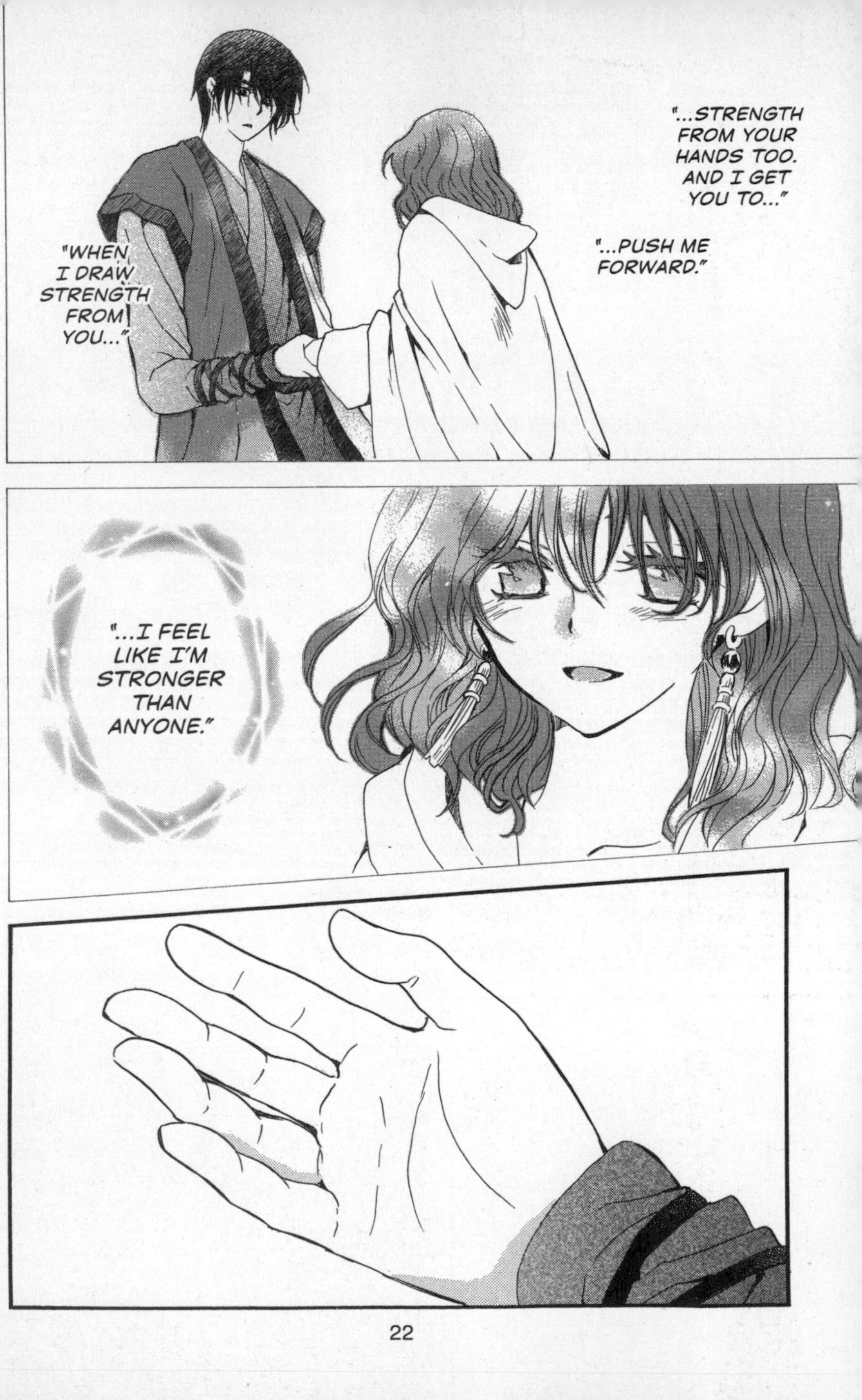
"...STRENGTH FROM YOUR HANDS TOO. AND I GET YOU TO..."
"...PUSH ME FORWARD."
"WHEN I DRAW STRENGTH FROM YOU..."
"...I FEEL LIKE I'M STRONGER THAN ANYONE."

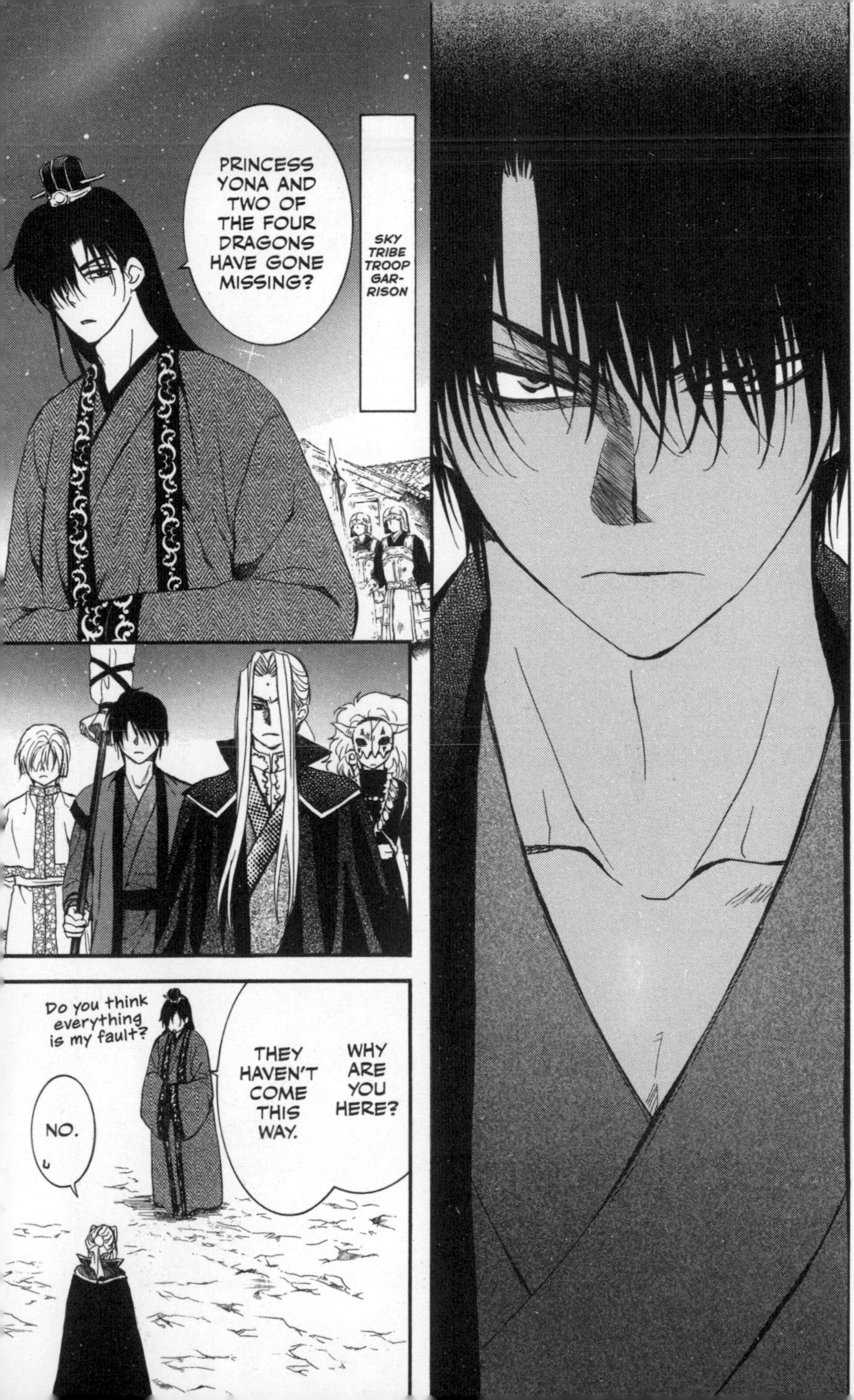
SKY TRIBE TROOP GARRISON
PRINCESS YONA AND TWO OF THE FOUR DRAGONS HAVE GONE MISSING?
WHY ARE YOU HERE?
THEY HAVEN'T COME THIS WAY.
Do you think everything is my fault?
NO.

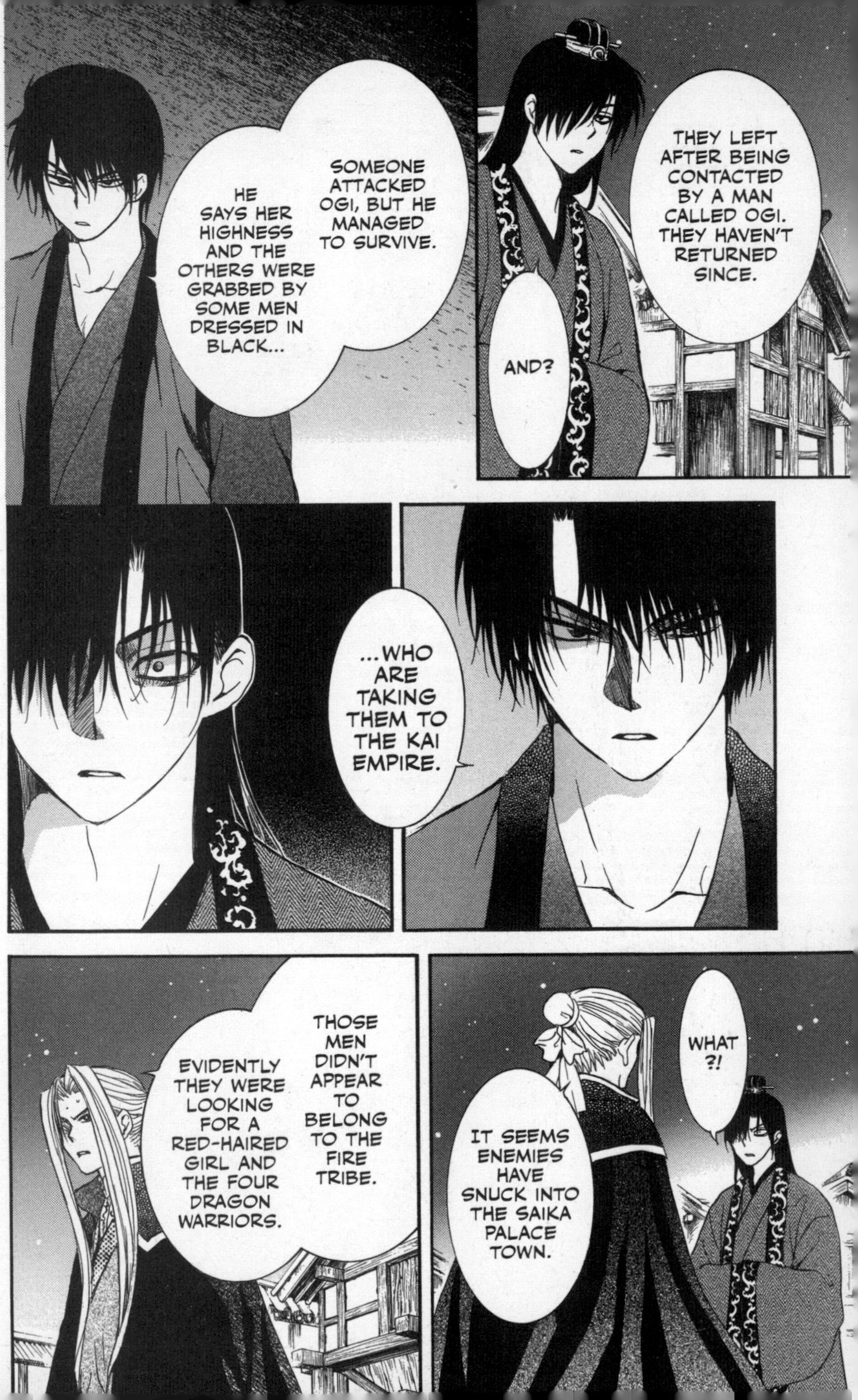
THEY LEFT AFTER BEING CONTACTED BY A MAN CALLED OGI. THEY HAVEN'T RETURNED SINCE.
AND?
SOMEONE ATTACKED OGI, BUT HE MANAGED TO SURVIVE.
HE SAYS HER HIGHNESS AND THE OTHERS WERE GRABBED BY SOME MEN DRESSED IN BLACK...
...WHO ARE TAKING THEM TO THE KAI EMPIRE.
WHAT?!
IT SEEMS ENEMIES HAVE SNUCK INTO THE SAIKA PALACE TOWN.
THOSE MEN DIDN'T APPEAR TO BELONG TO THE FIRE TRIBE.
EVIDENTLY THEY WERE LOOKING FOR A RED-HAIRED GIRL AND THE FOUR DRAGON WARRIORS.

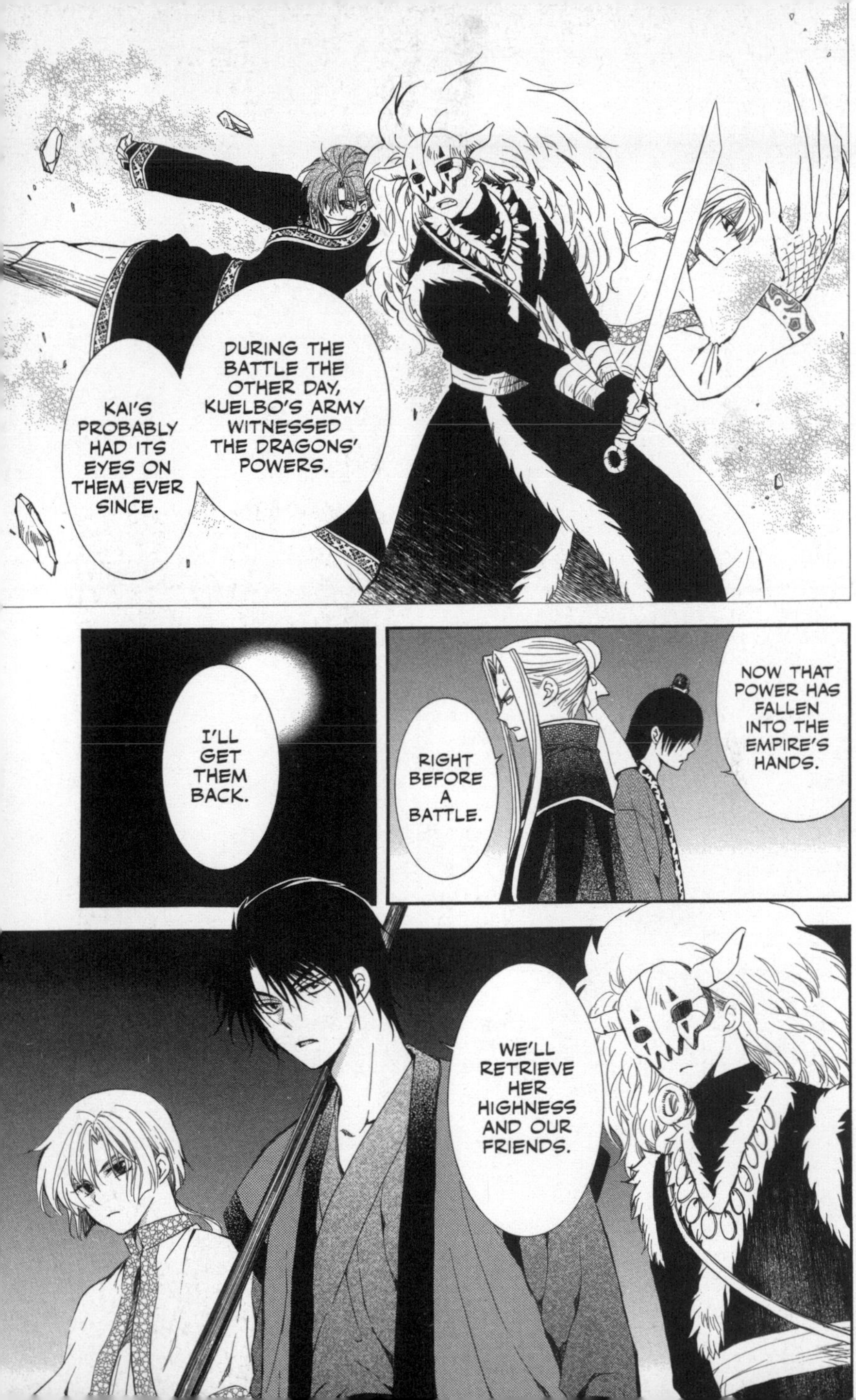

DURING THE BATTLE THE OTHER DAY, KUELBO'S ARMY WITNESSED THE DRAGONS' POWERS.
KAI'S PROBABLY HAD ITS EYES ON THEM EVER SINCE.
NOW THAT POWER HAS FALLEN INTO THE EMPIRE'S HANDS.
RIGHT BEFORE A BATTLE.
I'LL GET THEM BACK.
WE'LL RETRIEVE HER HIGHNESS AND OUR FRIENDS.

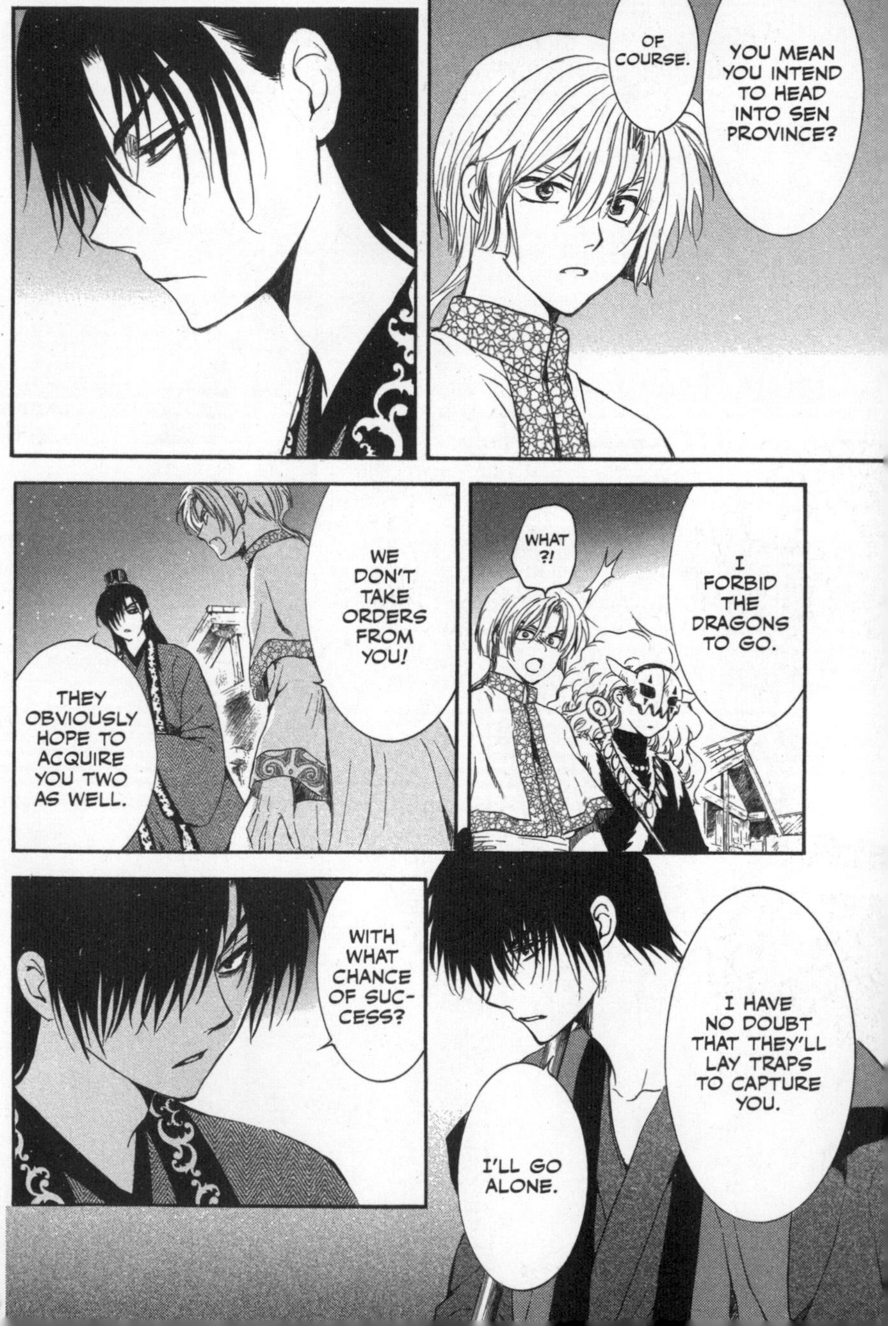
YOU MEAN YOU INTEND TO HEAD INTO SEN PROVINCE?
OF COURSE.
I FORBID THE DRAGONS TO GO.
WHAT?!
WE DON'T TAKE ORDERS FROM YOU!
THEY OBVIOUSLY HOPE TO ACQUIRE YOU TWO AS WELL.
I HAVE NO DOUBT THAT THEY'LL LAY TRAPS TO CAPTURE YOU.
I'LL GO ALONE.
WITH WHAT CHANCE OF SUC-CESS?

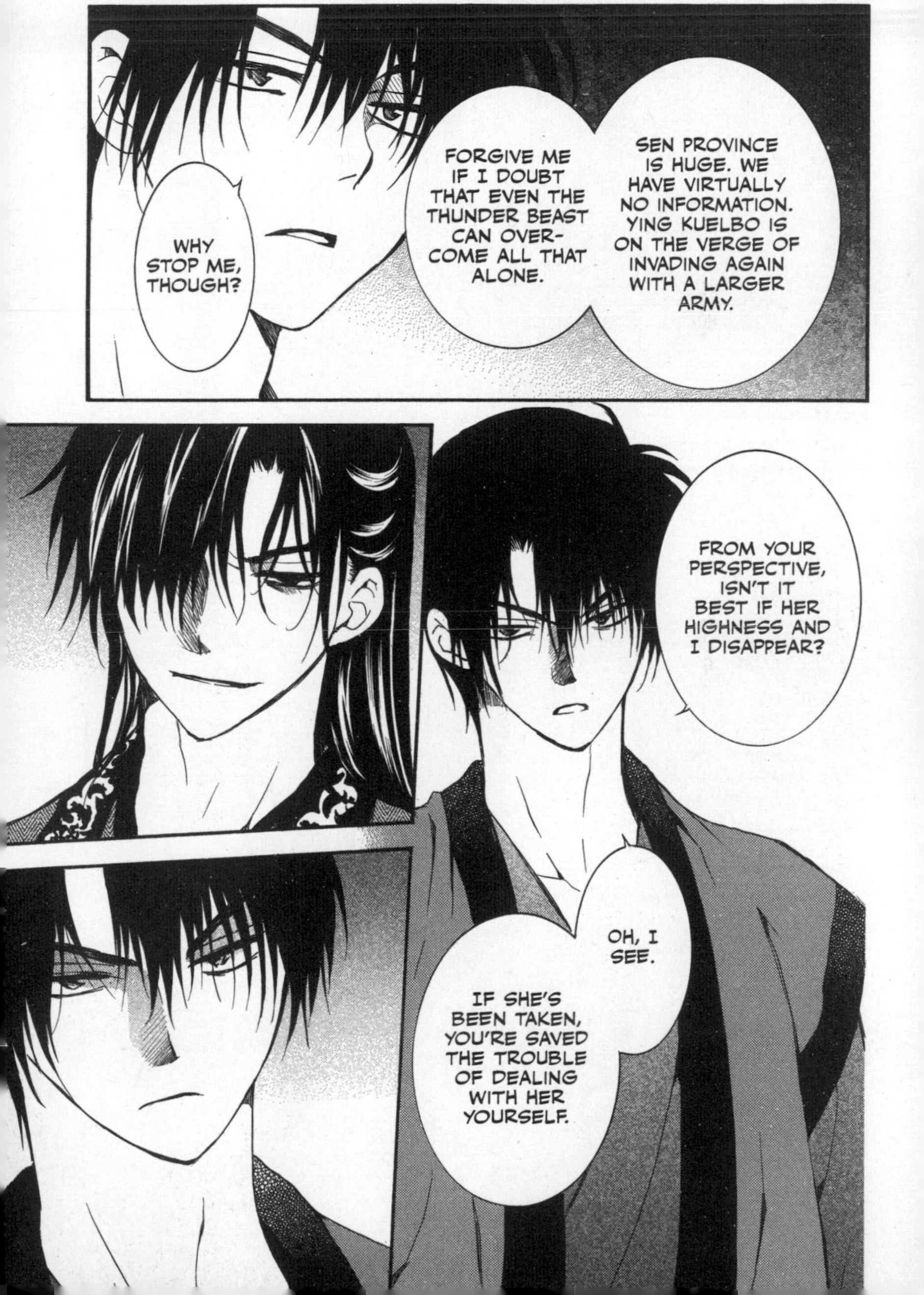
SEN PROVINCE IS HUGE. WE HAVE VIRTUALLY NO INFORMATION. YING KUELBO IS ON THE VERGE OF INVADING AGAIN WITH A LARGER ARMY.
FORGIVE ME IF I DOUBT THAT EVEN THE THUNDER BEAST CAN OVER-COME ALL THAT ALONE.
WHY STOP ME, THOUGH?
FROM YOUR PERSPECTIVE, ISN'T IT BEST IF HER HIGHNESS AND I DISAPPEAR?
OH, I SEE.
IF SHE'S BEEN TAKEN, YOU'RE SAVED THE TROUBLE OF DEALING WITH HER YOURSELF.

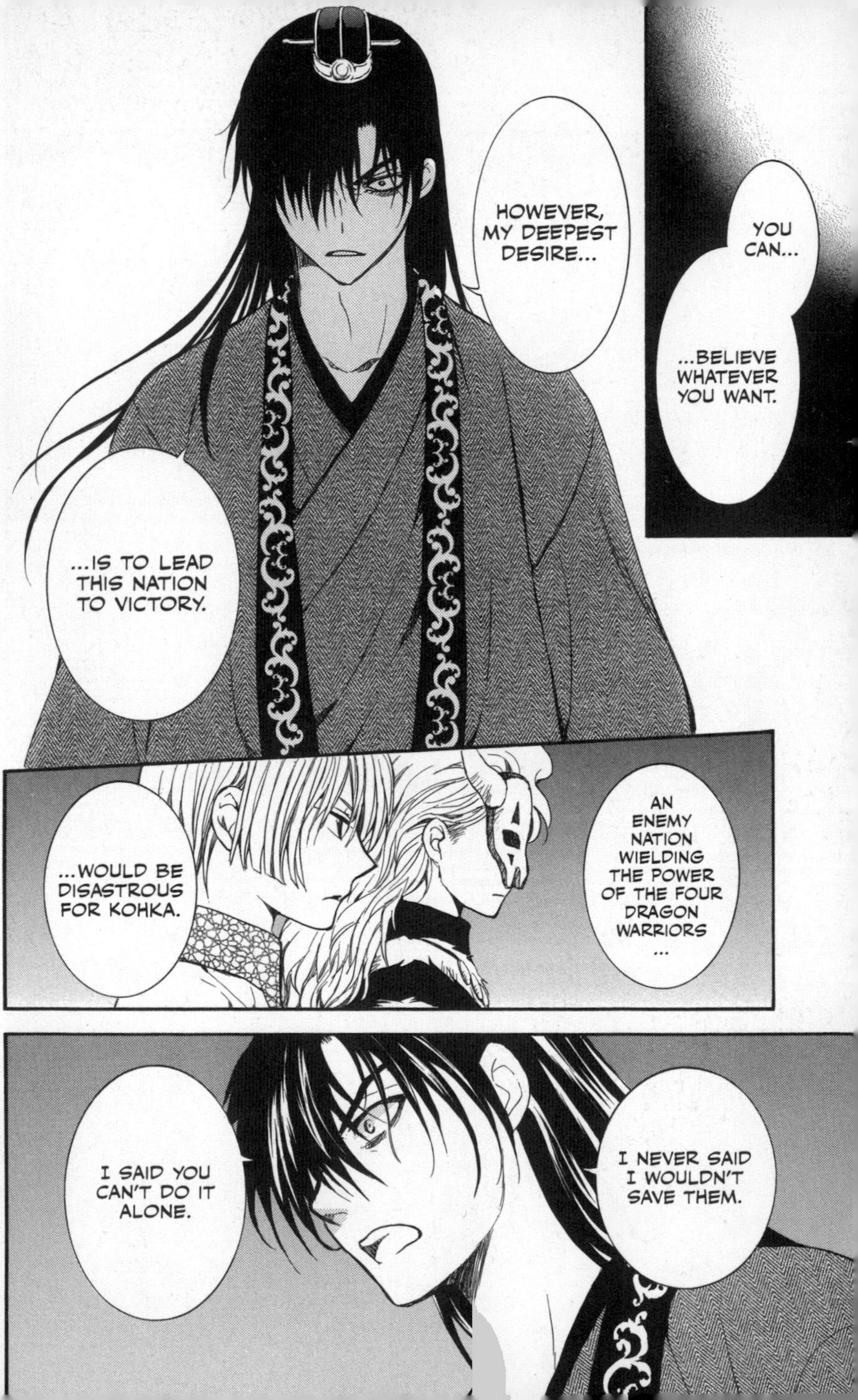
YOU CAN...
...BELIEVE WHATEVER YOU WANT.
HOWEVER, MY DEEPEST DESIRE...
...IS TO LEAD THIS NATION TO VICTORY.
AN ENEMY NATION WIELDING THE POWER OF THE FOUR DRAGON WARRIORS ...
...WOULD BE DISASTROUS FOR KOHKA.
I NEVER SAID I WOULDN'T SAVE THEM.
I SAID YOU CAN'T DO IT ALONE.

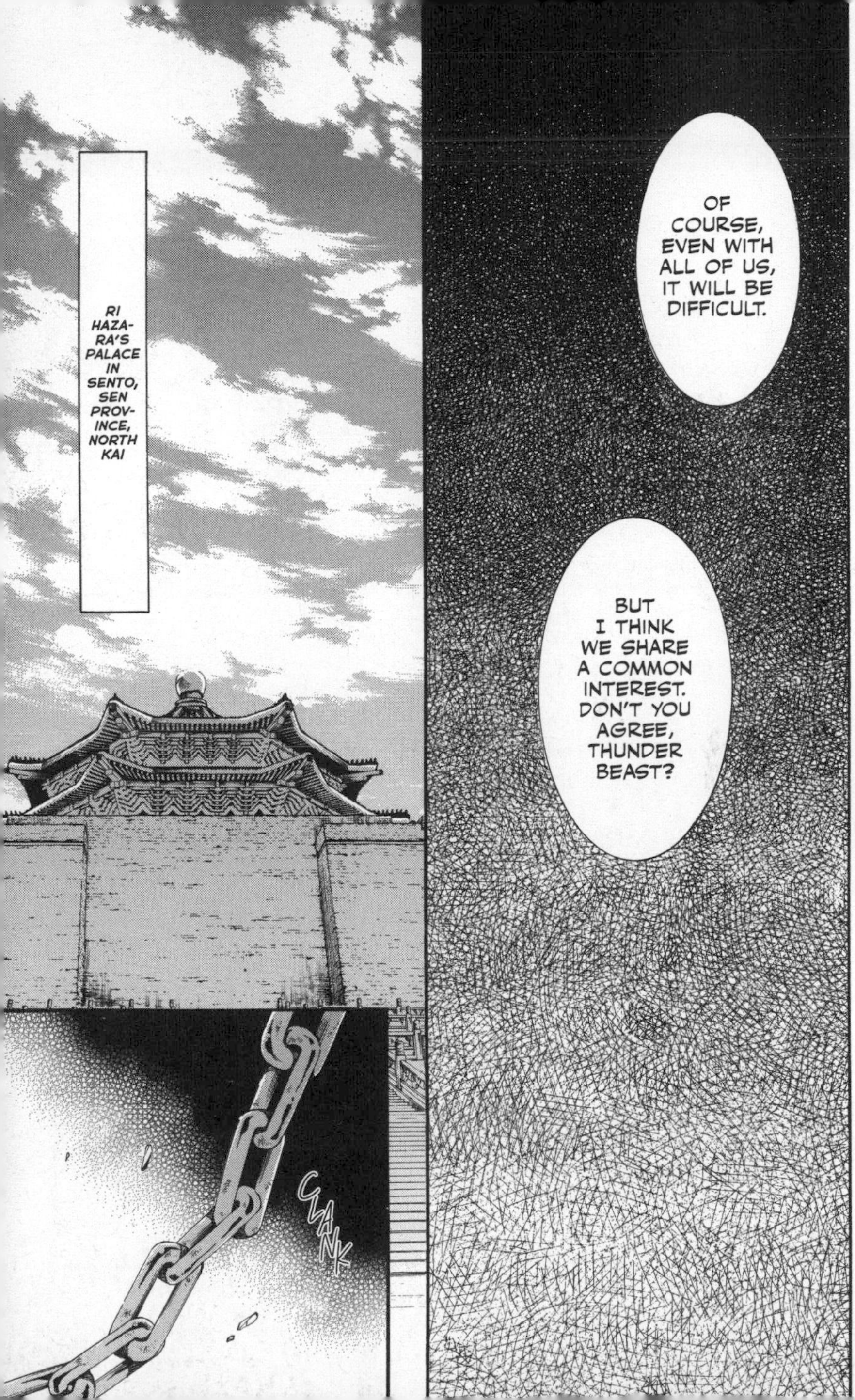
OF COURSE, EVEN WITH ALL OF US, IT WILL BE DIFFICULT.
BUT I THINK WE SHARE A COMMON INTEREST. DON'T YOU AGREE, THUNDER BEAST?
RI HAZARA'S PALACE IN SENTO, SEN PROVINCE, NORTH KAI
CLANK

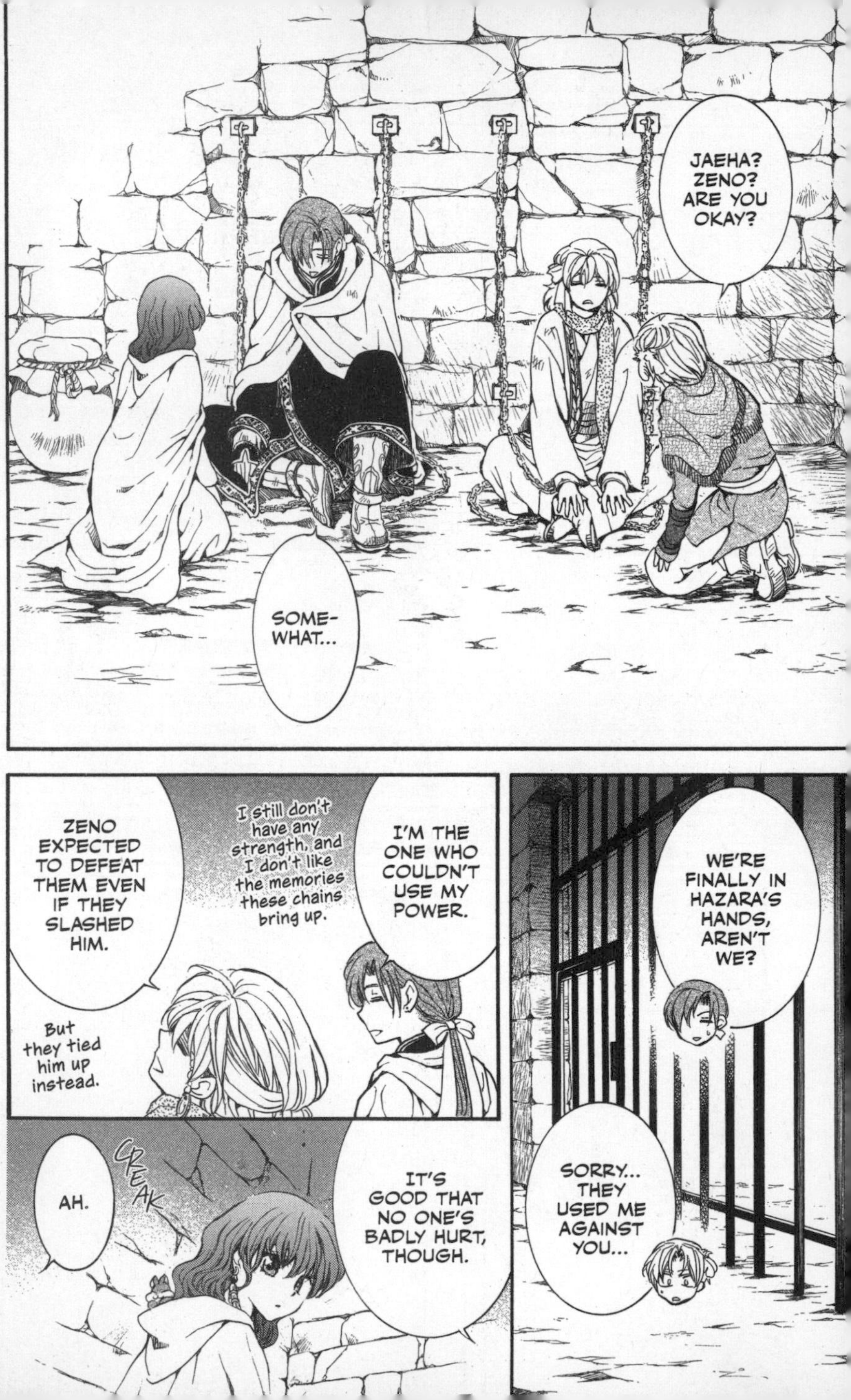
JAEHA? ZENO? ARE YOU OKAY?
SOME-WHAT...
WE'RE FINALLY IN HAZARA'S HANDS, AREN'T WE?
SORRY... THEY USED ME AGAINST YOU...
I'M THE ONE WHO COULDN'T USE MY POWER.
I still don't have any strength, and I don't like the memories these chains bring up.
ZENO EXPECTED TO DEFEAT THEM EVEN IF THEY SLASHED HIM.
But they tied him up instead.
IT'S GOOD THAT NO ONE'S BADLY HURT, THOUGH.
CREAK
AH.

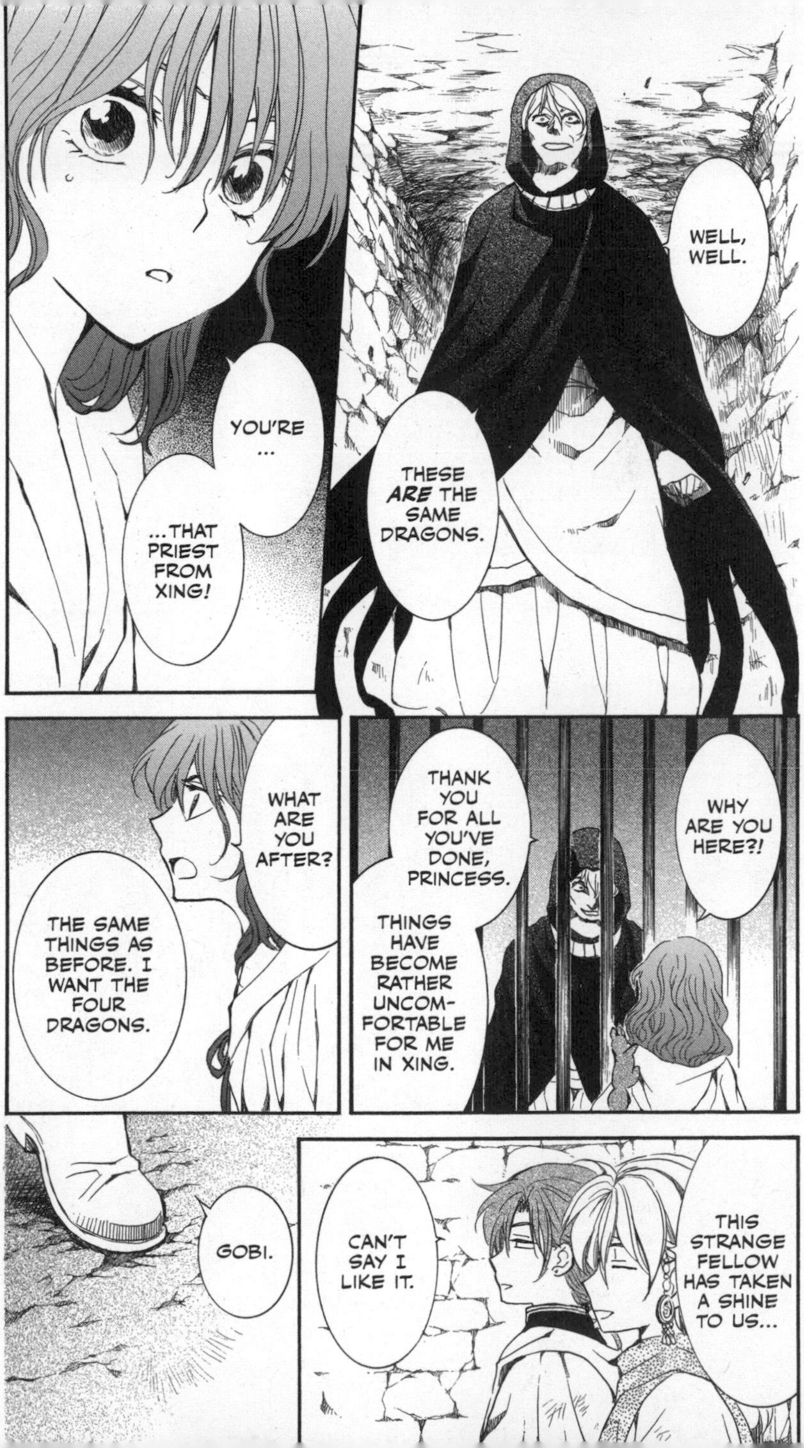
WELL, WELL.
THESE *ARE* THE SAME DRAGONS.
YOU'RE ...
...THAT PRIEST FROM XING!
WHY ARE YOU HERE?!
THANK YOU FOR ALL YOU'VE DONE, PRINCESS.
THINGS HAVE BECOME RATHER UNCOMFORTABLE FOR ME IN XING.
WHAT ARE YOU AFTER?
THE SAME THINGS AS BEFORE. I WANT THE FOUR DRAGONS.
THIS STRANGE FELLOW HAS TAKEN A SHINE TO US...
CAN'T SAY I LIKE IT.
GOBI.

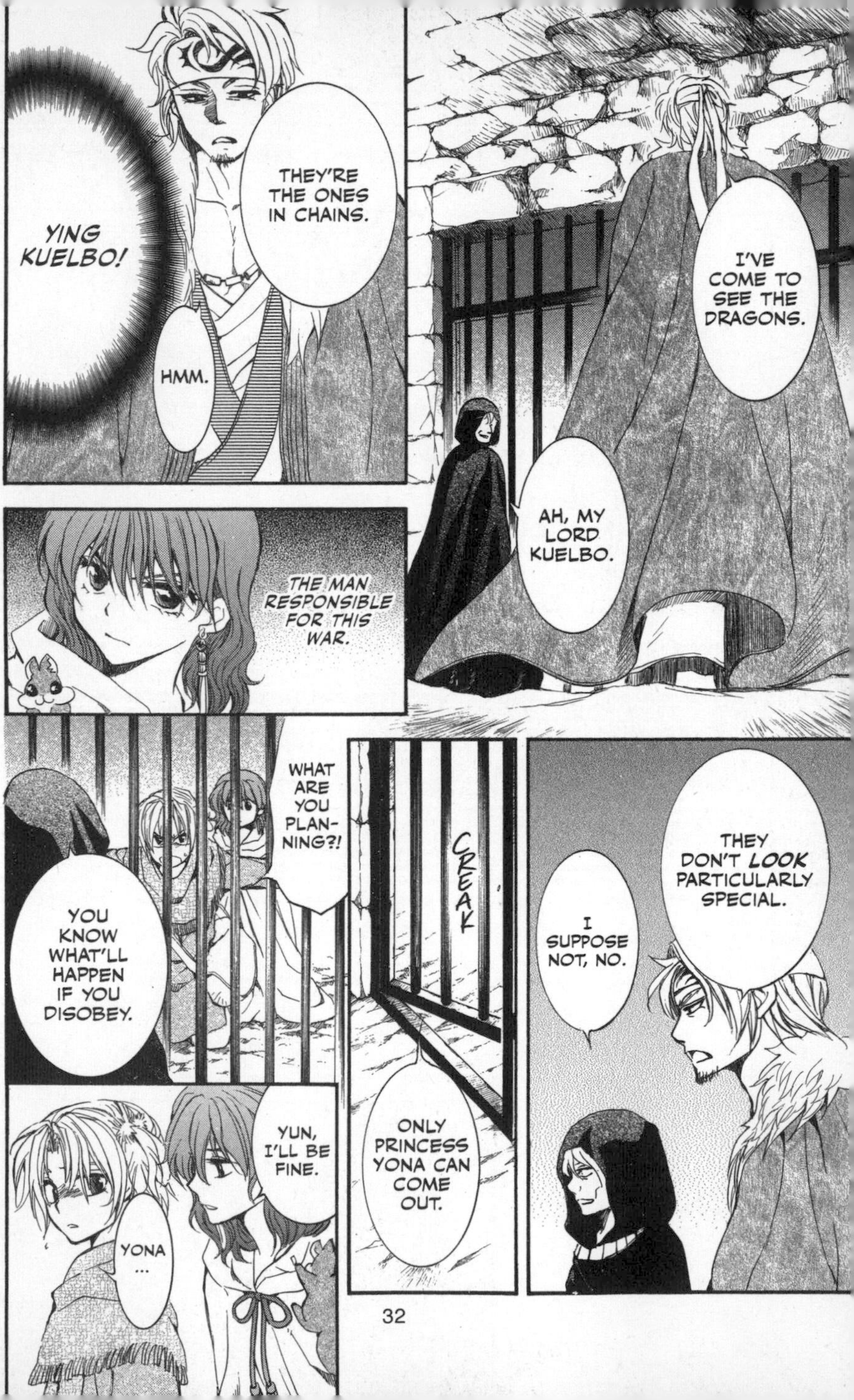
I'VE COME TO SEE THE DRAGONS.
AH, MY LORD KUELBO.
THEY'RE THE ONES IN CHAINS.
YING KUELBO!
HMM.
THE MAN RESPONSIBLE FOR THIS WAR.
THEY DON'T *LOOK* PARTICULARLY SPECIAL.
I SUPPOSE NOT, NO.
CREAK
ONLY PRINCESS YONA CAN COME OUT.
WHAT ARE YOU PLANNING?!
YOU KNOW WHAT'LL HAPPEN IF YOU DISOBEY.
YUN, I'LL BE FINE.
YONA ...

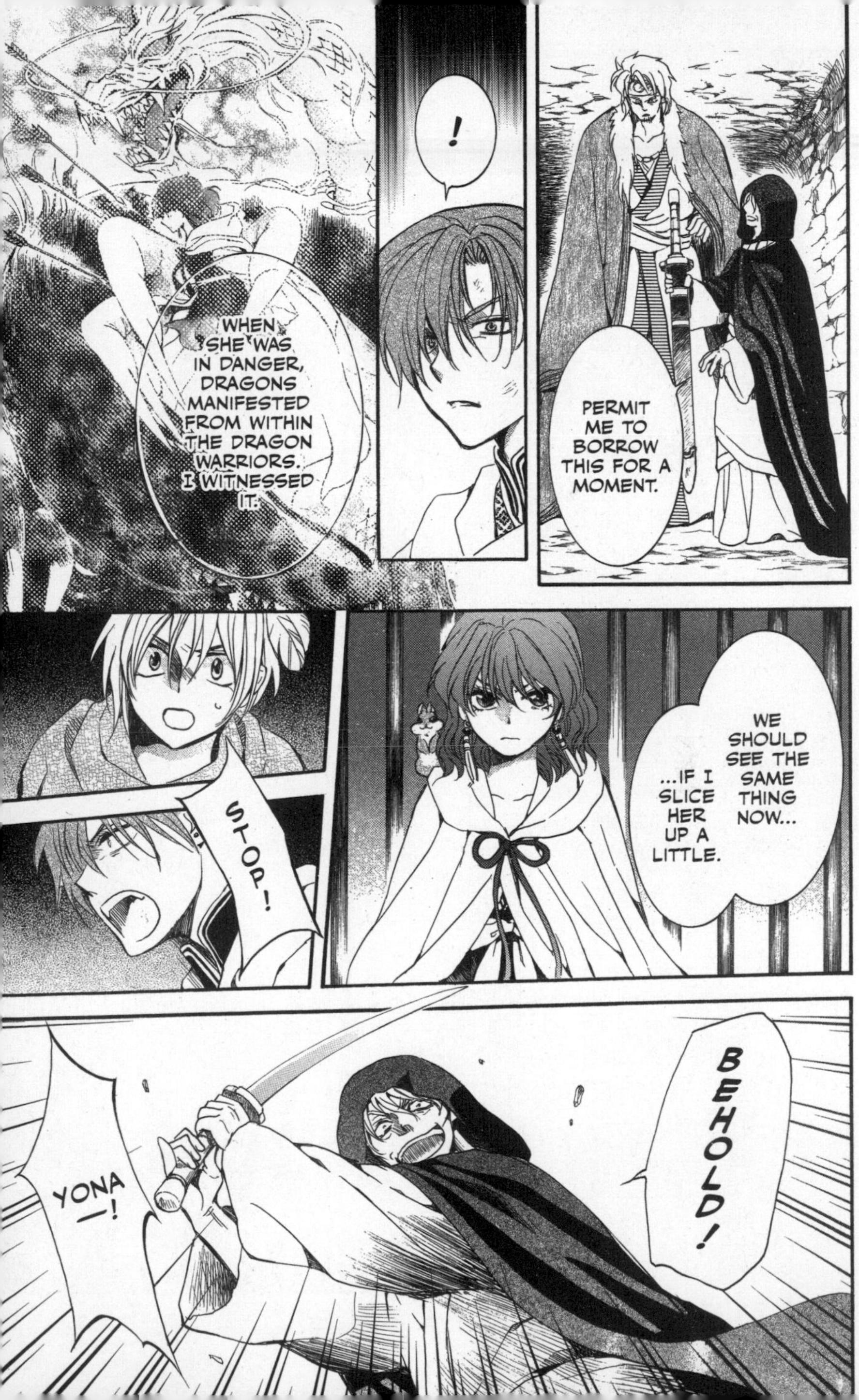
PERMIT ME TO BORROW THIS FOR A MOMENT.
!
WHEN SHE WAS IN DANGER, DRAGONS MANIFESTED FROM WITHIN THE DRAGON WARRIORS. I WITNESSED IT.
WE SHOULD SEE THE SAME THING NOW...
...IF I SLICE HER UP A LITTLE.
STOP!
BEHOLD!
YONA—!

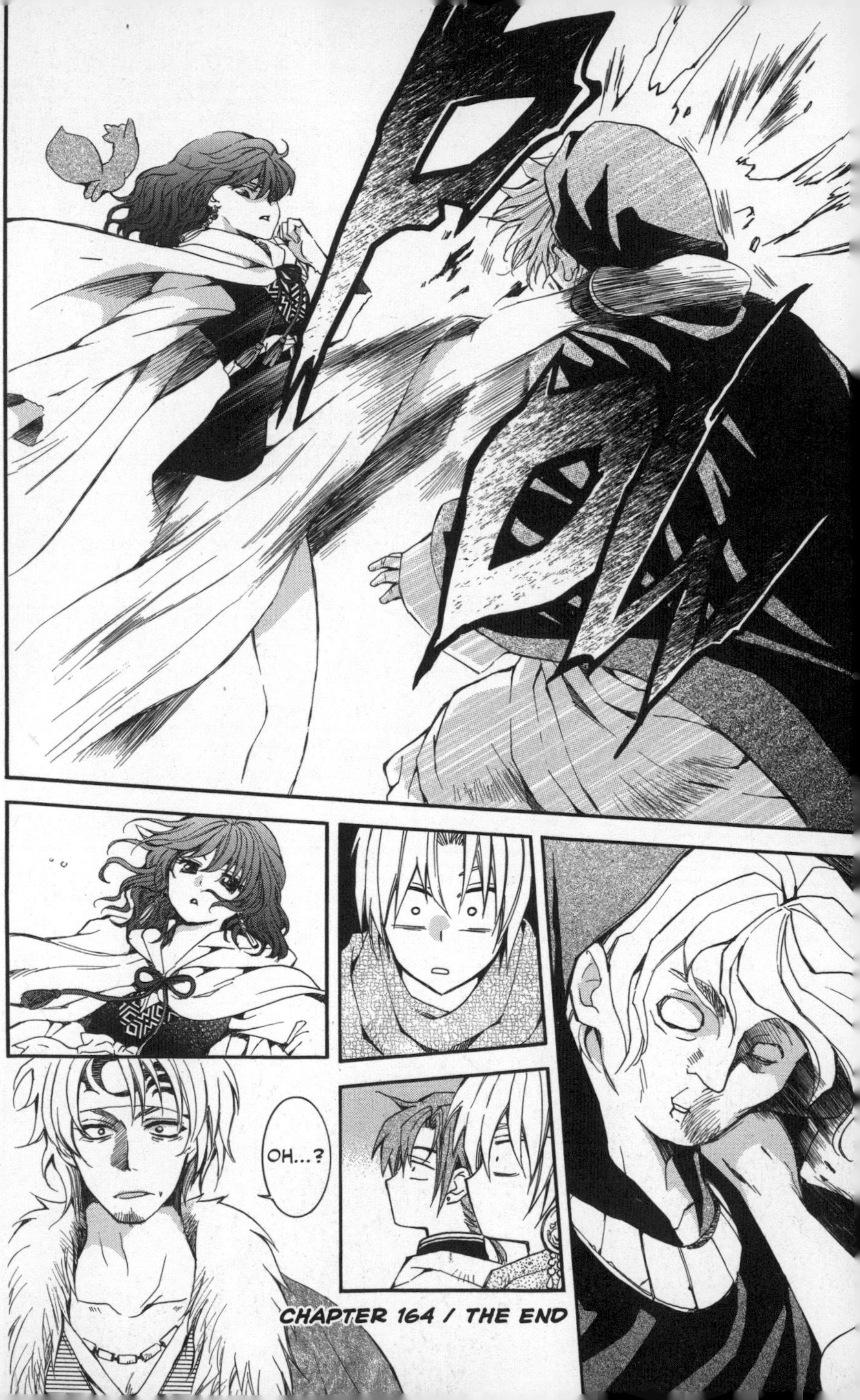
OH...?
CHAPTER 164 / THE END

CHAPTER 165: IN THE ENEMY'S HANDS

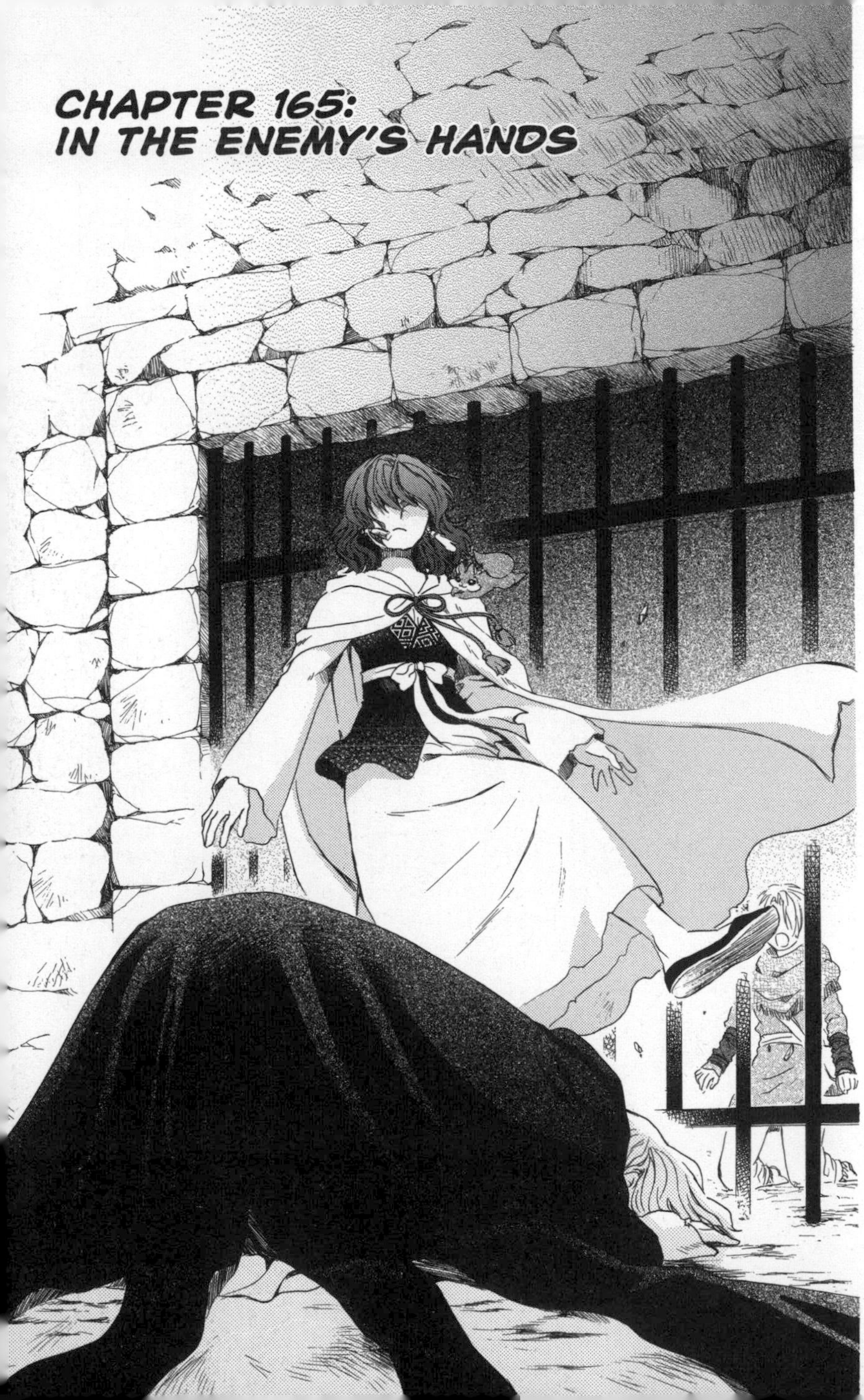

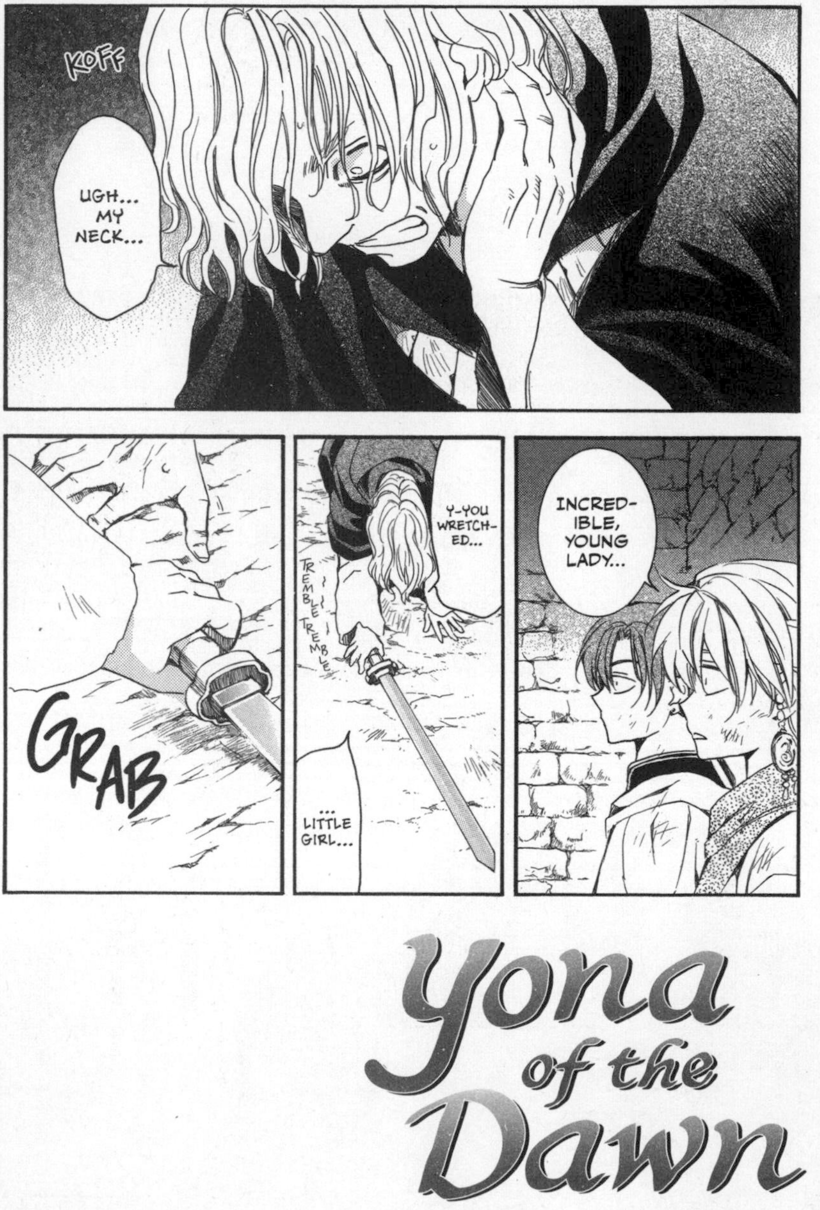
KOFF
UGH... MY NECK...
INCREDIBLE, YOUNG LADY...
Y-YOU WRETCHED...
TREMBLE TREMBLE
...LITTLE GIRL...
GRAB

Yona of the Dawn

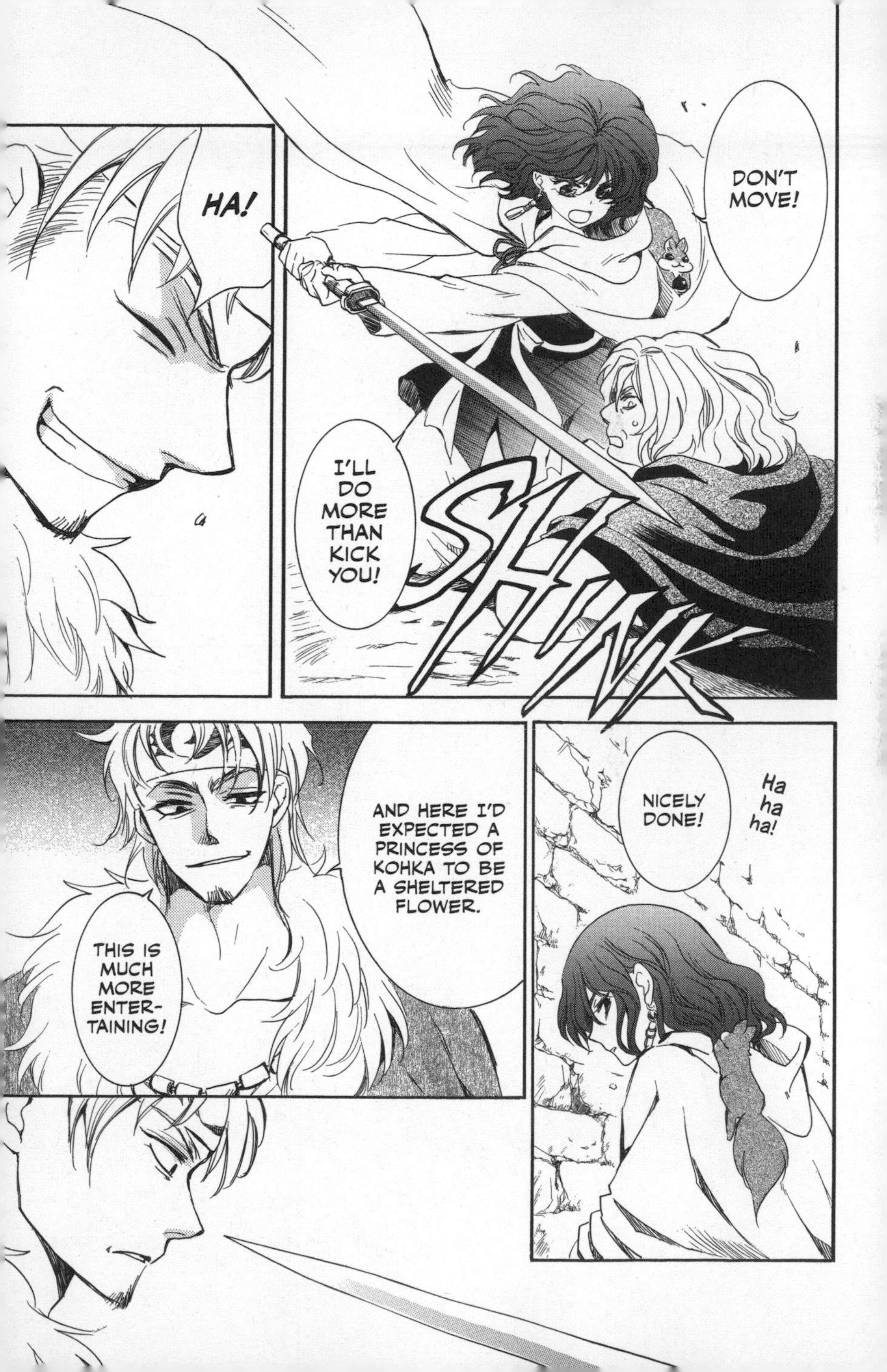
DON'T MOVE!
I'LL DO MORE THAN KICK YOU!
SHINK
HA!
NICELY DONE!
Ha ha ha!
AND HERE I'D EXPECTED A PRINCESS OF KOHKA TO BE A SHELTERED FLOWER.
THIS IS MUCH MORE ENTER-TAINING!

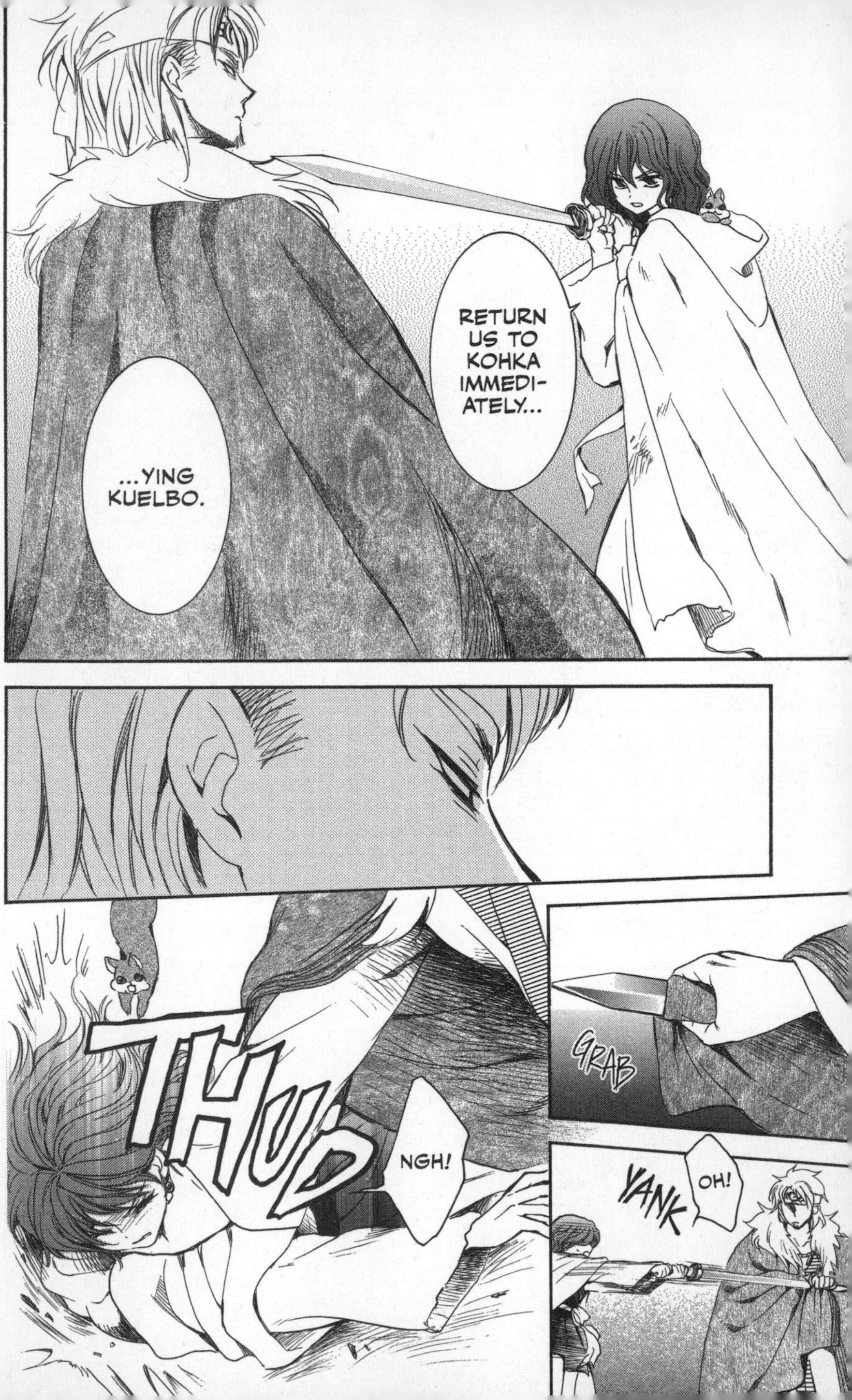
RETURN US TO KOHKA IMMEDI-ATELY...
...YING KUELBO.
GRAB
YANK
OH!
THUD
NGH!

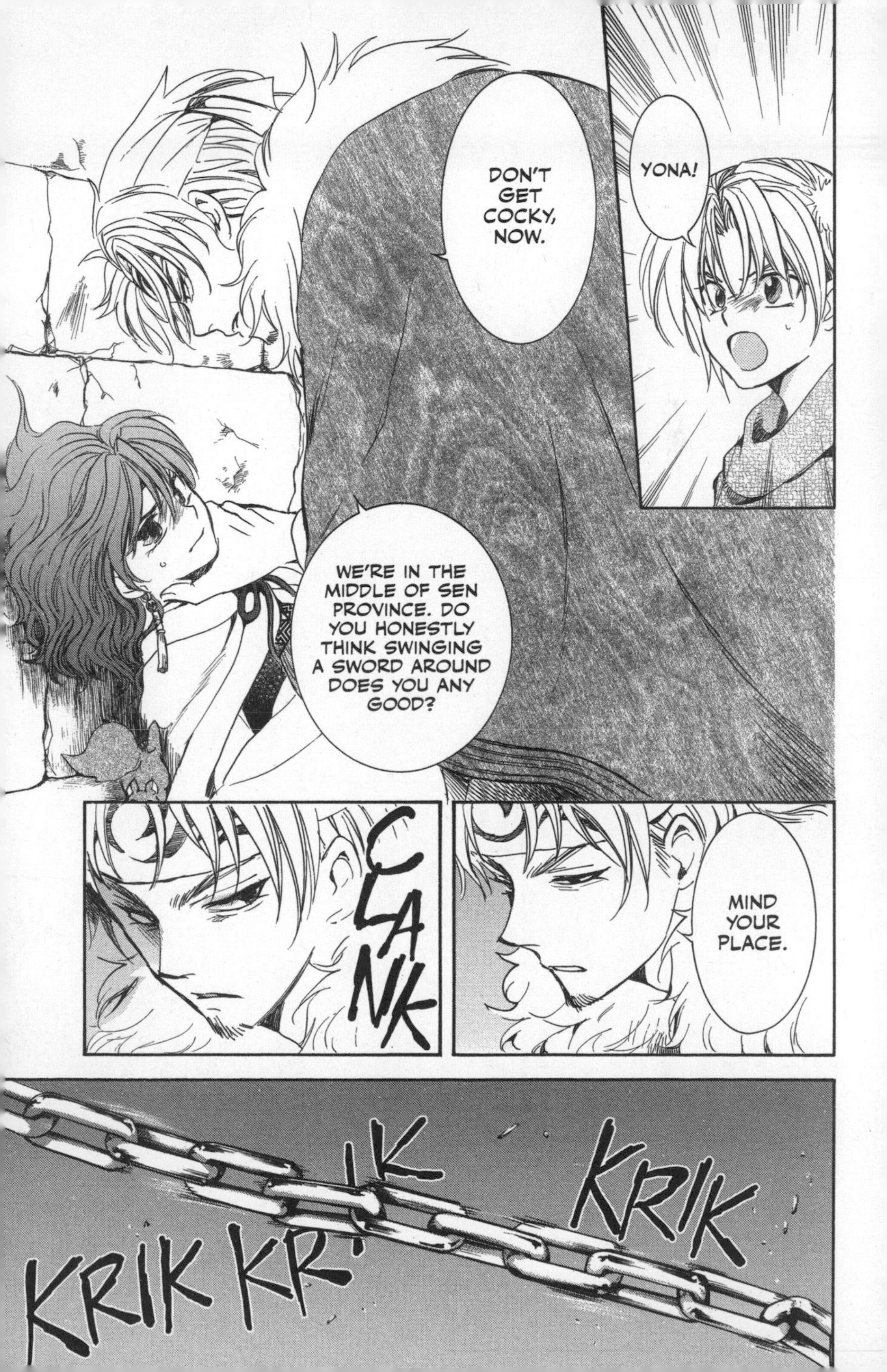
YONA!
DON'T GET COCKY, NOW.
WE'RE IN THE MIDDLE OF SEN PROVINCE. DO YOU HONESTLY THINK SWINGING A SWORD AROUND DOES YOU ANY GOOD?
MIND YOUR PLACE.
CLANK
KRIK
IK
KRIK KR

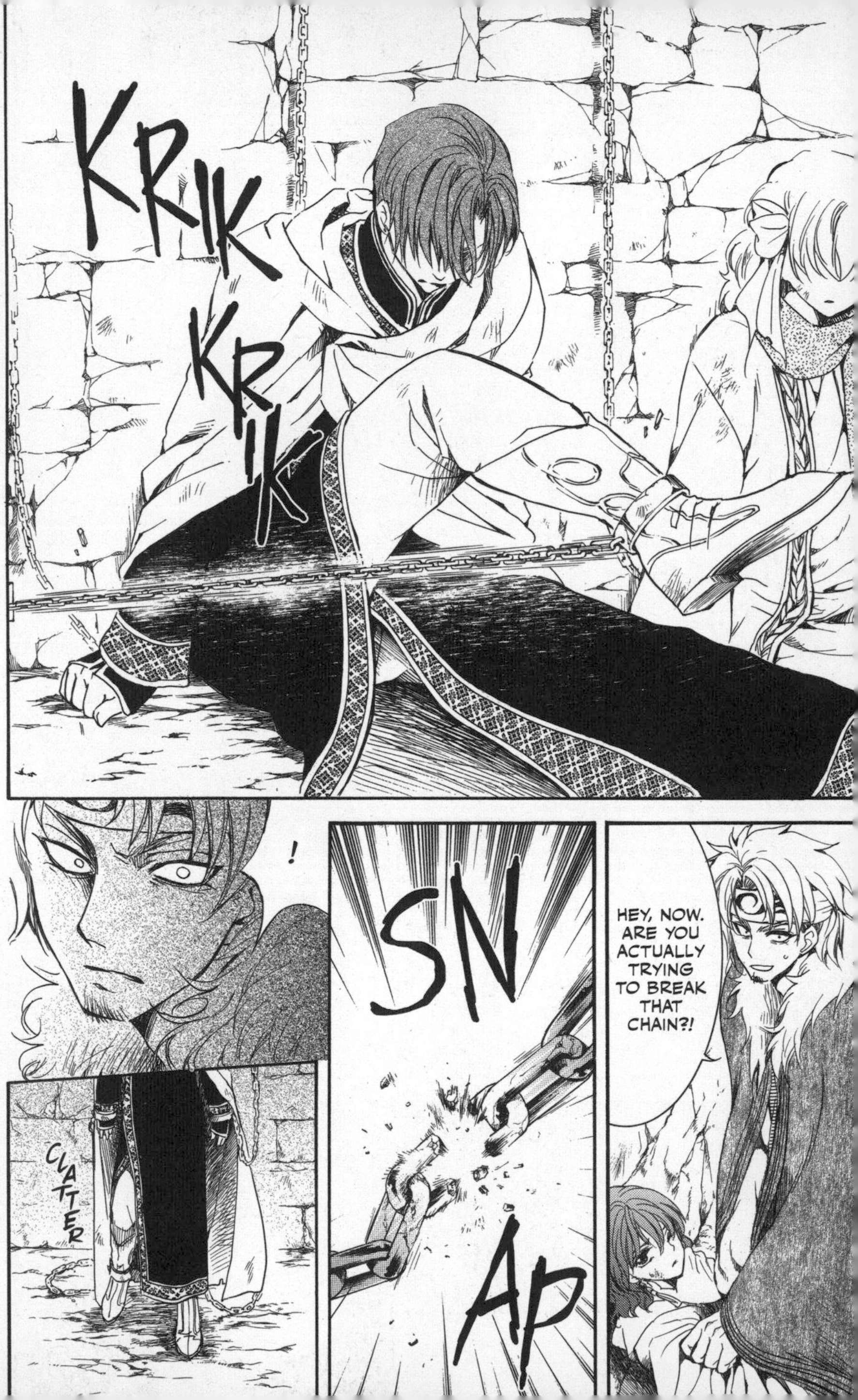
KRIK
KRIK
KRIK
HEY, NOW. ARE YOU ACTUALLY TRYING TO BREAK THAT CHAIN?!
SN
AP
!
CLATTER

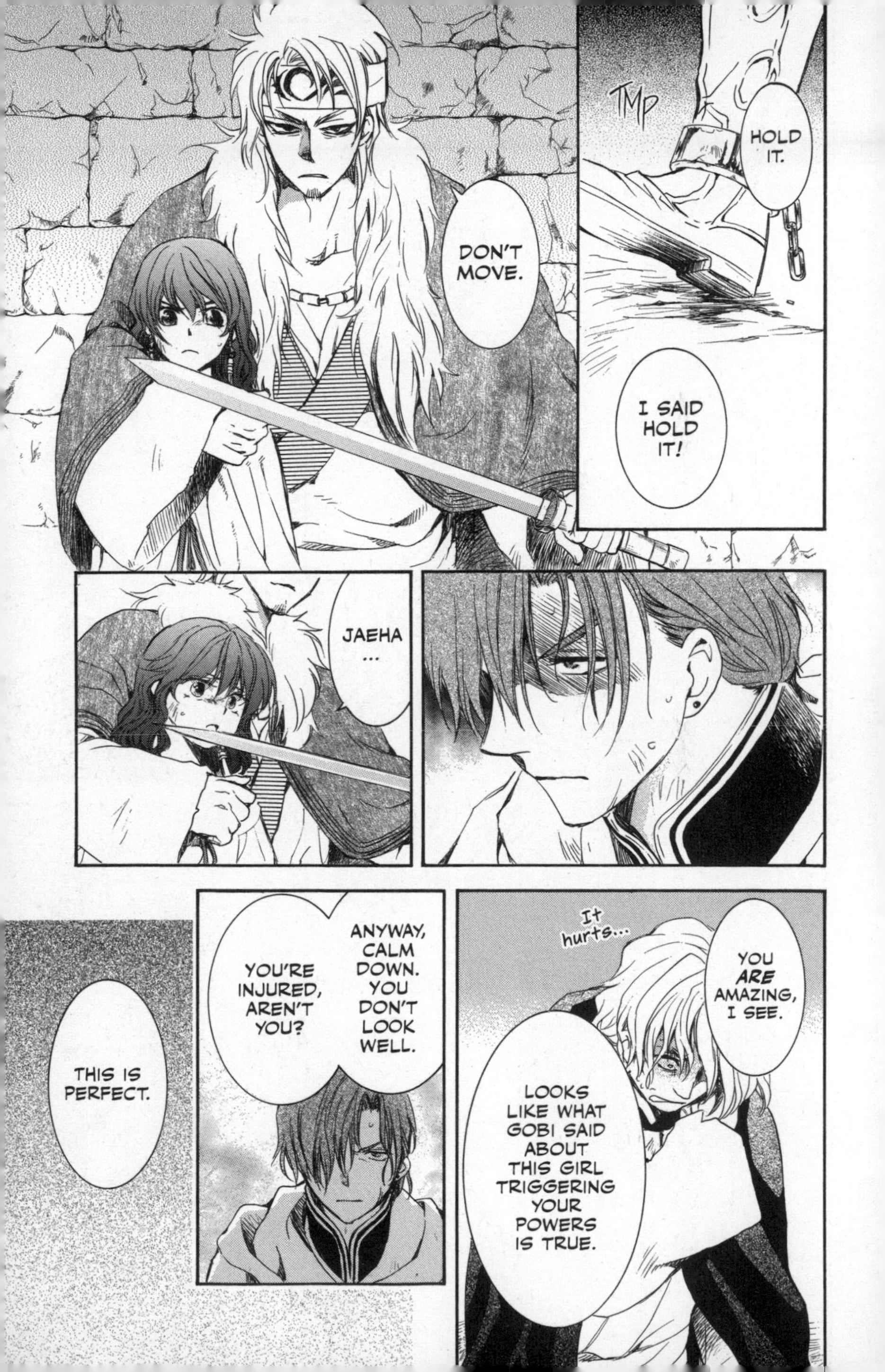
TMP
HOLD IT.
I SAID HOLD IT!
DON'T MOVE.
JAEHA...
It hurts...
YOU *ARE* AMAZING, I SEE.
LOOKS LIKE WHAT GOBI SAID ABOUT THIS GIRL TRIGGERING YOUR POWERS IS TRUE.
ANYWAY, CALM DOWN. YOU DON'T LOOK WELL.
YOU'RE INJURED, AREN'T YOU?
THIS IS PERFECT.

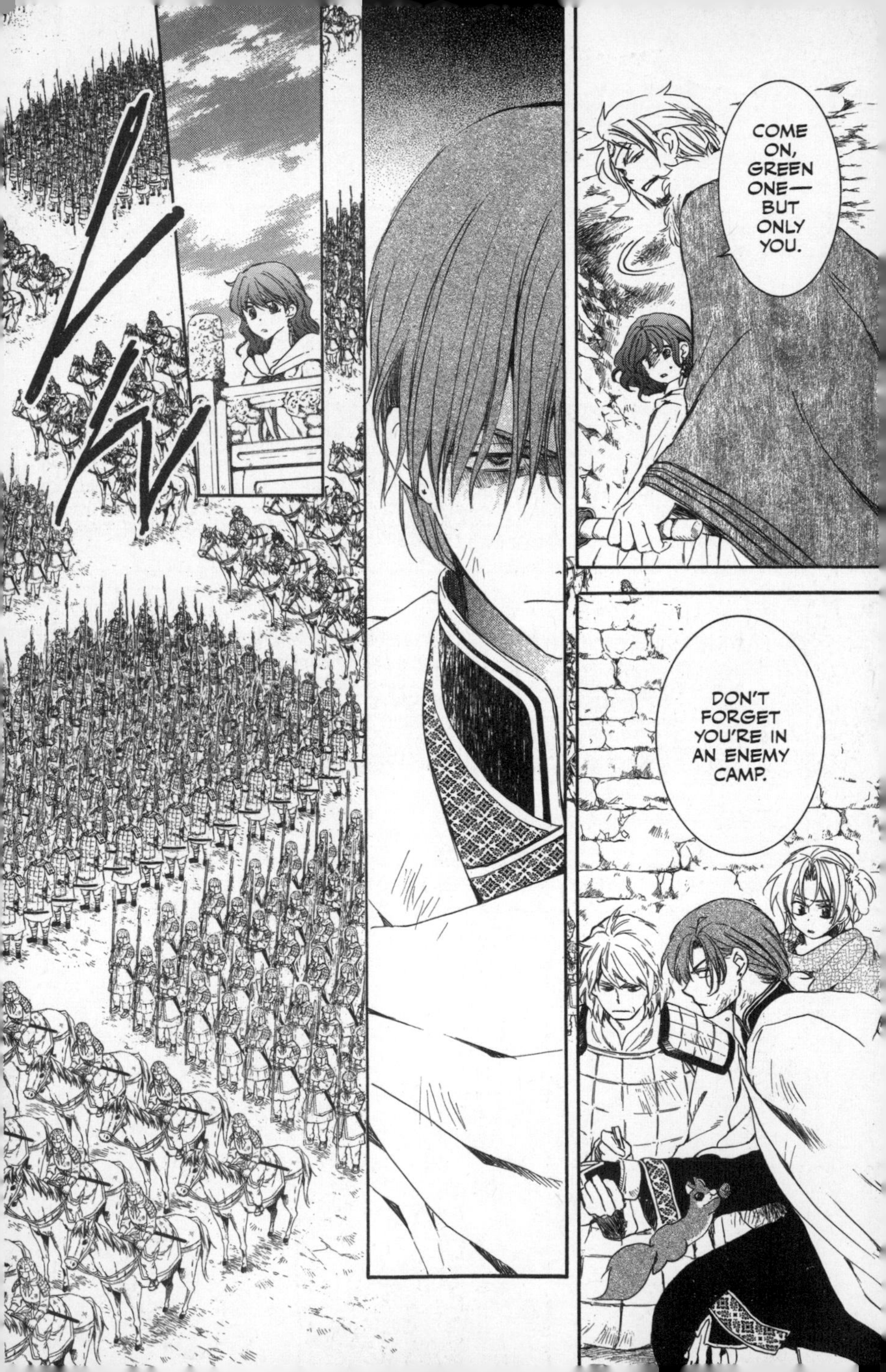
COME ON, GREEN ONE— BUT ONLY YOU.
DON'T FORGET YOU'RE IN AN ENEMY CAMP.

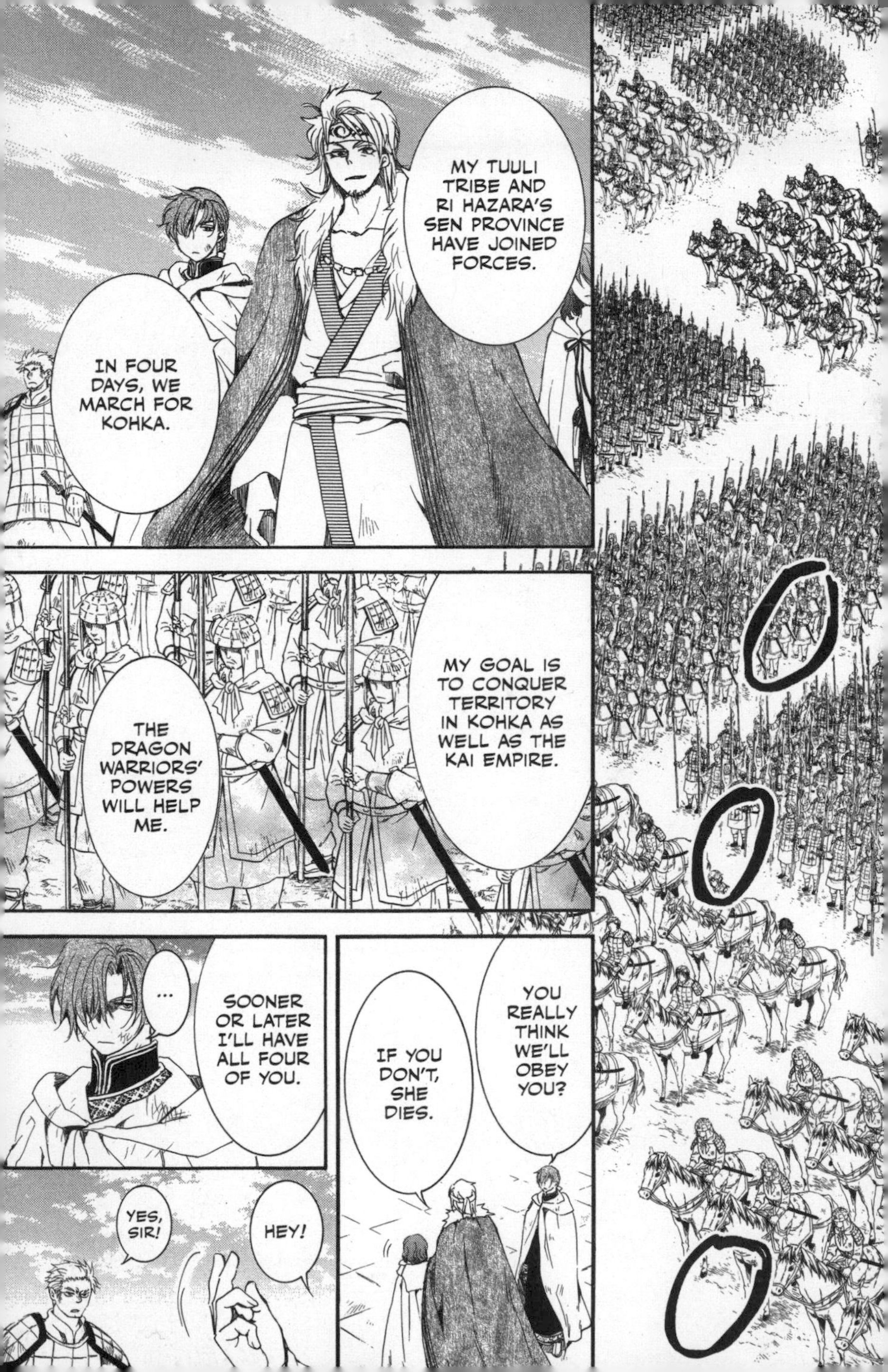
MY TUULI TRIBE AND RI HAZARA'S SEN PROVINCE HAVE JOINED FORCES.
IN FOUR DAYS, WE MARCH FOR KOHKA.
MY GOAL IS TO CONQUER TERRITORY IN KOHKA AS WELL AS THE KAI EMPIRE.
THE DRAGON WARRIORS' POWERS WILL HELP ME.
YOU REALLY THINK WE'LL OBEY YOU?
IF YOU DON'T, SHE DIES.
SOONER OR LATER I'LL HAVE ALL FOUR OF YOU.
...
HEY!
YES, SIR!

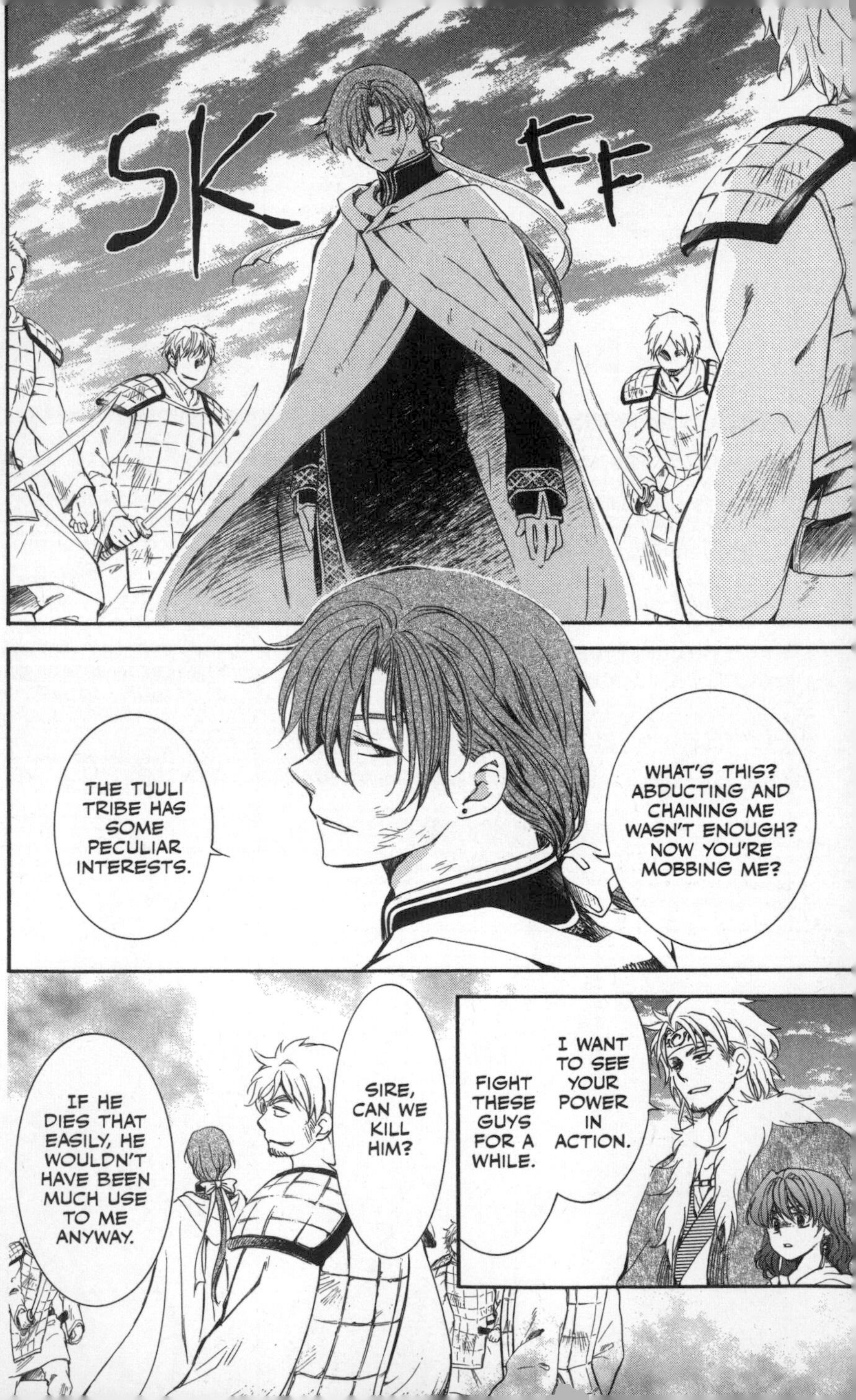
SK
FF
WHAT'S THIS? ABDUCTING AND CHAINING ME WASN'T ENOUGH? NOW YOU'RE MOBBING ME?
THE TUULI TRIBE HAS SOME PECULIAR INTERESTS.
I WANT TO SEE YOUR POWER IN ACTION.
FIGHT THESE GUYS FOR A WHILE.
SIRE, CAN WE KILL HIM?
IF HE DIES THAT EASILY, HE WOULDN'T HAVE BEEN MUCH USE TO ME ANYWAY.

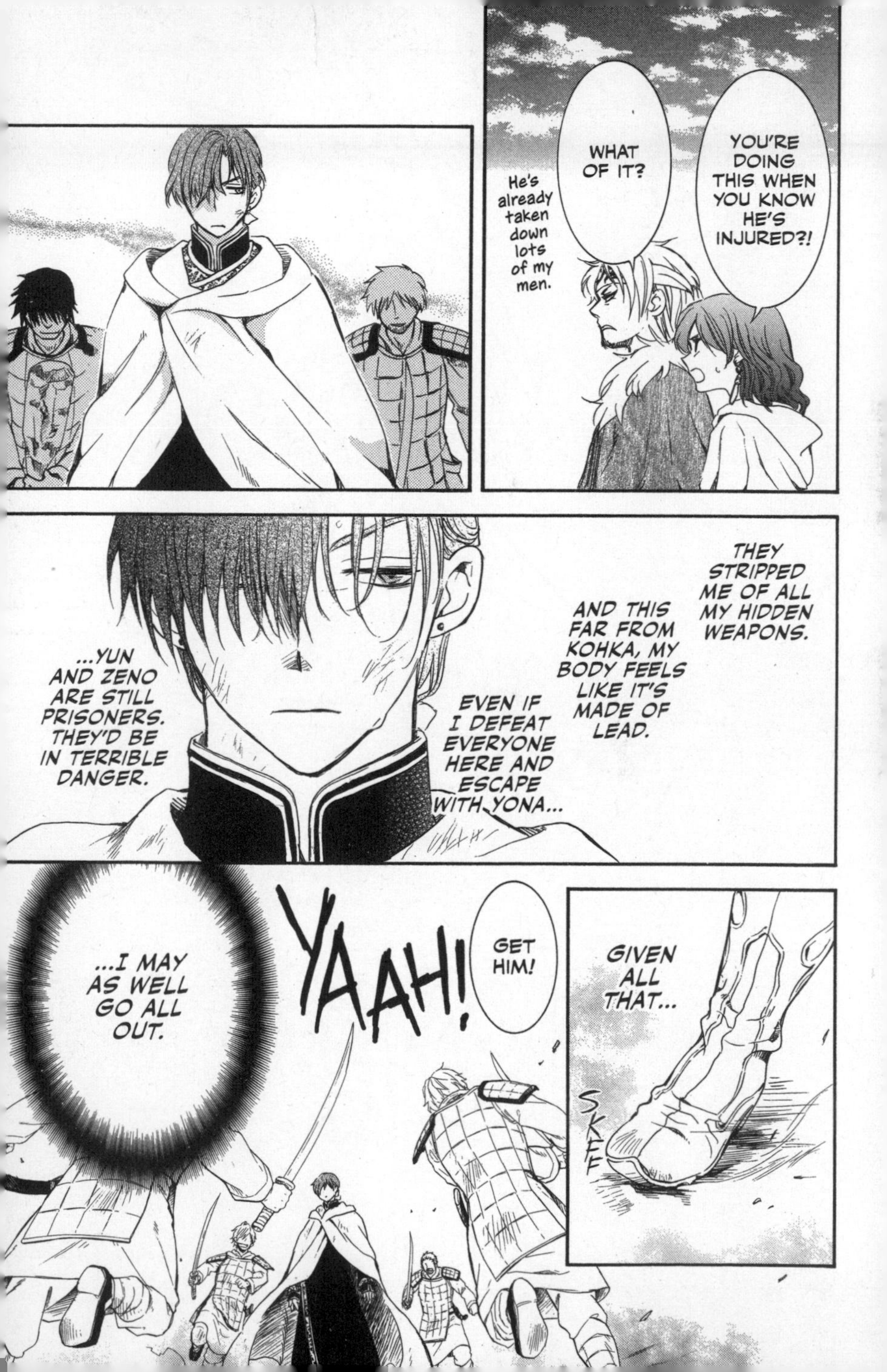
YOU'RE DOING THIS WHEN YOU KNOW HE'S INJURED?!
WHAT OF IT?
He's already taken down lots of my men.
THEY STRIPPED ME OF ALL MY HIDDEN WEAPONS.
AND THIS FAR FROM KOHKA, MY BODY FEELS LIKE IT'S MADE OF LEAD.
EVEN IF I DEFEAT EVERYONE HERE AND ESCAPE WITH YONA...
...YUN AND ZENO ARE STILL PRISONERS. THEY'D BE IN TERRIBLE DANGER.
GIVEN ALL THAT...
SKFF
GET HIM!
YAAH!
...I MAY AS WELL GO ALL OUT.

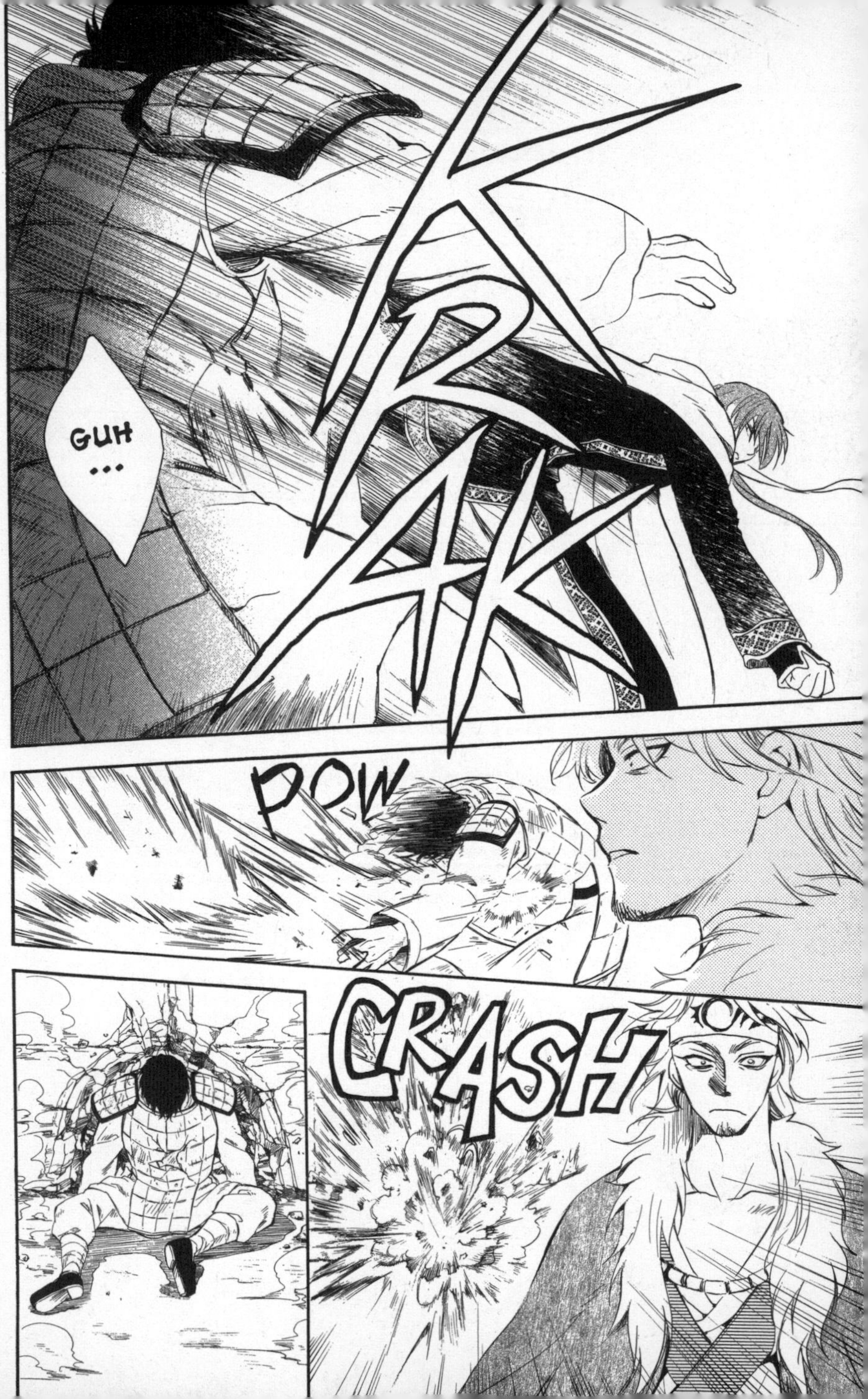
KRAAK
GUH ...
POW
CRASH

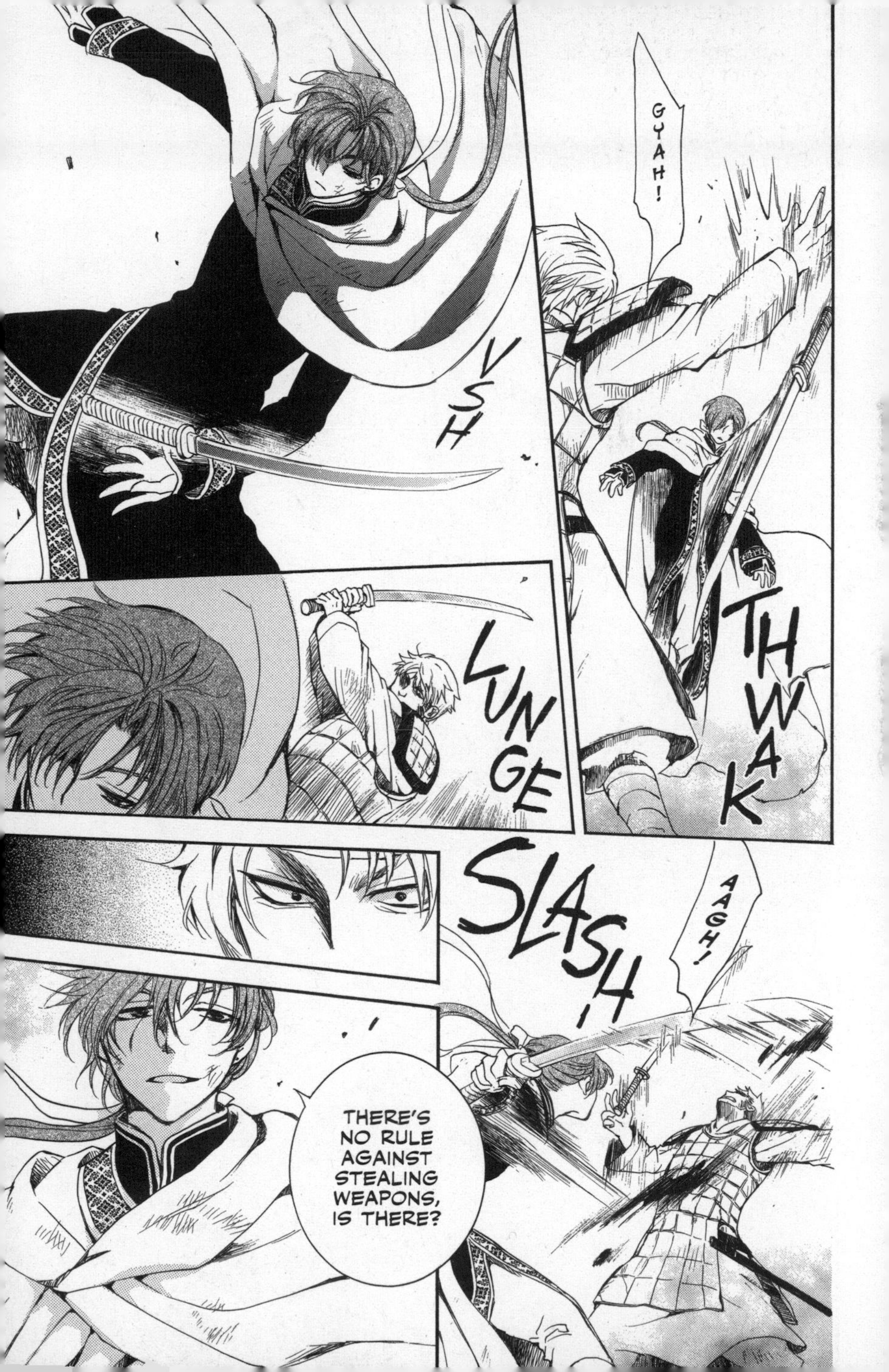
GYAH!
THWAK
VSH
LUNGE
SLASH!
AAGH!
THERE'S NO RULE AGAINST STEALING WEAPONS, IS THERE?

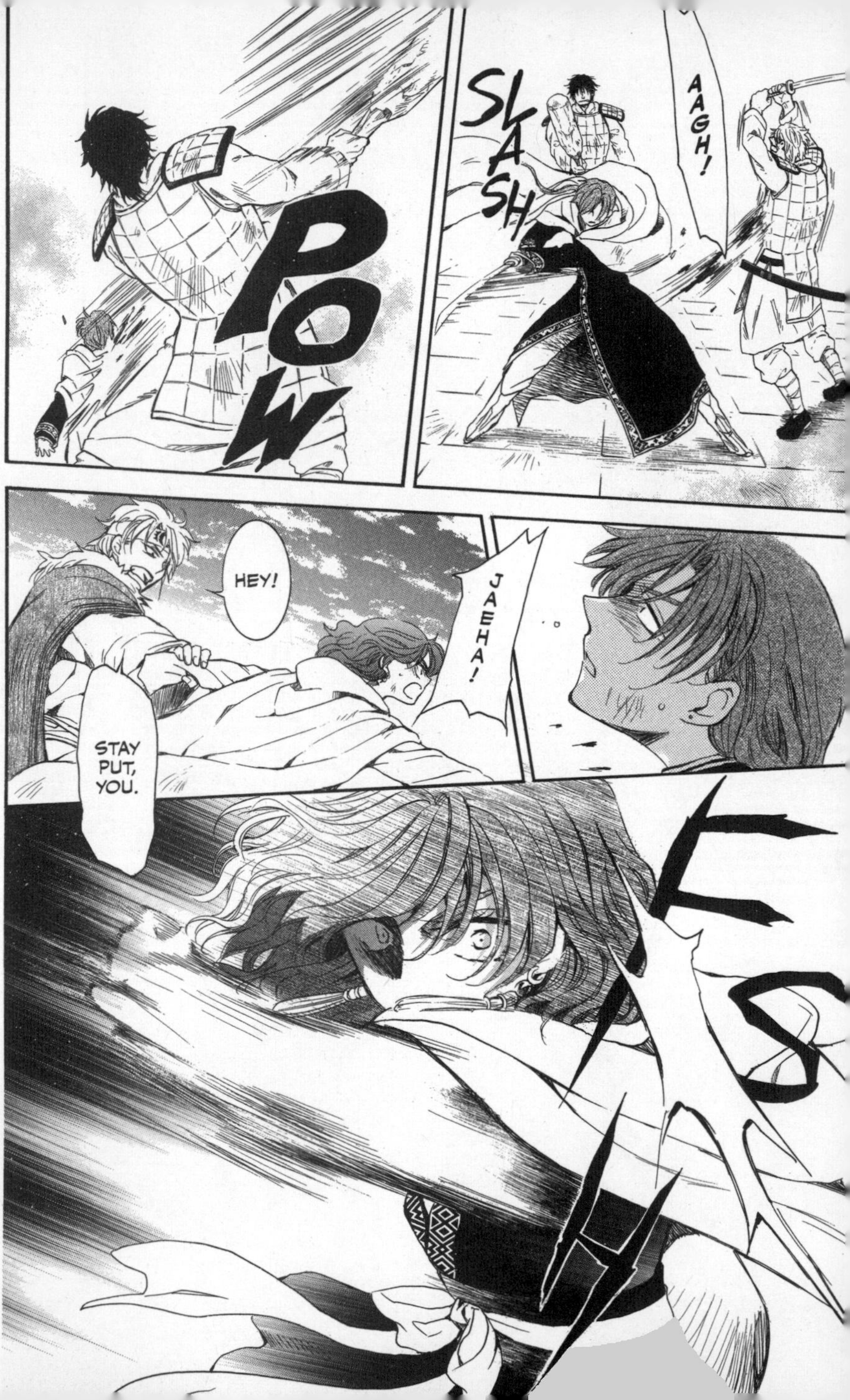
AAGH!
SLASH
POW
JAEHA!
HEY!
STAY PUT, YOU.

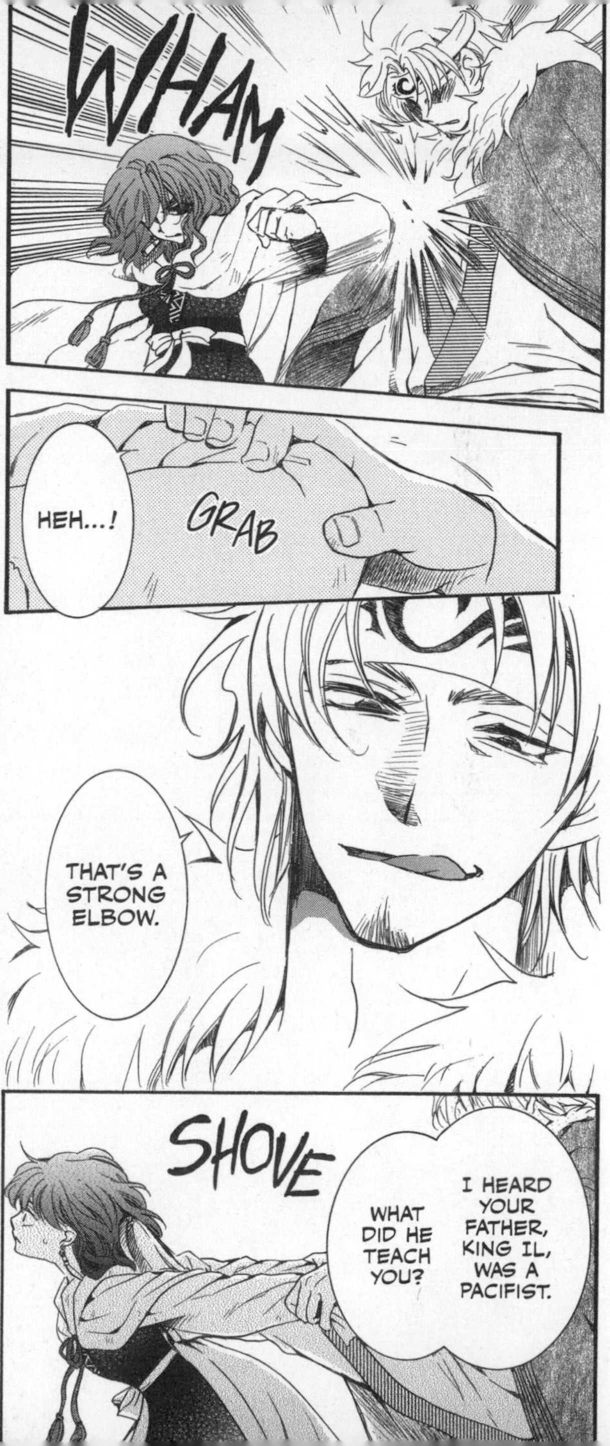
WHAM
GRAB
HEH...!
THAT'S A STRONG ELBOW.
SHOVE
I HEARD YOUR FATHER, KING IL, WAS A PACIFIST.
WHAT DID HE TEACH YOU?

Last December, I went in for my first physical exam in a while.

It was my first time having a gastroscopy and a colonoscopy.

I didn't want to feel any pain, so I chose a hospital that would do it under general anesthesia.

My vision and hearing tests were like orienteering, so that was fun.

I made some lucky guesses, but my sight was 20/13.

Right. CLICK

Down. CLICK

Left. CLICK

For the endoscopy, I was given a liter of laxatives.

Drank 200 milliliters of laxatives the day before. ↓

Drink it slowly over the next hour.

Ugh...

Some places make you drink two liters, so it was still better there than at other hospitals...

To be continued

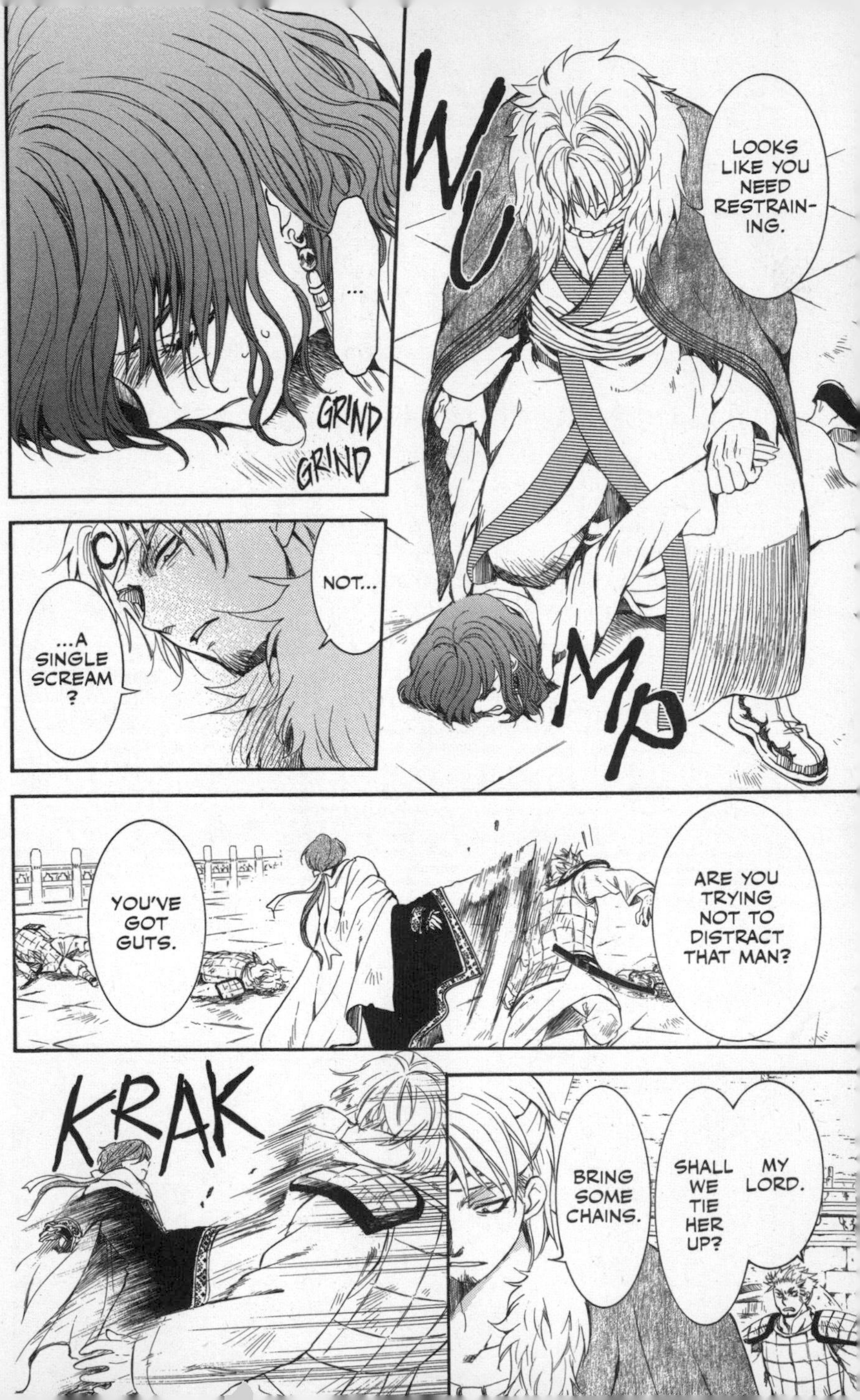
LOOKS LIKE YOU NEED RESTRAIN-ING.
WUMP
...
GRIND
GRIND
NOT...
...A SINGLE SCREAM?
ARE YOU TRYING NOT TO DISTRACT THAT MAN?
YOU'VE GOT GUTS.
MY LORD.
SHALL WE TIE HER UP?
BRING SOME CHAINS.
KRAK

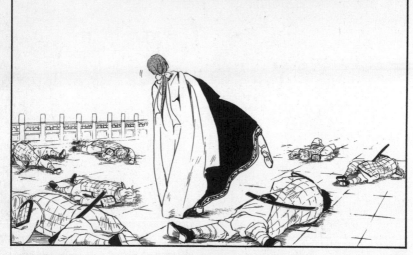

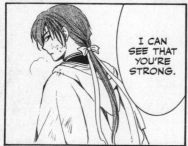

Huff
I CAN SEE THAT YOU'RE STRONG.
BUT I FEEL LIKE YOU STILL HAVEN'T SHOWN ME EVERY-THING.
NEVER MIND THAT.
WHAT HAVE YOU DONE TO HER?

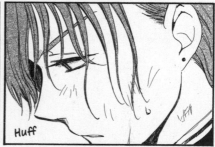

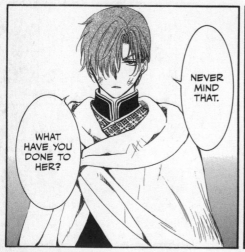

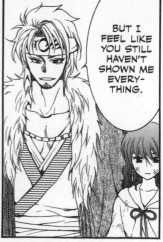

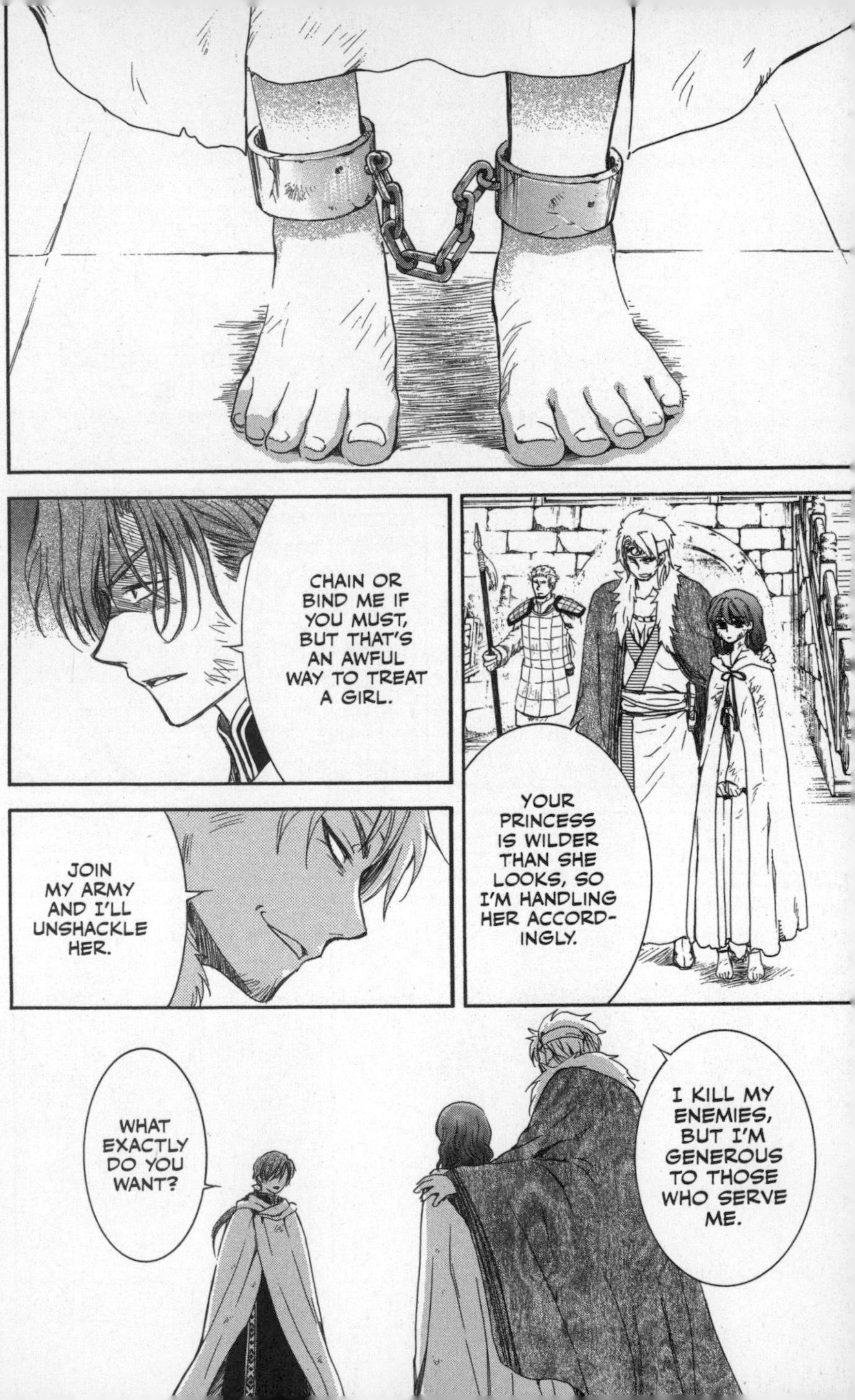

YOUR PRINCESS IS WILDER THAN SHE LOOKS, SO I'M HANDLING HER ACCORDINGLY.
CHAIN OR BIND ME IF YOU MUST, BUT THAT'S AN AWFUL WAY TO TREAT A GIRL.
JOIN MY ARMY AND I'LL UNSHACKLE HER.
I KILL MY ENEMIES, BUT I'M GENEROUS TO THOSE WHO SERVE ME.
WHAT EXACTLY DO YOU WANT?

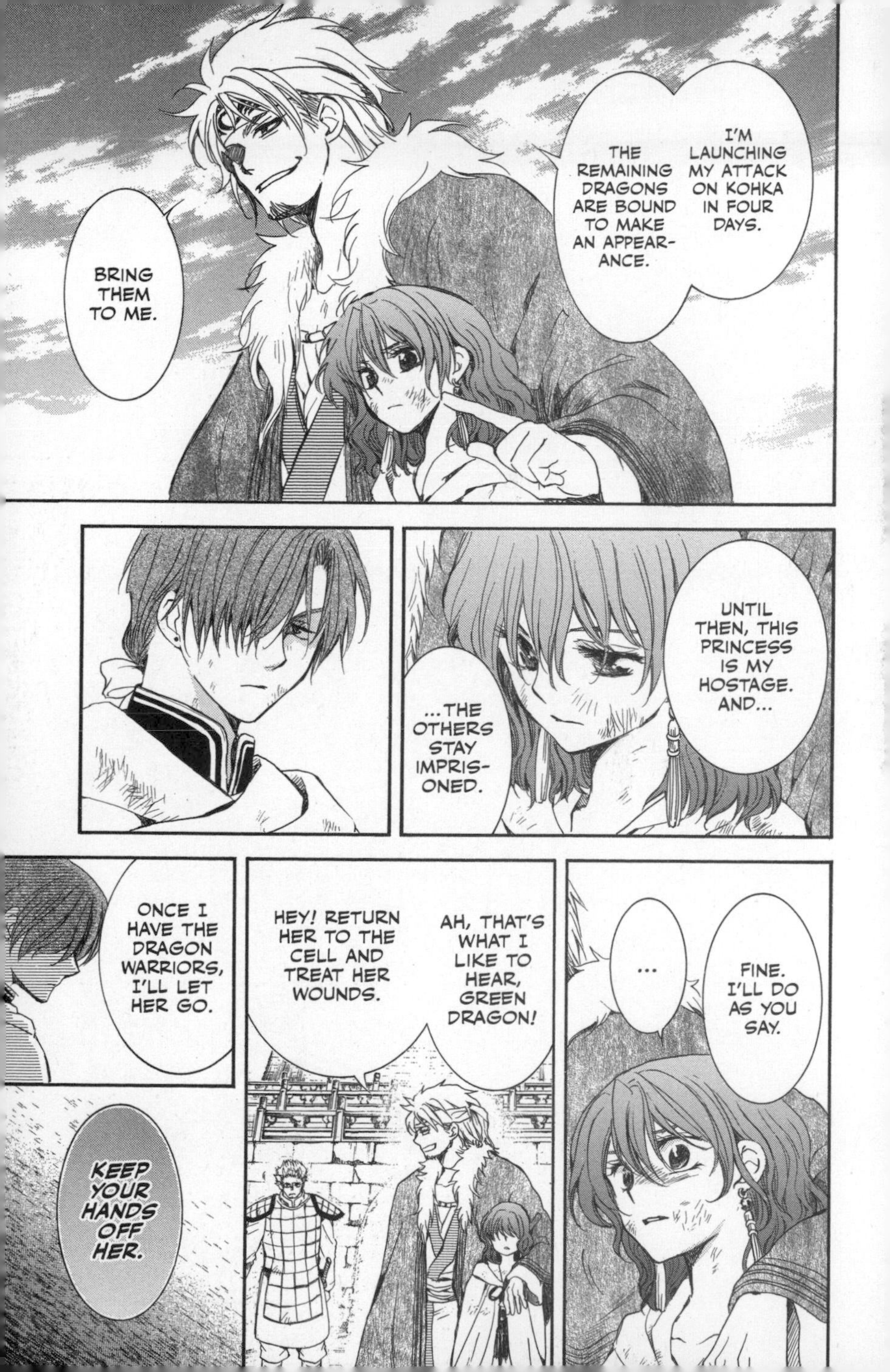
I'M LAUNCHING MY ATTACK ON KOHKA IN FOUR DAYS.
THE REMAINING DRAGONS ARE BOUND TO MAKE AN APPEAR-ANCE.
BRING THEM TO ME.
UNTIL THEN, THIS PRINCESS IS MY HOSTAGE. AND...
...THE OTHERS STAY IMPRIS-ONED.
FINE. I'LL DO AS YOU SAY.
...
AH, THAT'S WHAT I LIKE TO HEAR, GREEN DRAGON!
HEY! RETURN HER TO THE CELL AND TREAT HER WOUNDS.
ONCE I HAVE THE DRAGON WARRIORS, I'LL LET HER GO.
KEEP YOUR HANDS OFF HER.

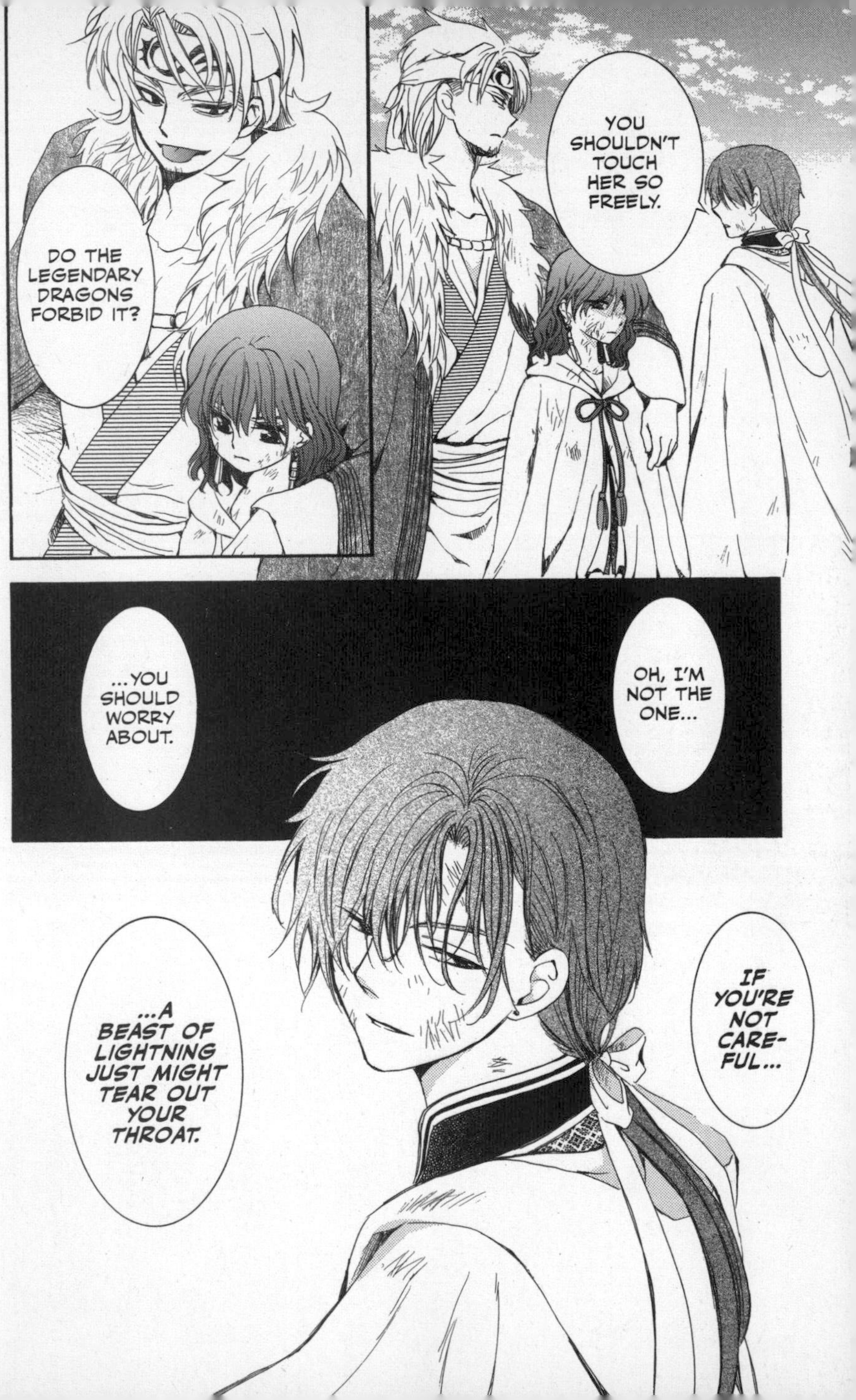
YOU SHOULDN'T TOUCH HER SO FREELY.
DO THE LEGENDARY DRAGONS FORBID IT?
OH, I'M NOT THE ONE...
...YOU SHOULD WORRY ABOUT.
IF YOU'RE NOT CARE-FUL...
...A BEAST OF LIGHTNING JUST MIGHT TEAR OUT YOUR THROAT.

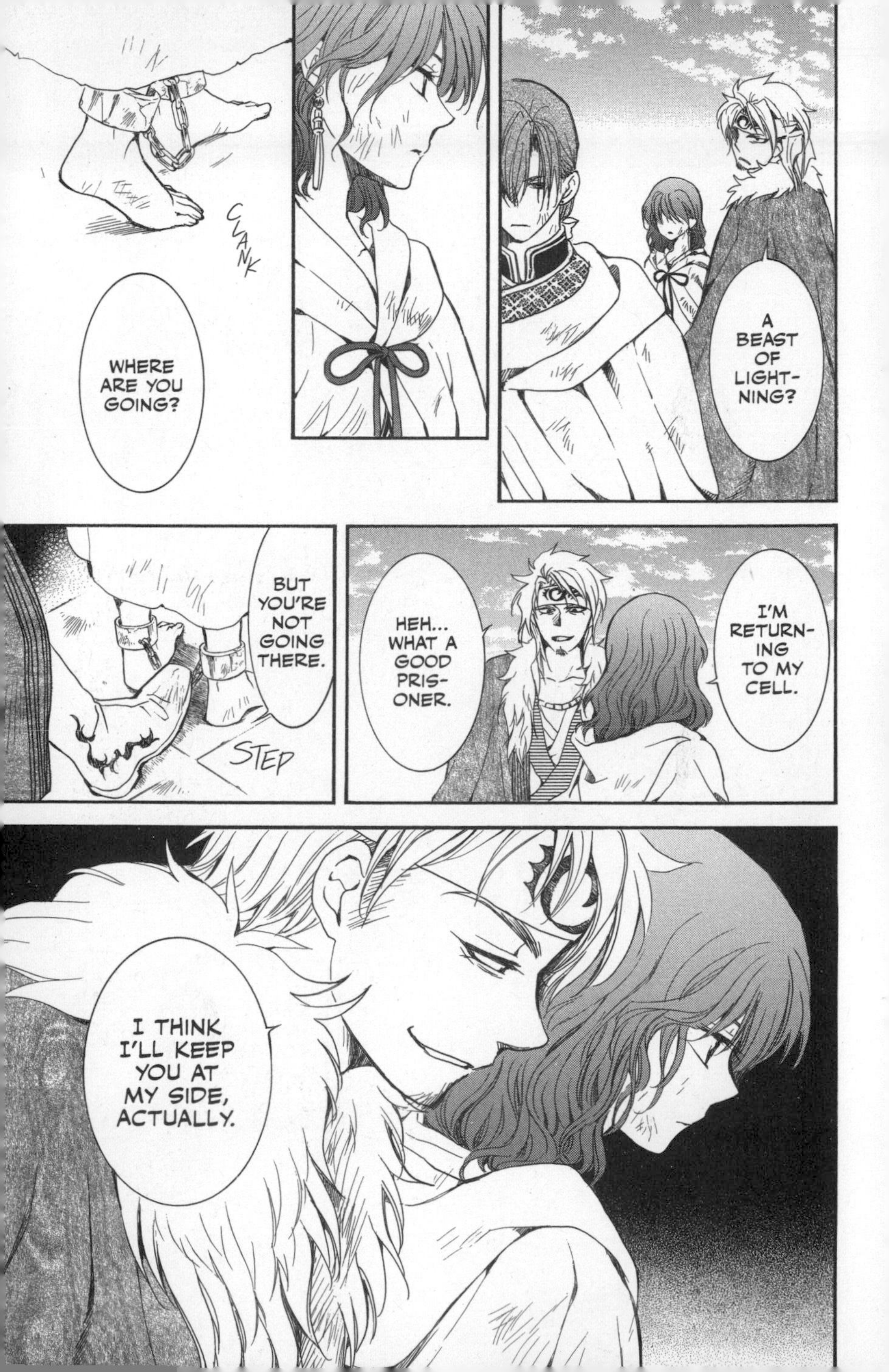
A BEAST OF LIGHTNING?
CLANK
WHERE ARE YOU GOING?
I'M RETURNING TO MY CELL.
HEH... WHAT A GOOD PRISONER.
BUT YOU'RE NOT GOING THERE.
STEP
I THINK I'LL KEEP YOU AT MY SIDE, ACTUALLY.

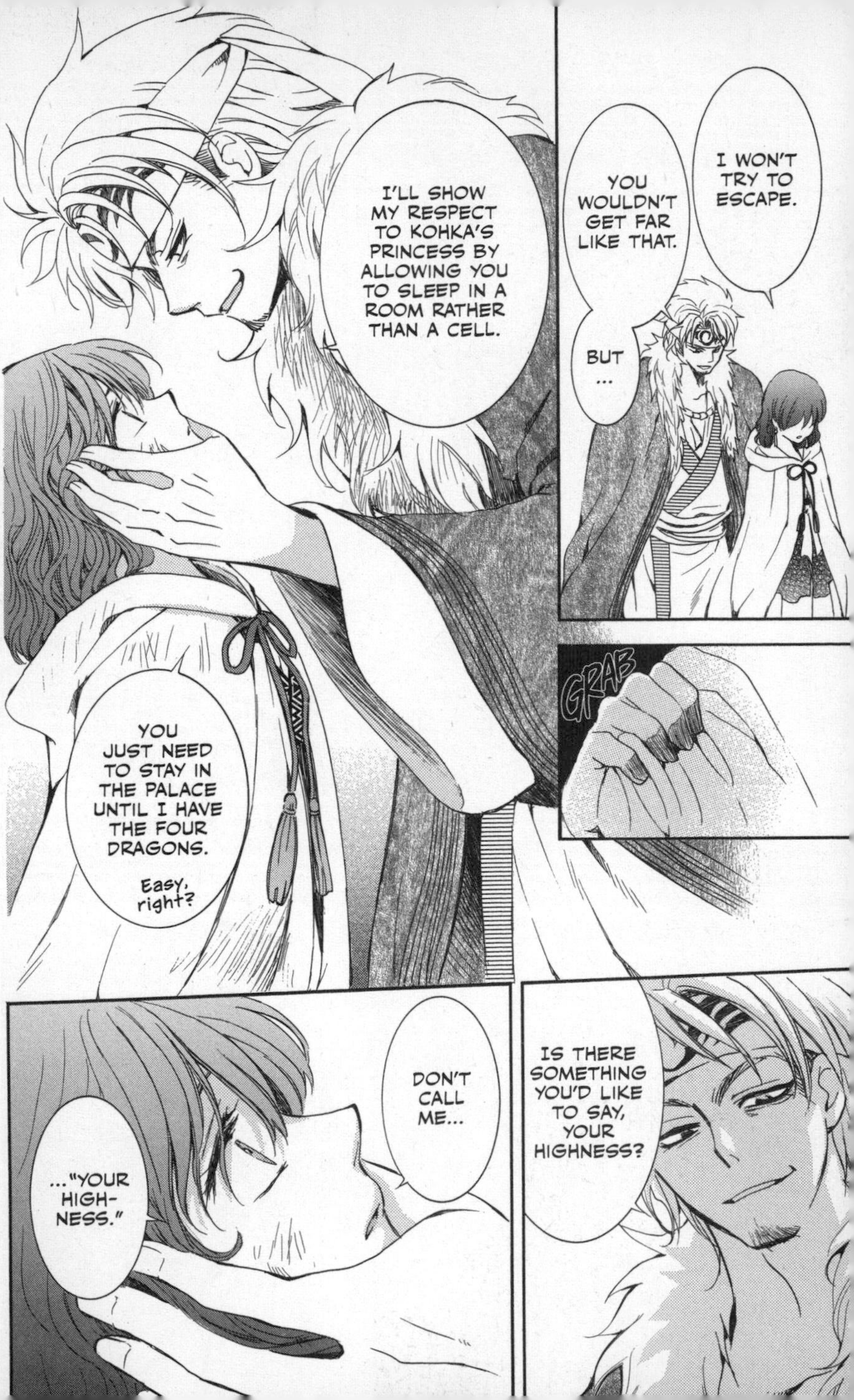
I WON'T TRY TO ESCAPE.
YOU WOULDN'T GET FAR LIKE THAT.
BUT ...
GRAB
I'LL SHOW MY RESPECT TO KOHKA'S PRINCESS BY ALLOWING YOU TO SLEEP IN A ROOM RATHER THAN A CELL.
YOU JUST NEED TO STAY IN THE PALACE UNTIL I HAVE THE FOUR DRAGONS.
Easy, right?
IS THERE SOMETHING YOU'D LIKE TO SAY, YOUR HIGHNESS?
DON'T CALL ME...
..."YOUR HIGH-NESS."

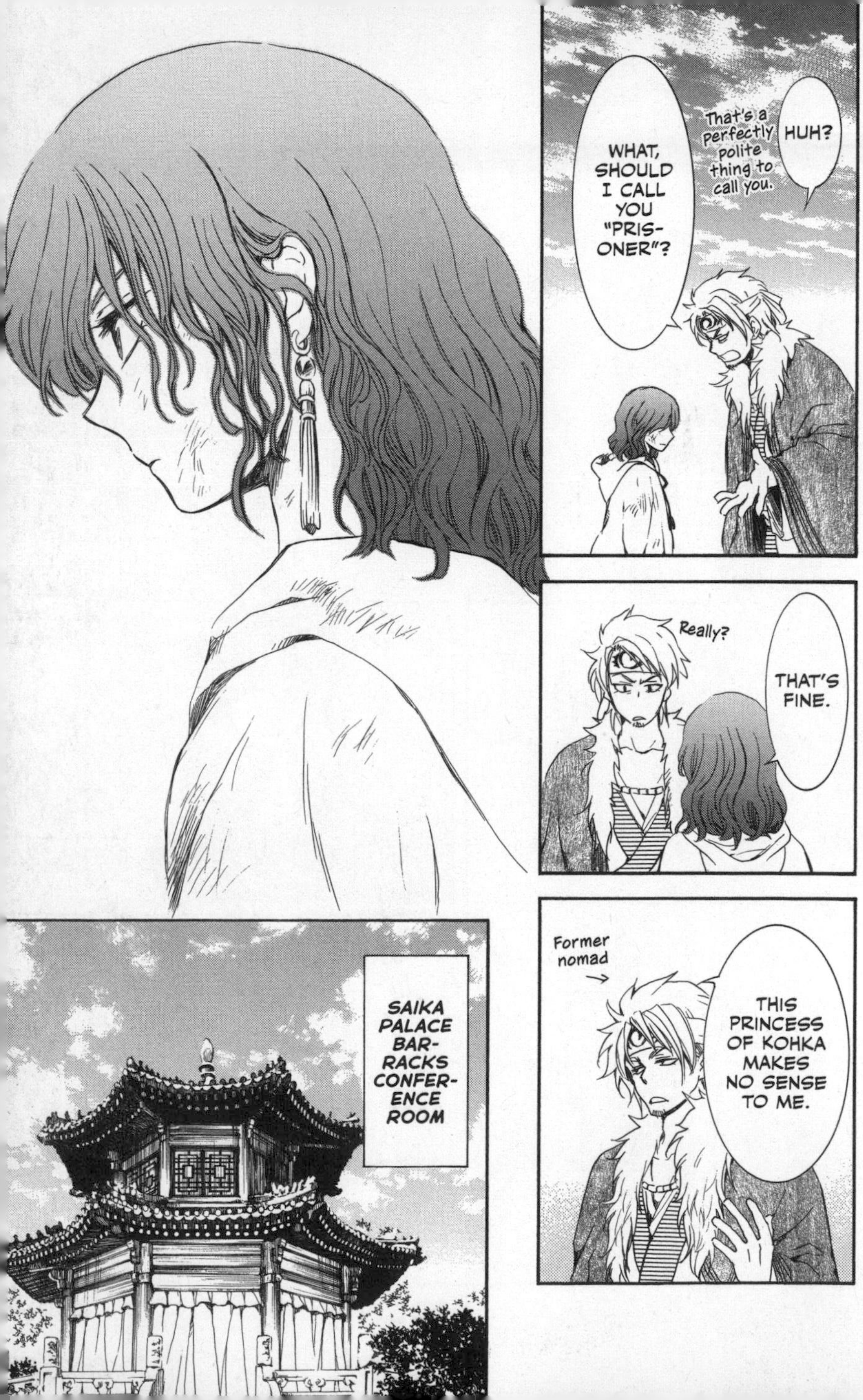
HUH?
That's a perfectly polite thing to call you.
WHAT, SHOULD I CALL YOU "PRIS-ONER"?
THAT'S FINE.
Really?
THIS PRINCESS OF KOHKA MAKES NO SENSE TO ME.
Former nomad
SAIKA PALACE BAR-RACKS CONFER-ENCE ROOM

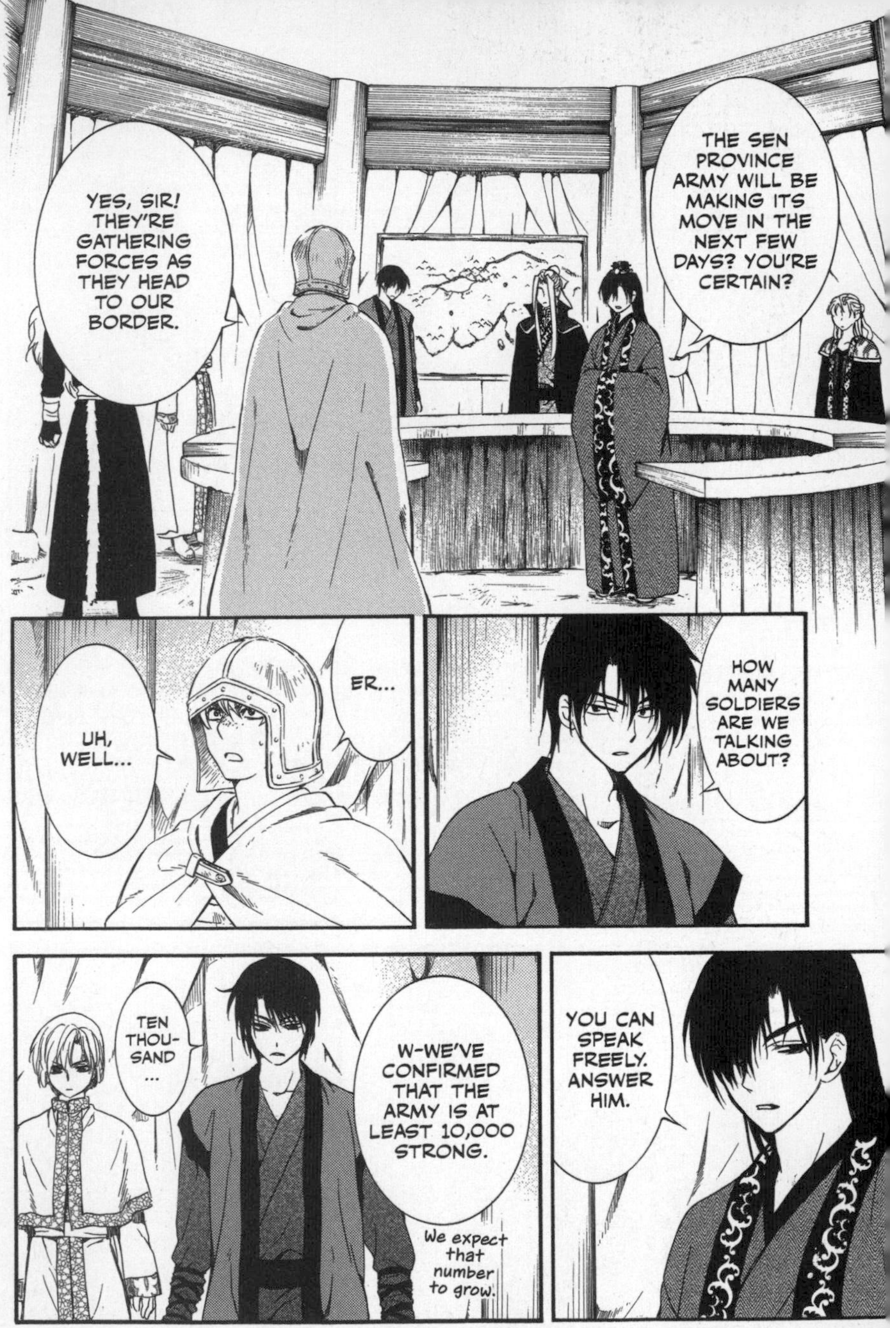
THE SEN PROVINCE ARMY WILL BE MAKING ITS MOVE IN THE NEXT FEW DAYS? YOU'RE CERTAIN?
YES, SIR! THEY'RE GATHERING FORCES AS THEY HEAD TO OUR BORDER.
HOW MANY SOLDIERS ARE WE TALKING ABOUT?
ER...
UH, WELL...
YOU CAN SPEAK FREELY. ANSWER HIM.
W-WE'VE CONFIRMED THAT THE ARMY IS AT LEAST 10,000 STRONG.
We expect that number to grow.
TEN THOU-SAND ...

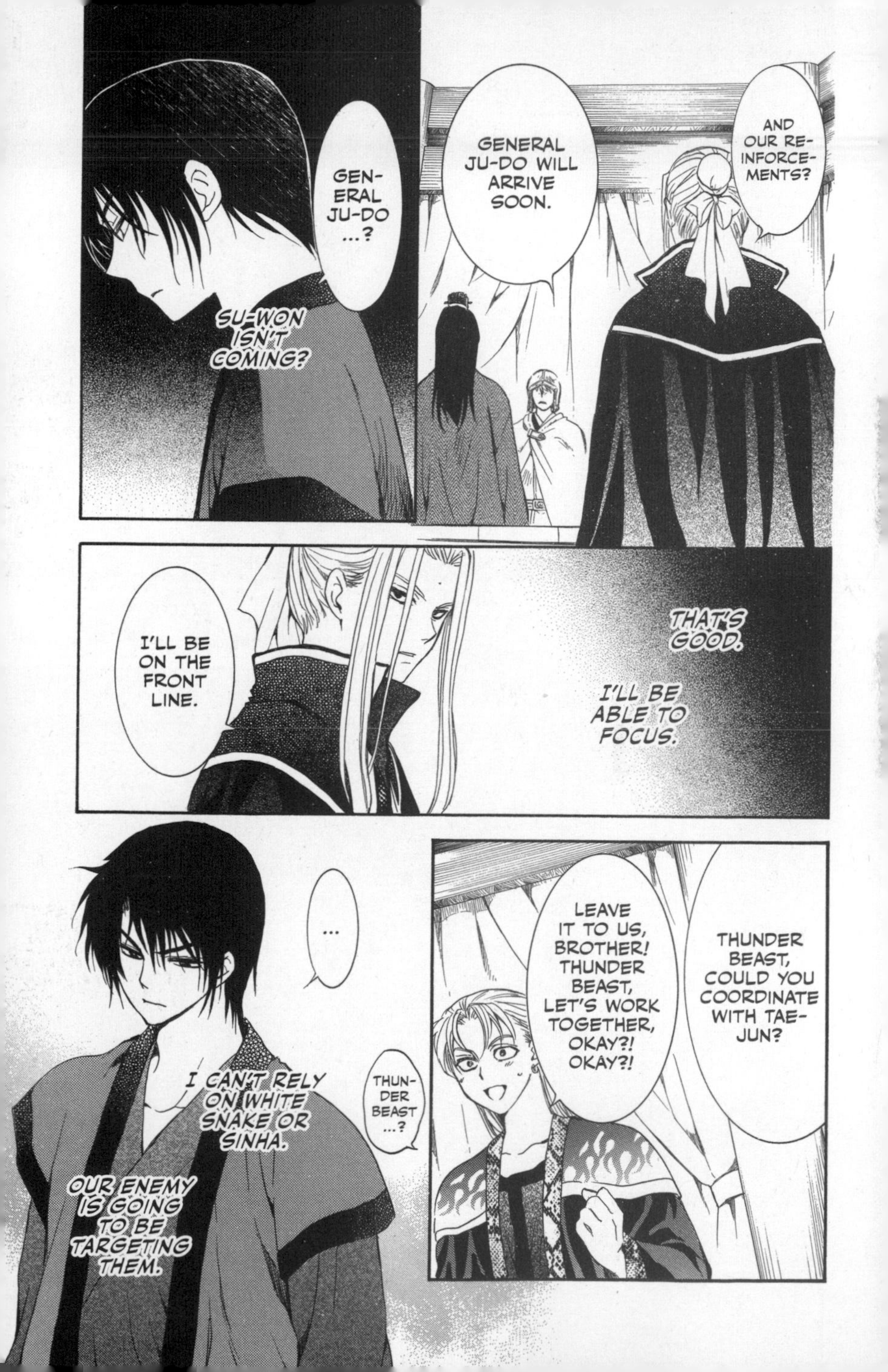

AND OUR RE-INFORCE-MENTS?
GENERAL JU-DO WILL ARRIVE SOON.
GEN-ERAL JU-DO ...?
SU-WON ISN'T COMING?
I'LL BE ON THE FRONT LINE.
THAT'S GOOD.
I'LL BE ABLE TO FOCUS.
THUNDER BEAST, COULD YOU COORDINATE WITH TAE-JUN?
LEAVE IT TO US, BROTHER! THUNDER BEAST, LET'S WORK TOGETHER, OKAY?! OKAY?!
...
THUN-DER BEAST ...?
I CAN'T RELY ON WHITE SNAKE OR SINHA.
OUR ENEMY IS GOING TO BE TARGETING THEM.

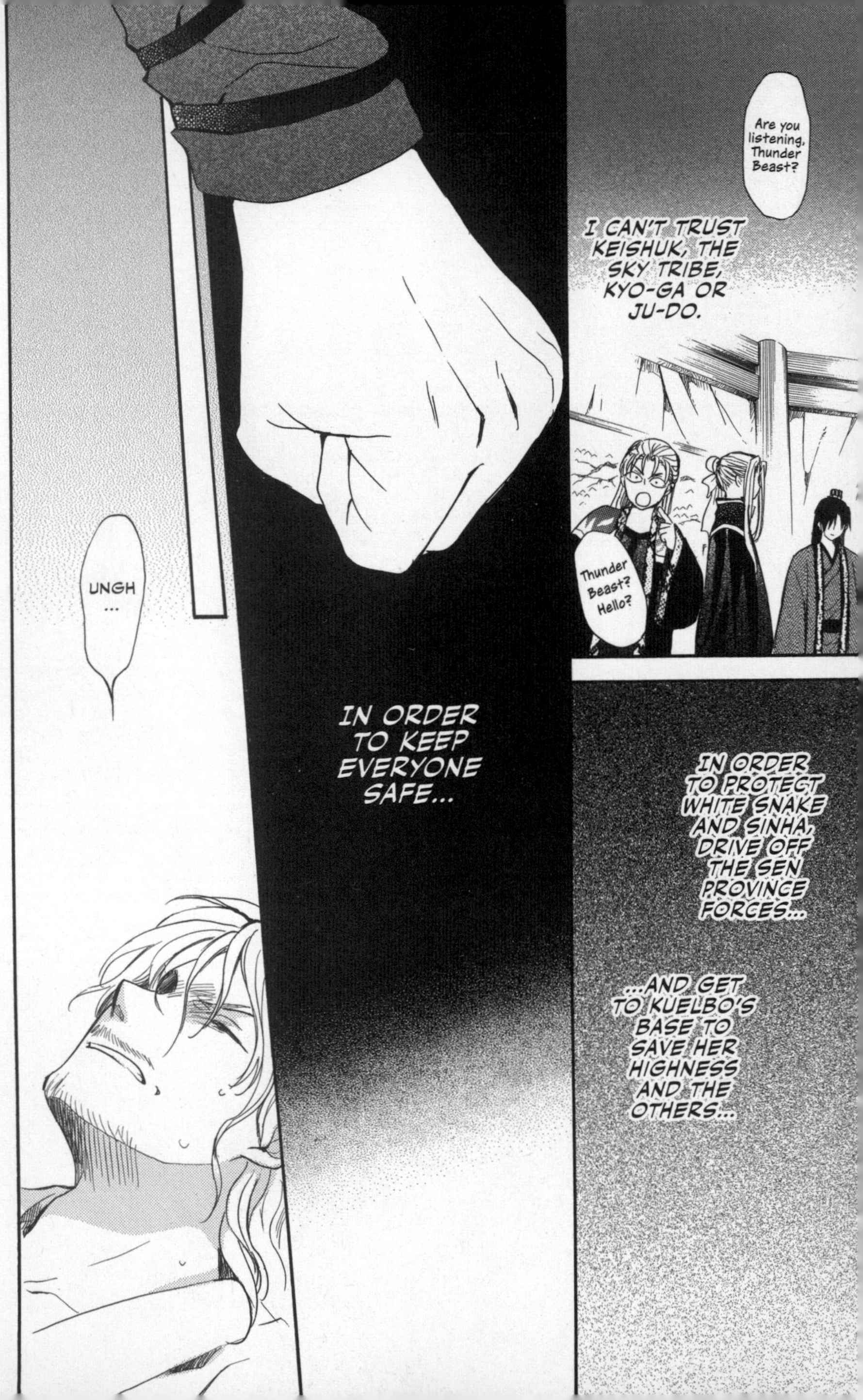
Are you listening, Thunder Beast?
I CAN'T TRUST KEISHUK, THE SKY TRIBE, KYO-GA OR JU-DO.
Thunder Beast? Hello?
IN ORDER TO PROTECT WHITE SNAKE AND SINHA, DRIVE OFF THE SEN PROVINCE FORCES...
...AND GET TO KUELBO'S BASE TO SAVE HER HIGHNESS AND THE OTHERS...
IN ORDER TO KEEP EVERYONE SAFE...
UNGH ...

HOW MANY DAYS AGO WAS I ATTACKED?

WHAT'S GOING ON OUT IN THE WORLD?

S-SOME-ONE...

OW...

...IS THERE?

SOME-ONE...

CLAK

UGH...

WHENEVER I SLEEP, I JUST DREAM ABOUT THOSE CLOAKED MEN...

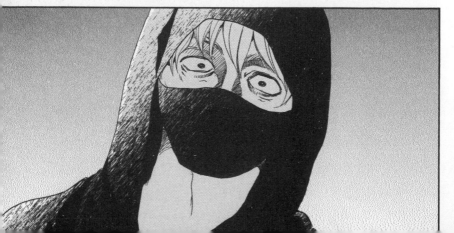

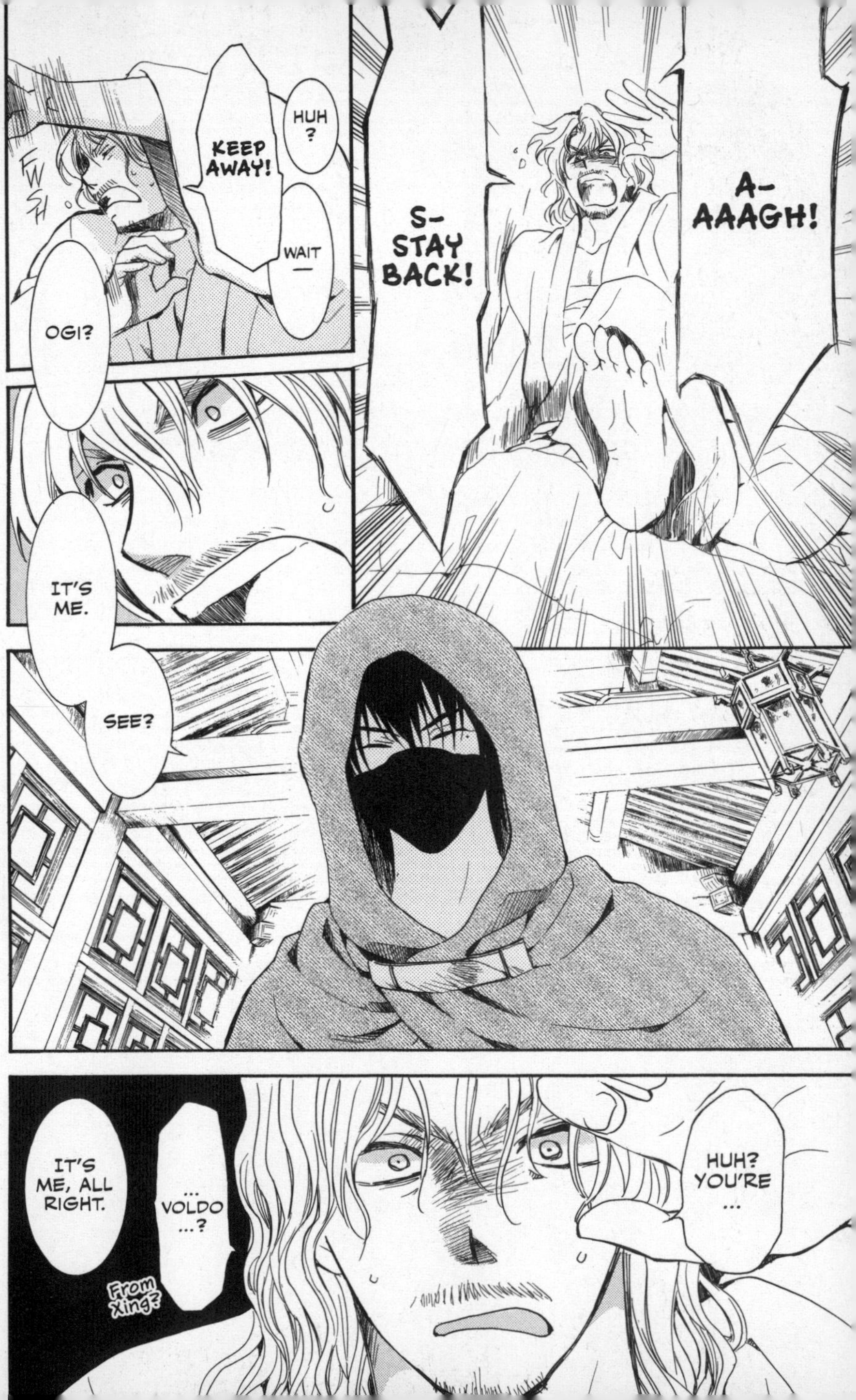
A- AAAGH!
S- STAY BACK!
HUH?
KEEP AWAY!
FWSH
WAIT —
OGI?
IT'S ME.
SEE?
HUH? YOU'RE ...
... VOLDO ...?
IT'S ME, ALL RIGHT.
From Xing?

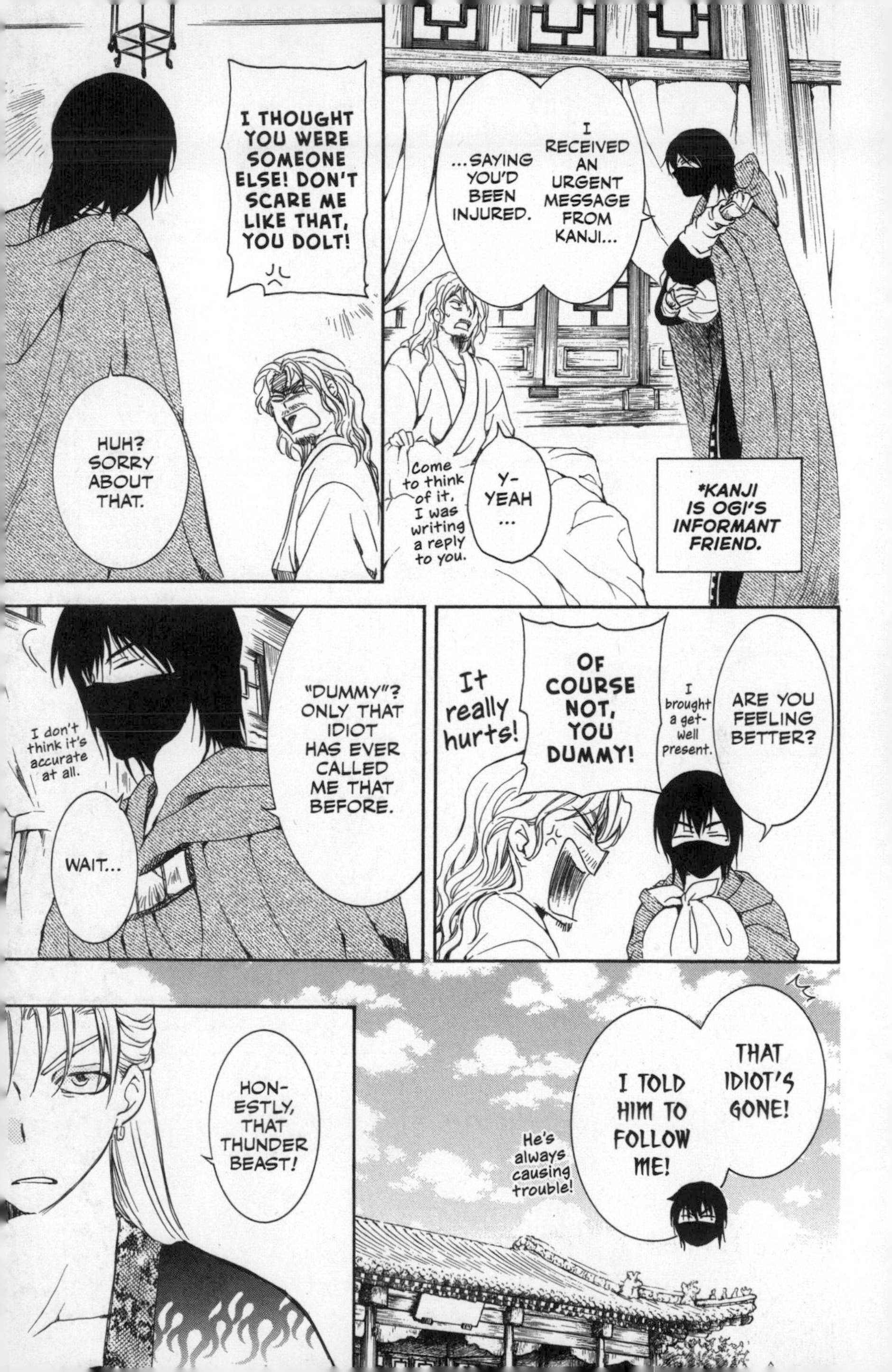
I RECEIVED AN URGENT MESSAGE FROM KANJI...
...SAYING YOU'D BEEN INJURED.
*KANJI IS OGI'S INFORMANT FRIEND.
Y-YEAH...
Come to think of it, I was writing a reply to you.
I THOUGHT YOU WERE SOMEONE ELSE! DON'T SCARE ME LIKE THAT, YOU DOLT!
HUH? SORRY ABOUT THAT.
ARE YOU FEELING BETTER?
I brought a get-well present.
OF COURSE NOT, YOU DUMMY!
It really hurts!
"DUMMY"? ONLY THAT IDIOT HAS EVER CALLED ME THAT BEFORE.
WAIT...
I don't think it's accurate at all.
THAT IDIOT'S GONE!
I TOLD HIM TO FOLLOW ME!
He's always causing trouble!
HONESTLY, THAT THUNDER BEAST!

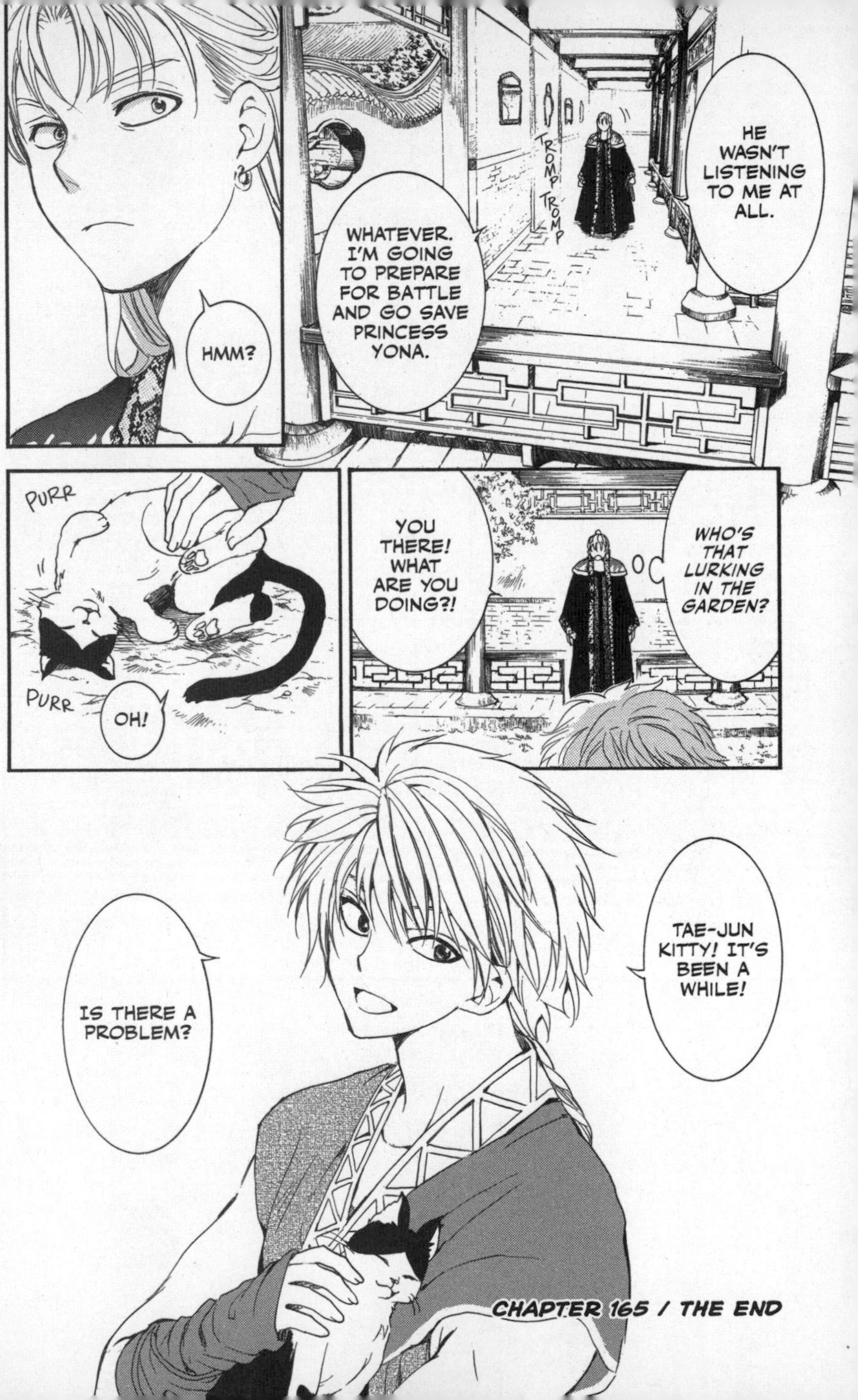
HE WASN'T LISTENING TO ME AT ALL.
TROMP TROMP
WHATEVER. I'M GOING TO PREPARE FOR BATTLE AND GO SAVE PRINCESS YONA.
HMM?
WHO'S THAT LURKING IN THE GARDEN?
YOU THERE! WHAT ARE YOU DOING?!
PURR
PURR
OH!
TAE-JUN KITTY! IT'S BEEN A WHILE!
IS THERE A PROBLEM?
CHAPTER 165 / THE END

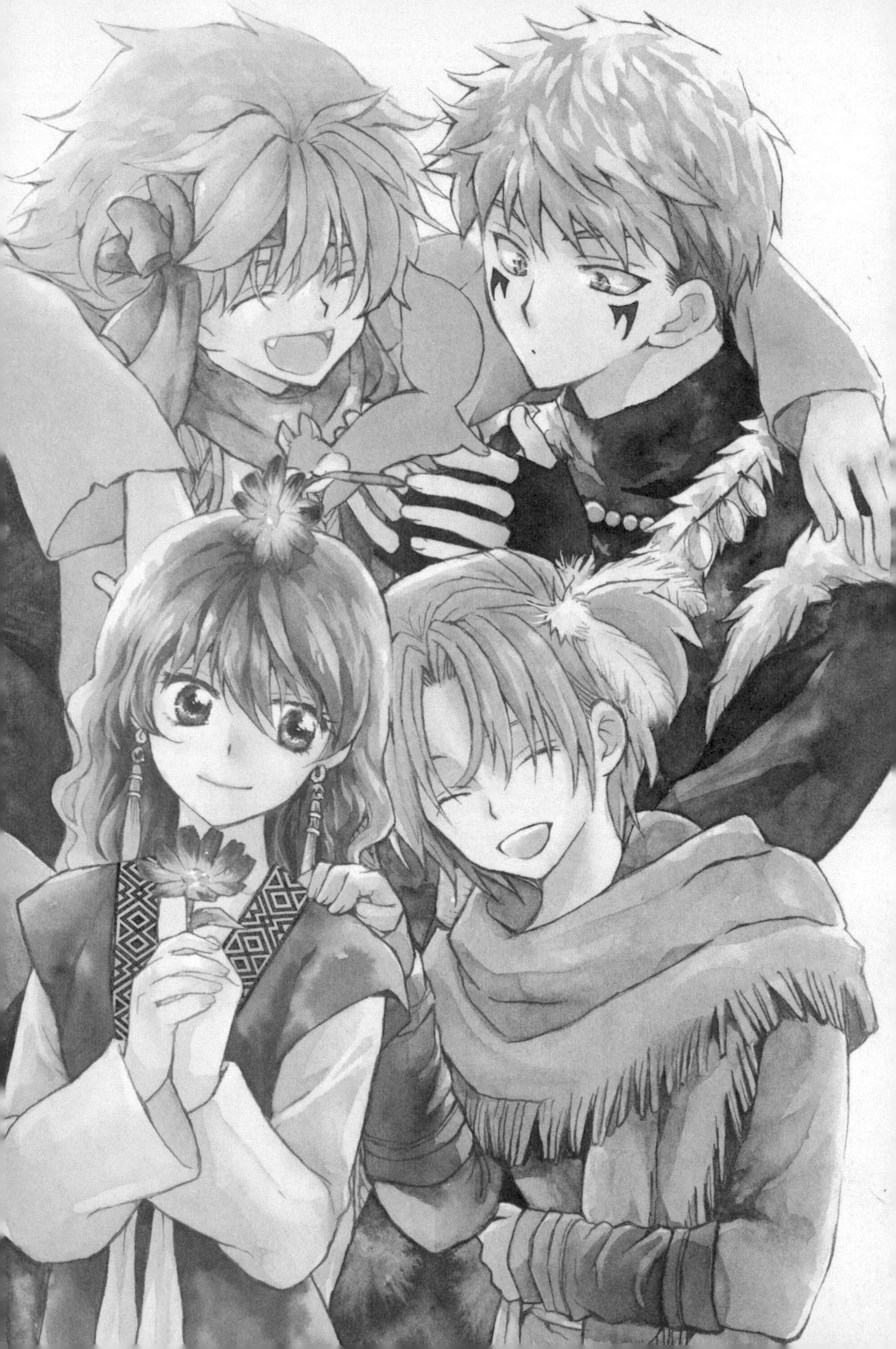

CHAPTER 166: MILITARY STRENGTH

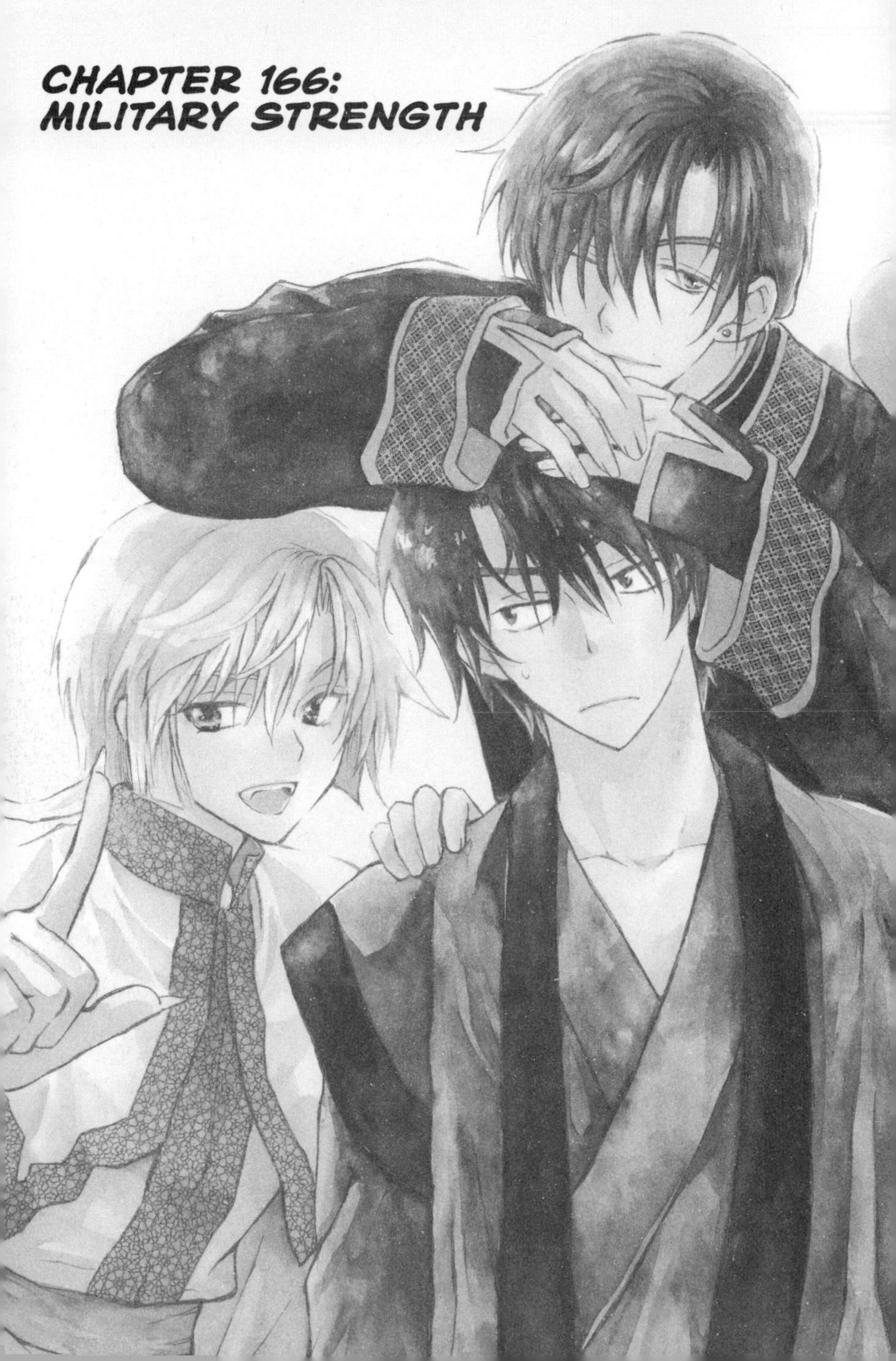

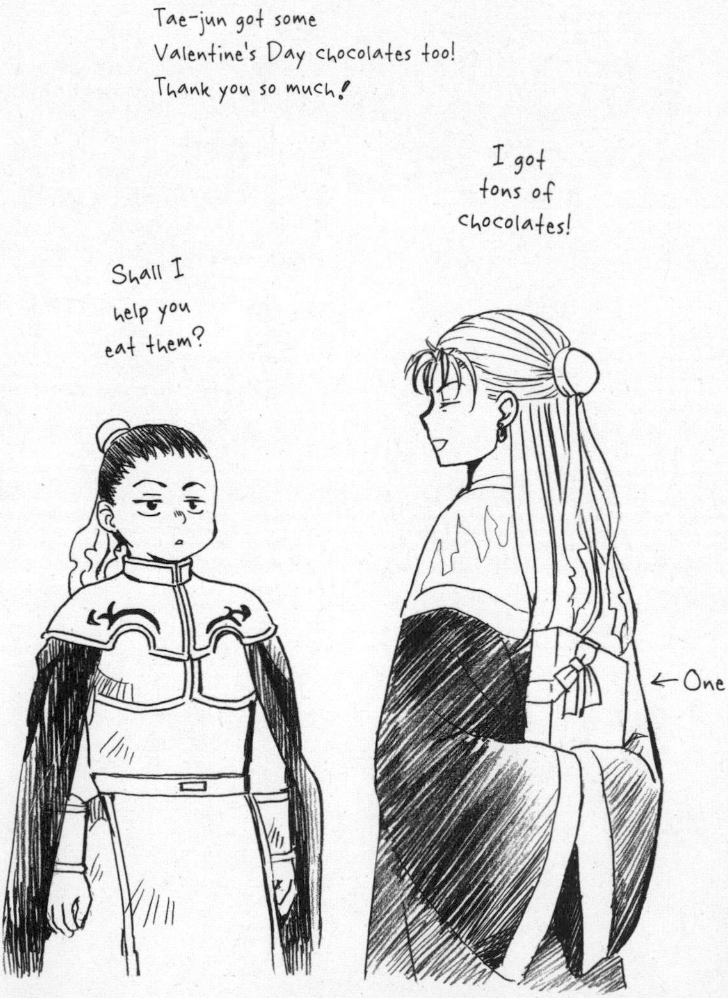

Tae-jun got some
Valentine's Day chocolates too!
Thank you so much!
I got
tons of
chocolates!
Shall I
help you
eat them?
← One

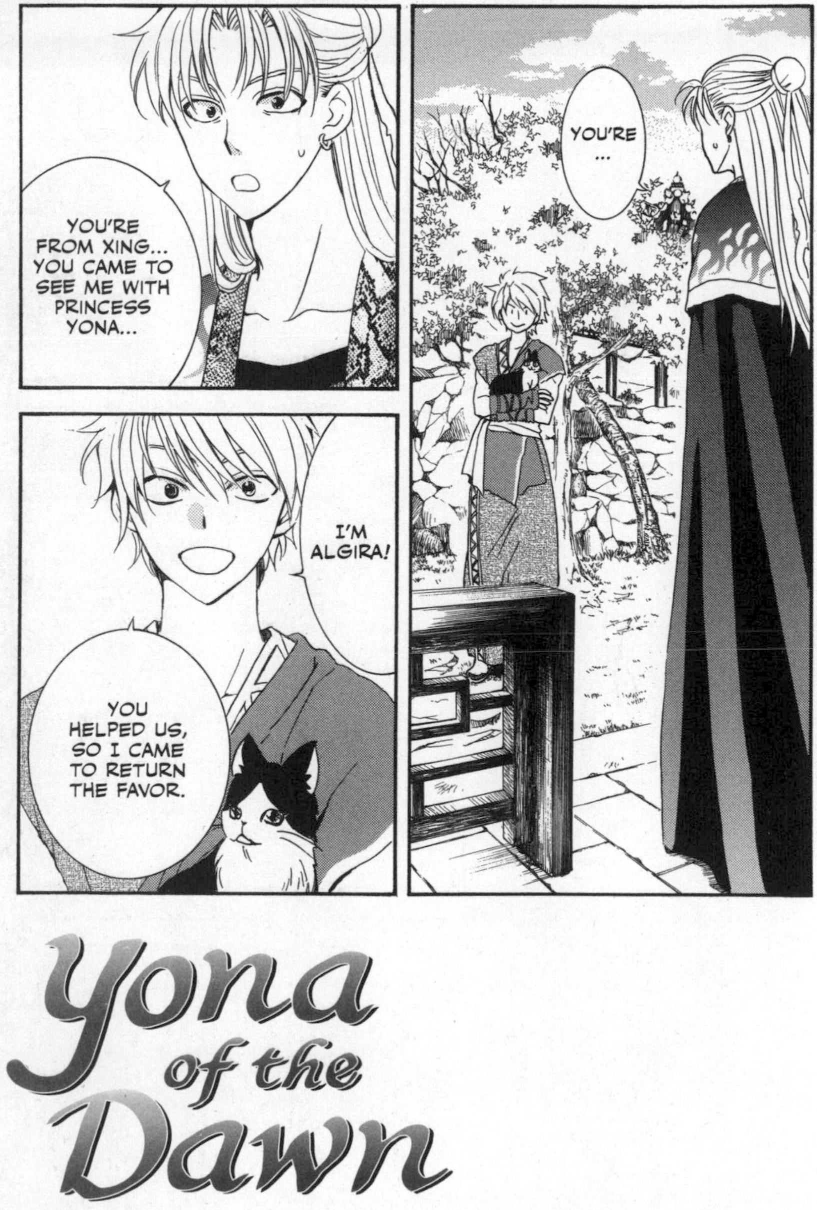
YOU'RE ...
YOU'RE FROM XING... YOU CAME TO SEE ME WITH PRINCESS YONA...
I'M ALGIRA!
YOU HELPED US, SO I CAME TO RETURN THE FAVOR.

Yona of the Dawn

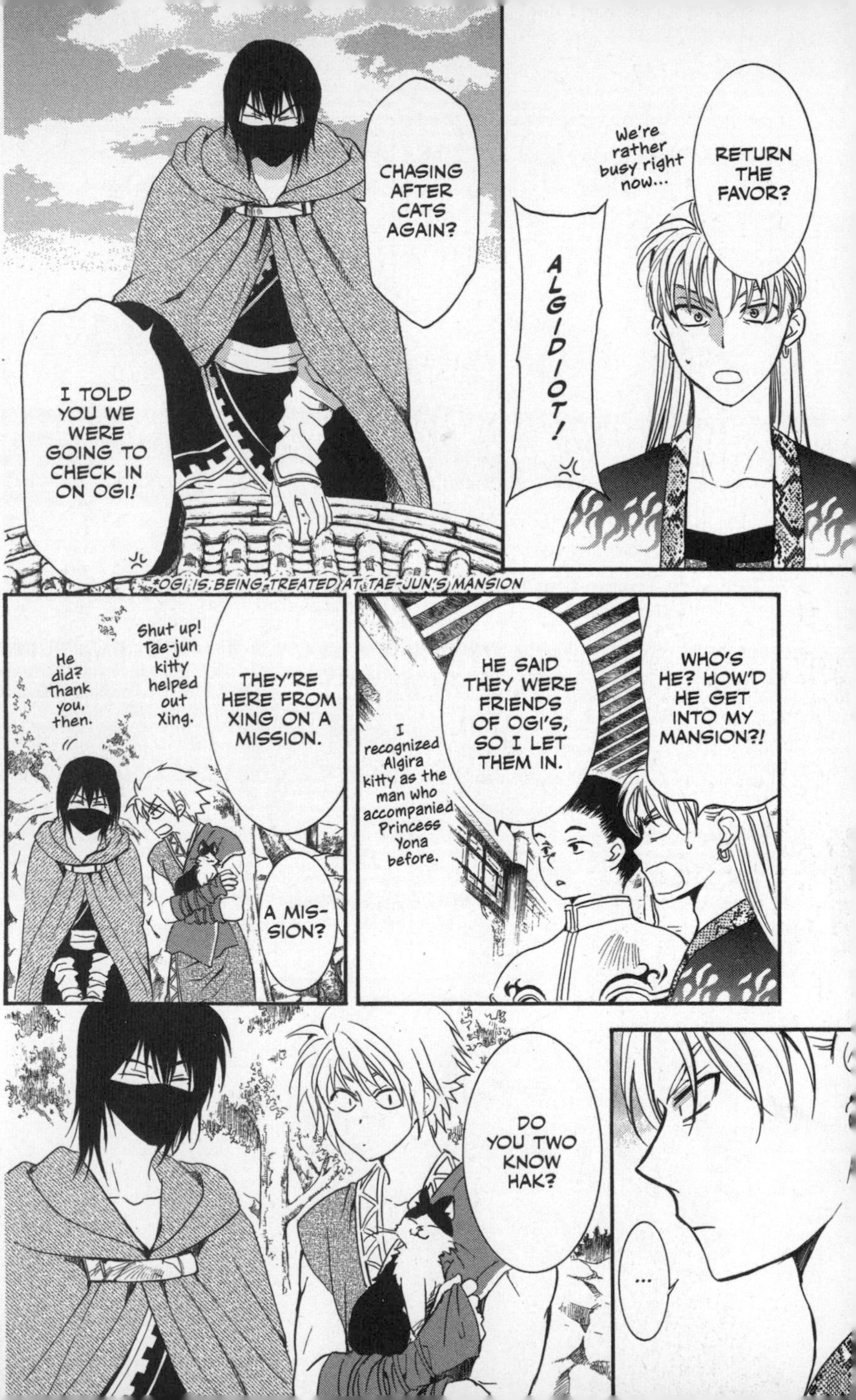
RETURN THE FAVOR?
We're rather busy right now...
ALGIDIOT!
CHASING AFTER CATS AGAIN?
I TOLD YOU WE WERE GOING TO CHECK IN ON OGI!
*OGI IS BEING TREATED AT TAE-JUN'S MANSION
WHO'S HE? HOW'D HE GET INTO MY MANSION?!
HE SAID THEY WERE FRIENDS OF OGI'S, SO I LET THEM IN.
I recognized Algira kitty as the man who accompanied Princess Yona before.
THEY'RE HERE FROM XING ON A MISSION.
Shut up! Tae-jun kitty helped out Xing.
He did? Thank you, then.
A MIS-SION?
...
DO YOU TWO KNOW HAK?

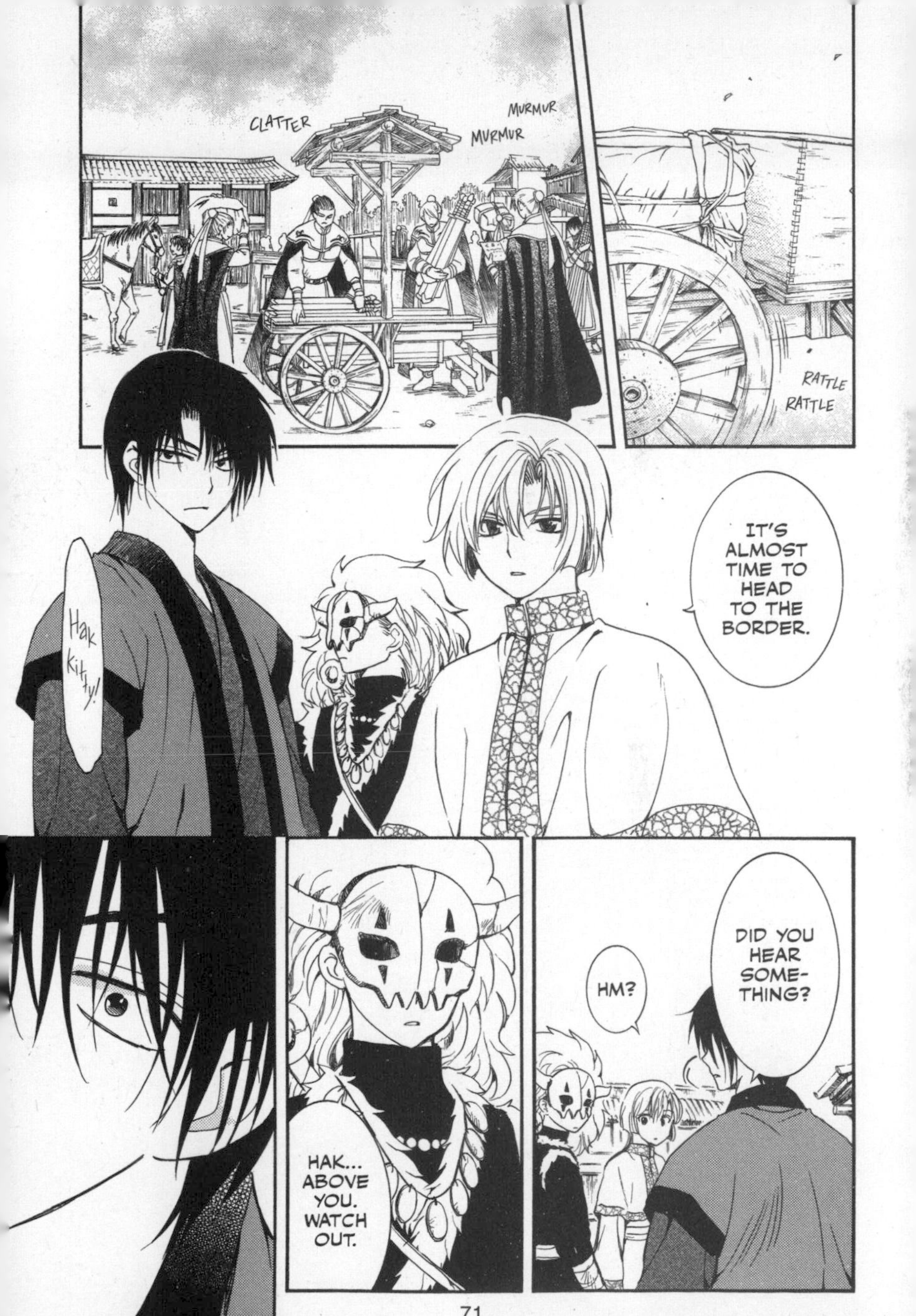
RATTLE
RATTLE
CLATTER
MURMUR
MURMUR
IT'S ALMOST TIME TO HEAD TO THE BORDER.
Hak kitty!
DID YOU HEAR SOME-THING?
HM?
HAK... ABOVE YOU. WATCH OUT.

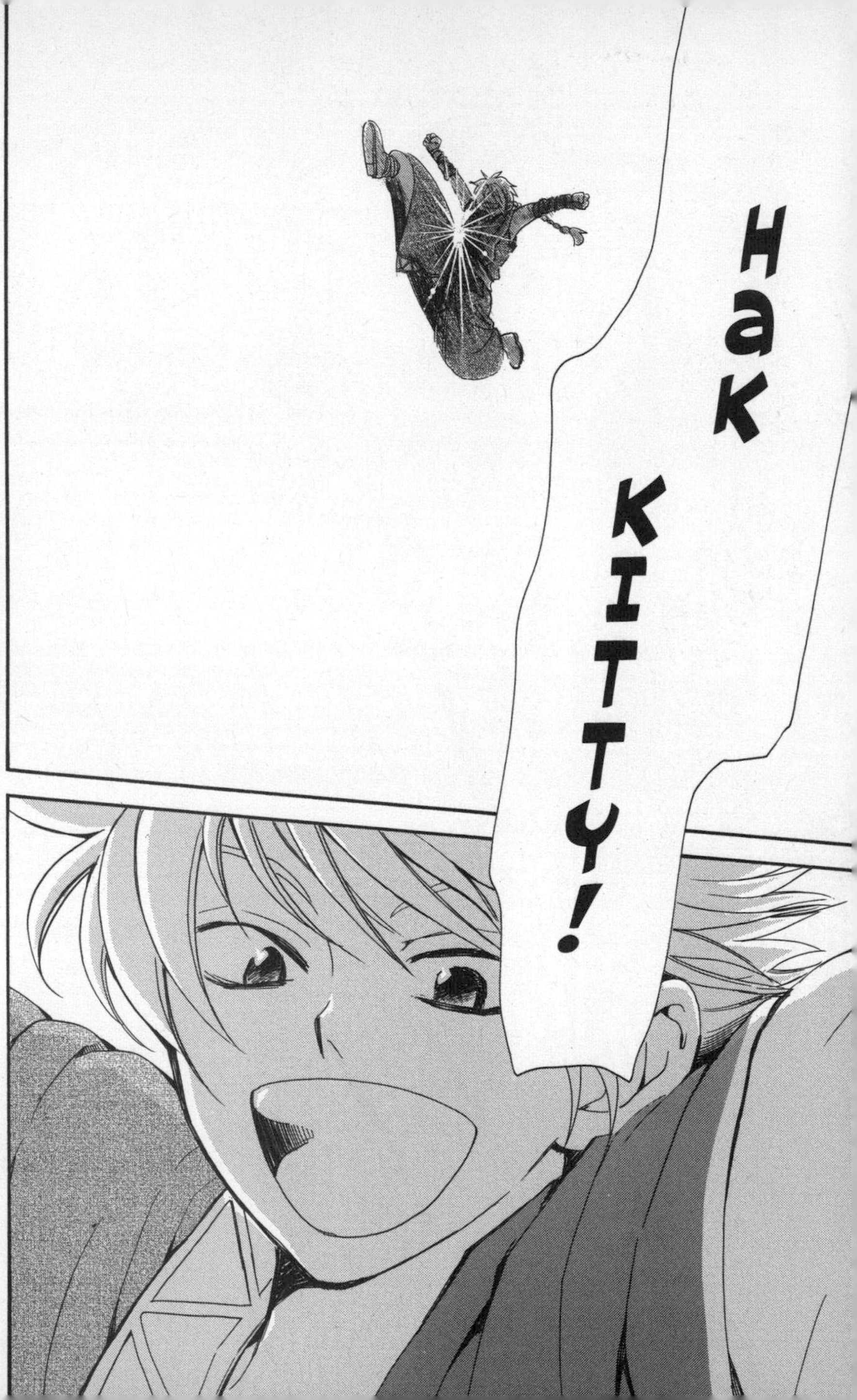
HaK KITTY!

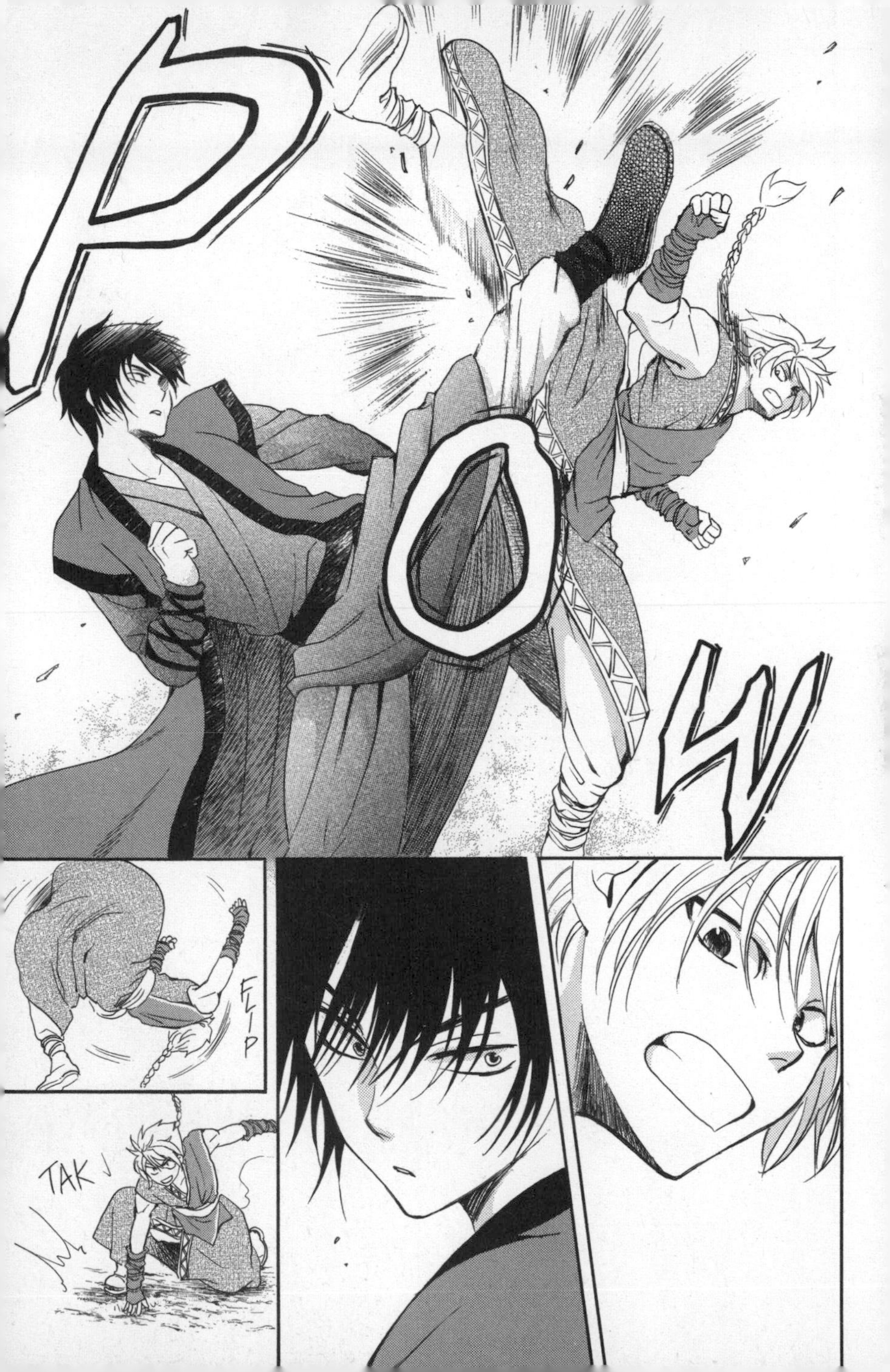
POW
FLIP
TAK

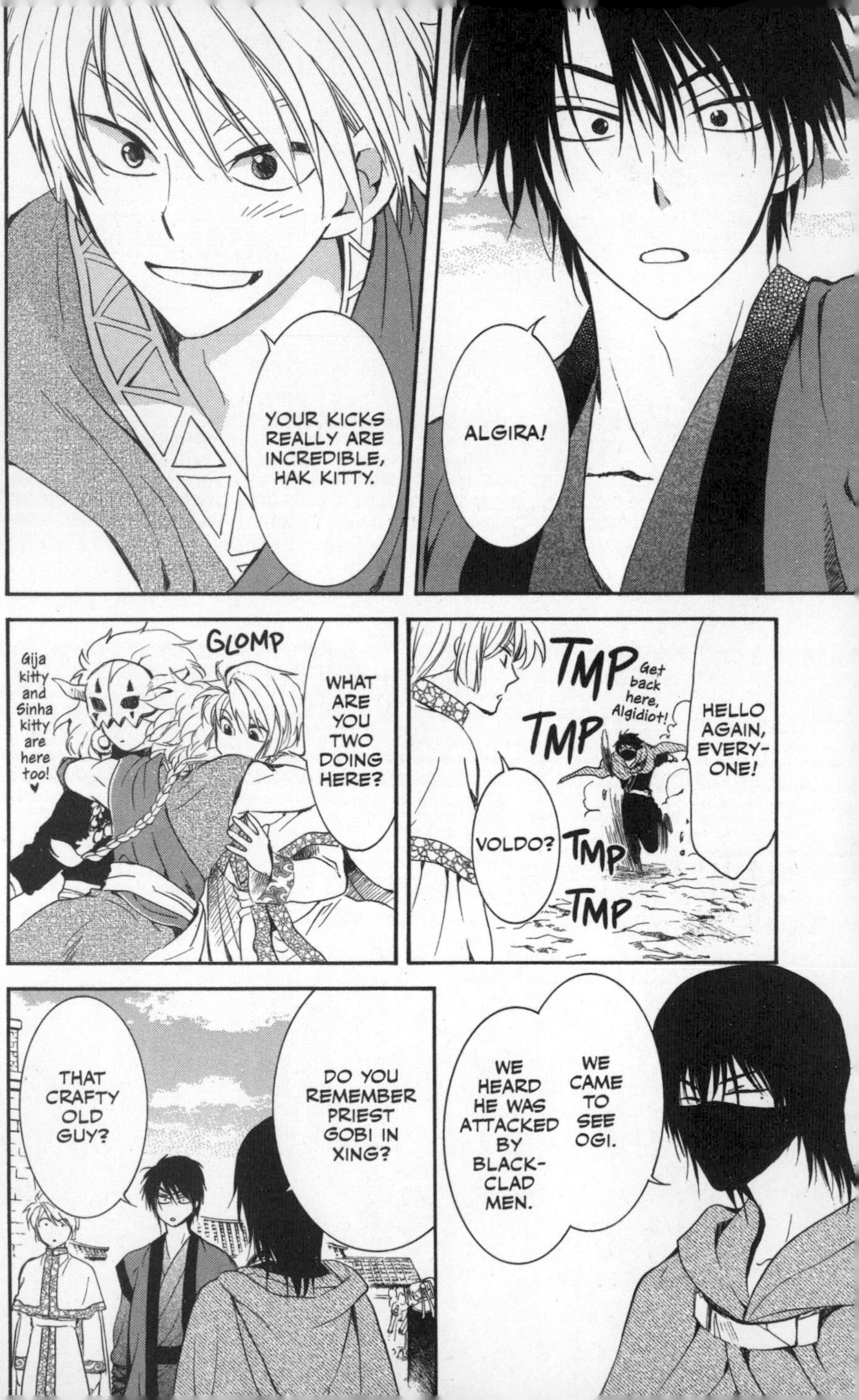
ALGIRA!
YOUR KICKS REALLY ARE INCREDIBLE, HAK KITTY.
HELLO AGAIN, EVERYONE!
Get back here, Algidiot!
TMP
TMP
VOLDO?
TMP
TMP
WHAT ARE YOU TWO DOING HERE?
GLOMP
Gija kitty and Sinha kitty are here too! ♥
WE CAME TO SEE OGI.
WE HEARD HE WAS ATTACKED BY BLACK-CLAD MEN.
DO YOU REMEMBER PRIEST GOBI IN XING?
THAT CRAFTY OLD GUY?

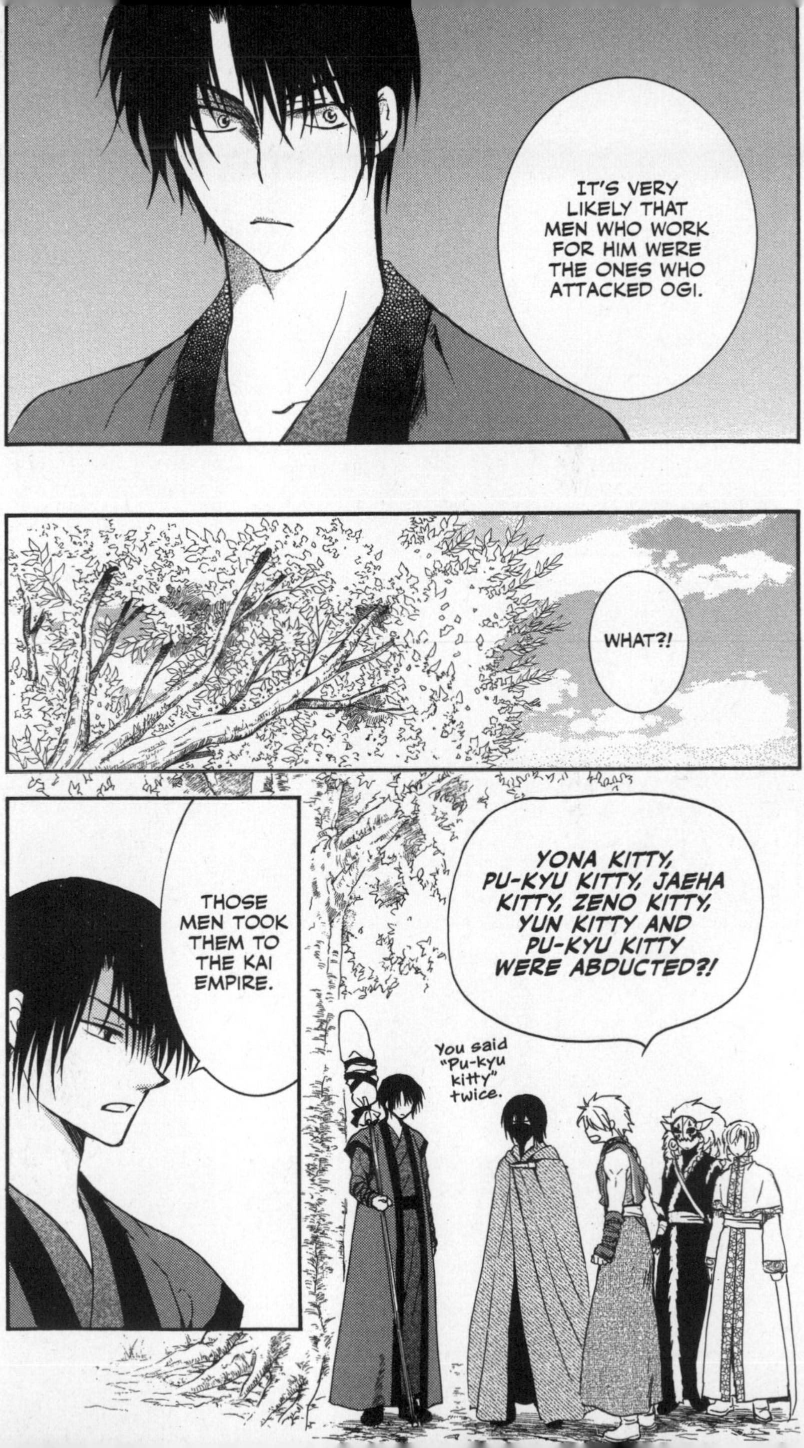
IT'S VERY LIKELY THAT MEN WHO WORK FOR HIM WERE THE ONES WHO ATTACKED OGI.
WHAT?!
YONA KITTY, PU-KYU KITTY, JAEHA KITTY, ZENO KITTY, YUN KITTY AND PU-KYU KITTY WERE ABDUCTED?!
You said "Pu-kyu kitty" twice.
THOSE MEN TOOK THEM TO THE KAI EMPIRE.

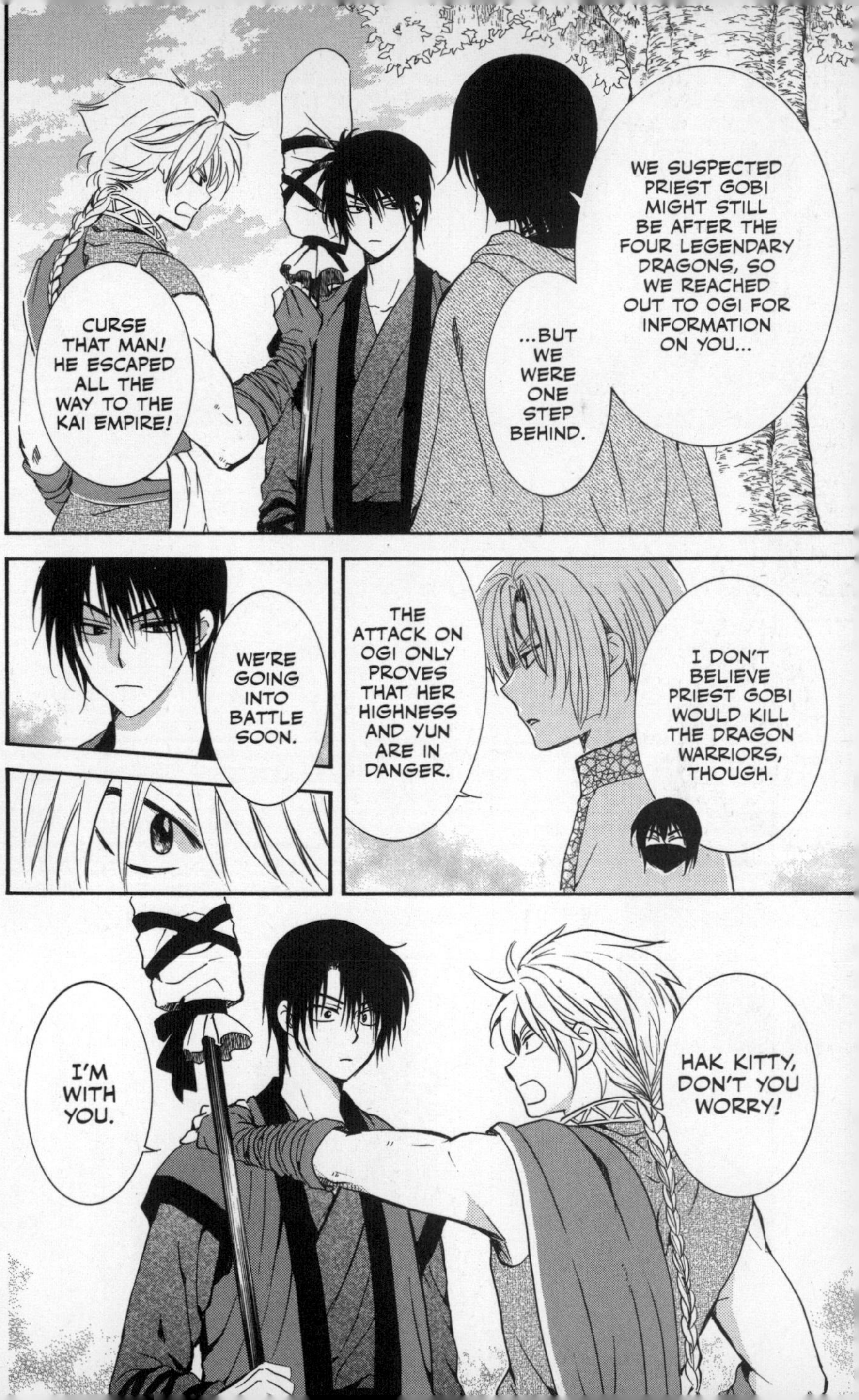
WE SUSPECTED PRIEST GOBI MIGHT STILL BE AFTER THE FOUR LEGENDARY DRAGONS, SO WE REACHED OUT TO OGI FOR INFORMATION ON YOU...
...BUT WE WERE ONE STEP BEHIND.
CURSE THAT MAN! HE ESCAPED ALL THE WAY TO THE KAI EMPIRE!
I DON'T BELIEVE PRIEST GOBI WOULD KILL THE DRAGON WARRIORS, THOUGH.
THE ATTACK ON OGI ONLY PROVES THAT HER HIGHNESS AND YUN ARE IN DANGER.
WE'RE GOING INTO BATTLE SOON.
HAK KITTY, DON'T YOU WORRY!
I'M WITH YOU.

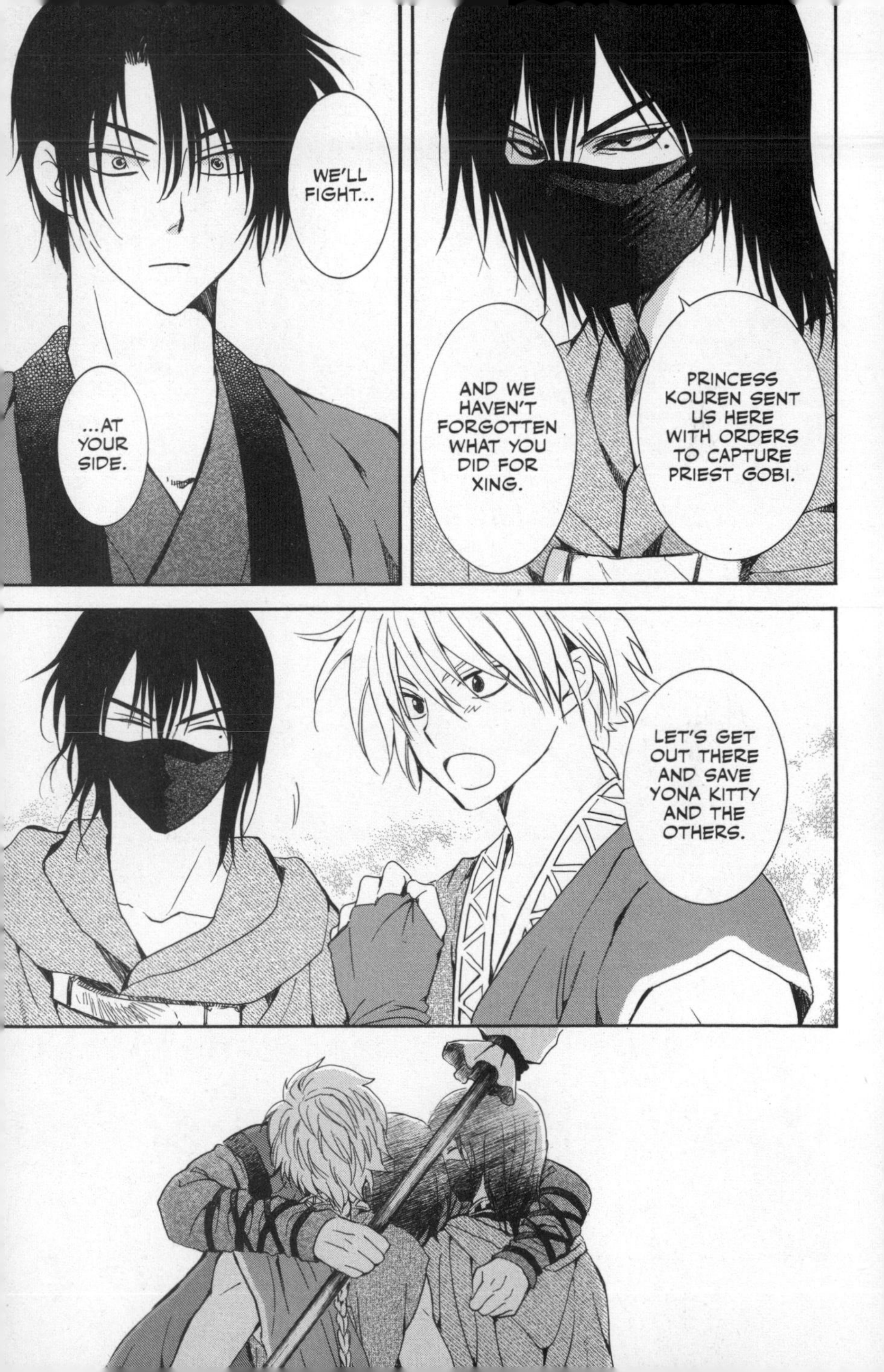
PRINCESS KOUREN SENT US HERE WITH ORDERS TO CAPTURE PRIEST GOBI.
AND WE HAVEN'T FORGOTTEN WHAT YOU DID FOR XING.
WE'LL FIGHT...
...AT YOUR SIDE.
LET'S GET OUT THERE AND SAVE YONA KITTY AND THE OTHERS.

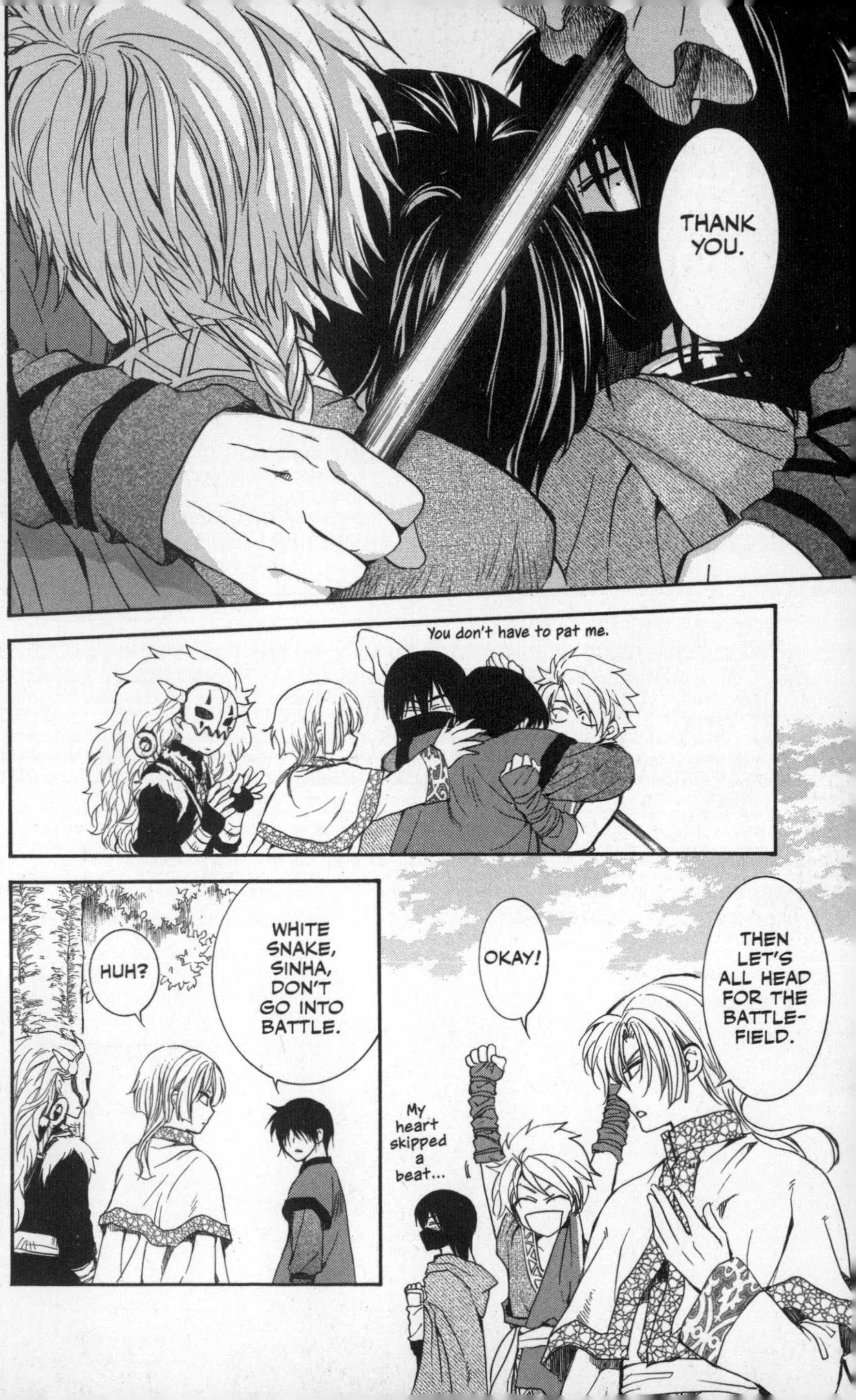
THANK YOU.
You don't have to pat me.
THEN LET'S ALL HEAD FOR THE BATTLE-FIELD.
OKAY!
WHITE SNAKE, SINHA, DON'T GO INTO BATTLE.
HUH?
My heart skipped a beat...

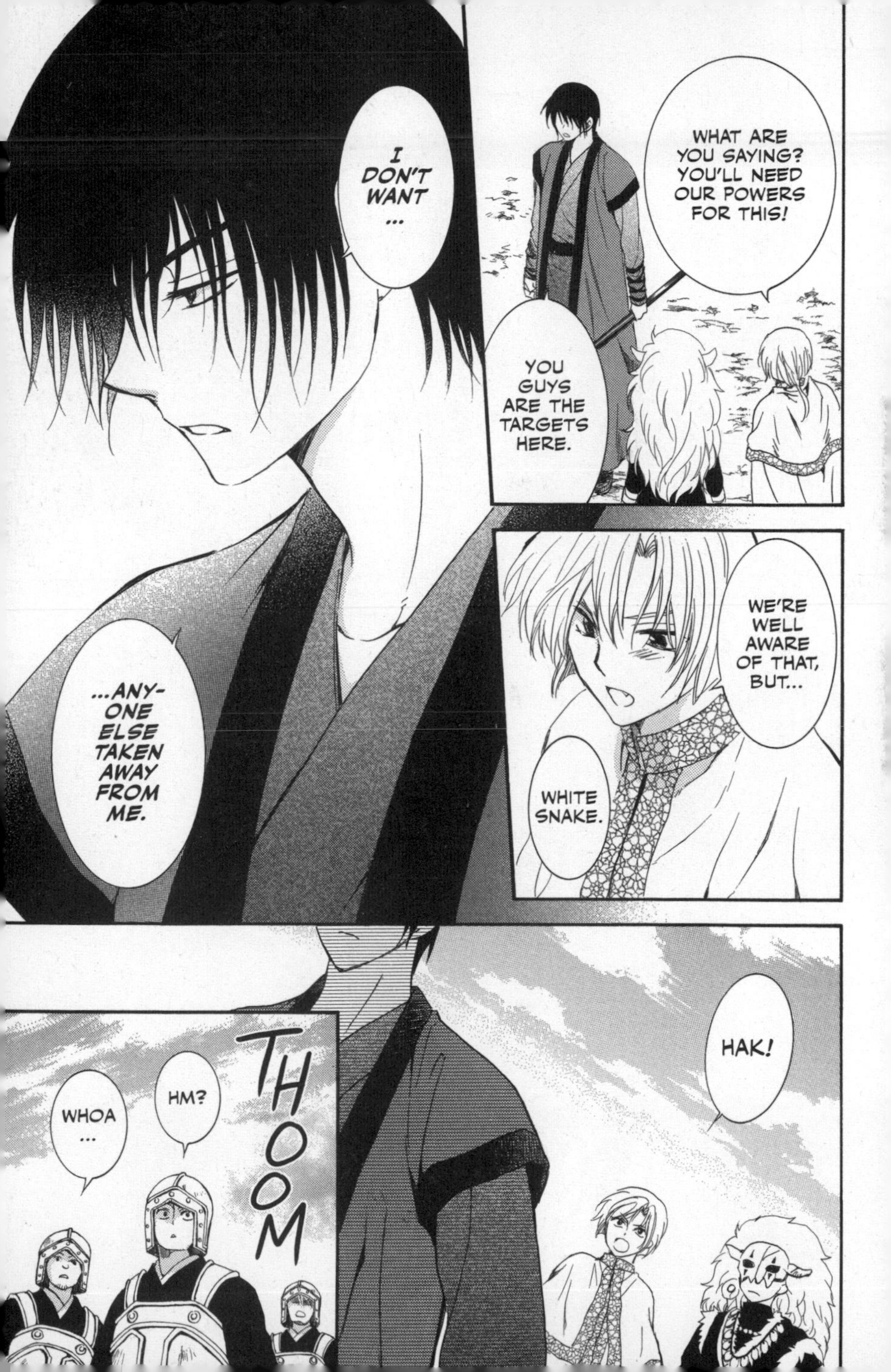
WHAT ARE YOU SAYING? YOU'LL NEED OUR POWERS FOR THIS!
YOU GUYS ARE THE TARGETS HERE.
WE'RE WELL AWARE OF THAT, BUT...
WHITE SNAKE.
I DON'T WANT ...
...ANYONE ELSE TAKEN AWAY FROM ME.
HAK!
THOOM
HM?
WHOA ...

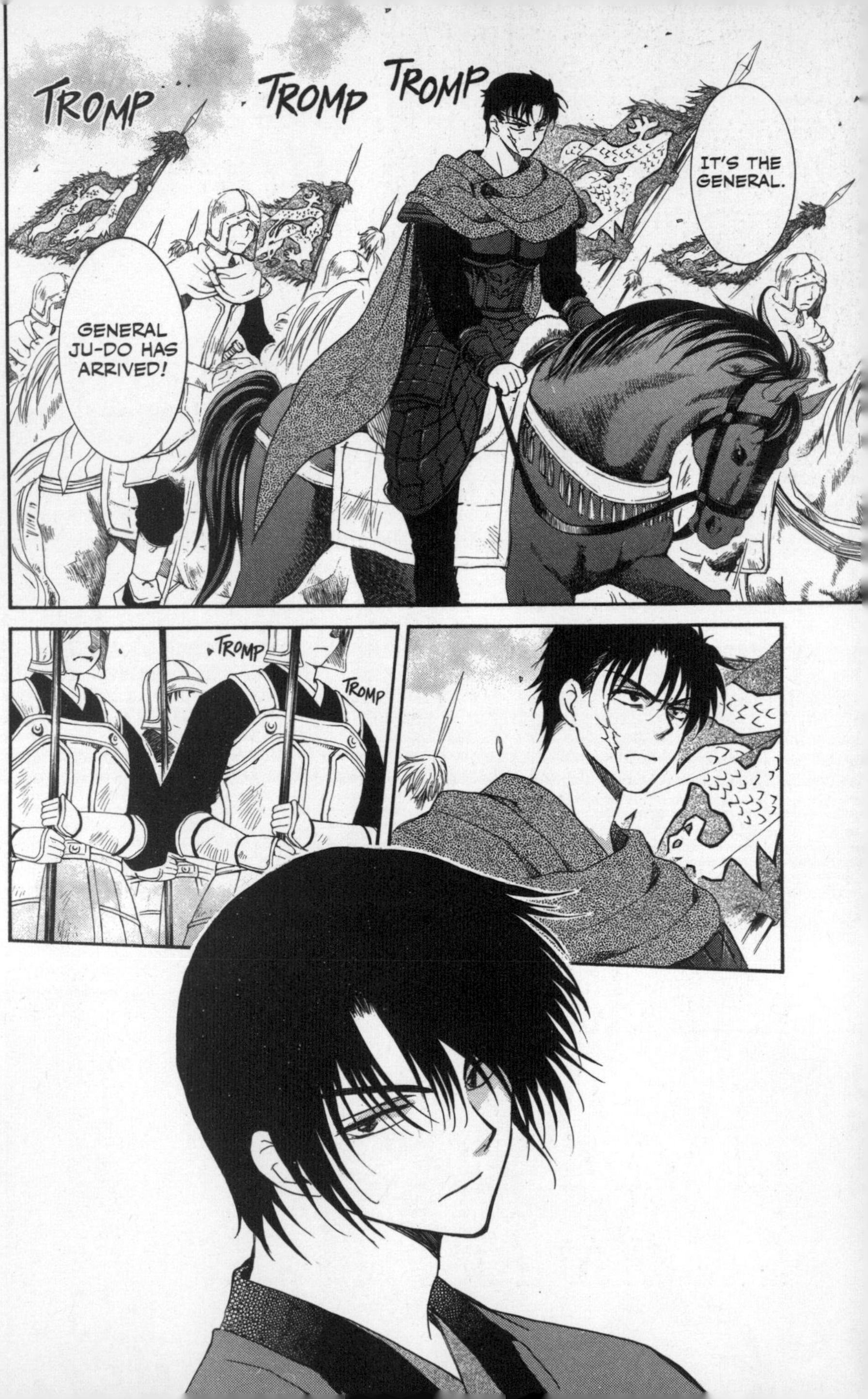
TROMP
TROMP
TROMP
IT'S THE GENERAL.
GENERAL JU-DO HAS ARRIVED!
TROMP
TROMP

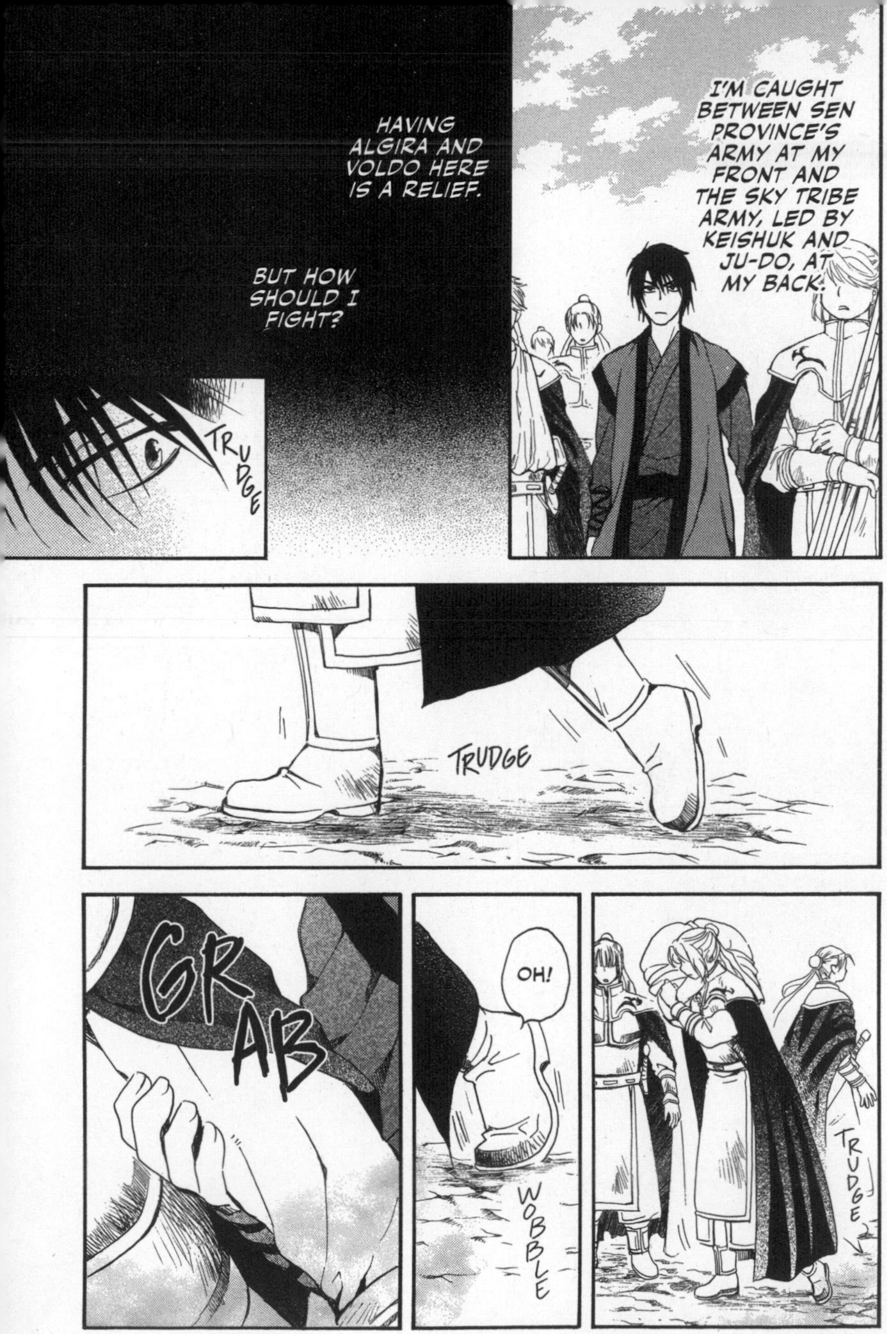
I'M CAUGHT BETWEEN SEN PROVINCE'S ARMY AT MY FRONT AND THE SKY TRIBE ARMY, LED BY KEISHUK AND JU-DO, AT MY BACK.
HAVING ALGIRA AND VOLDO HERE IS A RELIEF.
BUT HOW SHOULD I FIGHT?
TRUDGE
TRUDGE
TRUDGE
OH!
WOBBLE
GRAB

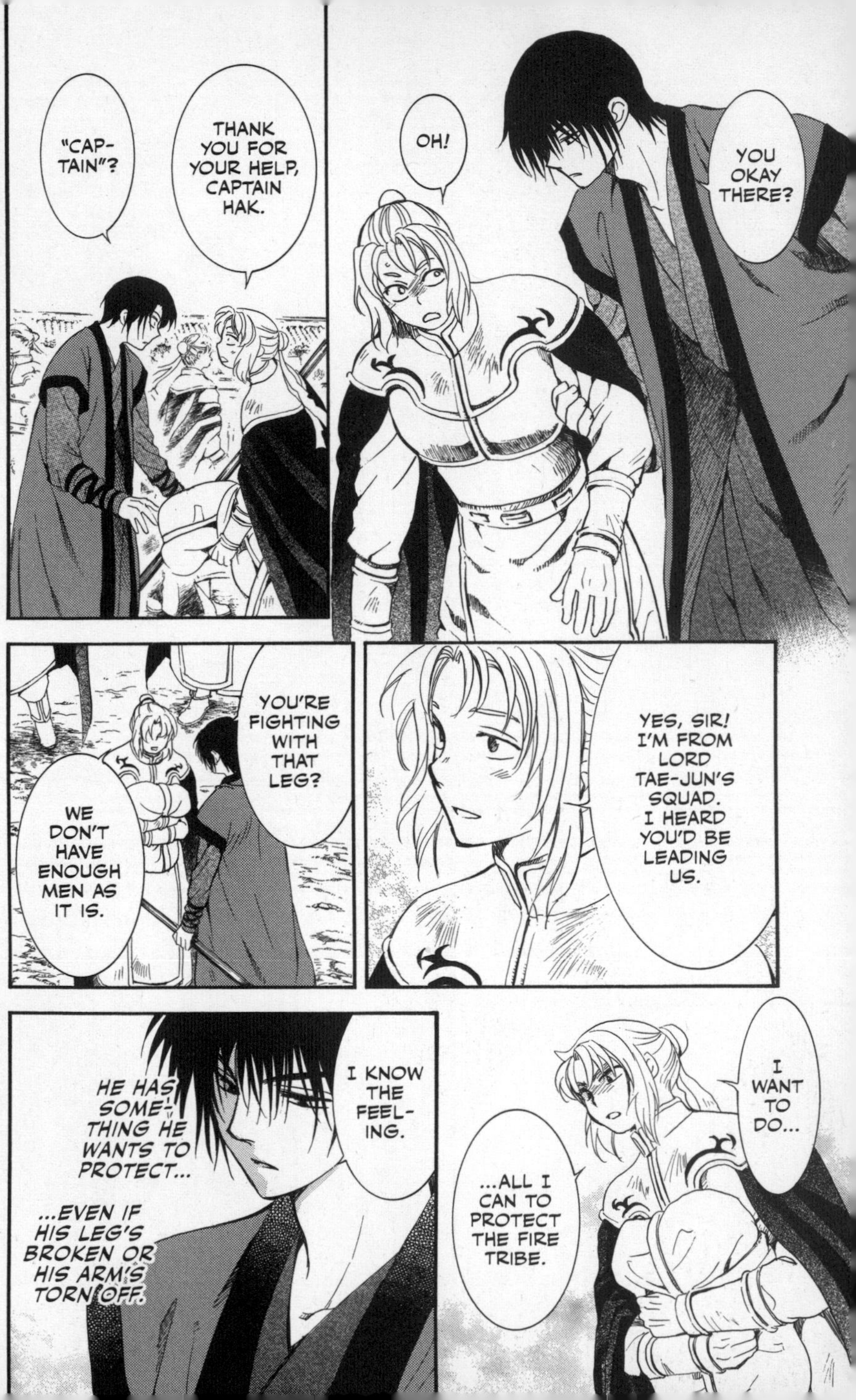
YOU OKAY THERE?
OH!
THANK YOU FOR YOUR HELP, CAPTAIN HAK.
"CAPTAIN"?
YES, SIR! I'M FROM LORD TAE-JUN'S SQUAD. I HEARD YOU'D BE LEADING US.
YOU'RE FIGHTING WITH THAT LEG?
WE DON'T HAVE ENOUGH MEN AS IT IS.
I WANT TO DO...
...ALL I CAN TO PROTECT THE FIRE TRIBE.
I KNOW THE FEELING.
HE HAS SOMETHING HE WANTS TO PROTECT...
...EVEN IF HIS LEG'S BROKEN OR HIS ARM'S TORN OFF.

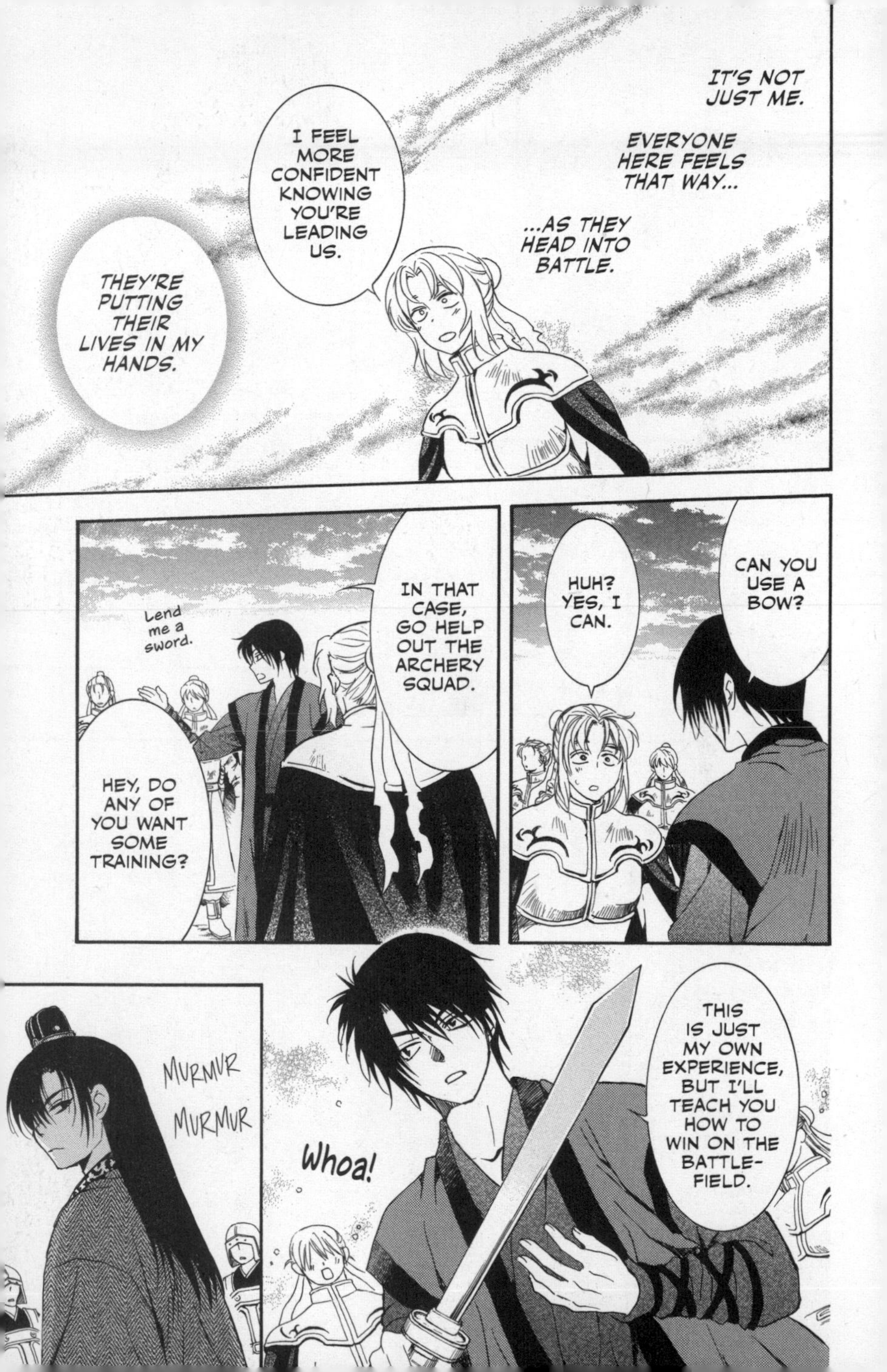
IT'S NOT JUST ME.
EVERYONE HERE FEELS THAT WAY...
...AS THEY HEAD INTO BATTLE.
I FEEL MORE CONFIDENT KNOWING YOU'RE LEADING US.
THEY'RE PUTTING THEIR LIVES IN MY HANDS.
CAN YOU USE A BOW?
HUH? YES, I CAN.
IN THAT CASE, GO HELP OUT THE ARCHERY SQUAD.
Lend me a sword.
HEY, DO ANY OF YOU WANT SOME TRAINING?
THIS IS JUST MY OWN EXPERIENCE, BUT I'LL TEACH YOU HOW TO WIN ON THE BATTLE-FIELD.
Whoa!
MURMUR
MURMUR

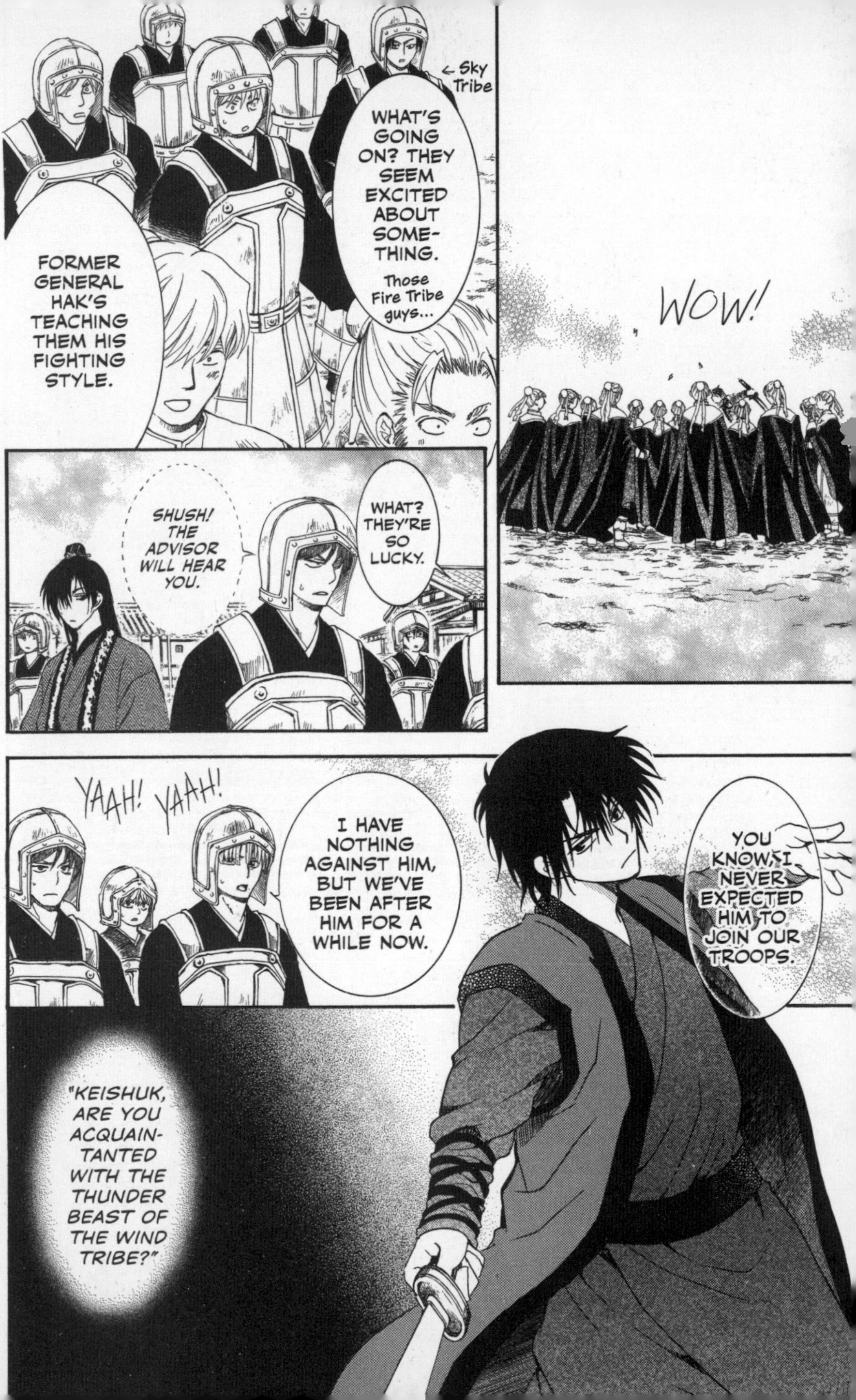
WOW!
← Sky Tribe
WHAT'S GOING ON? THEY SEEM EXCITED ABOUT SOME-THING.
Those Fire Tribe guys...
FORMER GENERAL HAK'S TEACHING THEM HIS FIGHTING STYLE.
WHAT? THEY'RE SO LUCKY.
SHUSH! THE ADVISOR WILL HEAR YOU.
YOU KNOW, I NEVER EXPECTED HIM TO JOIN OUR TROOPS.
YAAH! YAAH!
I HAVE NOTHING AGAINST HIM, BUT WE'VE BEEN AFTER HIM FOR A WHILE NOW.
"KEISHUK, ARE YOU ACQUAIN-TANTED WITH THE THUNDER BEAST OF THE WIND TRIBE?"

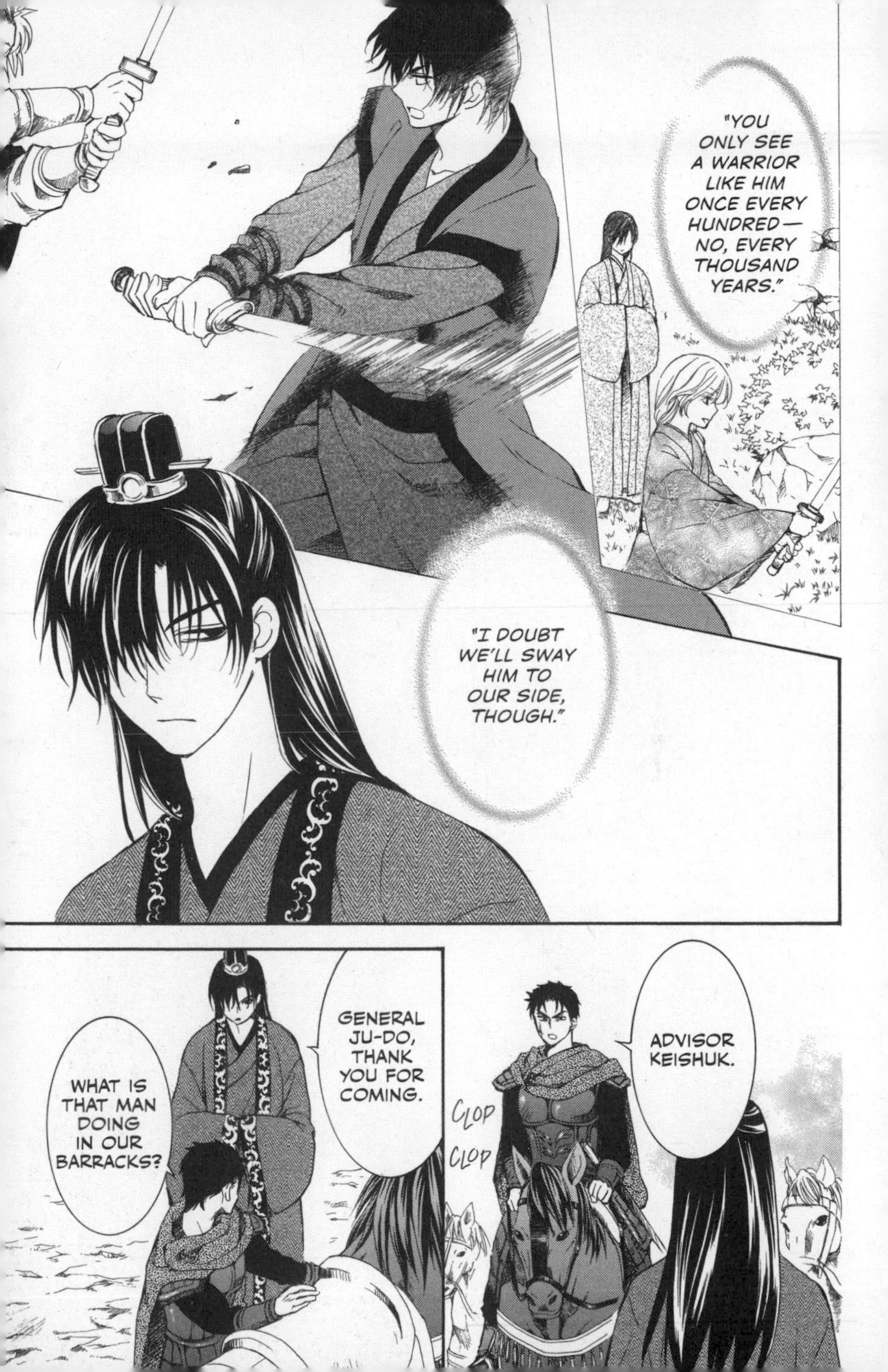
"YOU ONLY SEE A WARRIOR LIKE HIM ONCE EVERY HUNDRED—NO, EVERY THOUSAND YEARS."
"I DOUBT WE'LL SWAY HIM TO OUR SIDE, THOUGH."
ADVISOR KEISHUK.
CLOP
CLOP
GENERAL JU-DO, THANK YOU FOR COMING.
WHAT IS THAT MAN DOING IN OUR BARRACKS?

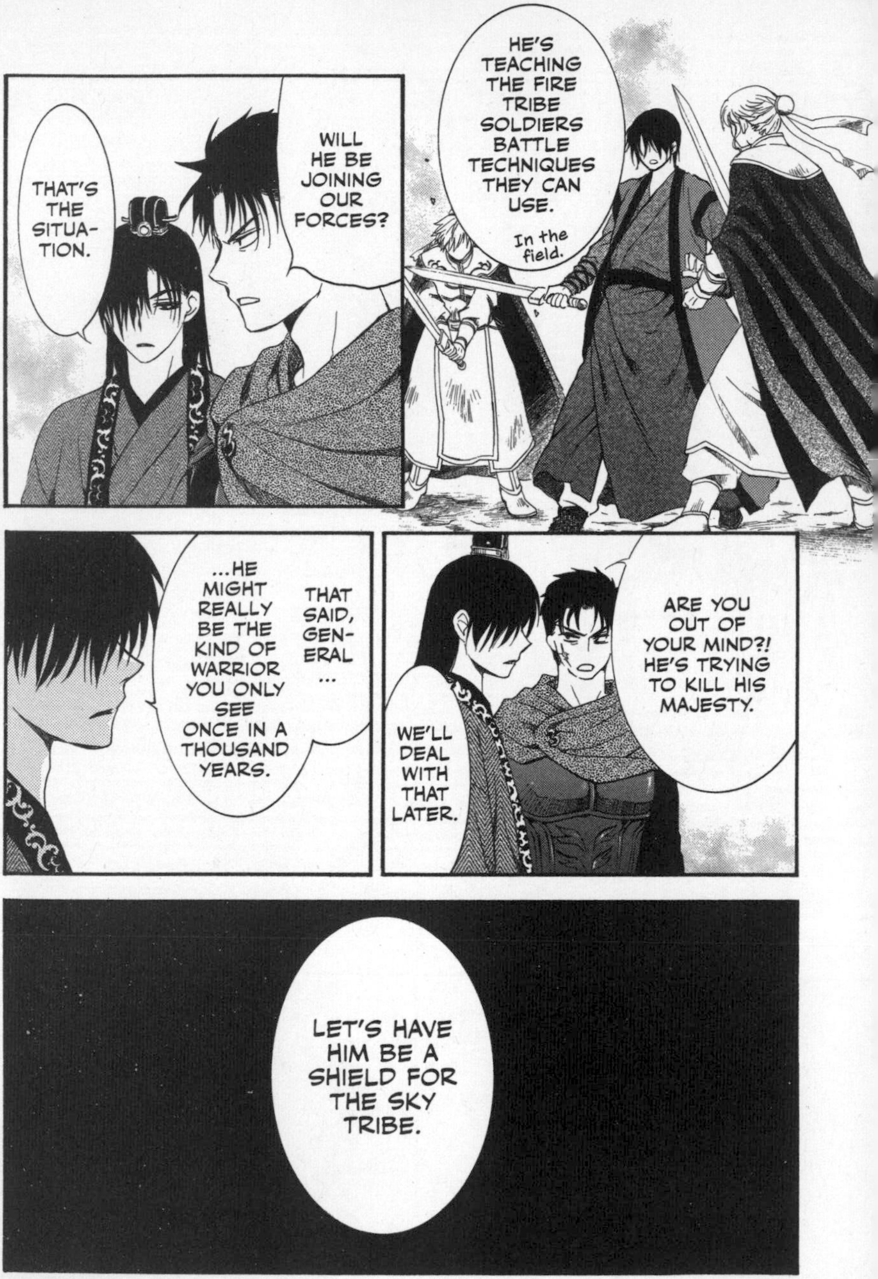
HE'S TEACHING THE FIRE TRIBE SOLDIERS BATTLE TECHNIQUES THEY CAN USE.
In the field.
WILL HE BE JOINING OUR FORCES?
THAT'S THE SITUA-TION.
ARE YOU OUT OF YOUR MIND?! HE'S TRYING TO KILL HIS MAJESTY.
WE'LL DEAL WITH THAT LATER.
THAT SAID, GEN-ERAL...
...HE MIGHT REALLY BE THE KIND OF WARRIOR YOU ONLY SEE ONCE IN A THOUSAND YEARS.
LET'S HAVE HIM BE A SHIELD FOR THE SKY TRIBE.

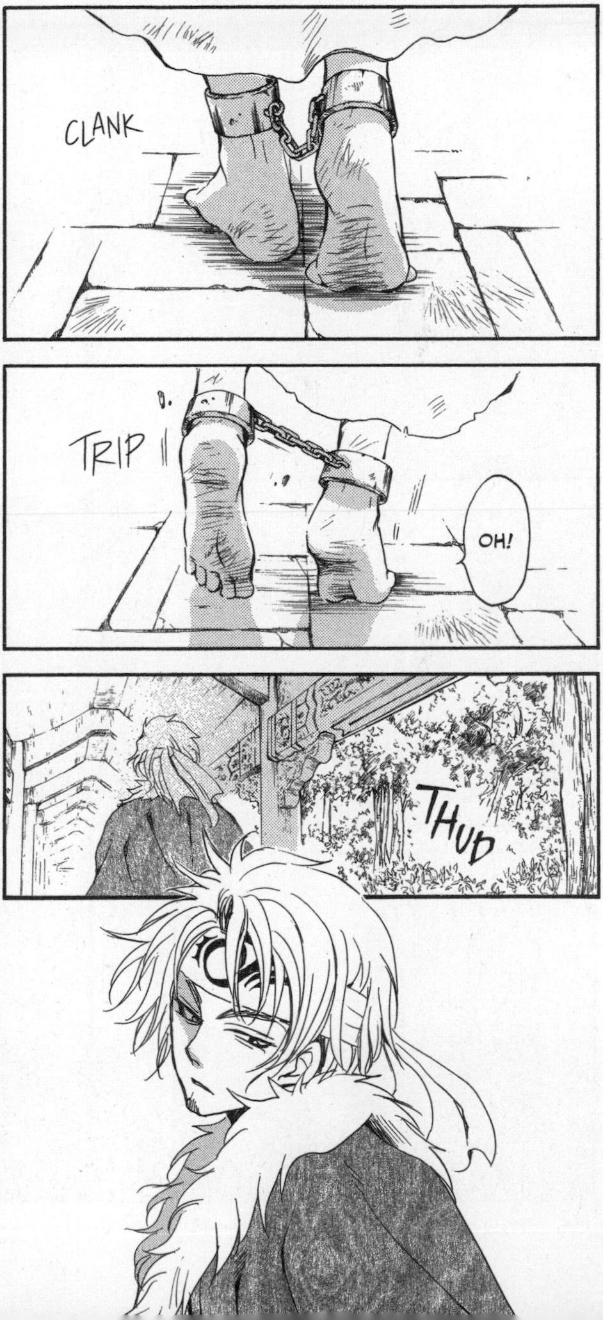
CLANK
TRIP
OH!
THUD

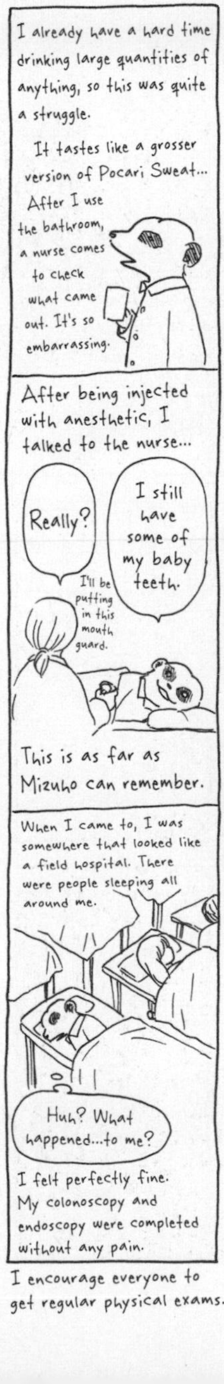
I already have a hard time drinking large quantities of anything, so this was quite a struggle.
It tastes like a grosser version of Pocari Sweat...
After I use the bathroom, a nurse comes to check what came out. It's so embarrassing.
After being injected with anesthetic, I talked to the nurse...
I still have some of my baby teeth.
Really?
I'll be putting in this mouth guard.
This is as far as Mizuho can remember.
When I came to, I was somewhere that looked like a field hospital. There were people sleeping all around me.
Huh? What happened...to me?
I felt perfectly fine. My colonoscopy and endoscopy were completed without any pain.
I encourage everyone to get regular physical exams.

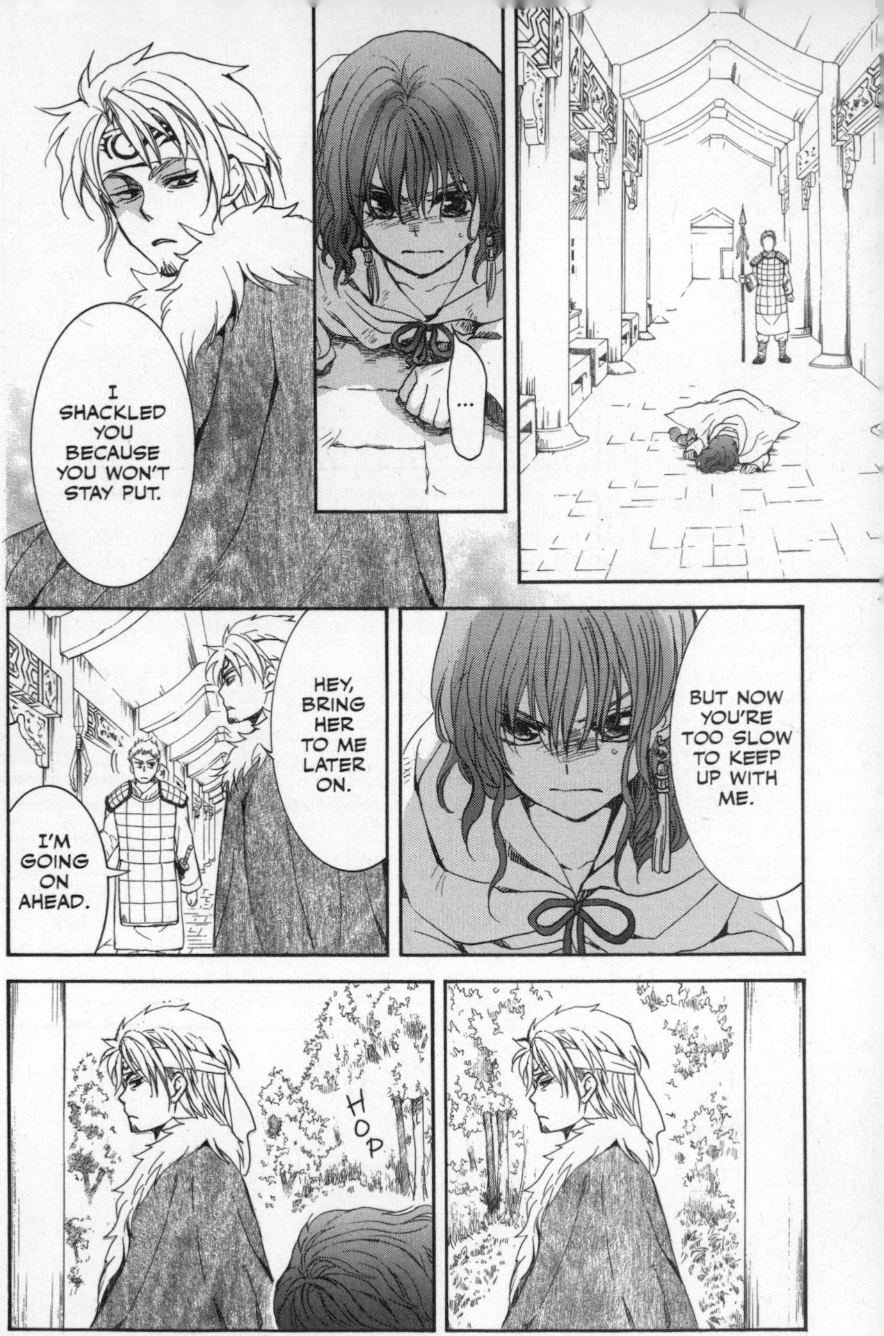
...
I SHACKLED YOU BECAUSE YOU WON'T STAY PUT.
BUT NOW YOU'RE TOO SLOW TO KEEP UP WITH ME.
HEY, BRING HER TO ME LATER ON.
I'M GOING ON AHEAD.
HOP

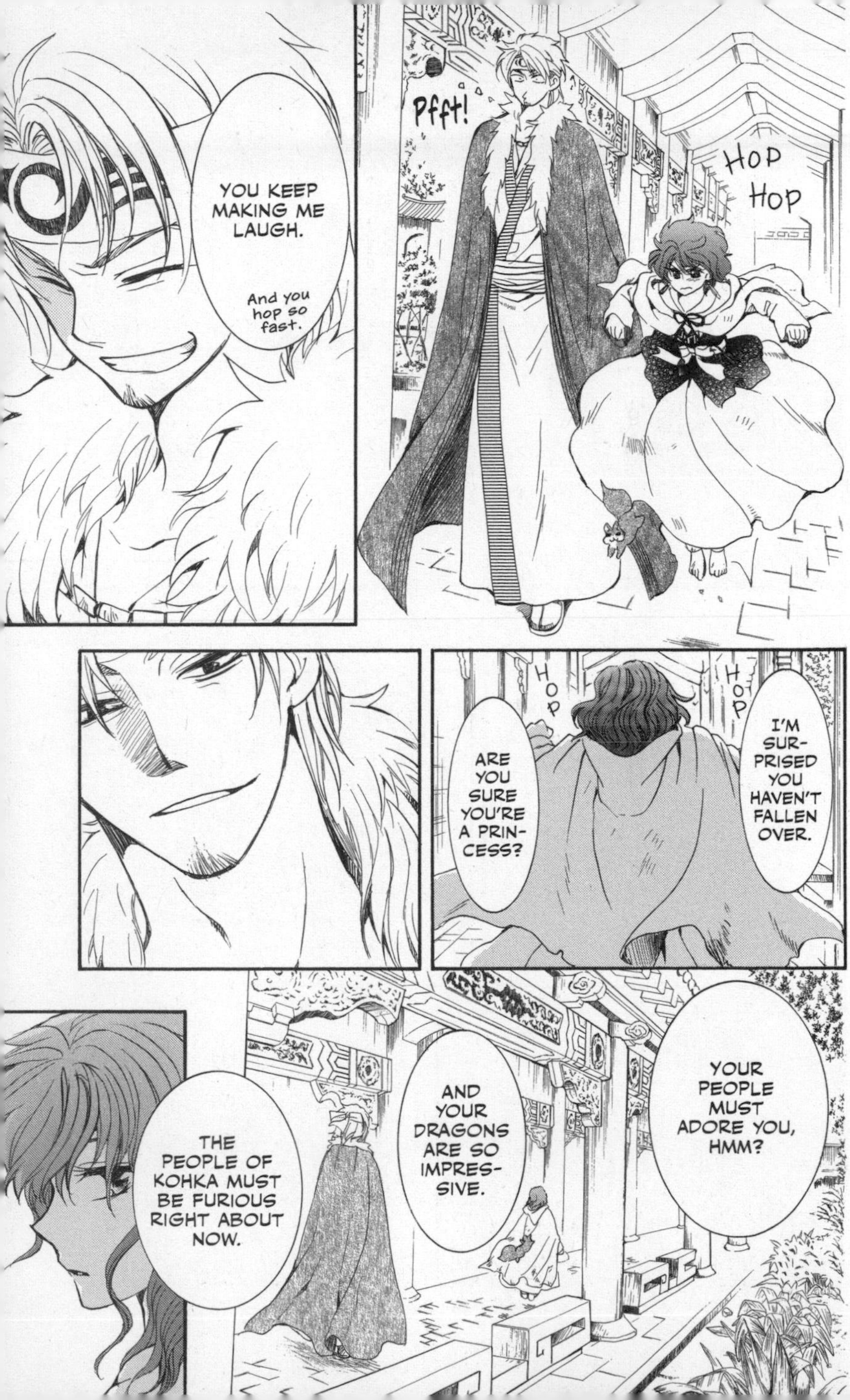
Pfft!
Hop
Hop
YOU KEEP MAKING ME LAUGH.
And you hop so fast.
HOP
I'M SURPRISED YOU HAVEN'T FALLEN OVER.
HOP
ARE YOU SURE YOU'RE A PRINCESS?
YOUR PEOPLE MUST ADORE YOU, HMM?
AND YOUR DRAGONS ARE SO IMPRESSIVE.
THE PEOPLE OF KOHKA MUST BE FURIOUS RIGHT ABOUT NOW.

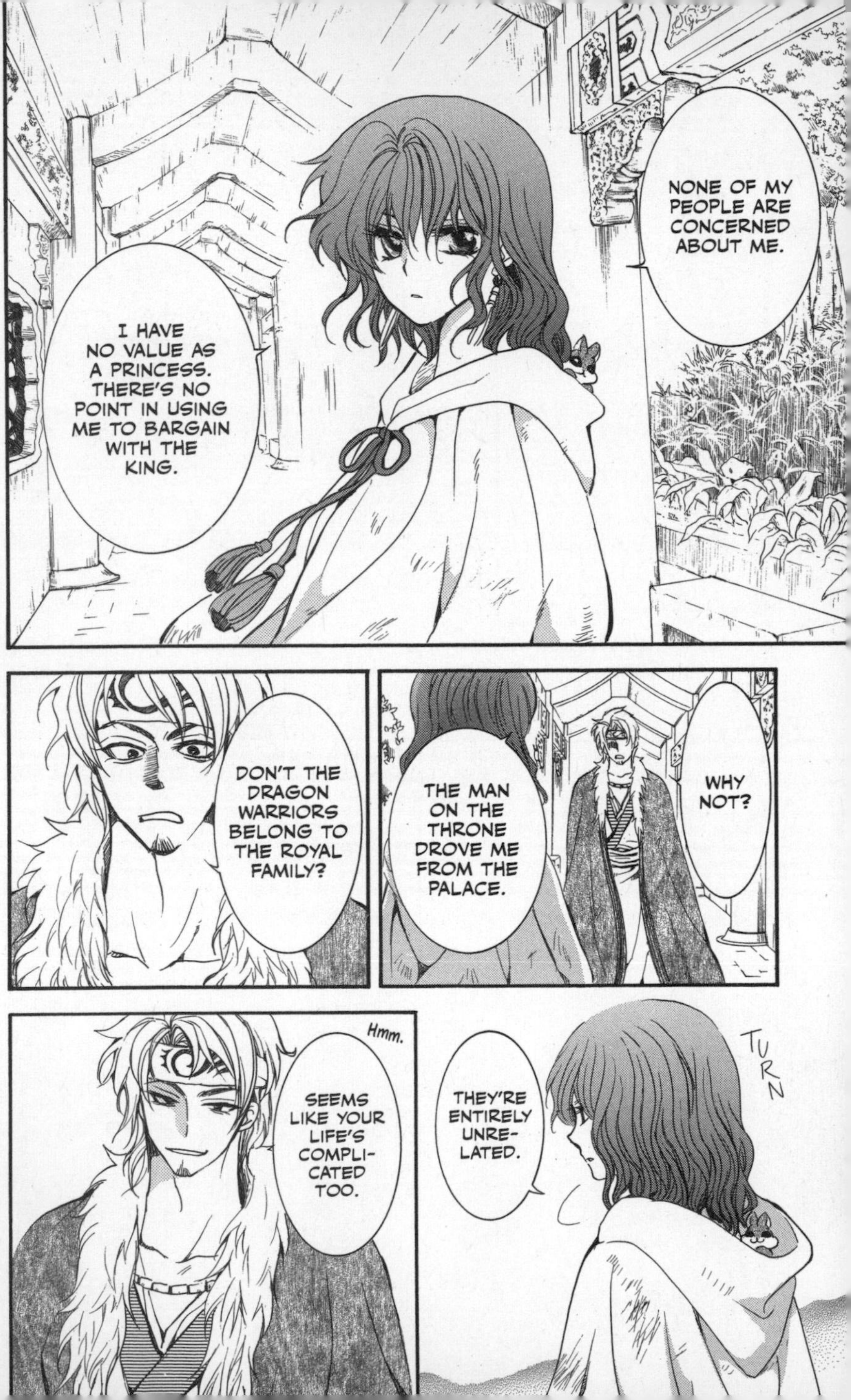
NONE OF MY PEOPLE ARE CONCERNED ABOUT ME.
I HAVE NO VALUE AS A PRINCESS. THERE'S NO POINT IN USING ME TO BARGAIN WITH THE KING.
WHY NOT?
THE MAN ON THE THRONE DROVE ME FROM THE PALACE.
DON'T THE DRAGON WARRIORS BELONG TO THE ROYAL FAMILY?
TURN
THEY'RE ENTIRELY UNRELATED.
Hmm.
SEEMS LIKE YOUR LIFE'S COMPLICATED TOO.

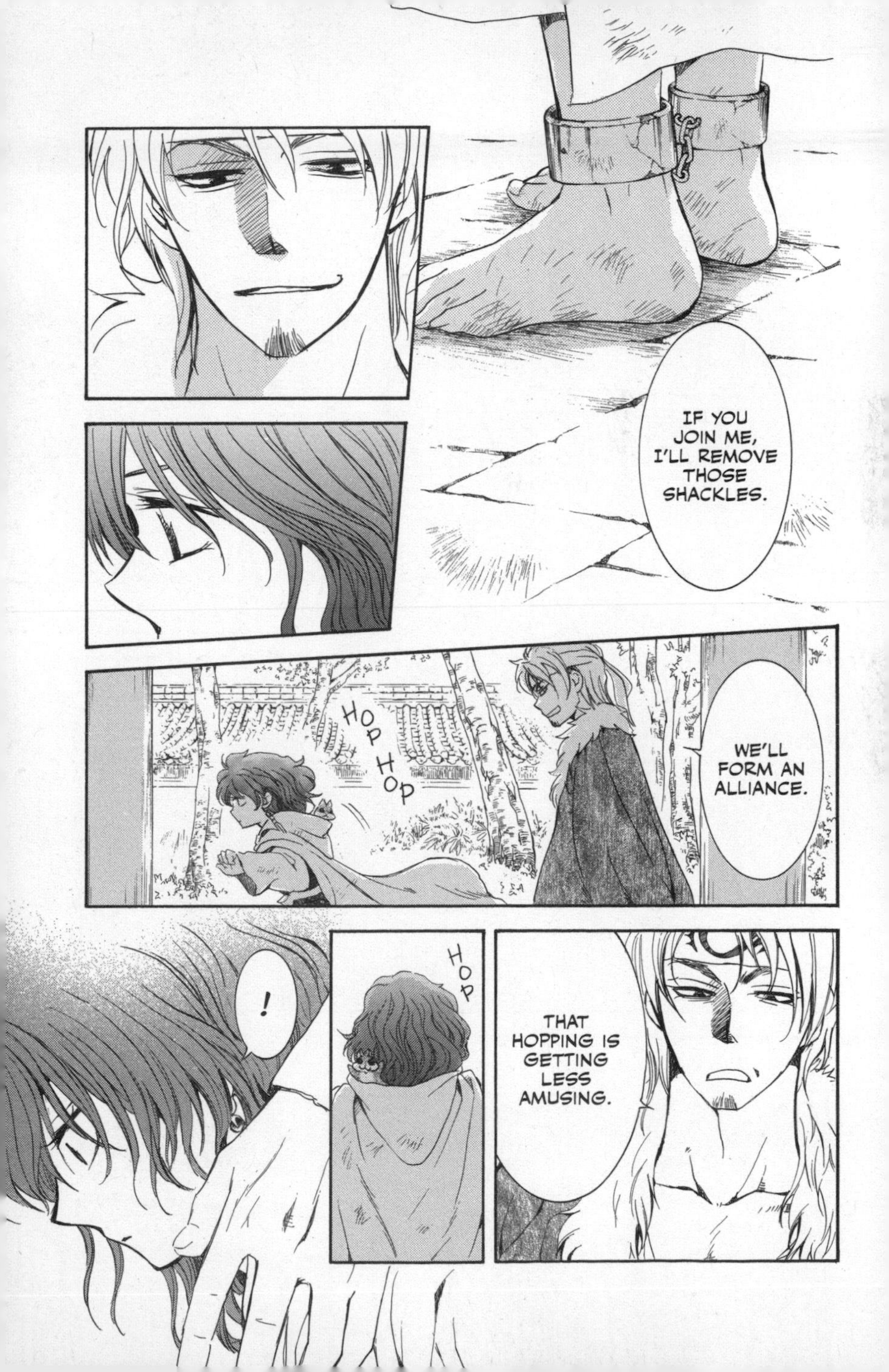
IF YOU JOIN ME, I'LL REMOVE THOSE SHACKLES.
WE'LL FORM AN ALLIANCE.
HOP HOP
THAT HOPPING IS GETTING LESS AMUSING.
HOP
!

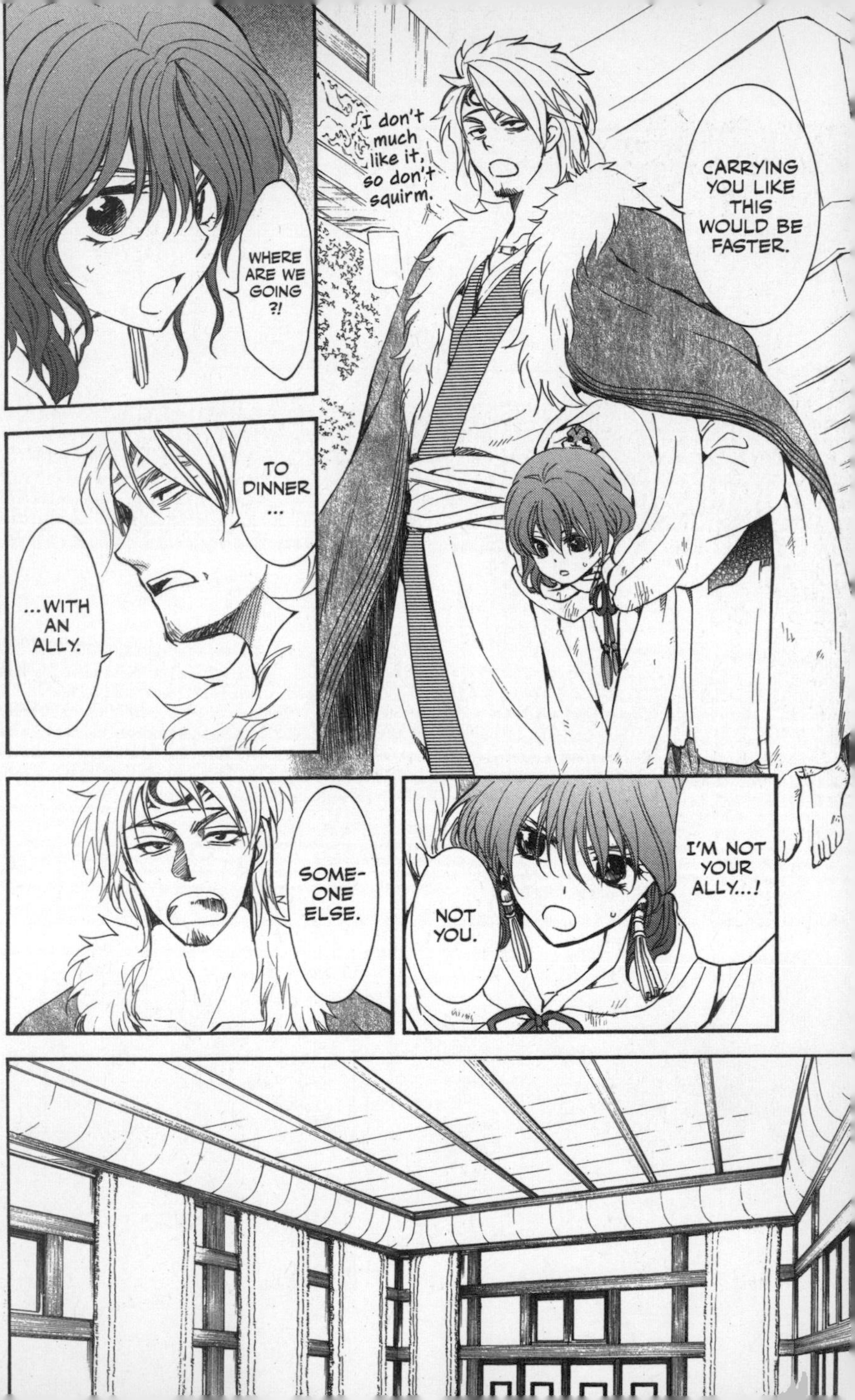
CARRYING YOU LIKE THIS WOULD BE FASTER.
I don't much like it, so don't squirm.
WHERE ARE WE GOING ?!
TO DINNER ...
...WITH AN ALLY.
I'M NOT YOUR ALLY...!
NOT YOU.
SOME-ONE ELSE.

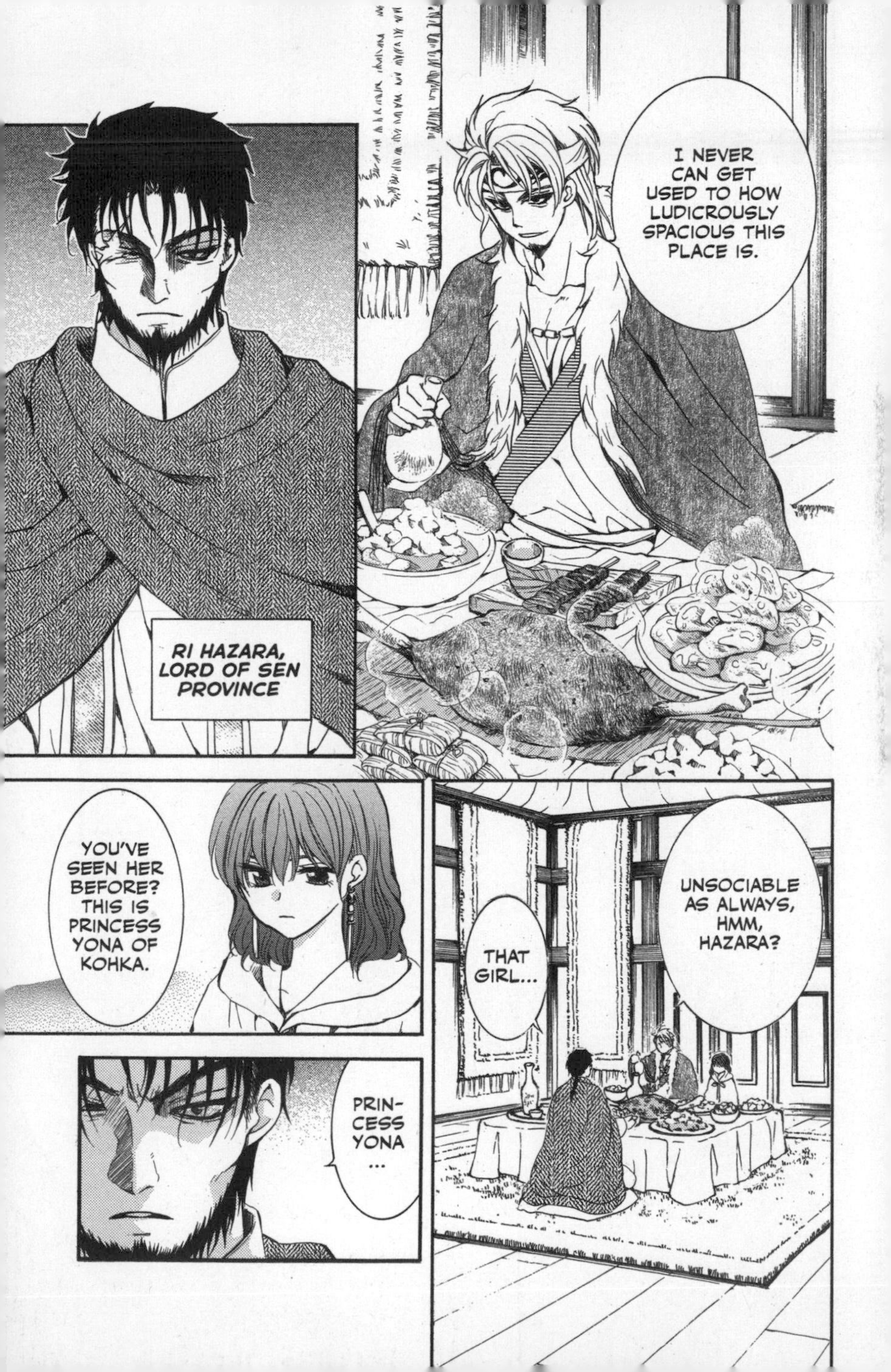
I NEVER CAN GET USED TO HOW LUDICROUSLY SPACIOUS THIS PLACE IS.
RI HAZARA, LORD OF SEN PROVINCE
UNSOCIABLE AS ALWAYS, HMM, HAZARA?
THAT GIRL...
YOU'VE SEEN HER BEFORE? THIS IS PRINCESS YONA OF KOHKA.
PRIN-CESS YONA...

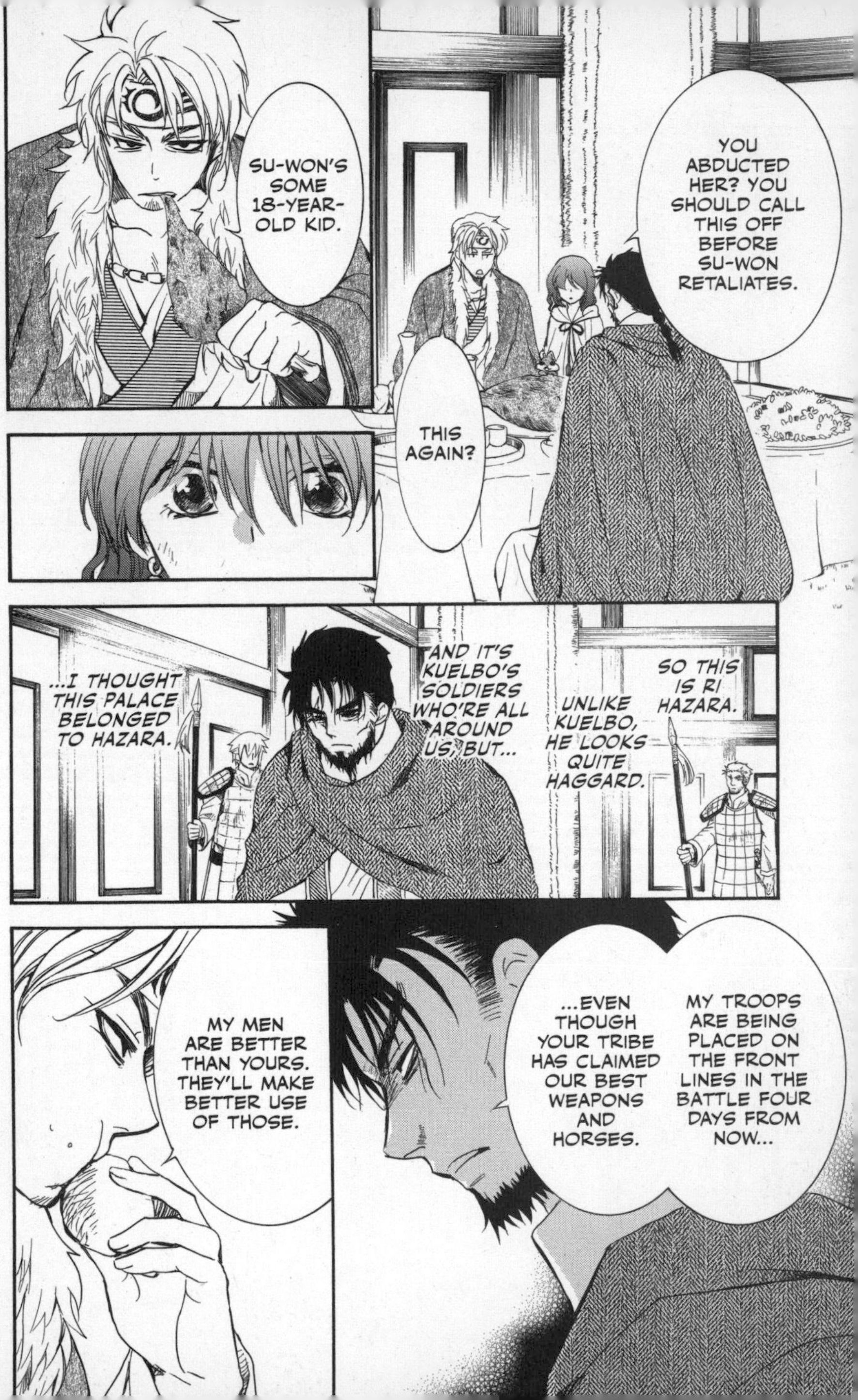
YOU ABDUCTED HER? YOU SHOULD CALL THIS OFF BEFORE SU-WON RETALIATES.
THIS AGAIN?
SU-WON'S SOME 18-YEAR-OLD KID.
SO THIS IS RI HAZARA.
UNLIKE KUELBO, HE LOOKS QUITE HAGGARD.
AND IT'S KUELBO'S SOLDIERS WHO'RE ALL AROUND US, BUT...
...I THOUGHT THIS PALACE BELONGED TO HAZARA.
MY TROOPS ARE BEING PLACED ON THE FRONT LINES IN THE BATTLE FOUR DAYS FROM NOW...
...EVEN THOUGH YOUR TRIBE HAS CLAIMED OUR BEST WEAPONS AND HORSES.
MY MEN ARE BETTER THAN YOURS. THEY'LL MAKE BETTER USE OF THOSE.

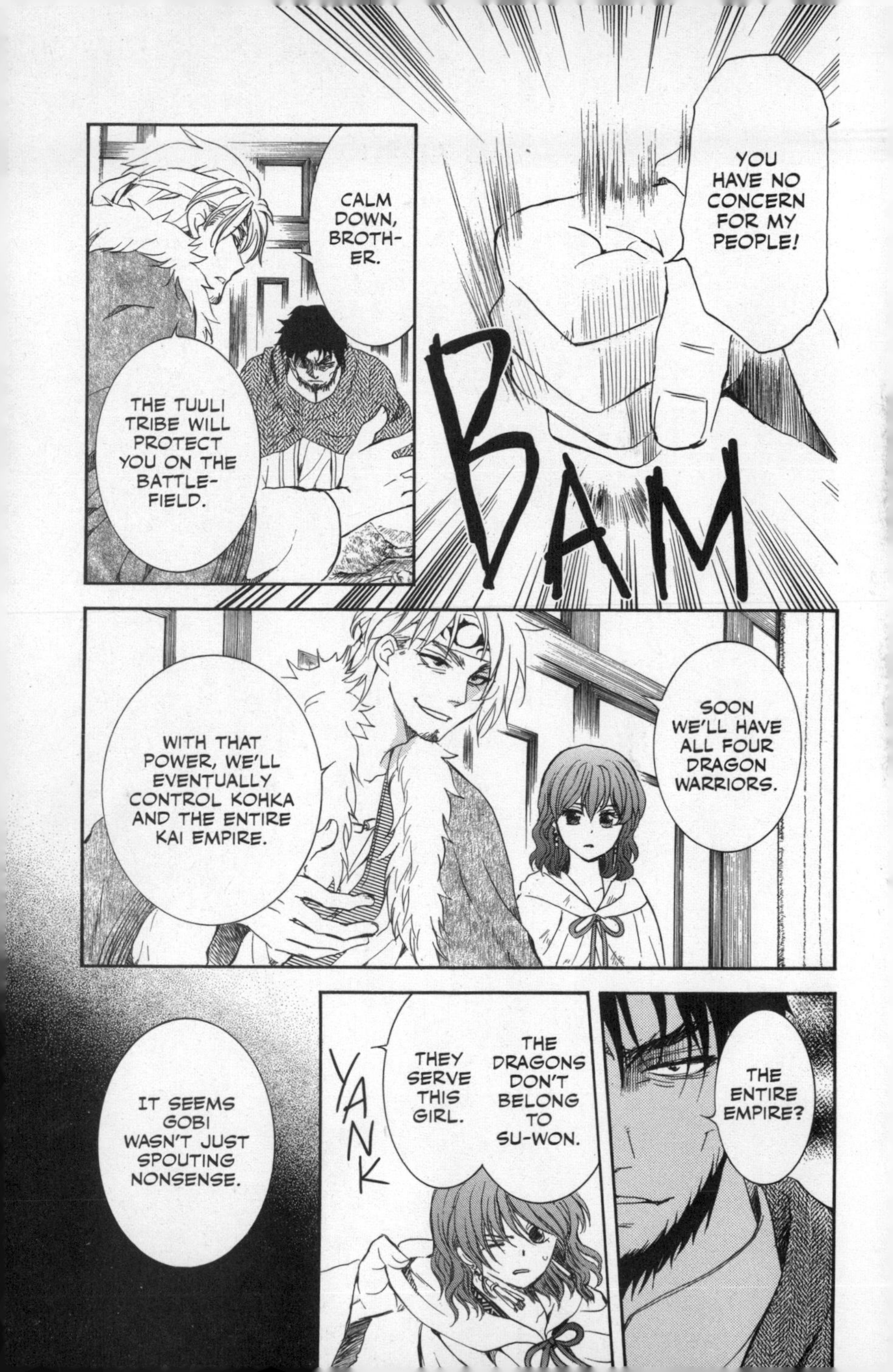
YOU HAVE NO CONCERN FOR MY PEOPLE!
BAM
CALM DOWN, BROTHER.
THE TUULI TRIBE WILL PROTECT YOU ON THE BATTLEFIELD.
SOON WE'LL HAVE ALL FOUR DRAGON WARRIORS.
WITH THAT POWER, WE'LL EVENTUALLY CONTROL KOHKA AND THE ENTIRE KAI EMPIRE.
THE ENTIRE EMPIRE?
THE DRAGONS DON'T BELONG TO SU-WON.
THEY SERVE THIS GIRL.
YANK
IT SEEMS GOBI WASN'T JUST SPOUTING NONSENSE.

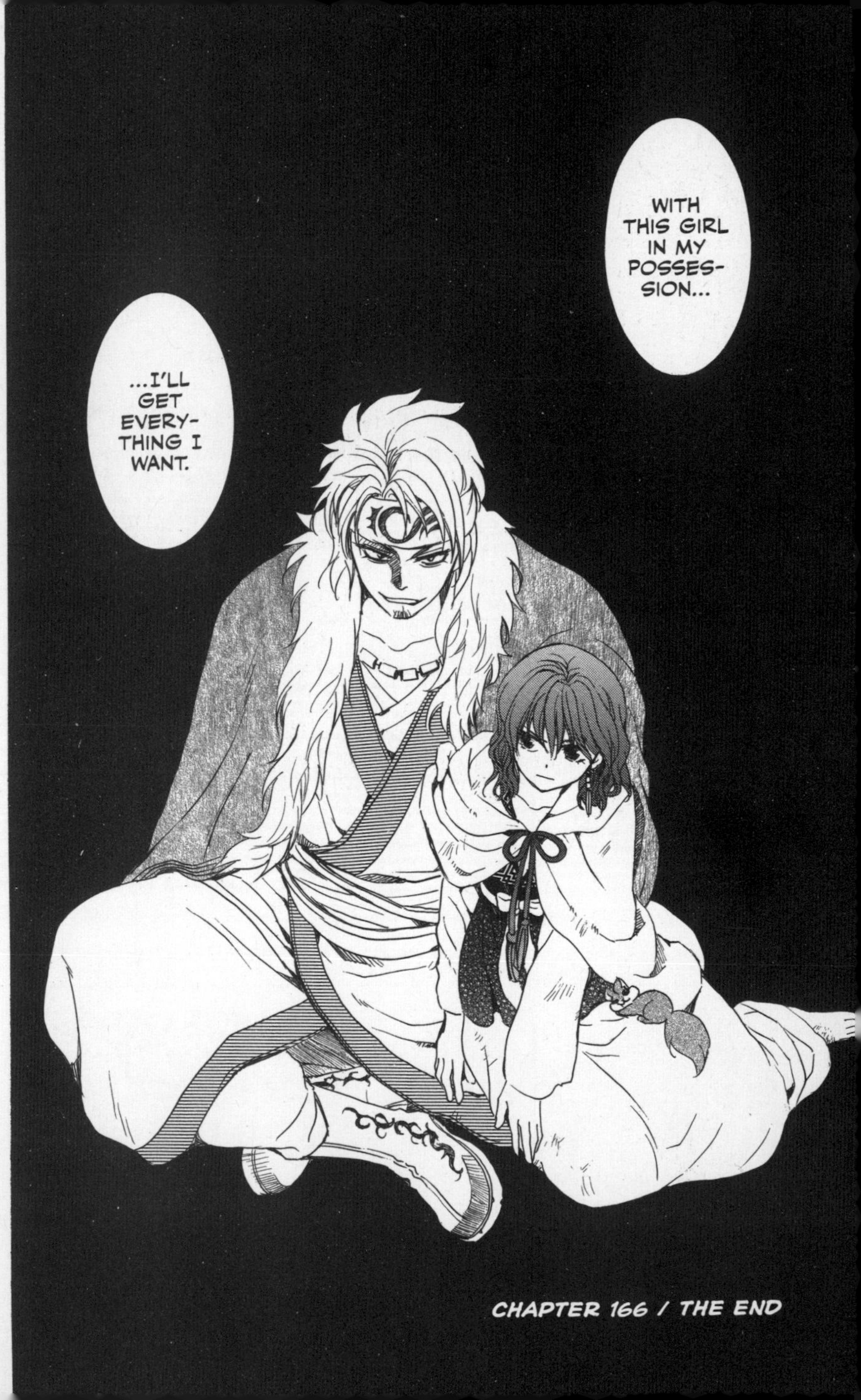
WITH THIS GIRL IN MY POSSESSION...
...I'LL GET EVERYTHING I WANT.
CHAPTER 166 / THE END

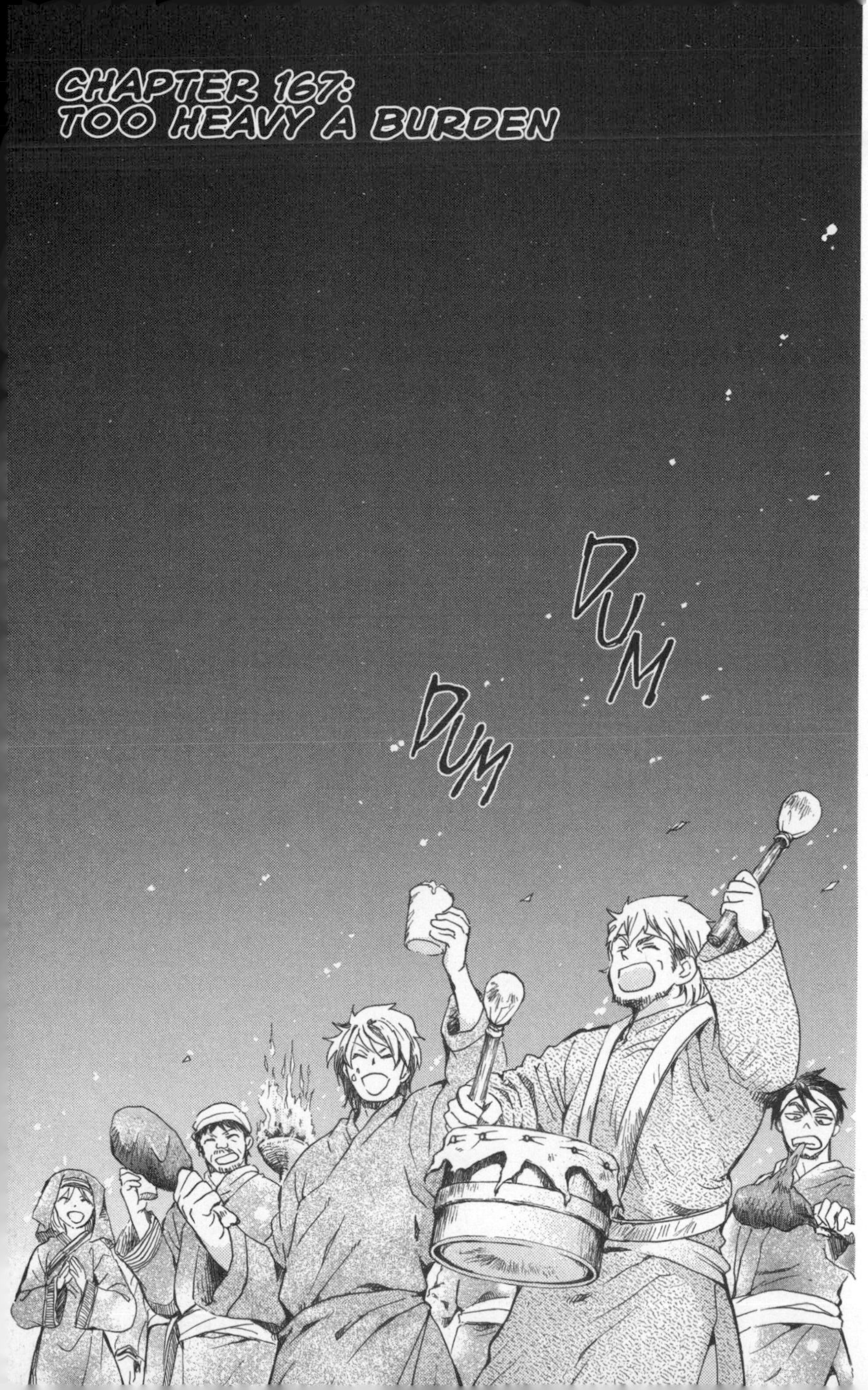
CHAPTER 167:
TOO HEAVY A BURDEN
DUM
DUM

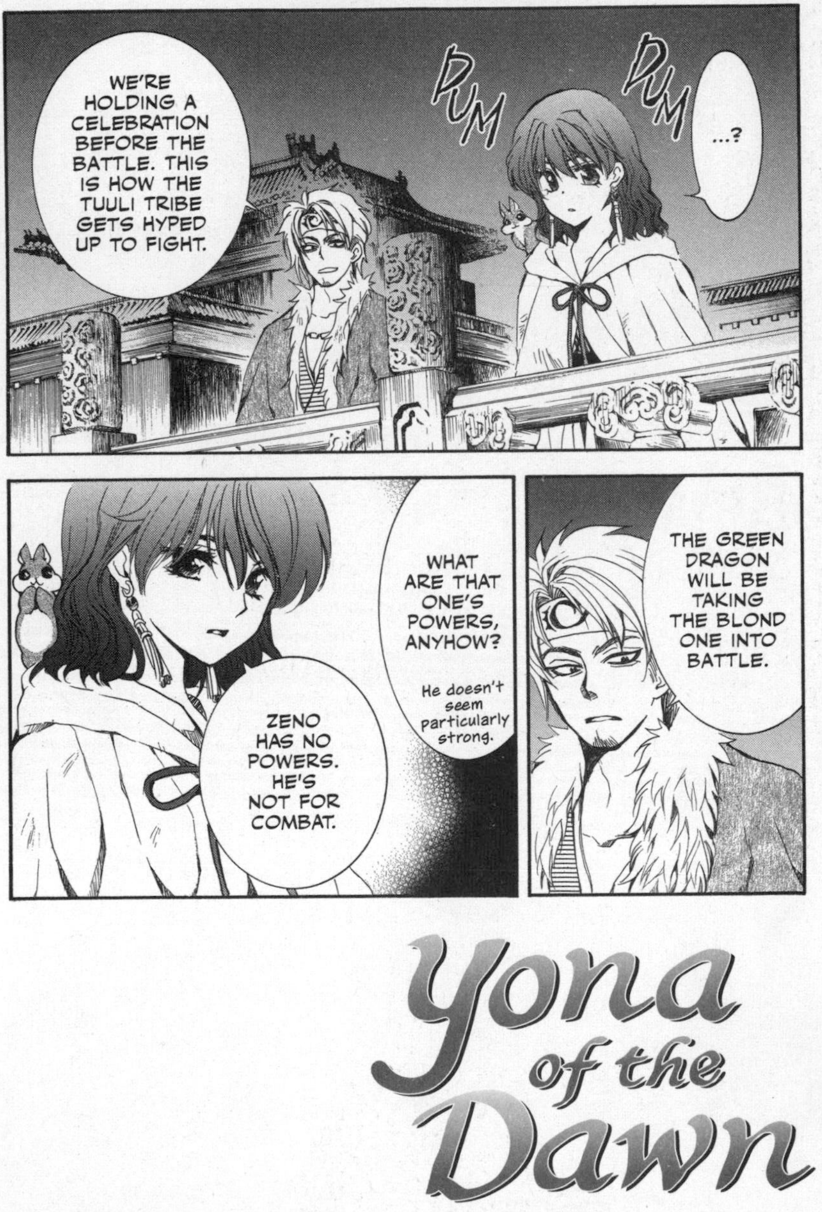
DUM DUM
...?
WE'RE HOLDING A CELEBRATION BEFORE THE BATTLE. THIS IS HOW THE TUULI TRIBE GETS HYPED UP TO FIGHT.
THE GREEN DRAGON WILL BE TAKING THE BLOND ONE INTO BATTLE.
WHAT ARE THAT ONE'S POWERS, ANYHOW?
He doesn't seem particularly strong.
ZENO HAS NO POWERS. HE'S NOT FOR COMBAT.

Yona of the Dawn

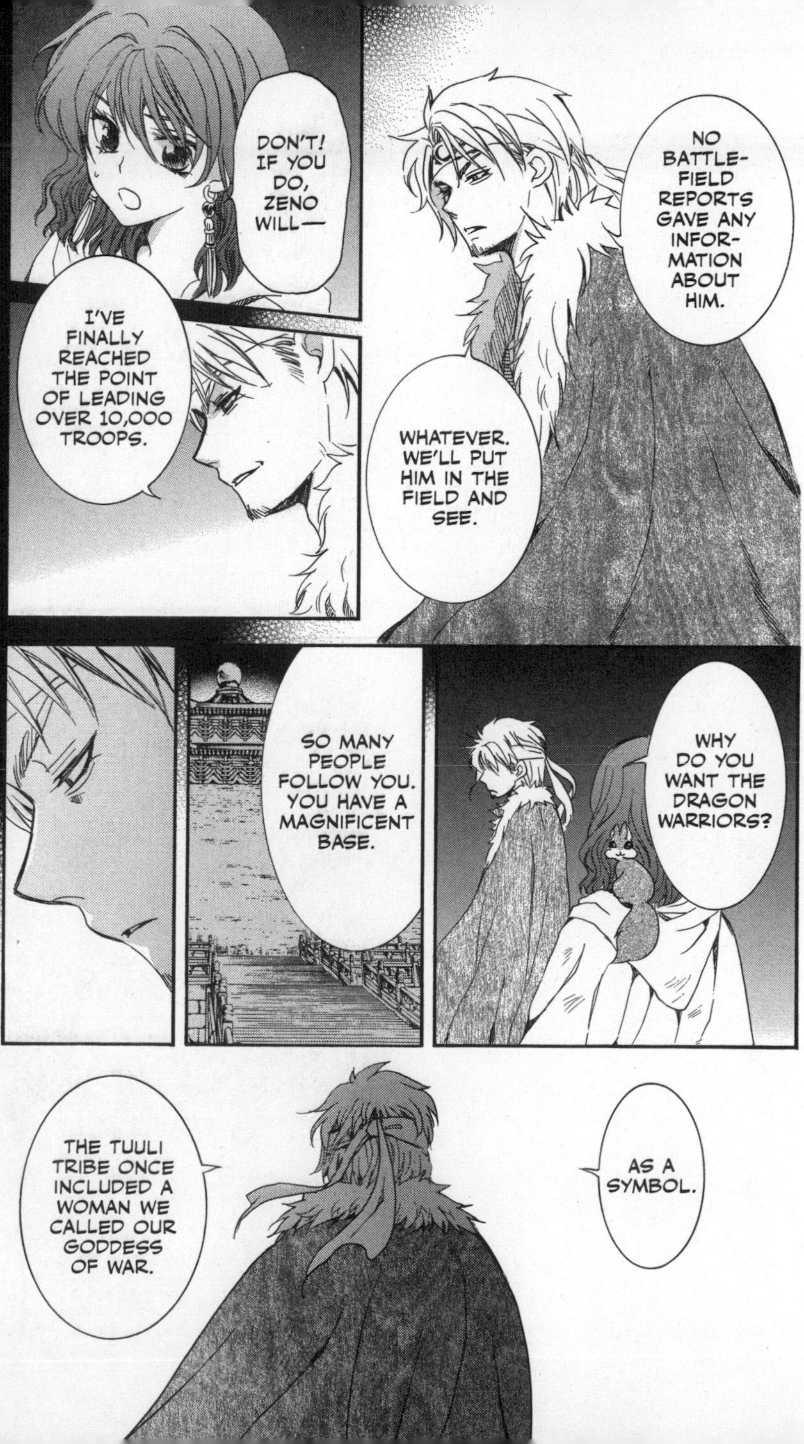
NO BATTLE-FIELD REPORTS GAVE ANY INFOR-MATION ABOUT HIM.
WHATEVER. WE'LL PUT HIM IN THE FIELD AND SEE.
DON'T! IF YOU DO, ZENO WILL—
I'VE FINALLY REACHED THE POINT OF LEADING OVER 10,000 TROOPS.
WHY DO YOU WANT THE DRAGON WARRIORS?
SO MANY PEOPLE FOLLOW YOU. YOU HAVE A MAGNIFICENT BASE.
AS A SYMBOL.
THE TUULI TRIBE ONCE INCLUDED A WOMAN WE CALLED OUR GODDESS OF WAR.

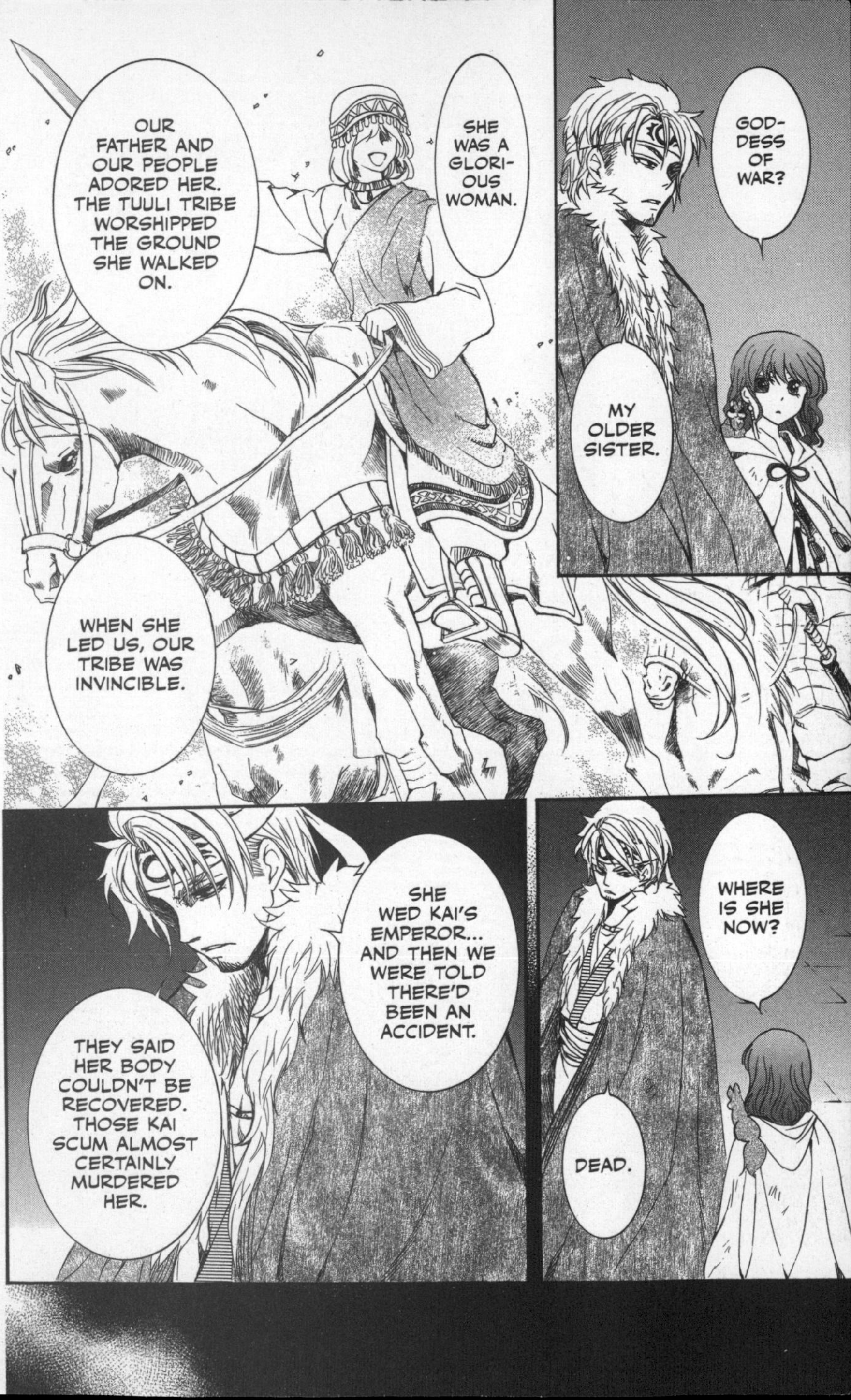
GOD-DESS OF WAR?
MY OLDER SISTER.
SHE WAS A GLORIOUS WOMAN.
OUR FATHER AND OUR PEOPLE ADORED HER. THE TUULI TRIBE WORSHIPPED THE GROUND SHE WALKED ON.
WHEN SHE LED US, OUR TRIBE WAS INVINCIBLE.
WHERE IS SHE NOW?
DEAD.
SHE WED KAI'S EMPEROR... AND THEN WE WERE TOLD THERE'D BEEN AN ACCIDENT.
THEY SAID HER BODY COULDN'T BE RECOVERED. THOSE KAI SCUM ALMOST CERTAINLY MURDERED HER.

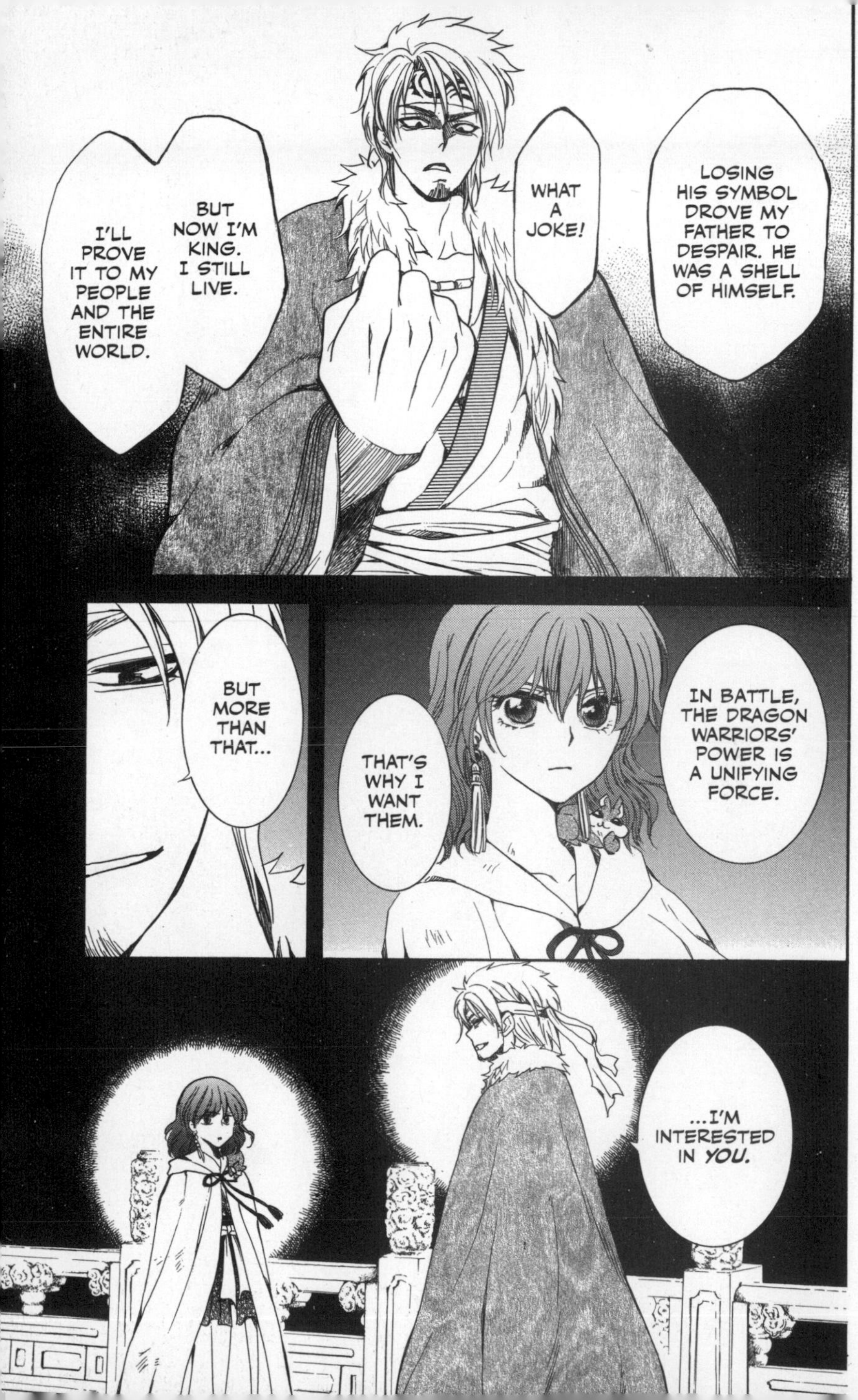
LOSING HIS SYMBOL DROVE MY FATHER TO DESPAIR. HE WAS A SHELL OF HIMSELF.
WHAT A JOKE!
BUT NOW I'M KING. I STILL LIVE.
I'LL PROVE IT TO MY PEOPLE AND THE ENTIRE WORLD.
IN BATTLE, THE DRAGON WARRIORS' POWER IS A UNIFYING FORCE.
THAT'S WHY I WANT THEM.
BUT MORE THAN THAT...
...I'M INTERESTED IN *YOU*.

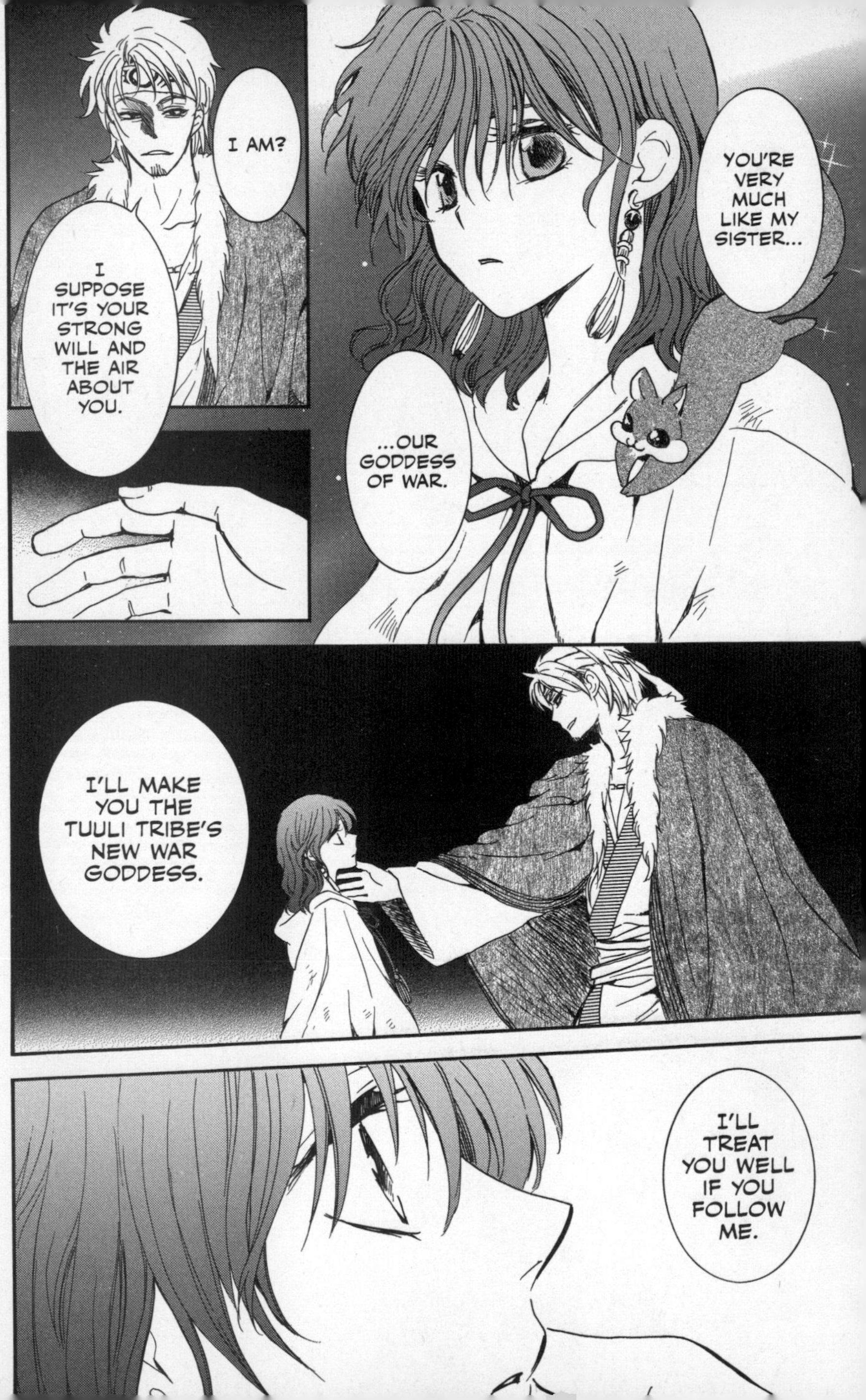
YOU'RE VERY MUCH LIKE MY SISTER...
...OUR GODDESS OF WAR.
I AM?
I SUPPOSE IT'S YOUR STRONG WILL AND THE AIR ABOUT YOU.
I'LL MAKE YOU THE TUULI TRIBE'S NEW WAR GODDESS.
I'LL TREAT YOU WELL IF YOU FOLLOW ME.

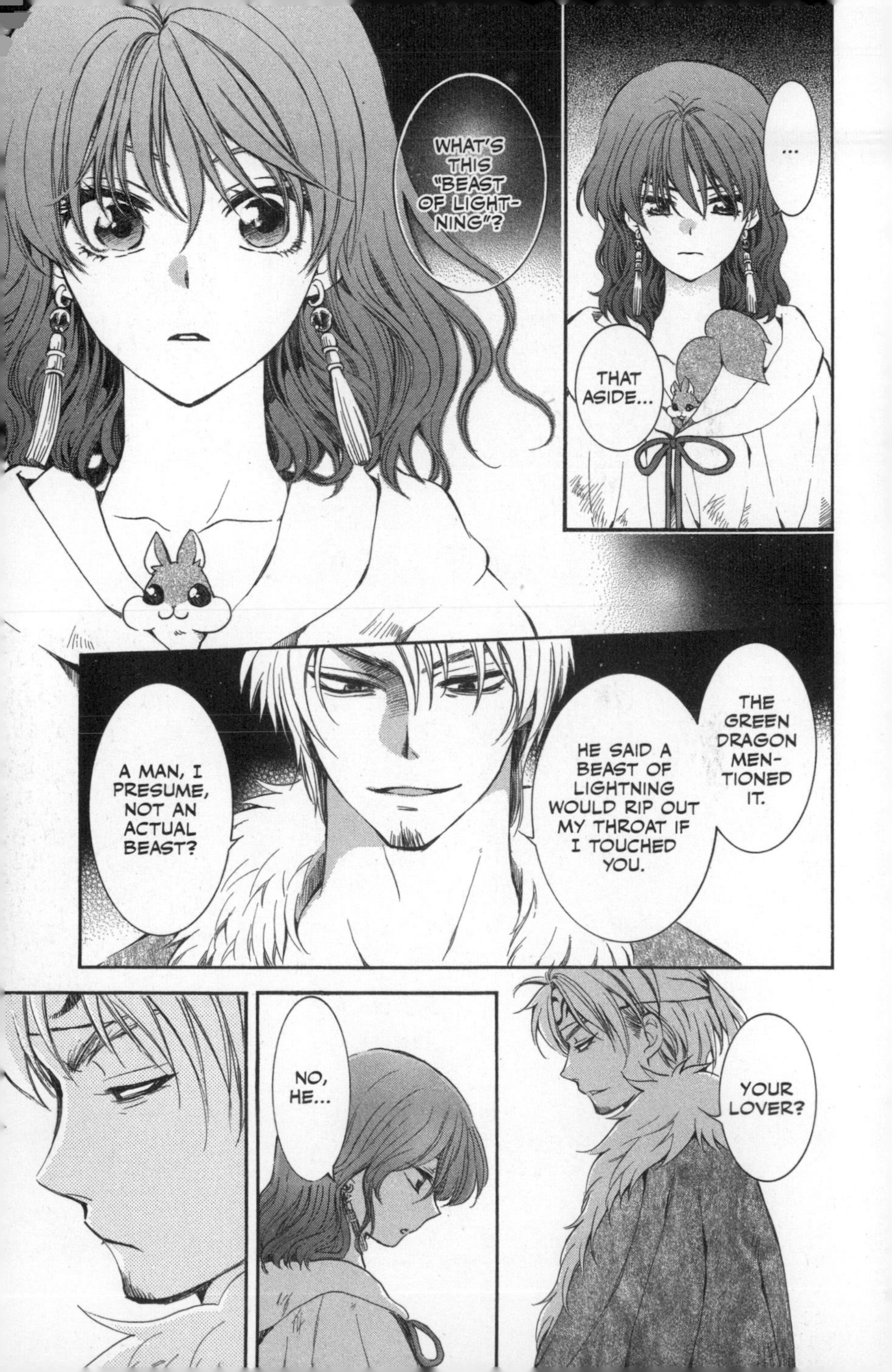
...
THAT ASIDE...
WHAT'S THIS "BEAST OF LIGHTNING"?
THE GREEN DRAGON MENTIONED IT.
HE SAID A BEAST OF LIGHTNING WOULD RIP OUT MY THROAT IF I TOUCHED YOU.
A MAN, I PRESUME, NOT AN ACTUAL BEAST?
YOUR LOVER?
NO, HE...

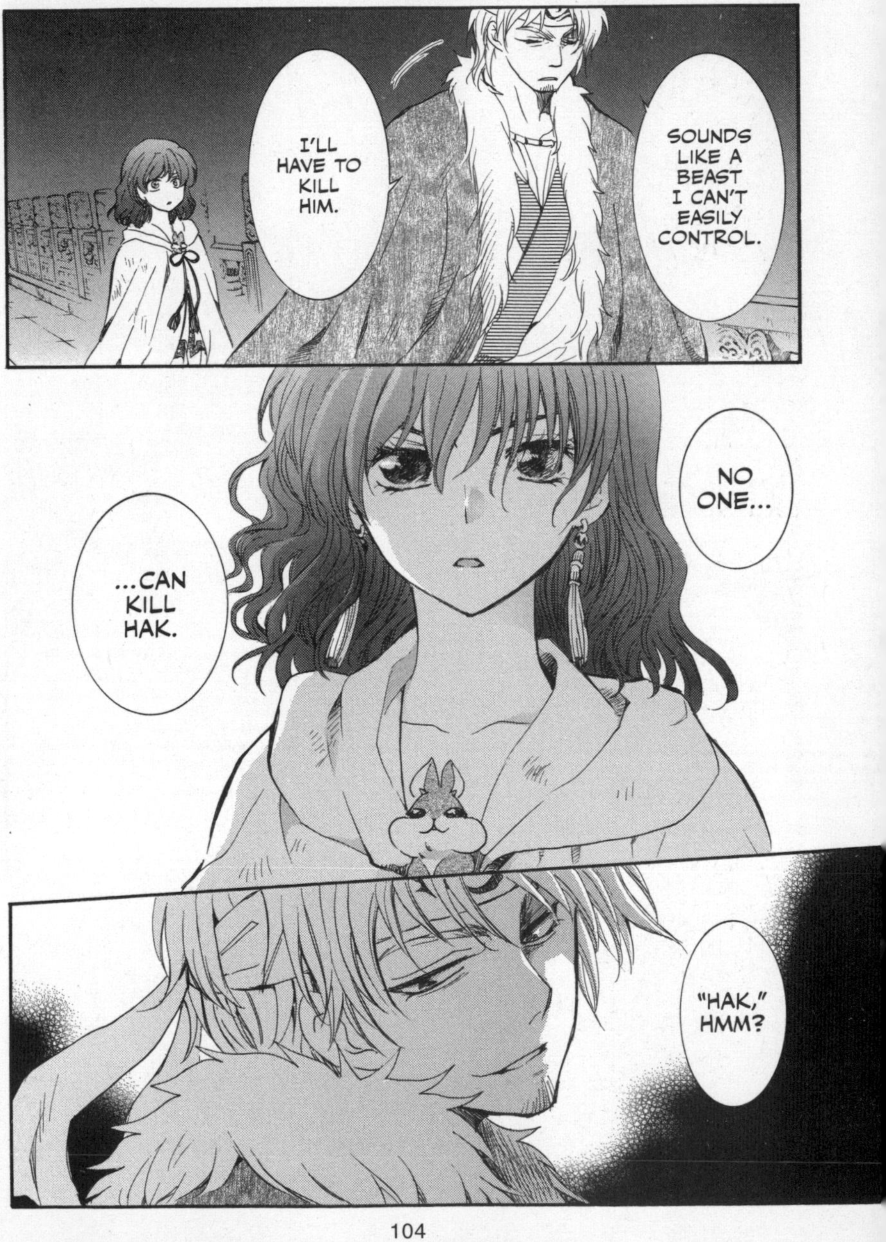
SOUNDS LIKE A BEAST I CAN'T EASILY CONTROL.
I'LL HAVE TO KILL HIM.
NO ONE...
...CAN KILL HAK.
"HAK," HMM?

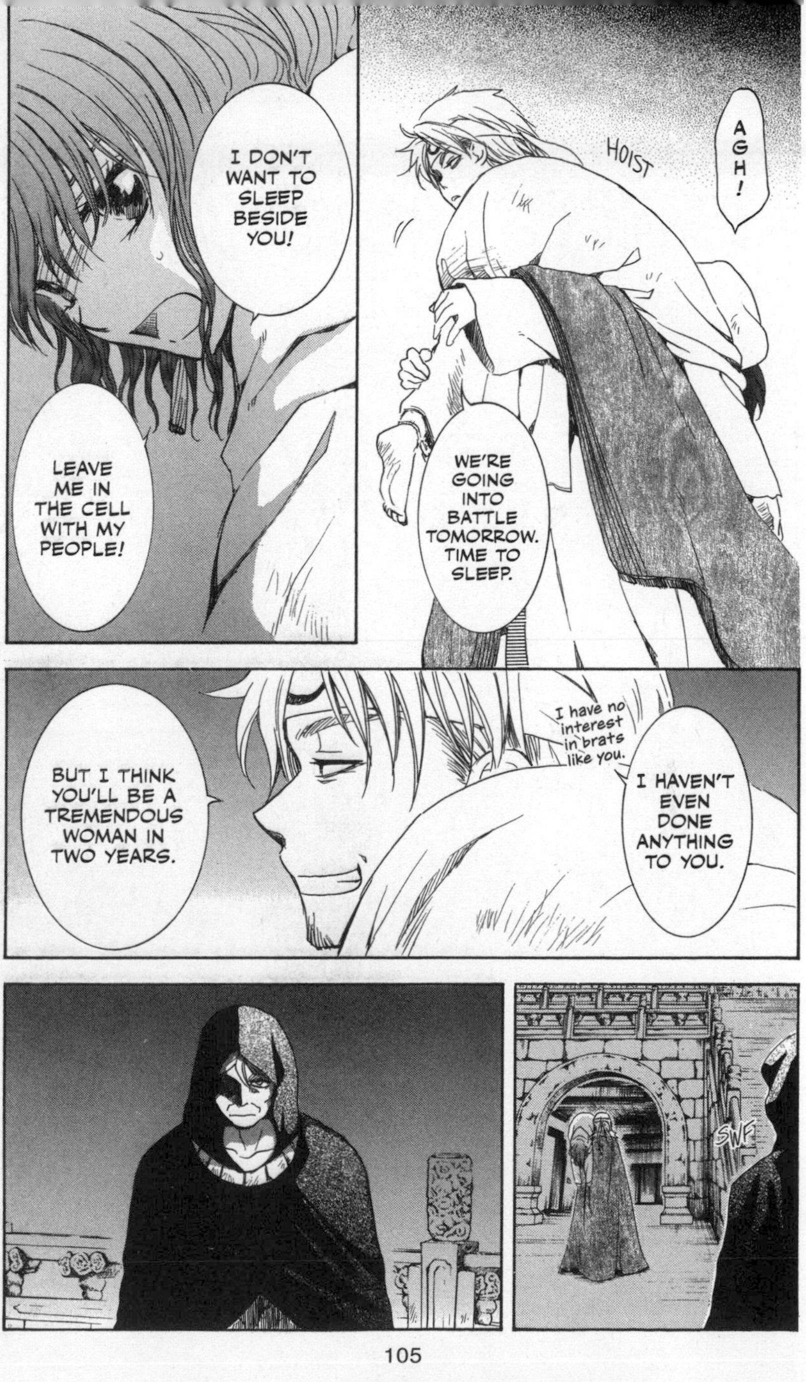
AGH!
HOIST
WE'RE GOING INTO BATTLE TOMORROW. TIME TO SLEEP.
I DON'T WANT TO SLEEP BESIDE YOU!
LEAVE ME IN THE CELL WITH MY PEOPLE!
I HAVEN'T EVEN DONE ANYTHING TO YOU.
I have no interest in brats like you.
BUT I THINK YOU'LL BE A TREMENDOUS WOMAN IN TWO YEARS.
SWF

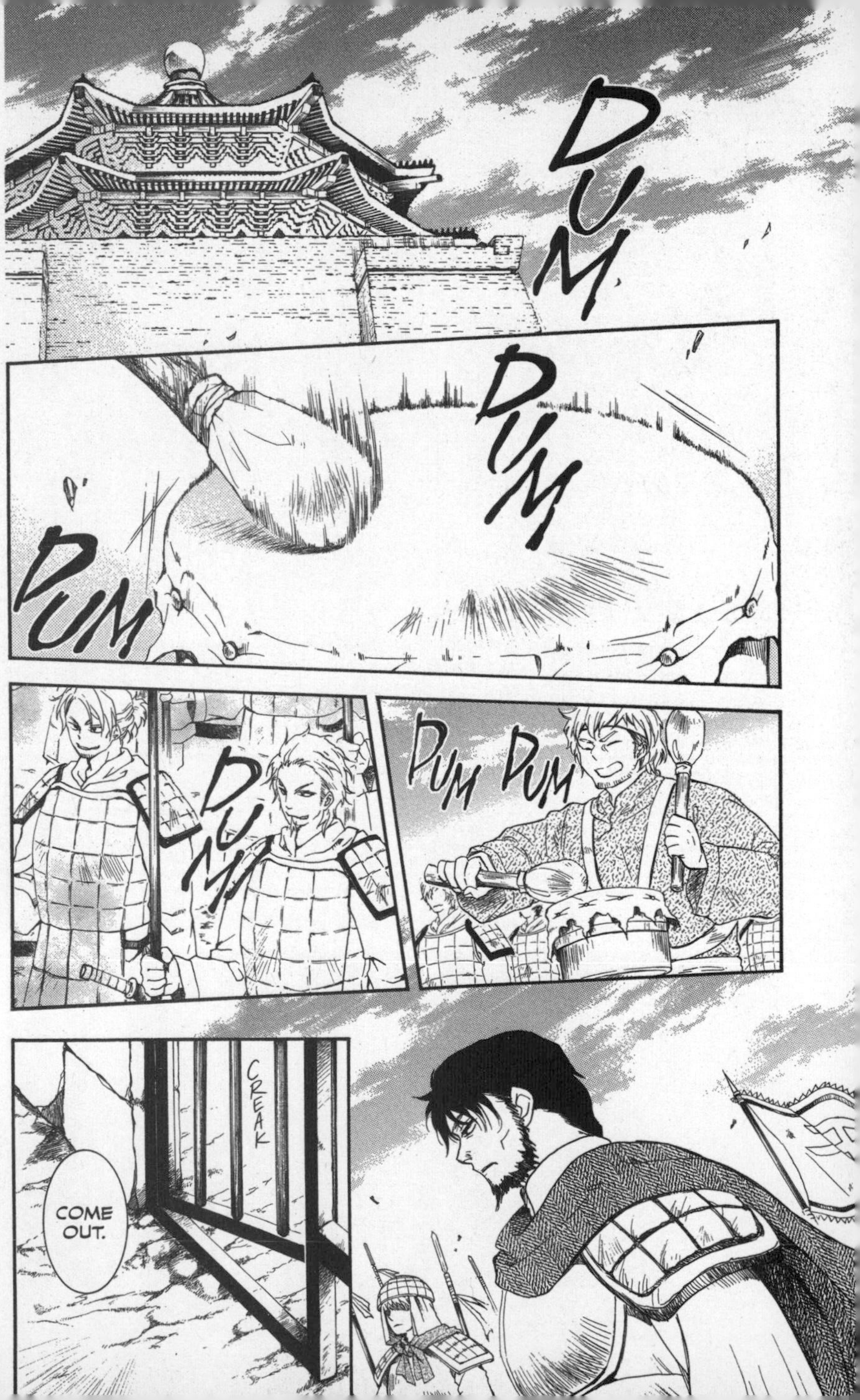
DUM
DUM
DUM
DUM DUM
DUM
CREAK
COME OUT.

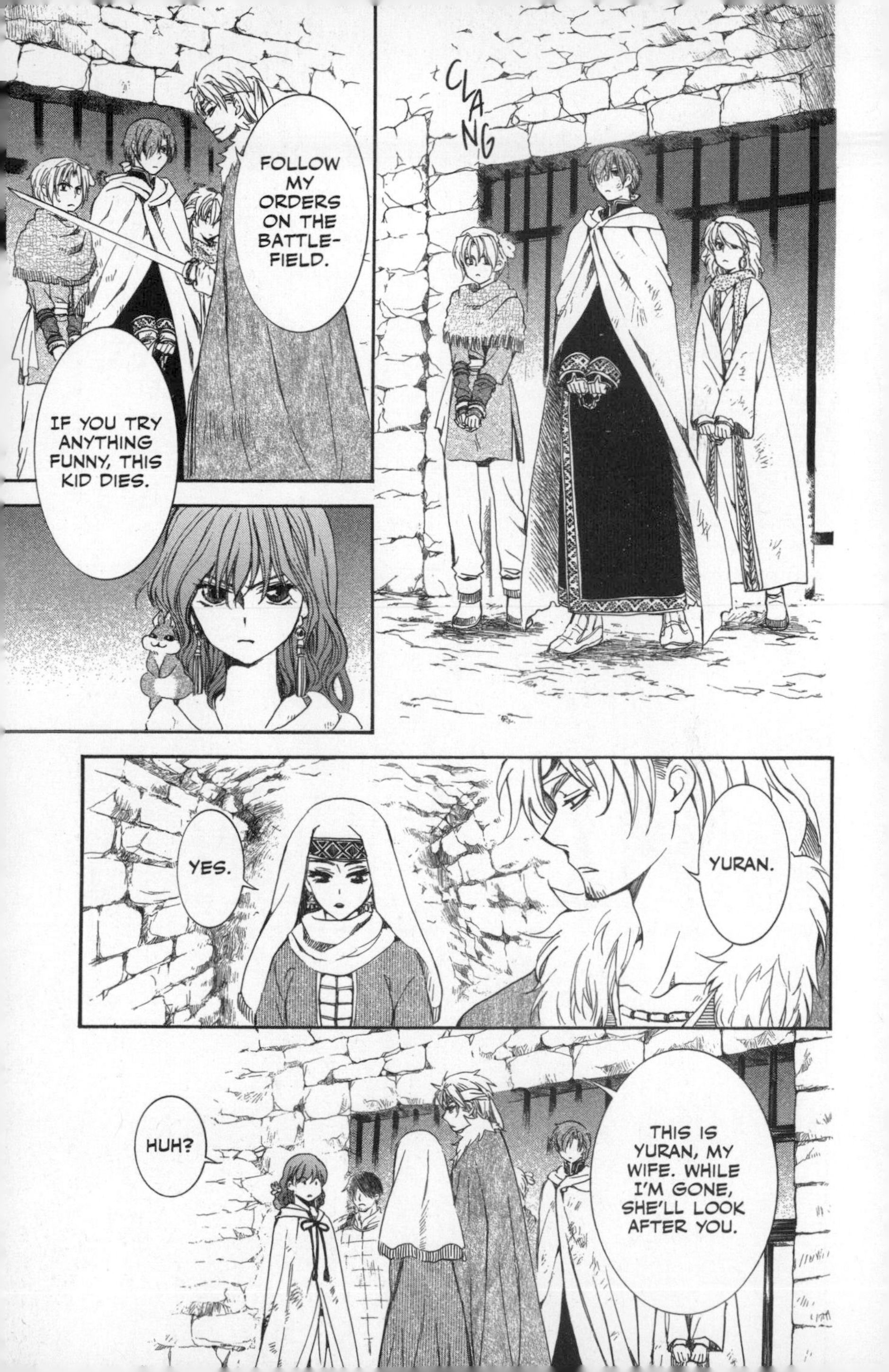
CLANG
FOLLOW MY ORDERS ON THE BATTLE-FIELD.
IF YOU TRY ANYTHING FUNNY, THIS KID DIES.
YURAN.
YES.
THIS IS YURAN, MY WIFE. WHILE I'M GONE, SHE'LL LOOK AFTER YOU.
HUH?

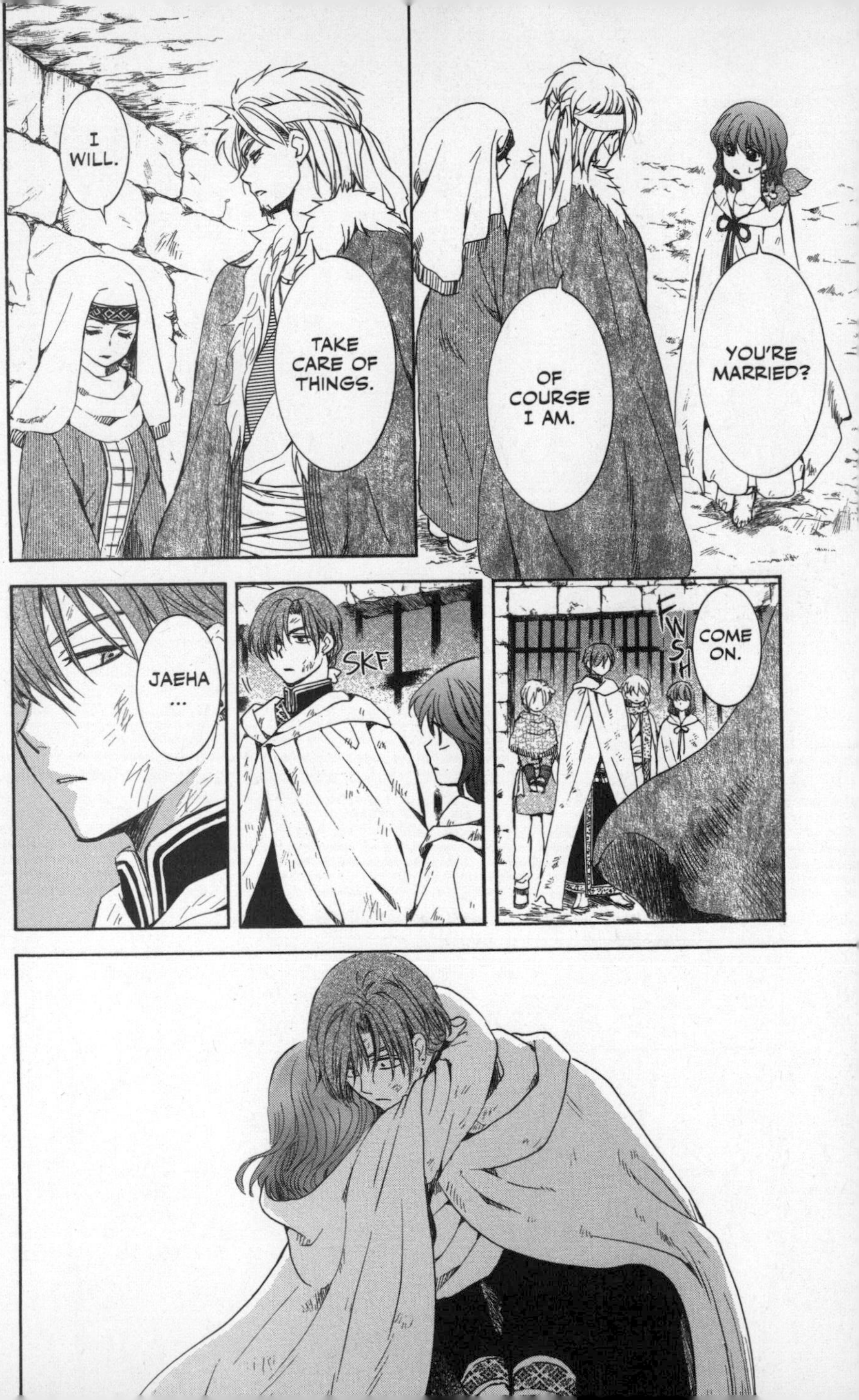
YOU'RE MARRIED?
OF COURSE I AM.
TAKE CARE OF THINGS.
I WILL.
FWSH
COME ON.
SKF
JAEHA ...

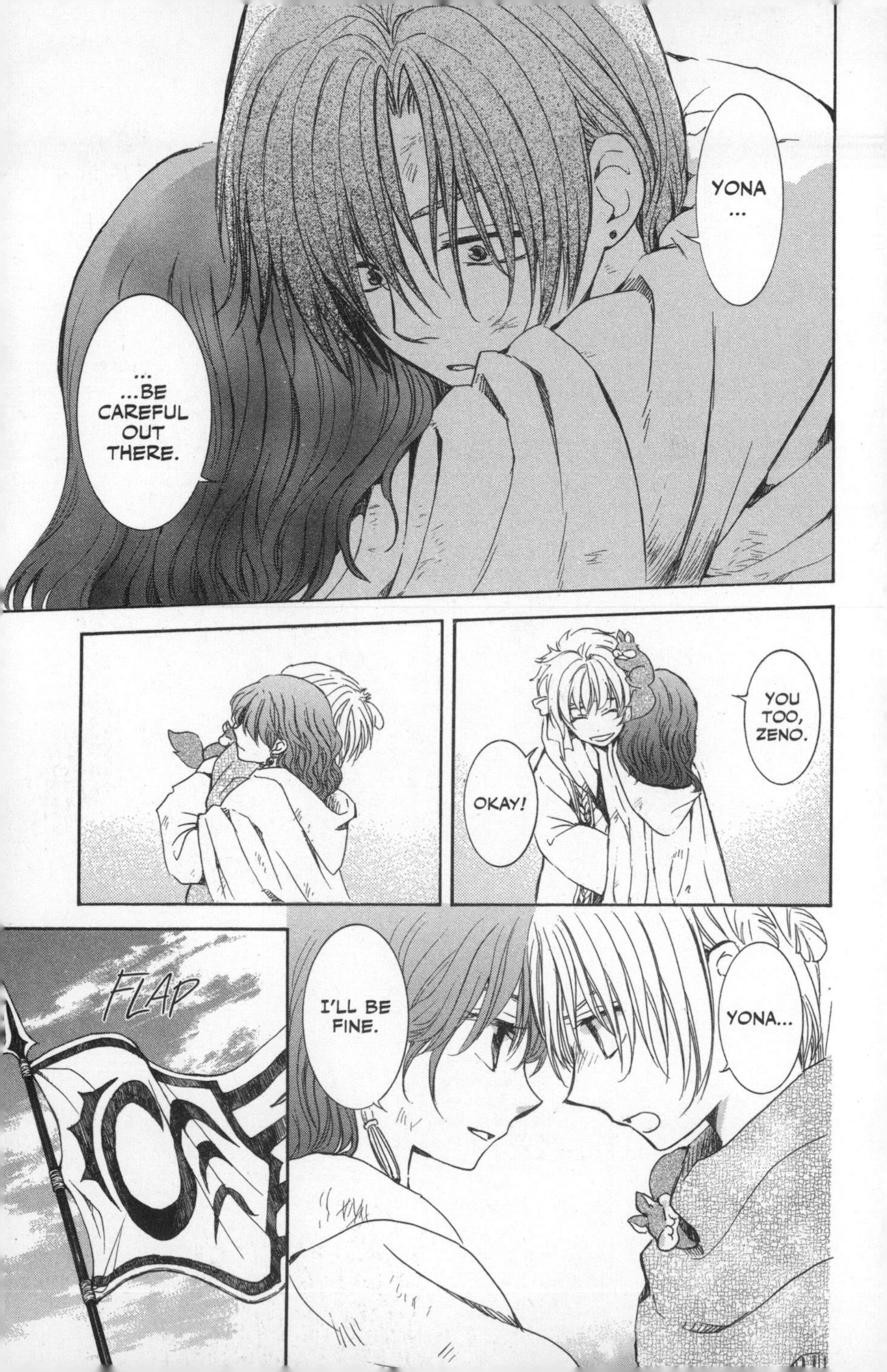
YONA ...
... ...BE CAREFUL OUT THERE.
YOU TOO, ZENO.
OKAY!
YONA...
I'LL BE FINE.
FLAP

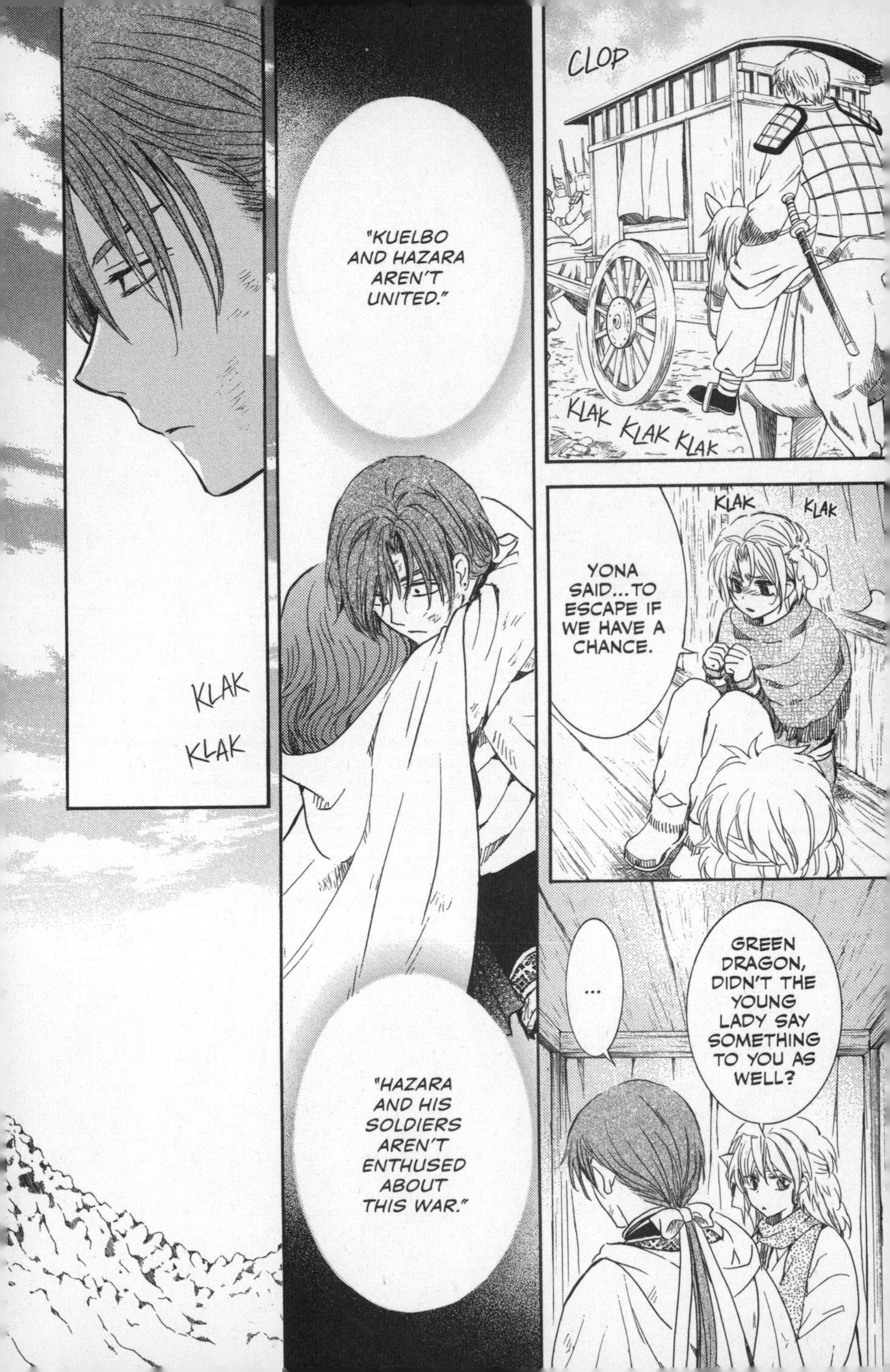
CLOP
KLAK KLAK KLAK
KLAK KLAK
YONA SAID...TO ESCAPE IF WE HAVE A CHANCE.
GREEN DRAGON, DIDN'T THE YOUNG LADY SAY SOMETHING TO YOU AS WELL?
...
"KUELBO AND HAZARA AREN'T UNITED."
"HAZARA AND HIS SOLDIERS AREN'T ENTHUSED ABOUT THIS WAR."
KLAK
KLAK

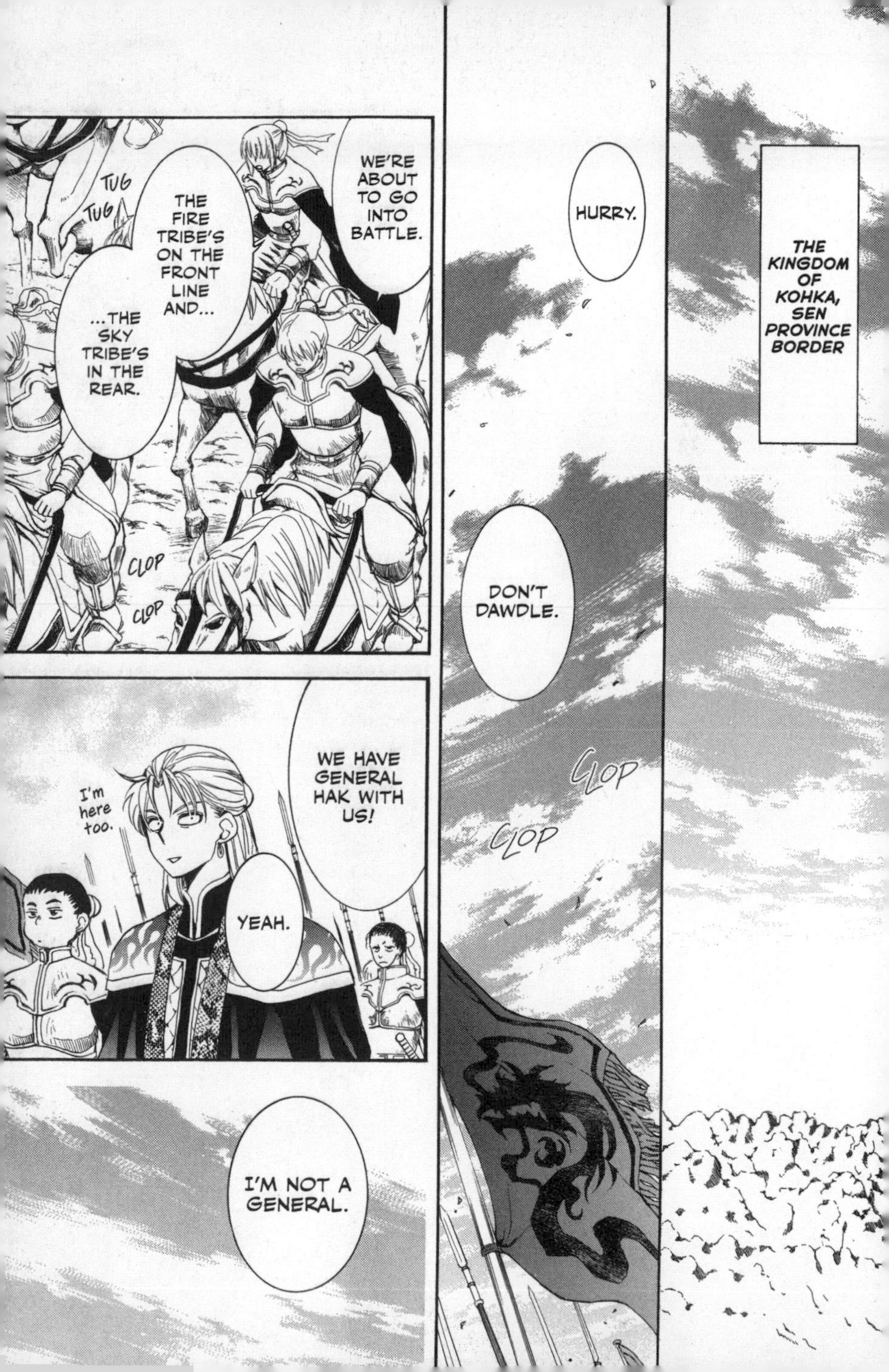
THE KINGDOM OF KOHKA, SEN PROVINCE BORDER
HURRY.
DON'T DAWDLE.
CLOP
CLOP
WE'RE ABOUT TO GO INTO BATTLE.
THE FIRE TRIBE'S ON THE FRONT LINE AND...
...THE SKY TRIBE'S IN THE REAR.
TUG
TUG
CLOP
CLOP
WE HAVE GENERAL HAK WITH US!
YEAH.
I'm here too.
I'M NOT A GENERAL.

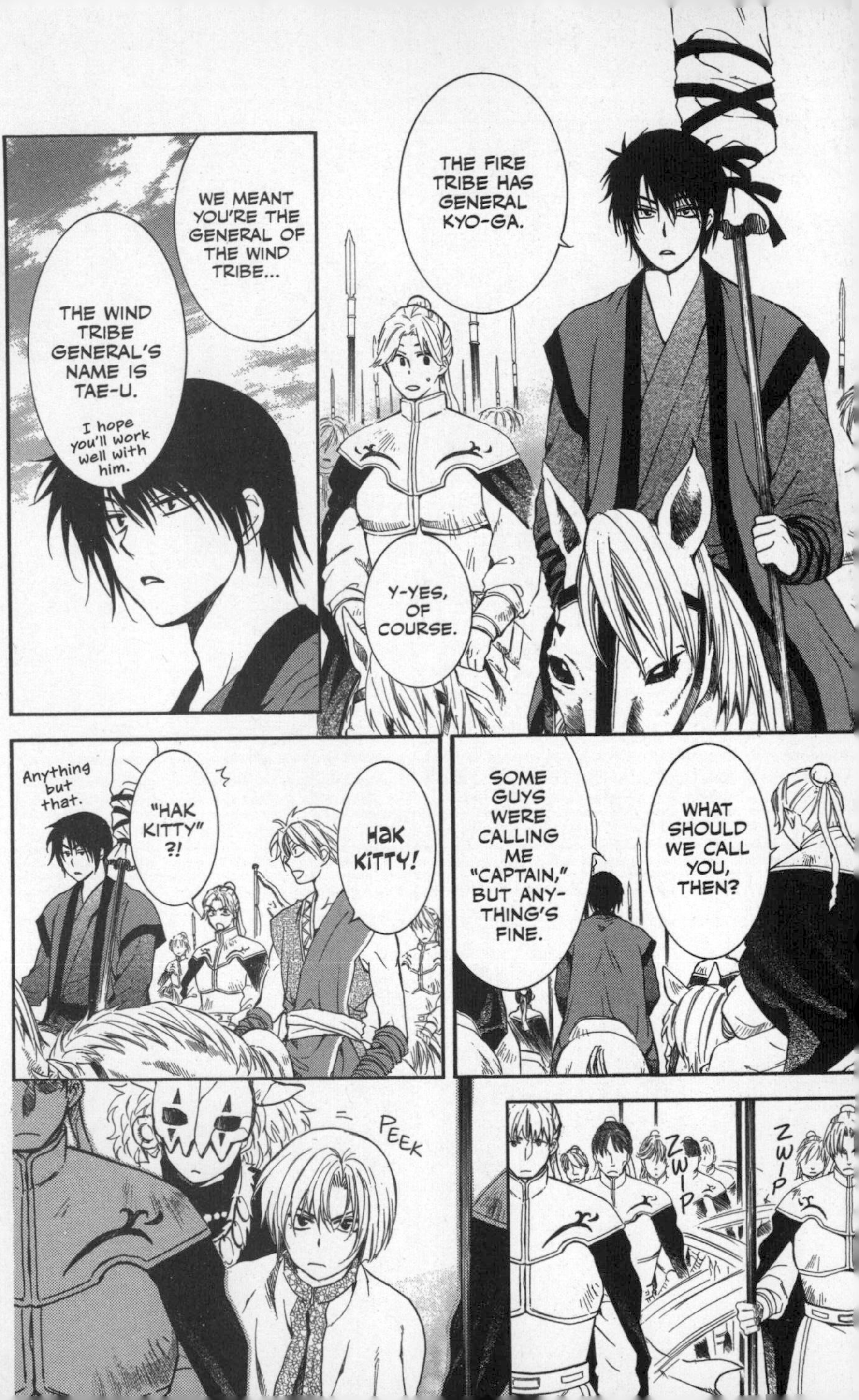
THE FIRE TRIBE HAS GENERAL KYO-GA.
Y-YES, OF COURSE.
WE MEANT YOU'RE THE GENERAL OF THE WIND TRIBE...
THE WIND TRIBE GENERAL'S NAME IS TAE-U.
I hope you'll work well with him.
WHAT SHOULD WE CALL YOU, THEN?
SOME GUYS WERE CALLING ME "CAPTAIN," BUT ANY-THING'S FINE.
HAK KITTY!
"HAK KITTY"?!
Anything but that.
ZWIP
ZWIP
PEEK

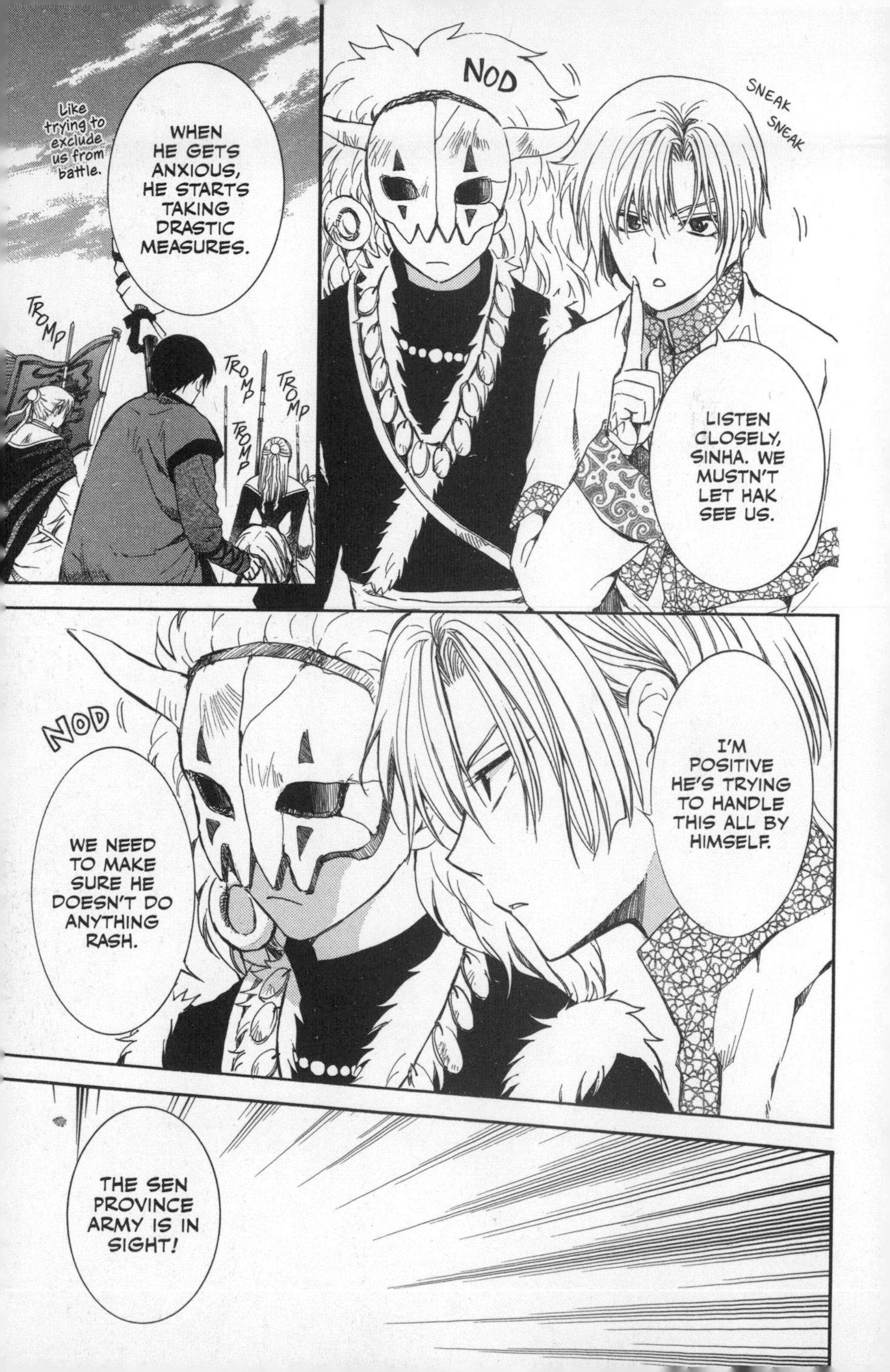
SNEAK
SNEAK
NOD
LISTEN CLOSELY, SINHA. WE MUSTN'T LET HAK SEE US.
WHEN HE GETS ANXIOUS, HE STARTS TAKING DRASTIC MEASURES.
Like trying to exclude us from battle.
TROMP
TROMP
TROMP
TROMP
I'M POSITIVE HE'S TRYING TO HANDLE THIS ALL BY HIMSELF.
NOD
WE NEED TO MAKE SURE HE DOESN'T DO ANYTHING RASH.
THE SEN PROVINCE ARMY IS IN SIGHT!

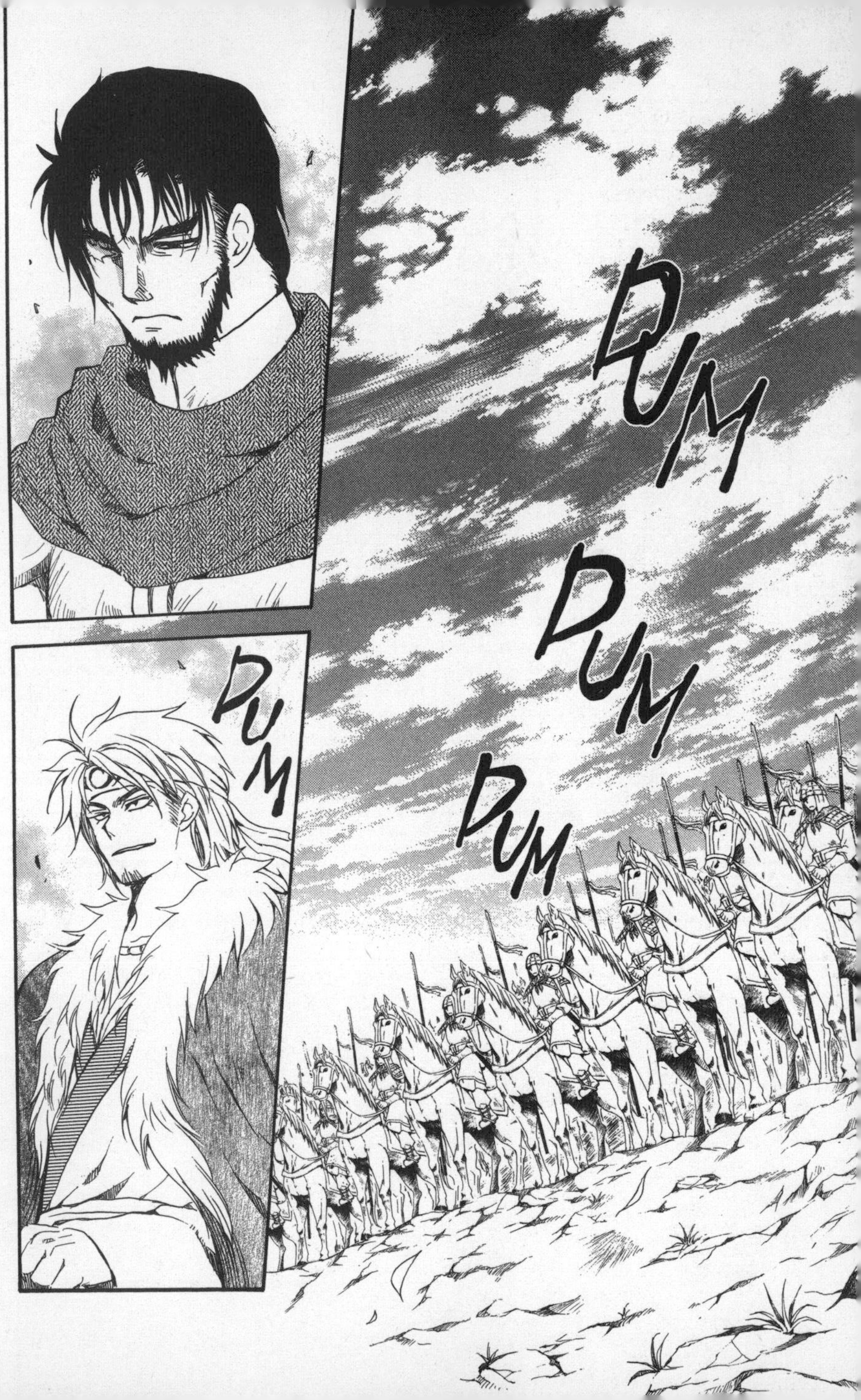
DUM
DUM
DUM
DUM

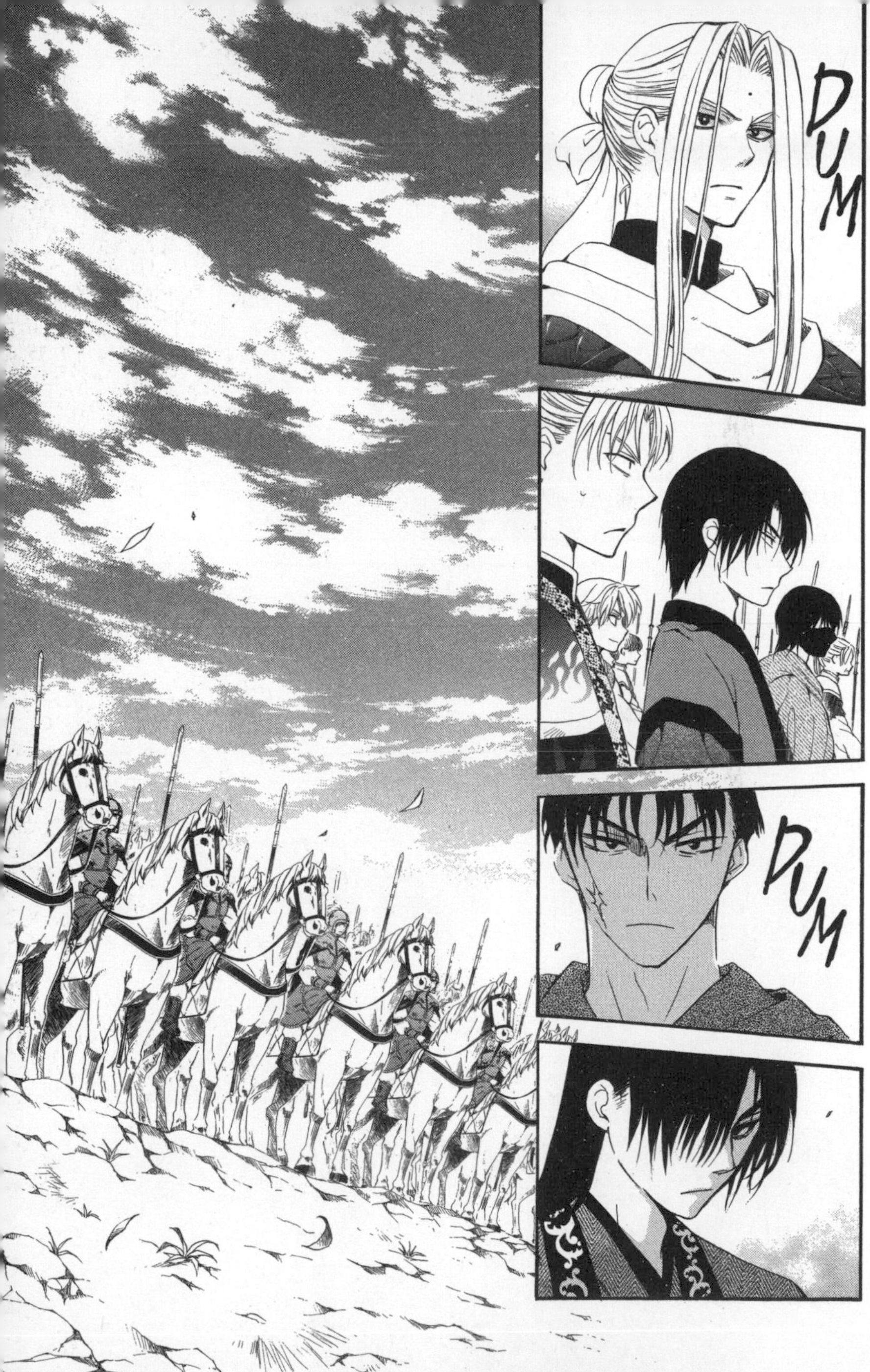
DUM
DUM

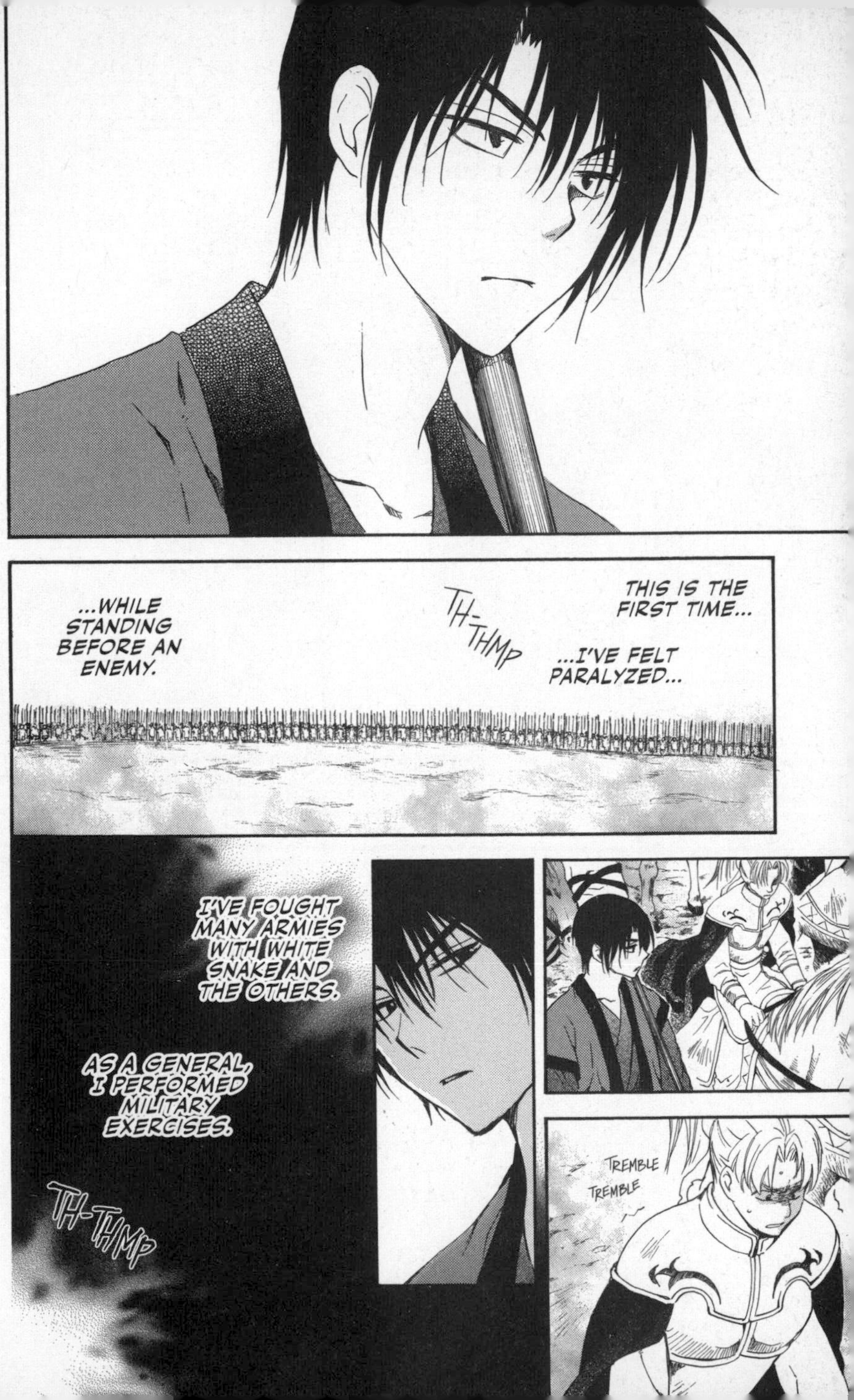
THIS IS THE FIRST TIME...
...I'VE FELT PARALYZED...
TH-THMP
...WHILE STANDING BEFORE AN ENEMY.
TREMBLE
TREMBLE
I'VE FOUGHT MANY ARMIES WITH WHITE SNAKE AND THE OTHERS.
AS A GENERAL, I PERFORMED MILITARY EXERCISES.
TH-THMP

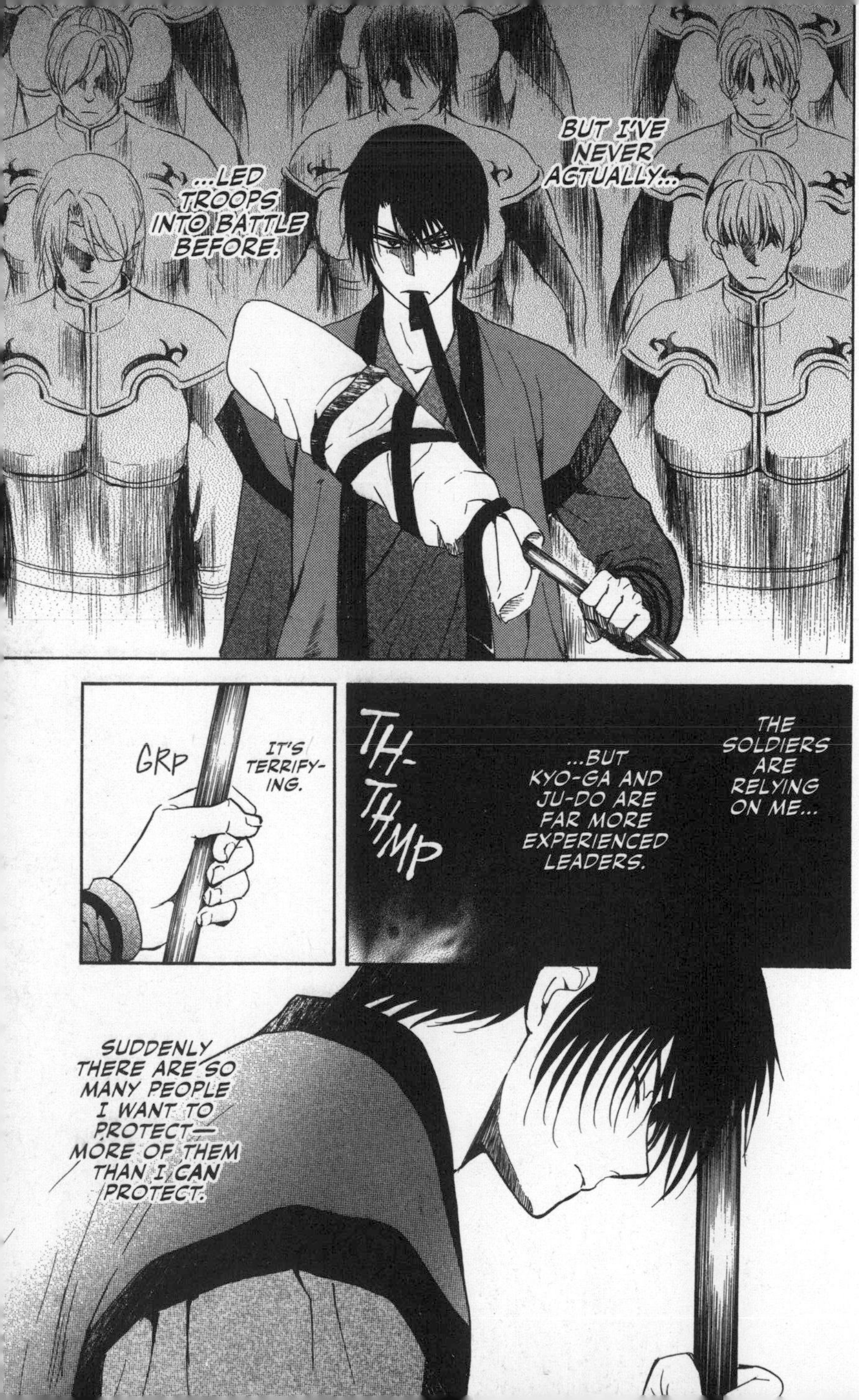
BUT I'VE NEVER ACTUALLY...
...LED TROOPS INTO BATTLE BEFORE.
THE SOLDIERS ARE RELYING ON ME...
...BUT KYO-GA AND JU-DO ARE FAR MORE EXPERIENCED LEADERS.
TH-THMP
IT'S TERRIFY-ING.
GRP
SUDDENLY THERE ARE SO MANY PEOPLE I WANT TO PROTECT— MORE OF THEM THAN I CAN PROTECT.

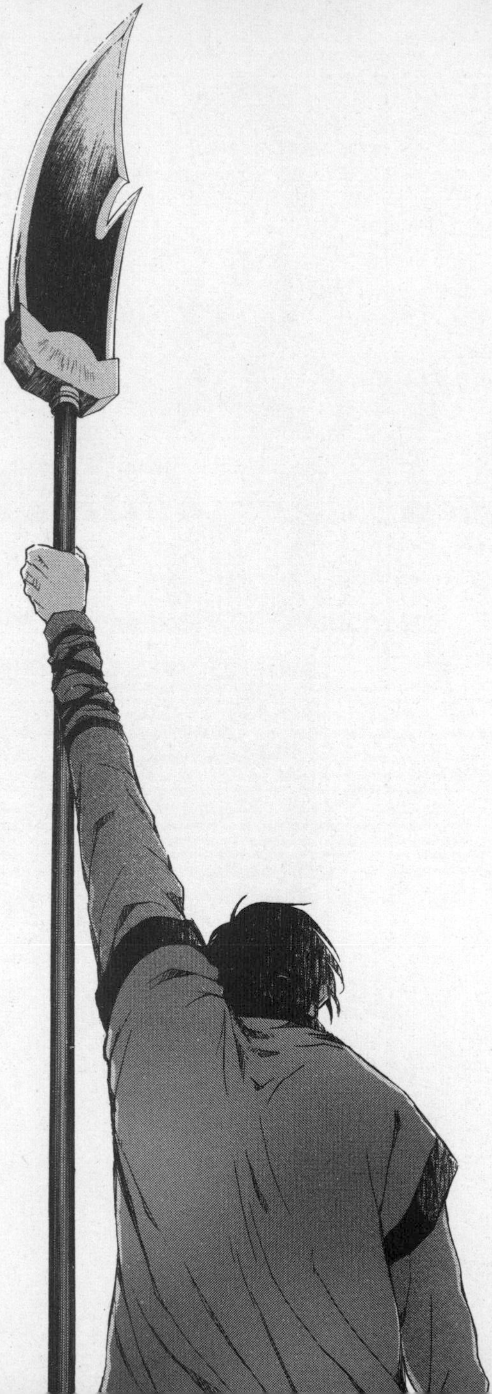

Last November, the second Yona stage play was performed! It adapted material from volumes 1-7.

The script was packed. There were tons of fight scenes. The actors did their best to play their roles, and everyone got along so well. It was as if the Happy Hungry Bunch was actually there. That's the feeling I got from it. I was very glad that the audiences enjoyed it.

Thank you so much to everyone involved in the production!

The first and second Yona stage plays taught me the joys of the stage.

Yona of the Dawn is very lucky to have this opportunity.

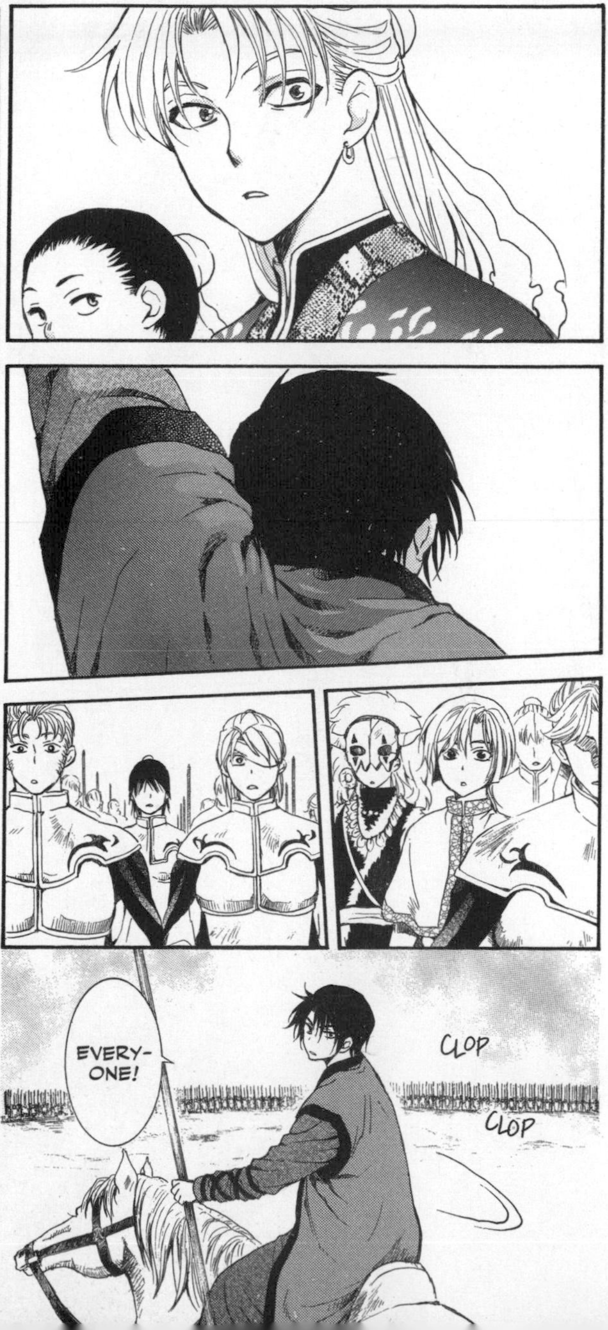

EVERY-ONE!
CLOP
CLOP

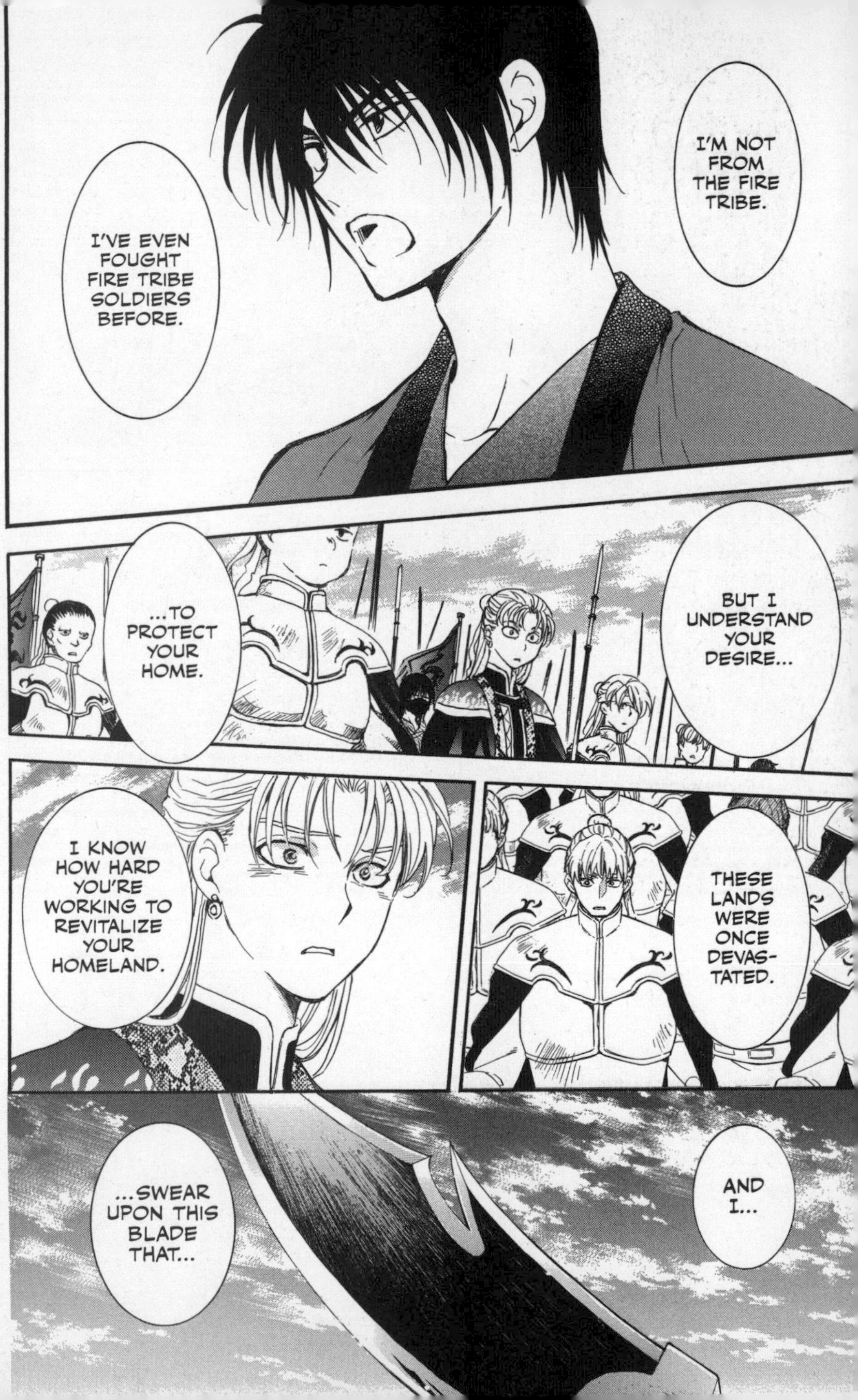
I'M NOT FROM THE FIRE TRIBE.
I'VE EVEN FOUGHT FIRE TRIBE SOLDIERS BEFORE.
BUT I UNDERSTAND YOUR DESIRE...
...TO PROTECT YOUR HOME.
THESE LANDS WERE ONCE DEVAS-TATED.
I KNOW HOW HARD YOU'RE WORKING TO REVITALIZE YOUR HOMELAND.
AND I...
...SWEAR UPON THIS BLADE THAT...

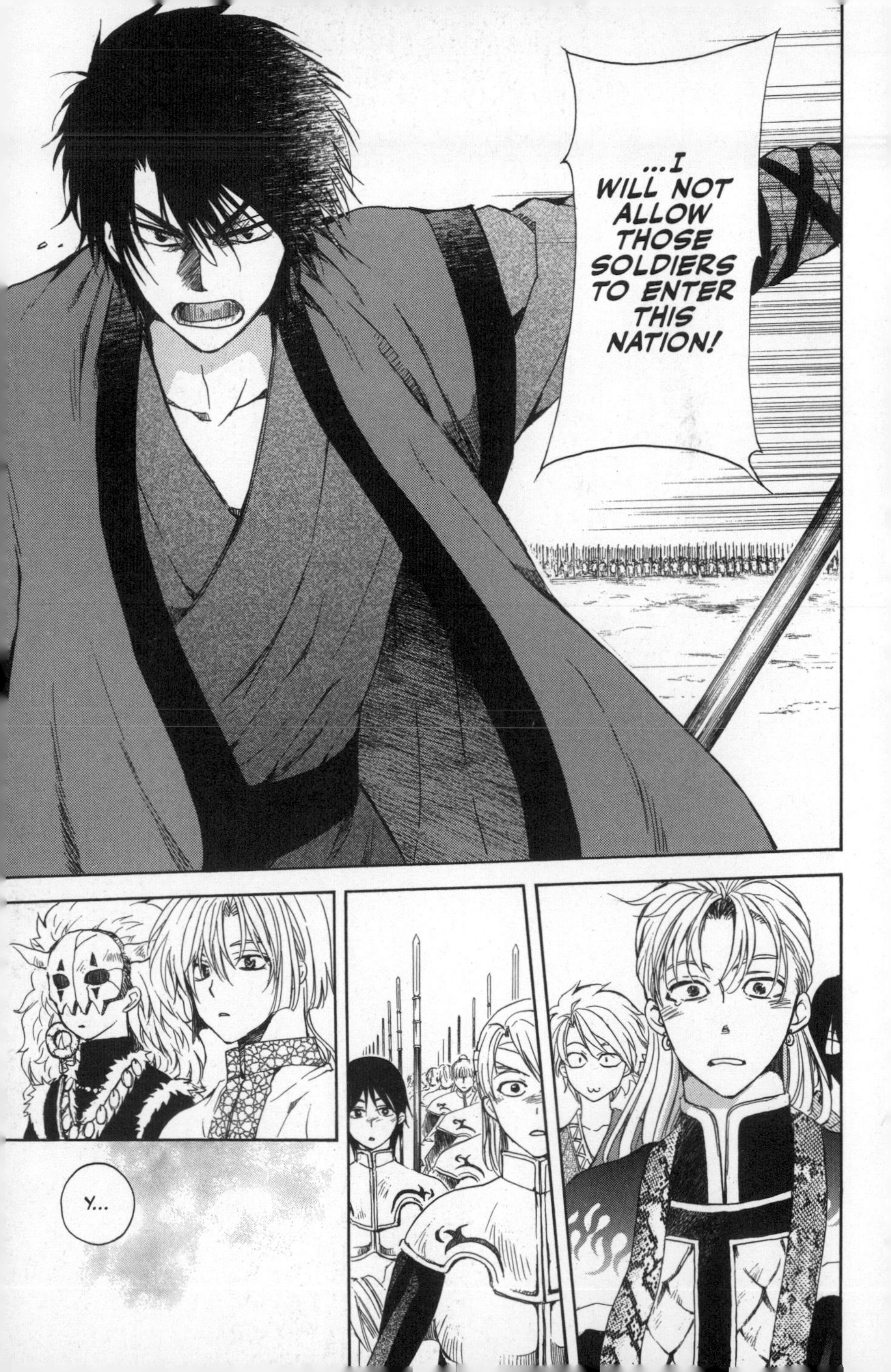
...I WILL NOT ALLOW THOSE SOLDIERS TO ENTER THIS NATION!
Y...

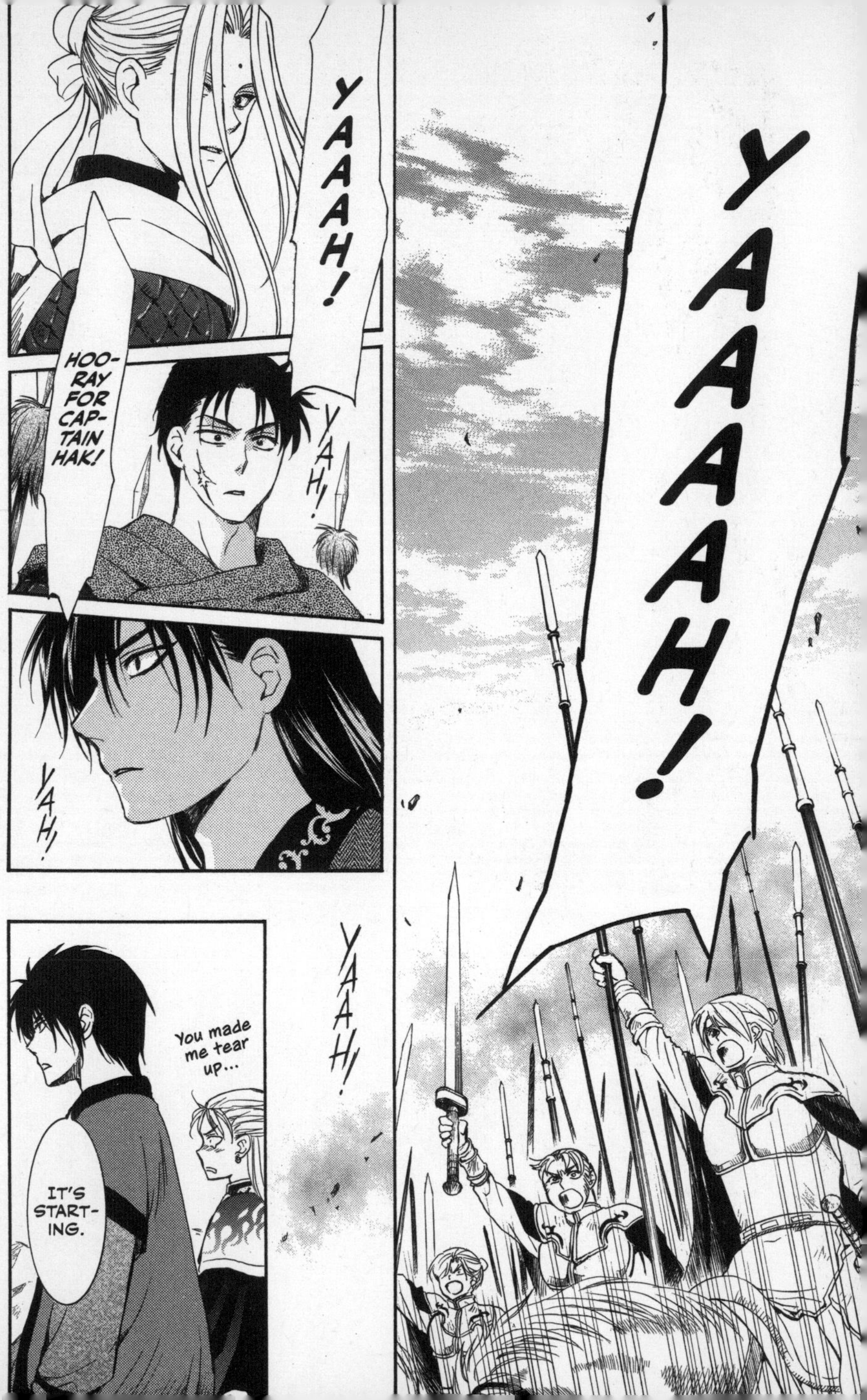
YAAAAH!
YAAAAH!
HOORAY FOR CAPTAIN HAK!
YAAH!
YAAH!
YAAAH!
You made me tear up...
IT'S STARTING.

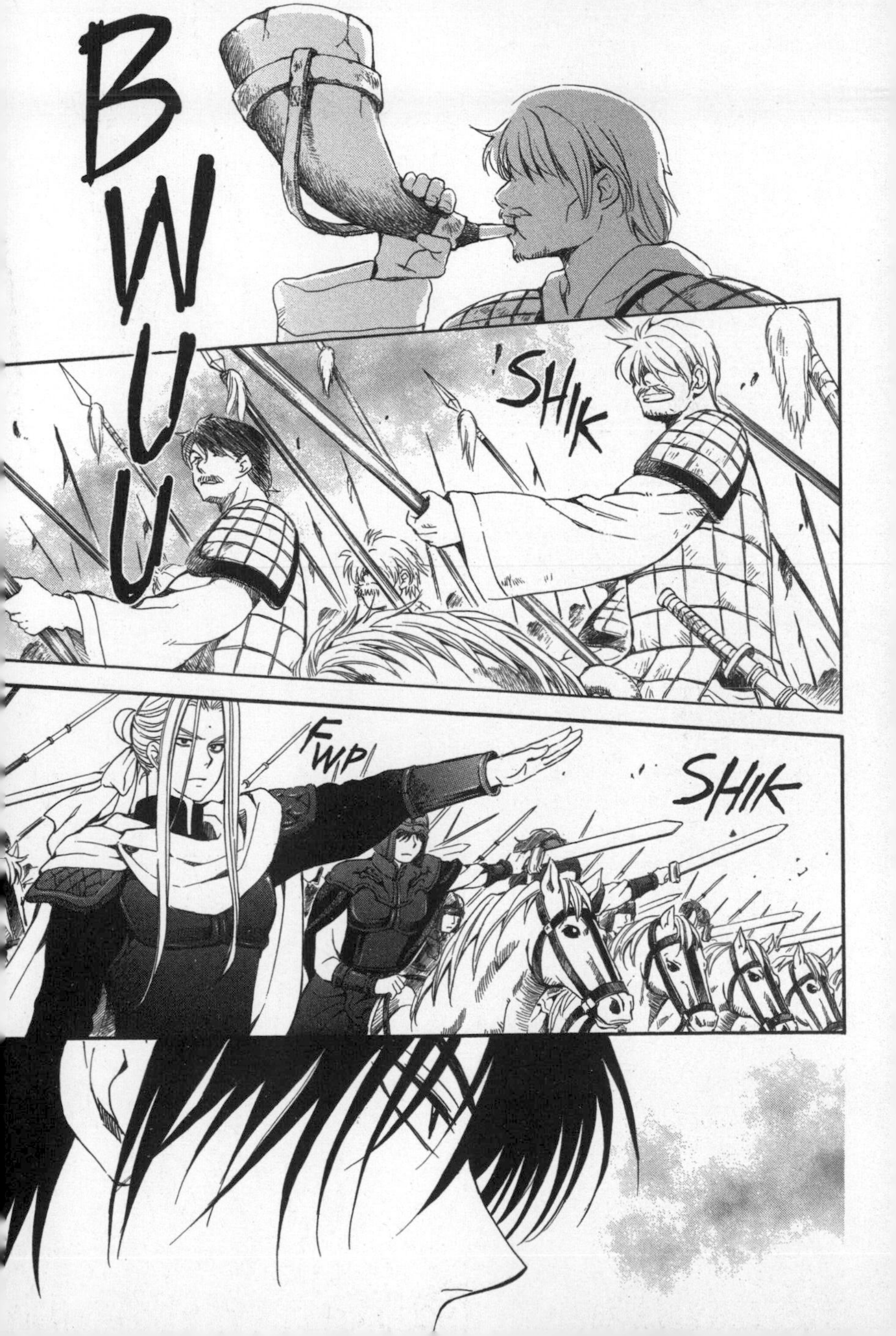
BWUU
SHIK
SHIK
FWP

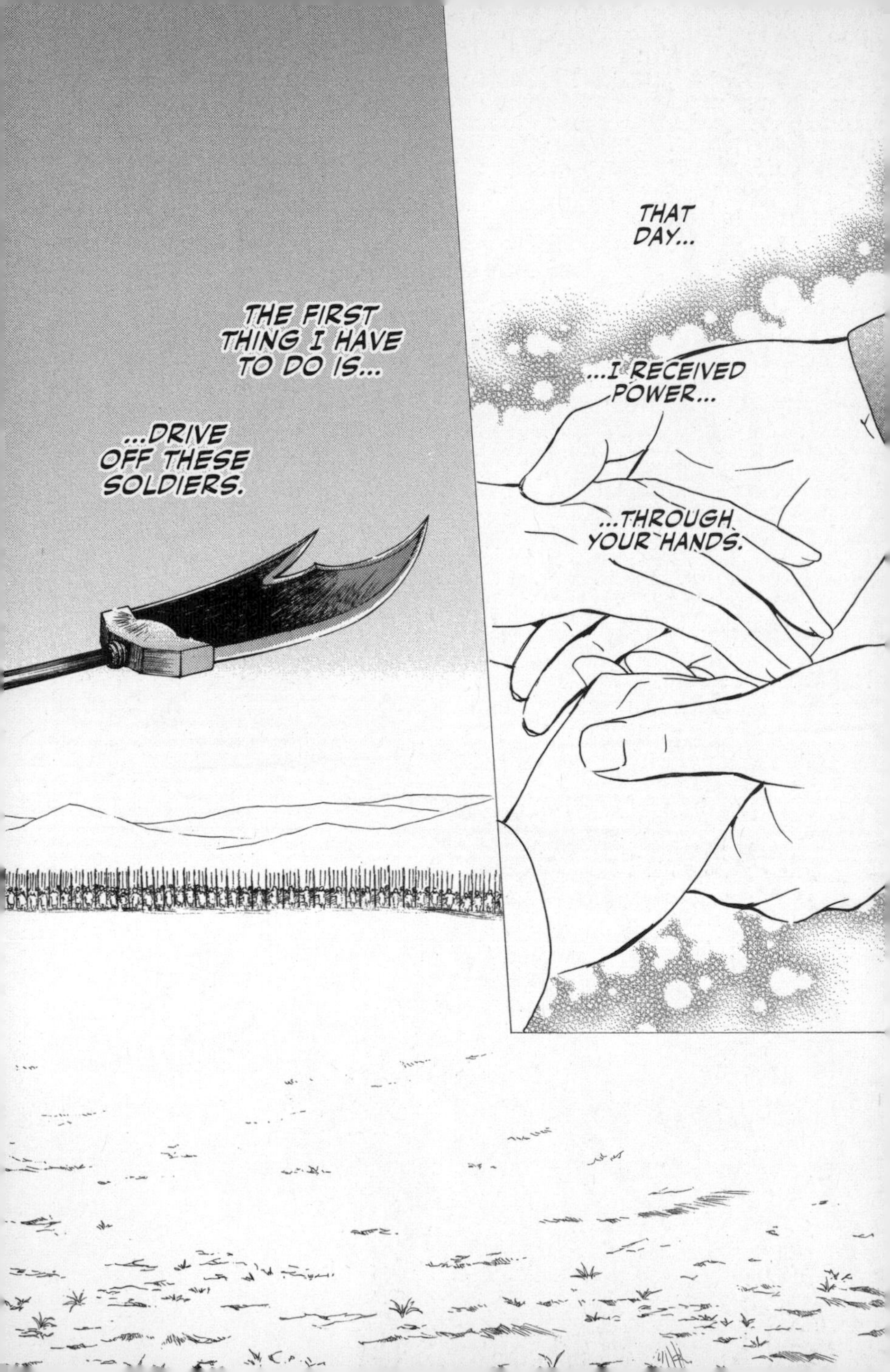
THAT DAY...
...I RECEIVED POWER...
...THROUGH YOUR HANDS.
THE FIRST THING I HAVE TO DO IS...
...DRIVE OFF THESE SOLDIERS.

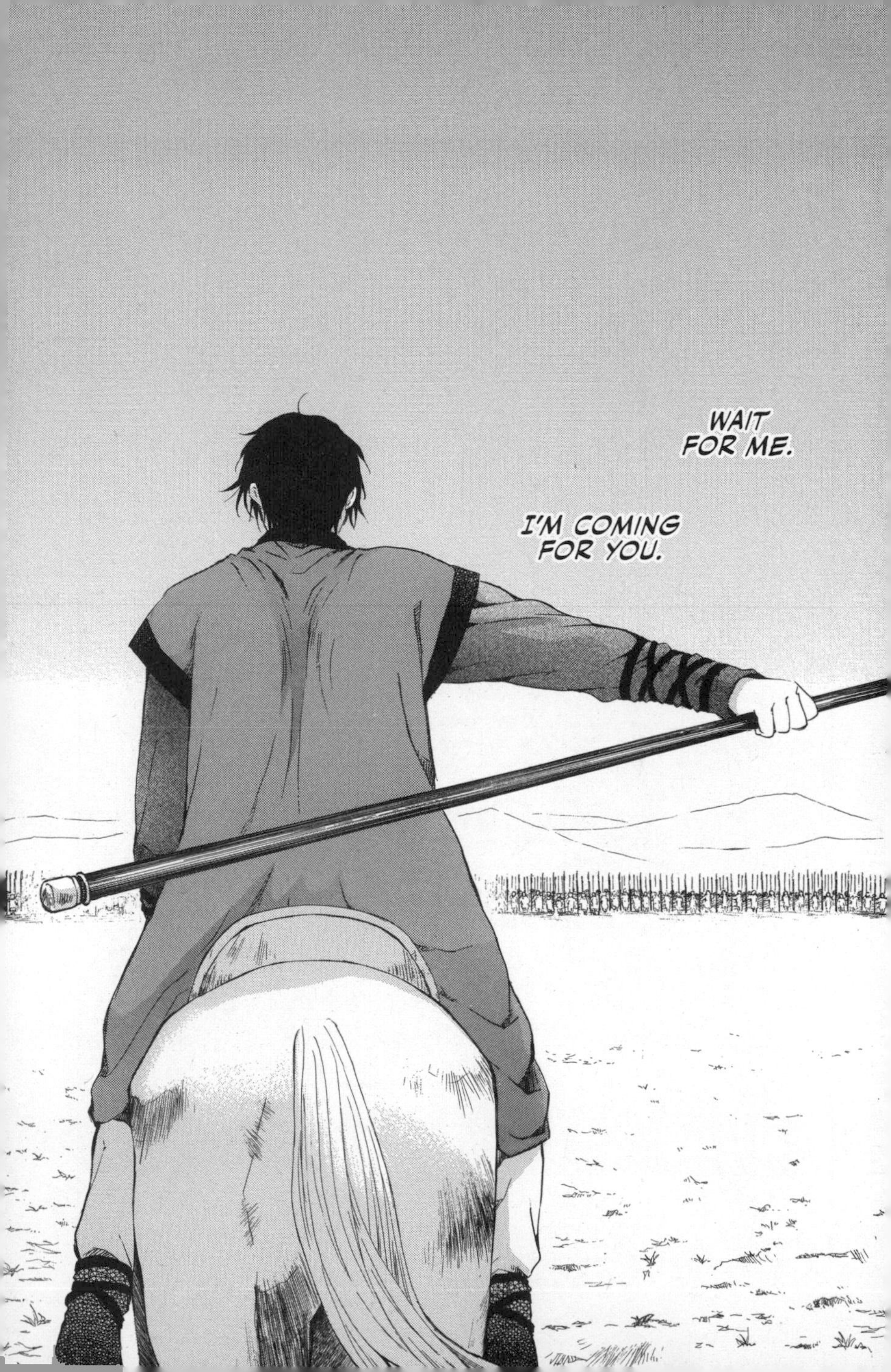
WAIT FOR ME.
I'M COMING FOR YOU.

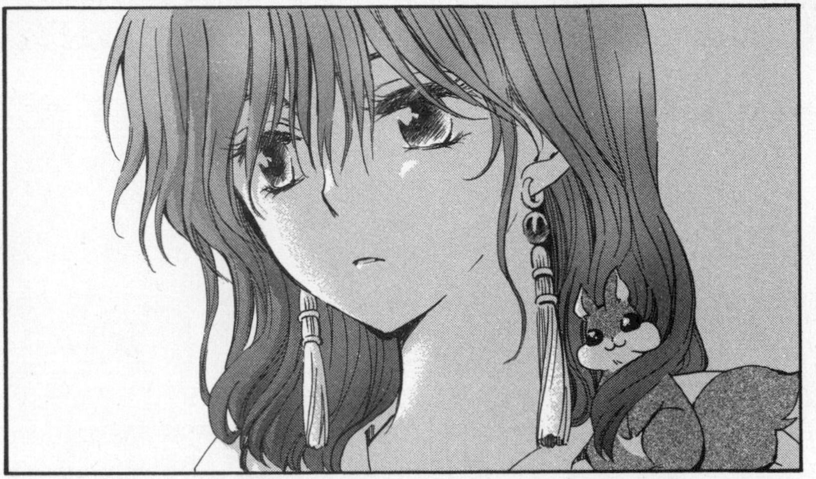

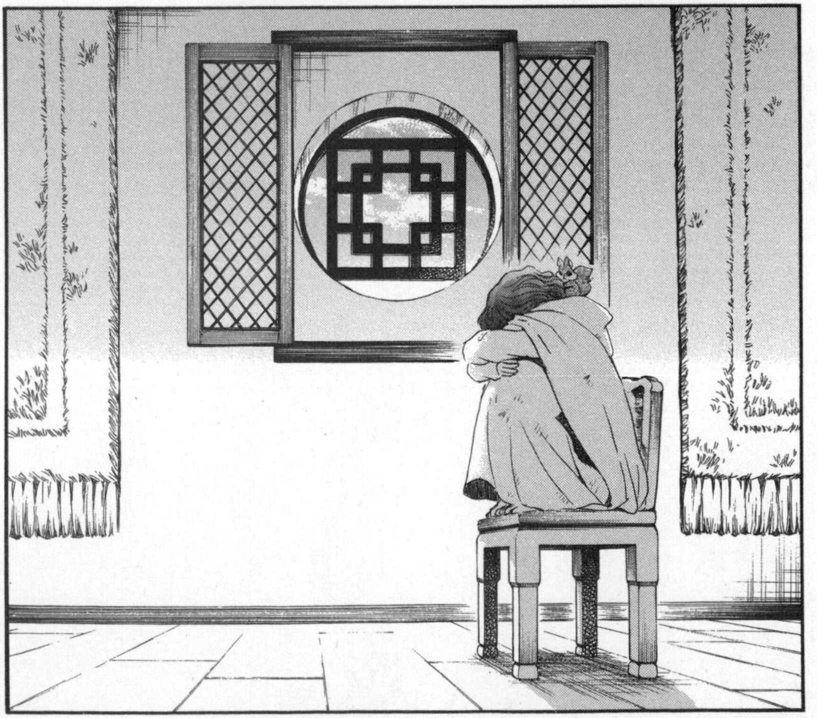

CHAPTER 167 / THE END

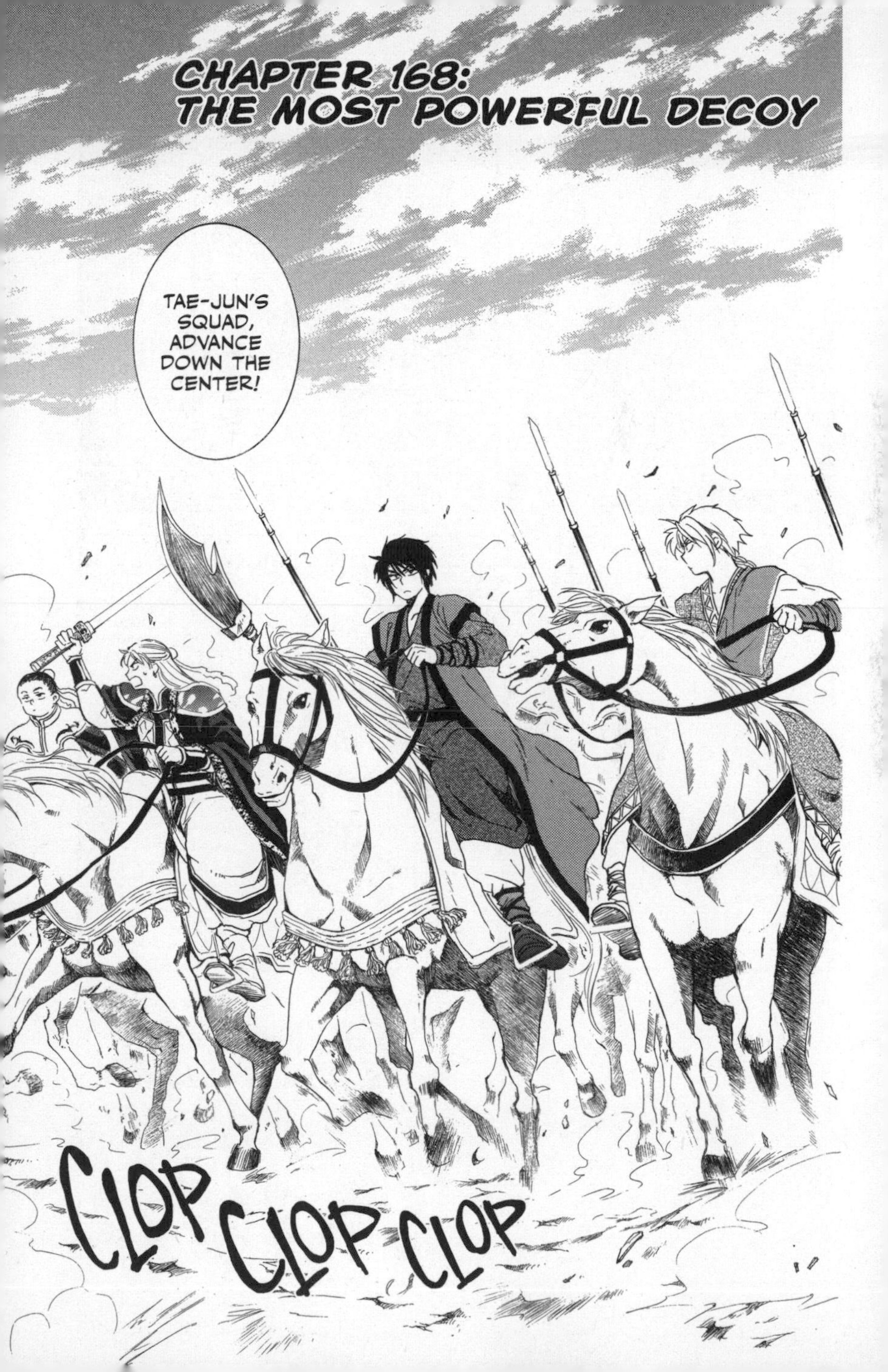
CHAPTER 168:
THE MOST POWERFUL DECOY
TAE-JUN'S SQUAD, ADVANCE DOWN THE CENTER!
CLOP CLOP CLOP

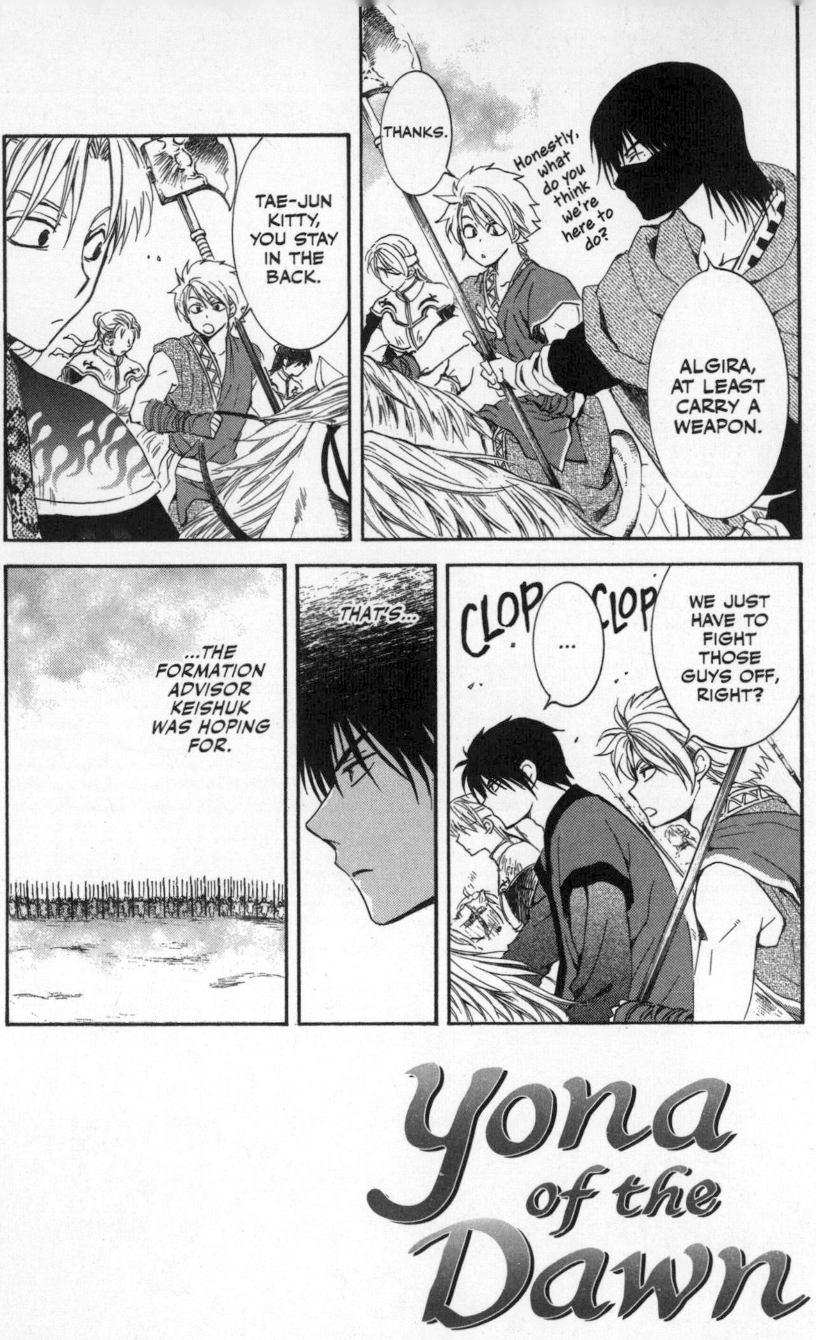
ALGIRA, AT LEAST CARRY A WEAPON.
THANKS.
Honestly, what do you think we're here to do?
TAE-JUN KITTY, YOU STAY IN THE BACK.
WE JUST HAVE TO FIGHT THOSE GUYS OFF, RIGHT?
CLOP
...
CLOP
THAT'S...
...THE FORMATION ADVISOR KEISHUK WAS HOPING FOR.

Yona of the Dawn

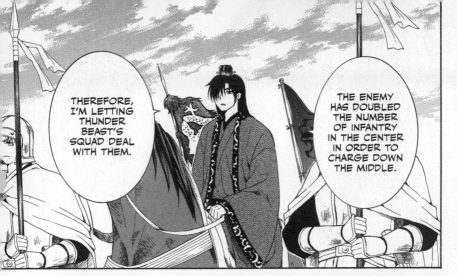

THE ENEMY HAS DOUBLED THE NUMBER OF INFANTRY IN THE CENTER IN ORDER TO CHARGE DOWN THE MIDDLE.
THEREFORE, I'M LETTING THUNDER BEAST'S SQUAD DEAL WITH THEM.
WHILE THUNDER BEAST AND HIS SQUAD DEFEND AGAINST THE ATTACK CONCENTRATED IN THE MIDDLE, OUR MOST POWERFUL CAVALRY SQUAD, LED BY GENERAL JU-DO, WILL DESTROY THE ENEMY'S RIGHT FLANK.
SEN PROVINCE ARMY: ABOUT 12,000
KOHKA ARMY: ABOUT 8,000
KUELBO'S CAVALRY
KUELBO'S INFANTRY
HAZARA'S INFANTRY
HAZARA'S INFANTRY
COMMANDER KUELBO
KUELBO'S CAVALRY
THE KOHKA ARMY'S STRONGEST UNITS ARE CONCENTRATED HERE.
JU-DO'S CAVALRY
INFANTRY
HAK/TAE-JUN SQUAD + INFANTRY
INFANTRY
KYO-GA'S CAVALRY
COMMANDER KEISHUK
GENERAL JU-DO'S CAVALRY WILL THEN CIRCLE BEHIND THE SEN PROVINCE ARMY TO ASSIST KYO-GA'S CAVALRY.
JU-DO'S CAVALRY
KUELBO'S INFANTRY
HAZARA'S INFANTRY
HAZARA'S INFANTRY
KUELBO'S CAVALRY
INFANTRY
HAK/TAE-JUN SQUAD + INFANTRY
INFANTRY
KYO-GA'S CAVALRY
IN THE END, WE'LL SURROUND THE SEN PROVINCE ARMY FROM THE FRONT AND THE SIDES.

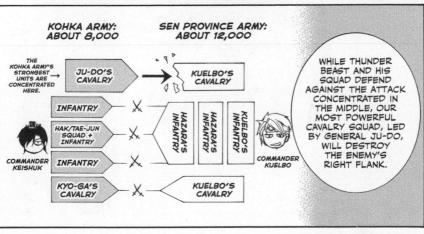

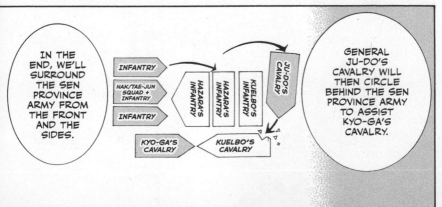

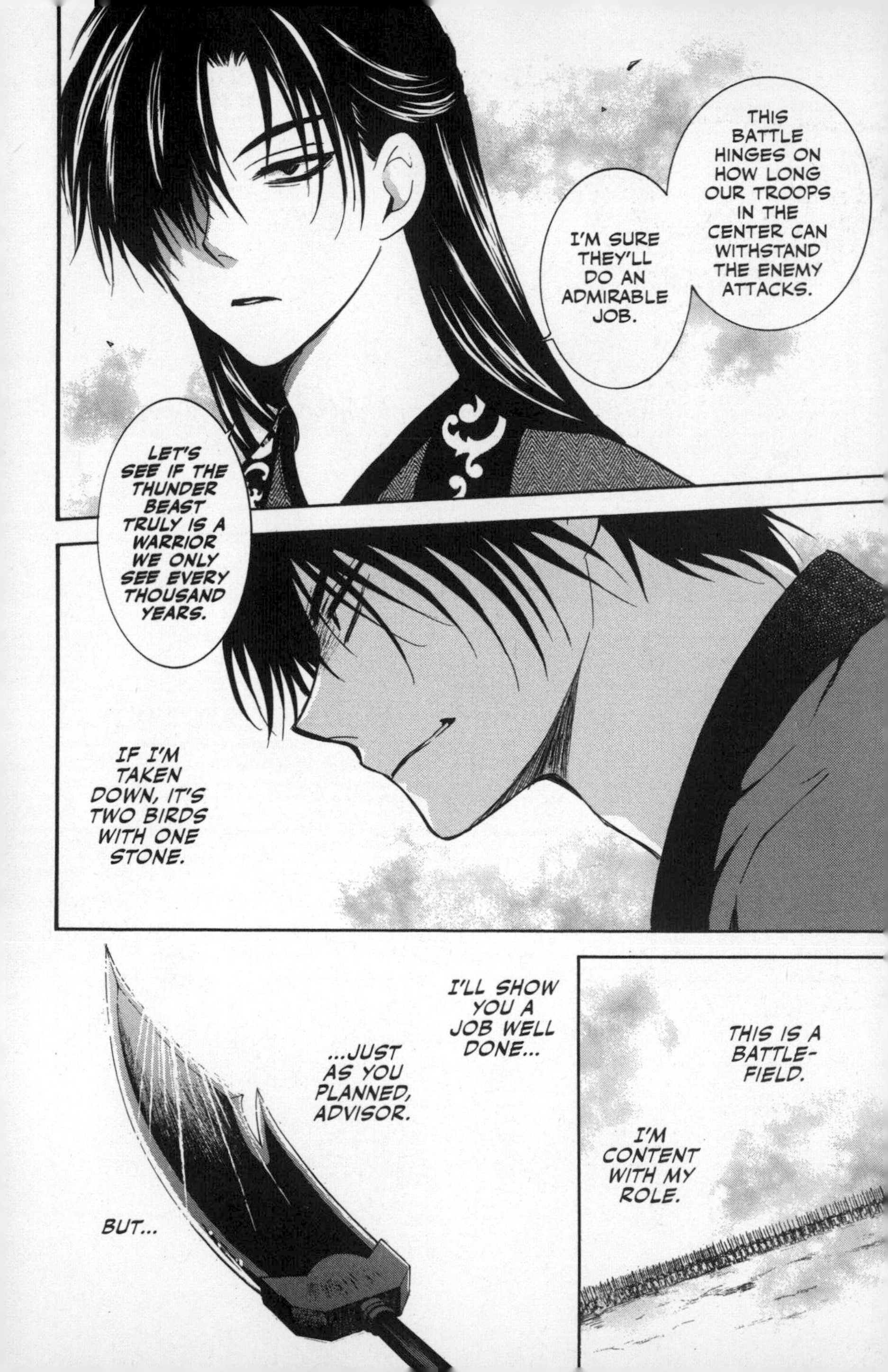
THIS BATTLE HINGES ON HOW LONG OUR TROOPS IN THE CENTER CAN WITHSTAND THE ENEMY ATTACKS.
I'M SURE THEY'LL DO AN ADMIRABLE JOB.
LET'S SEE IF THE THUNDER BEAST TRULY IS A WARRIOR WE ONLY SEE EVERY THOUSAND YEARS.
IF I'M TAKEN DOWN, IT'S TWO BIRDS WITH ONE STONE.
THIS IS A BATTLE-FIELD.
I'M CONTENT WITH MY ROLE.
I'LL SHOW YOU A JOB WELL DONE...
...JUST AS YOU PLANNED, ADVISOR.
BUT...

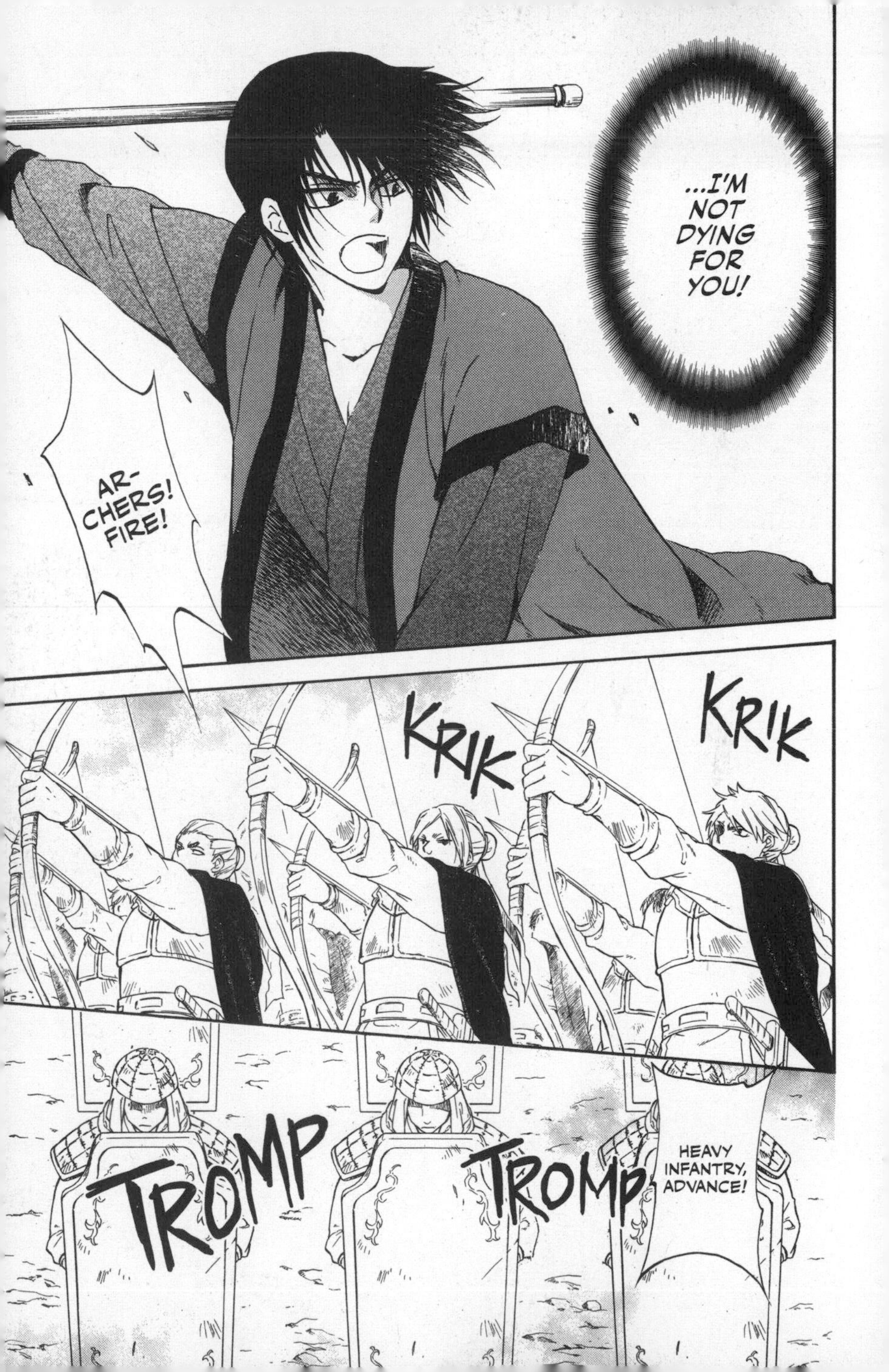
...I'M NOT DYING FOR YOU!
AR-CHERS! FIRE!
KRIK
KRIK
HEAVY INFANTRY, ADVANCE!
TROMP
TROMP

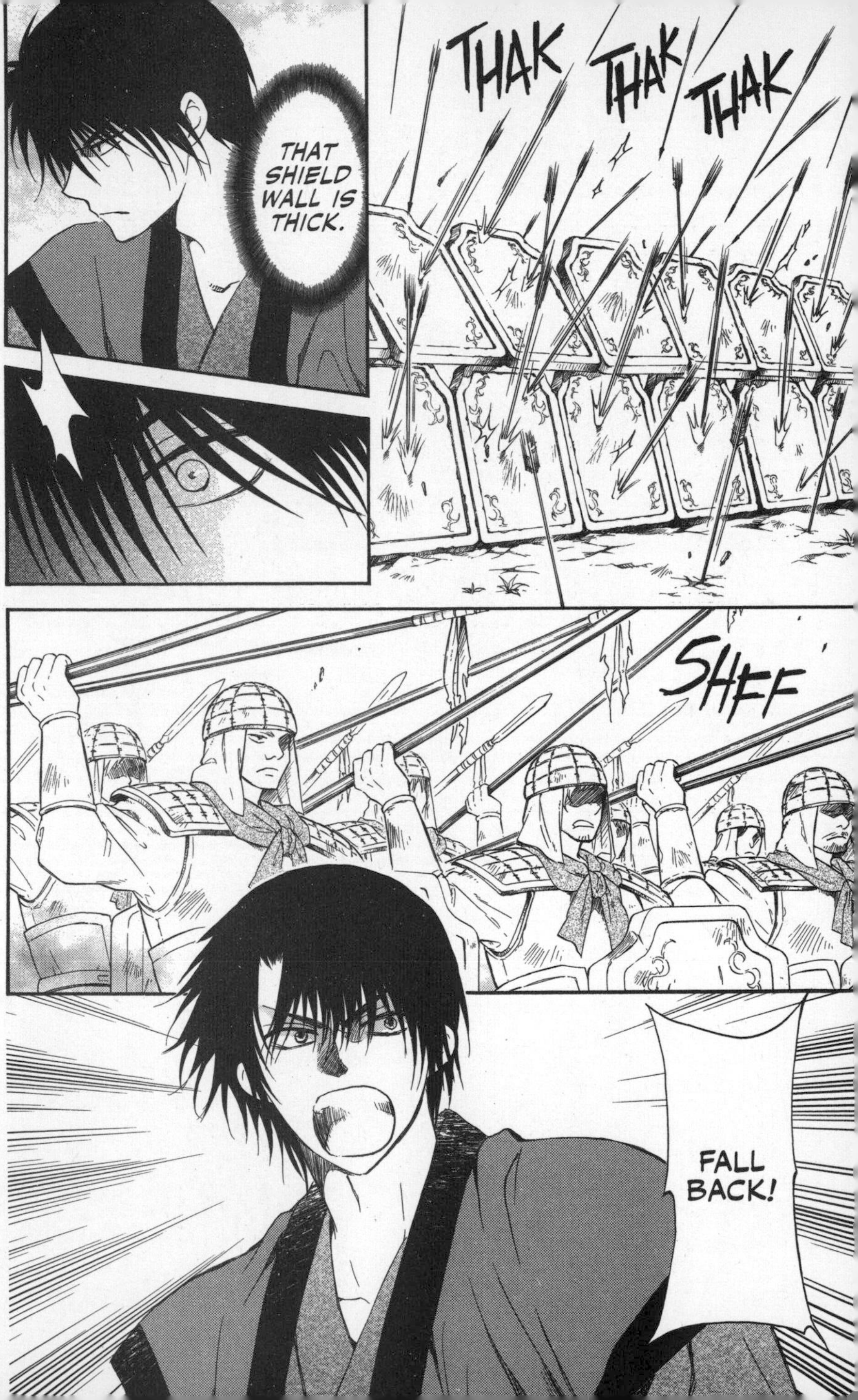
THAK THAK THAK
THAT SHIELD WALL IS THICK.
SHFF
FALL BACK!

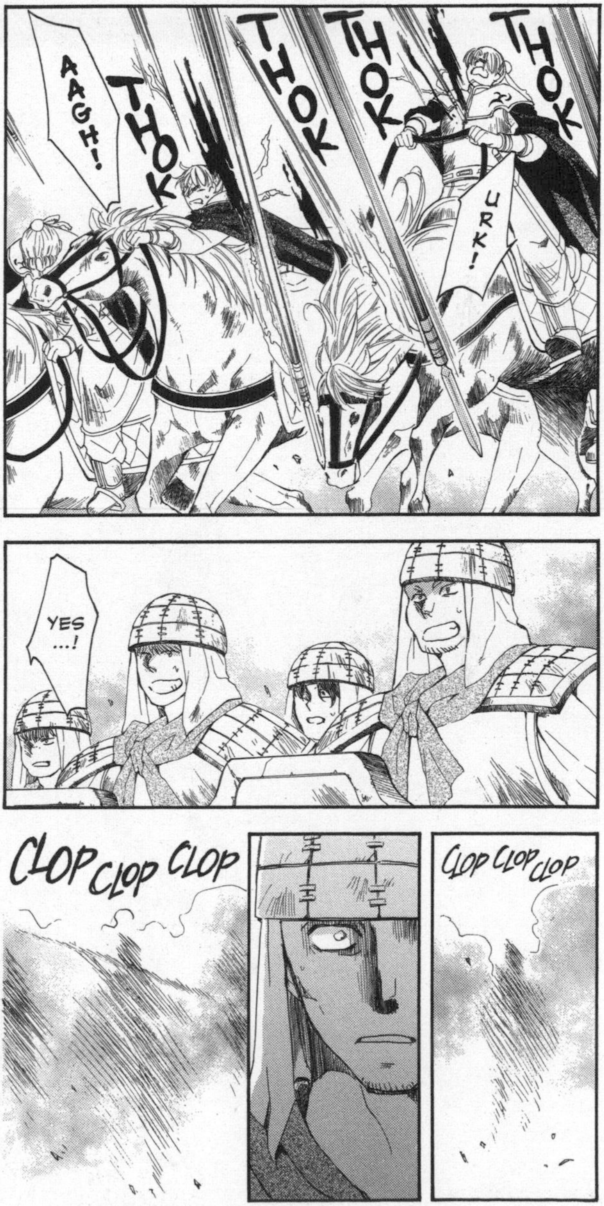
THOK
URK!
THOK
THOK
THOK
AAGH!
YES ...!
CLOP CLOP CLOP
CLOP CLOP CLOP

Some people's letters have said that they thought Priest Gobi was an old woman. The husband of one of my assistants said the same thing. Priest Gobi is a man. (*Ha.*) I should have made it slightly more obvious that he's an old man by his attire!

Also, Keishuk first appeared in this series way back in chapter 2. It's just that he's only recently had the chance to stand out. Speaking of him, in episode 6 of the anime, when Su-won was purifying himself, Keishuk spoke to him in a very kind voice. I remember being shocked by how cute his voice was. (He was voiced by the director.)

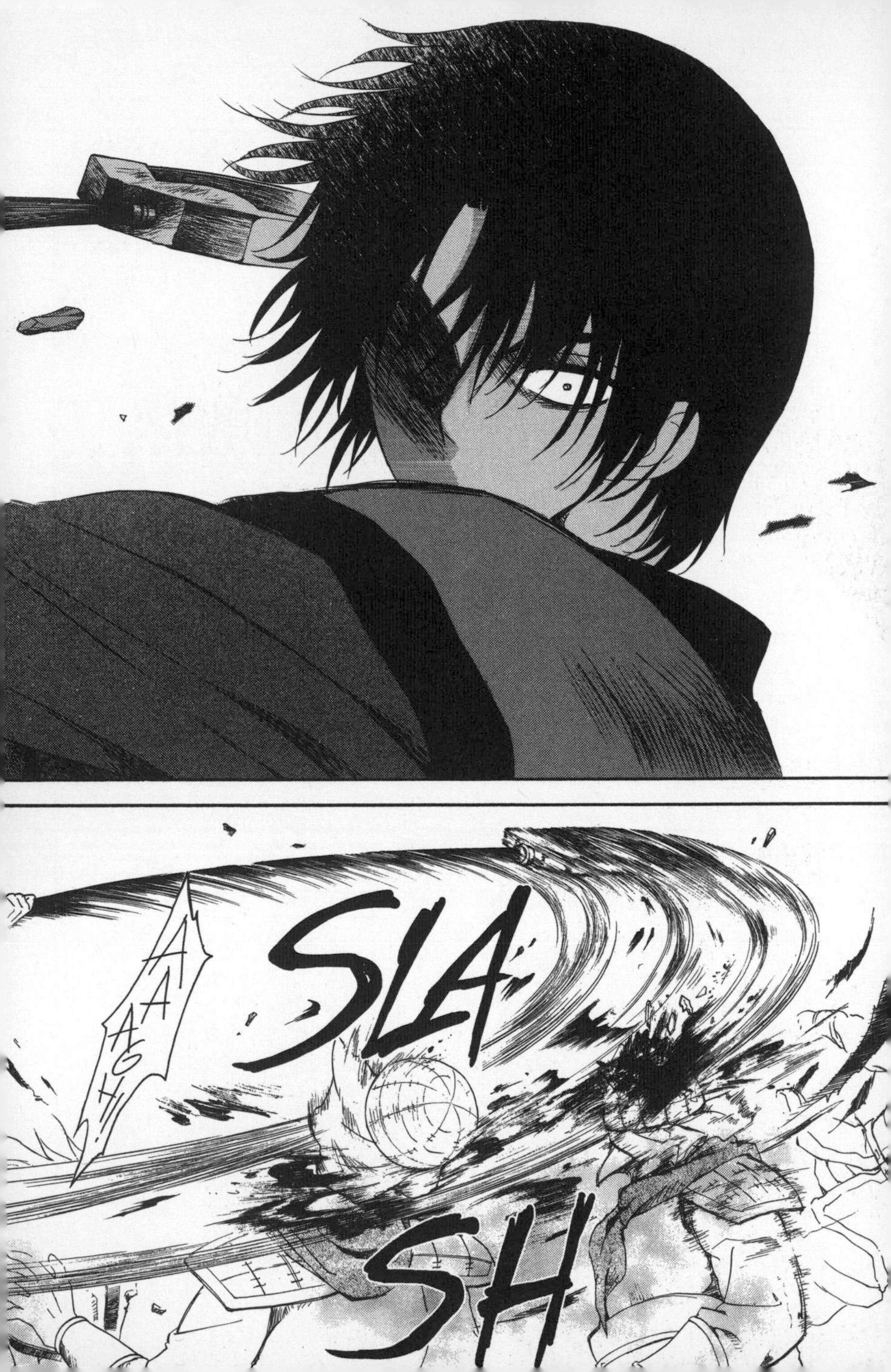
SLASH
AAAGH!

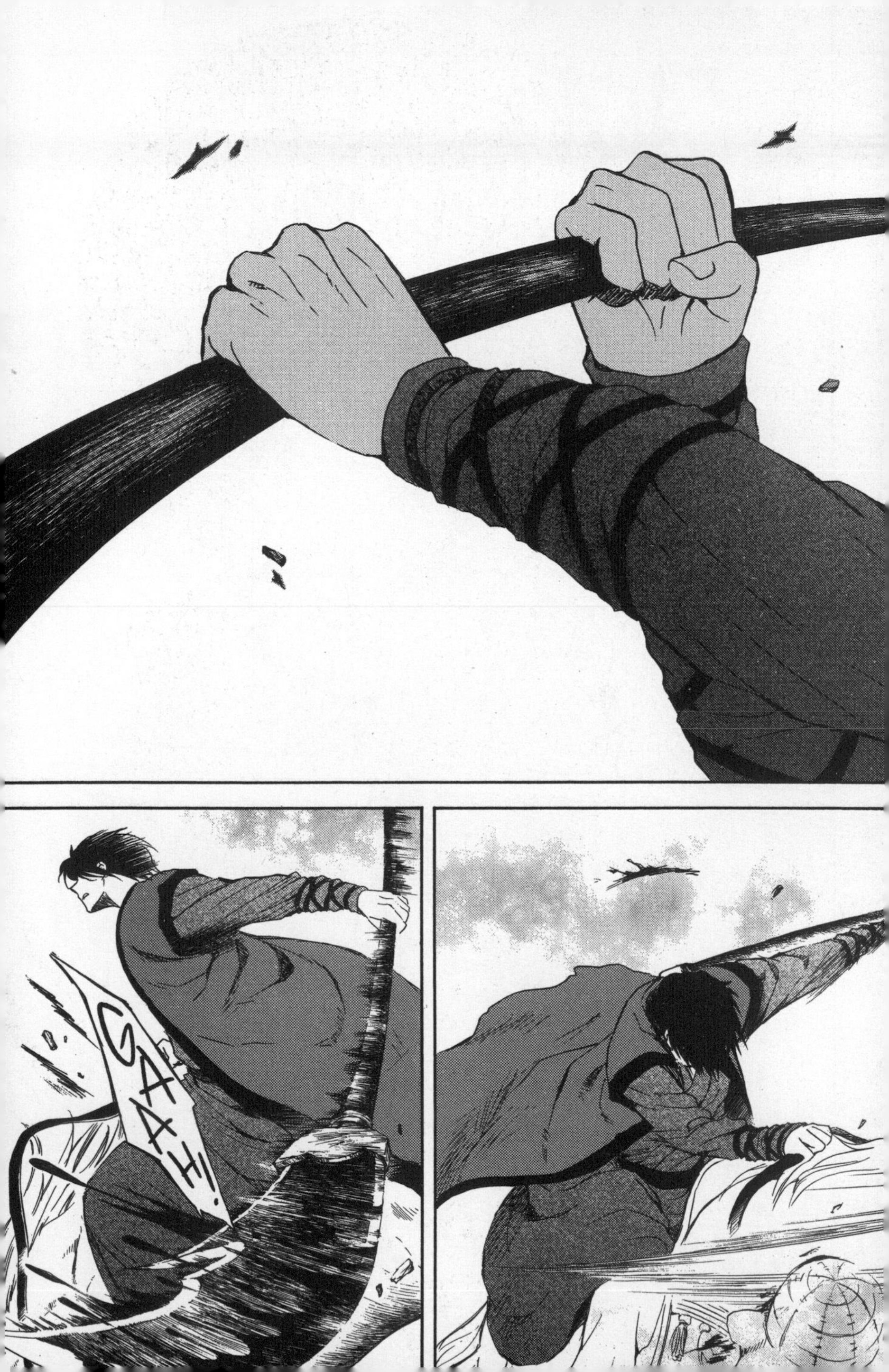
GAAH!

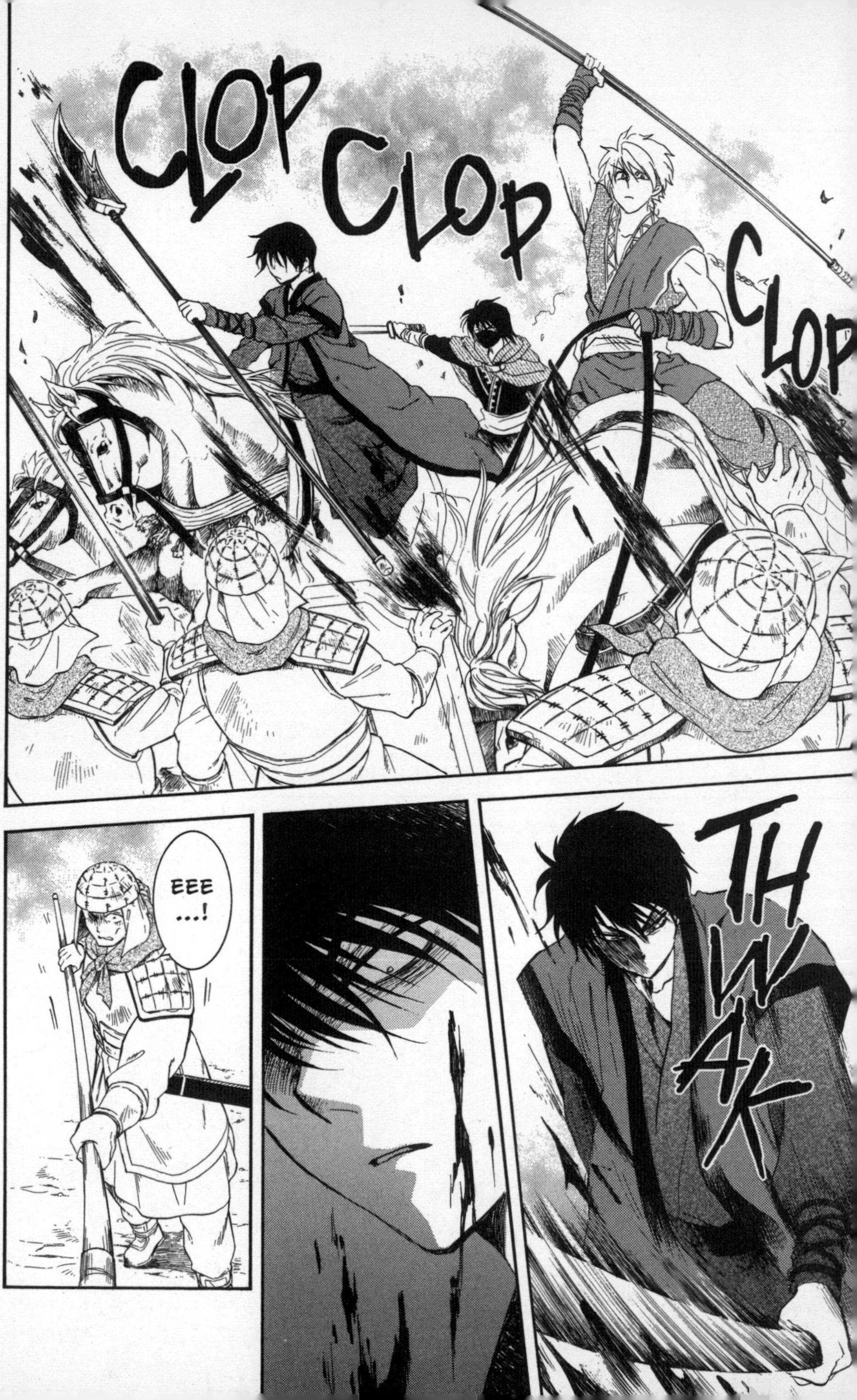
CLOP
CLOP
CLOP
THWAK
EEE ...!

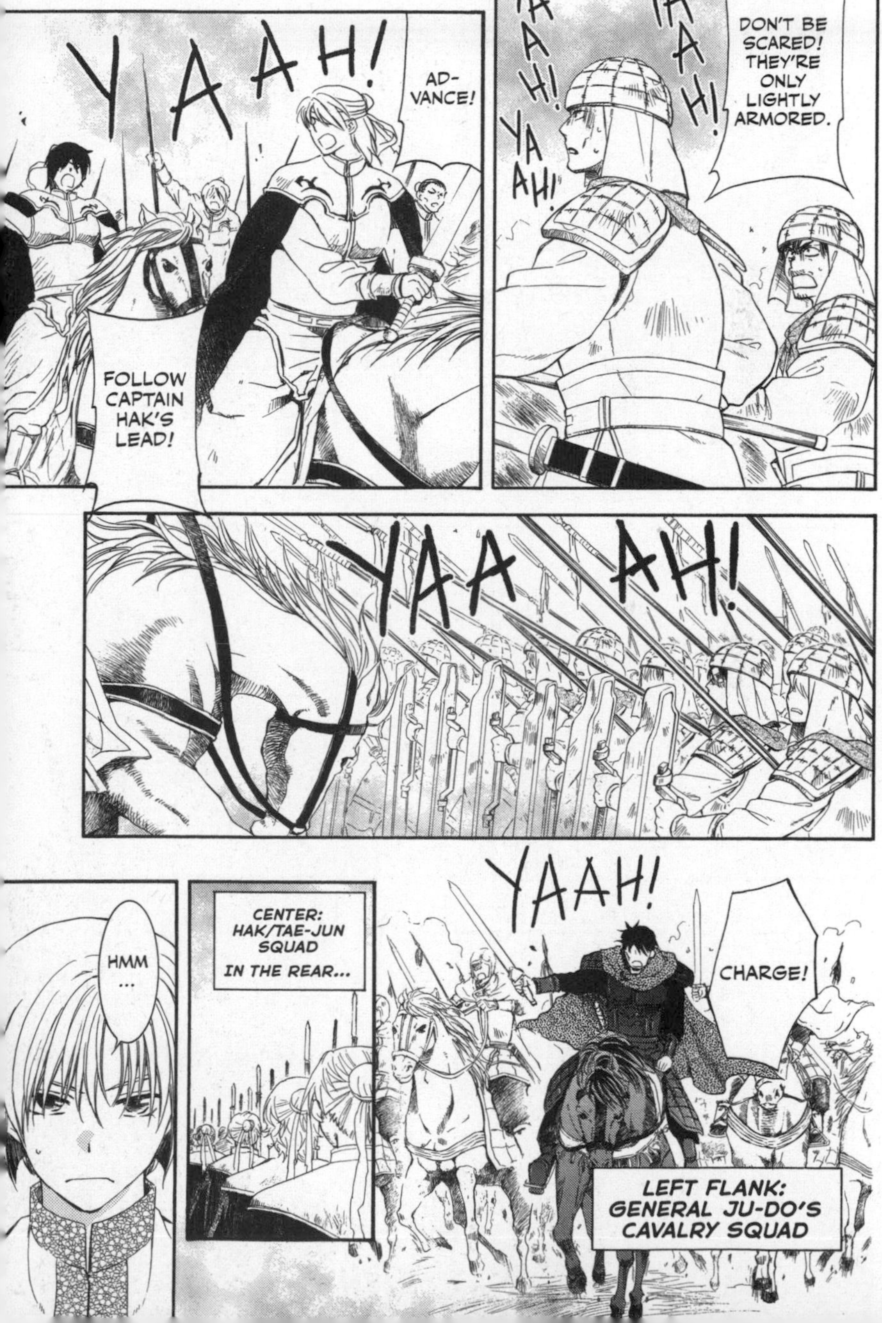
YAAAH!
YAAAH!
YAAH!
DON'T BE SCARED! THEY'RE ONLY LIGHTLY ARMORED.
YAAH!
ADVANCE!
FOLLOW CAPTAIN HAK'S LEAD!
YAAA AH!
YAAH!
CHARGE!
LEFT FLANK: GENERAL JU-DO'S CAVALRY SQUAD
CENTER: HAK/TAE-JUN SQUAD
IN THE REAR...
HMM ...

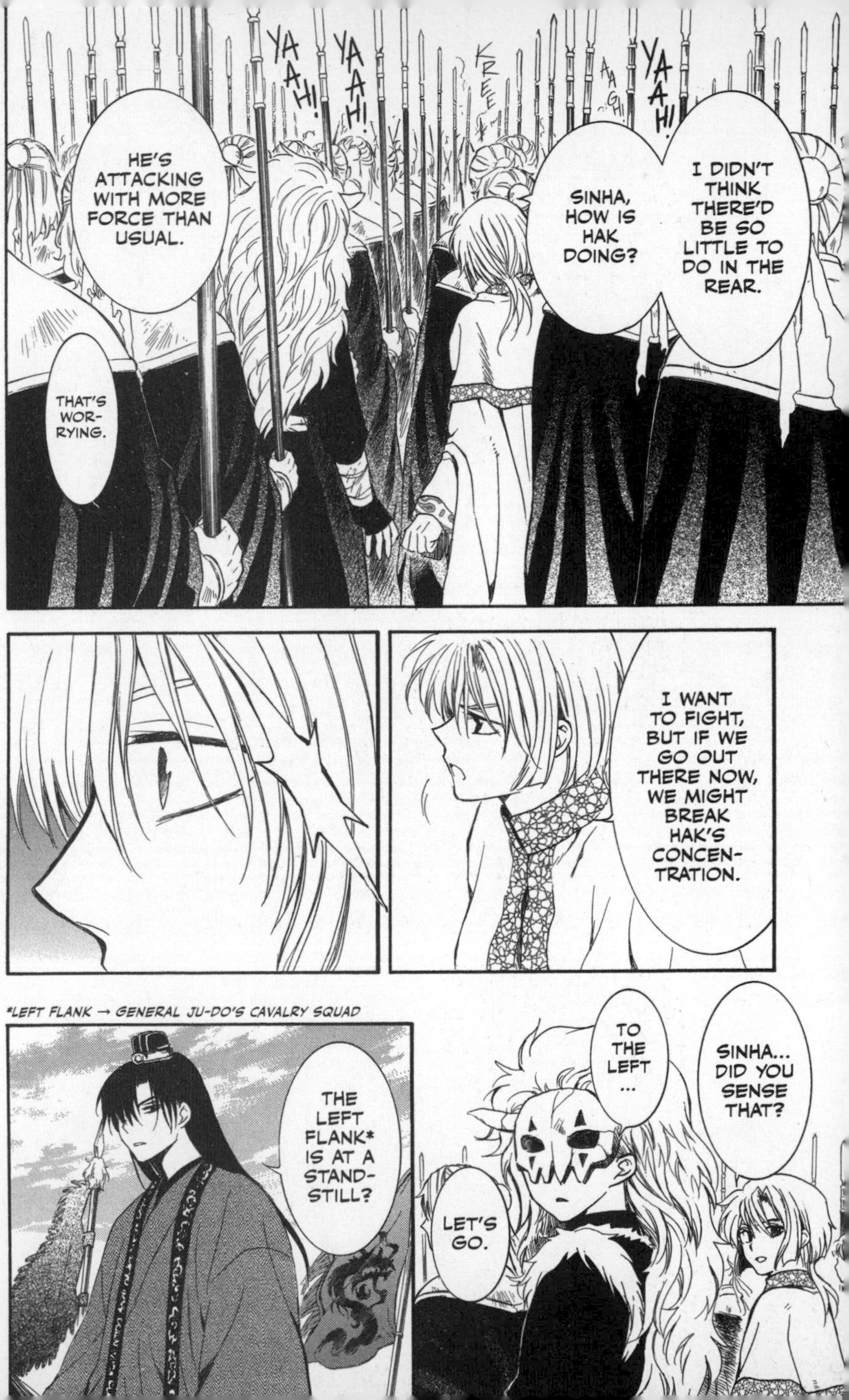
YAAH!
AAGH!
KREE
YAAH!
YAAH!
I DIDN'T THINK THERE'D BE SO LITTLE TO DO IN THE REAR.
SINHA, HOW IS HAK DOING?
HE'S ATTACKING WITH MORE FORCE THAN USUAL.
THAT'S WOR-RYING.
I WANT TO FIGHT, BUT IF WE GO OUT THERE NOW, WE MIGHT BREAK HAK'S CONCEN-TRATION.
SINHA... DID YOU SENSE THAT?
TO THE LEFT ...
LET'S GO.
THE LEFT FLANK* IS AT A STAND-STILL?
*LEFT FLANK → GENERAL JU-DO'S CAVALRY SQUAD

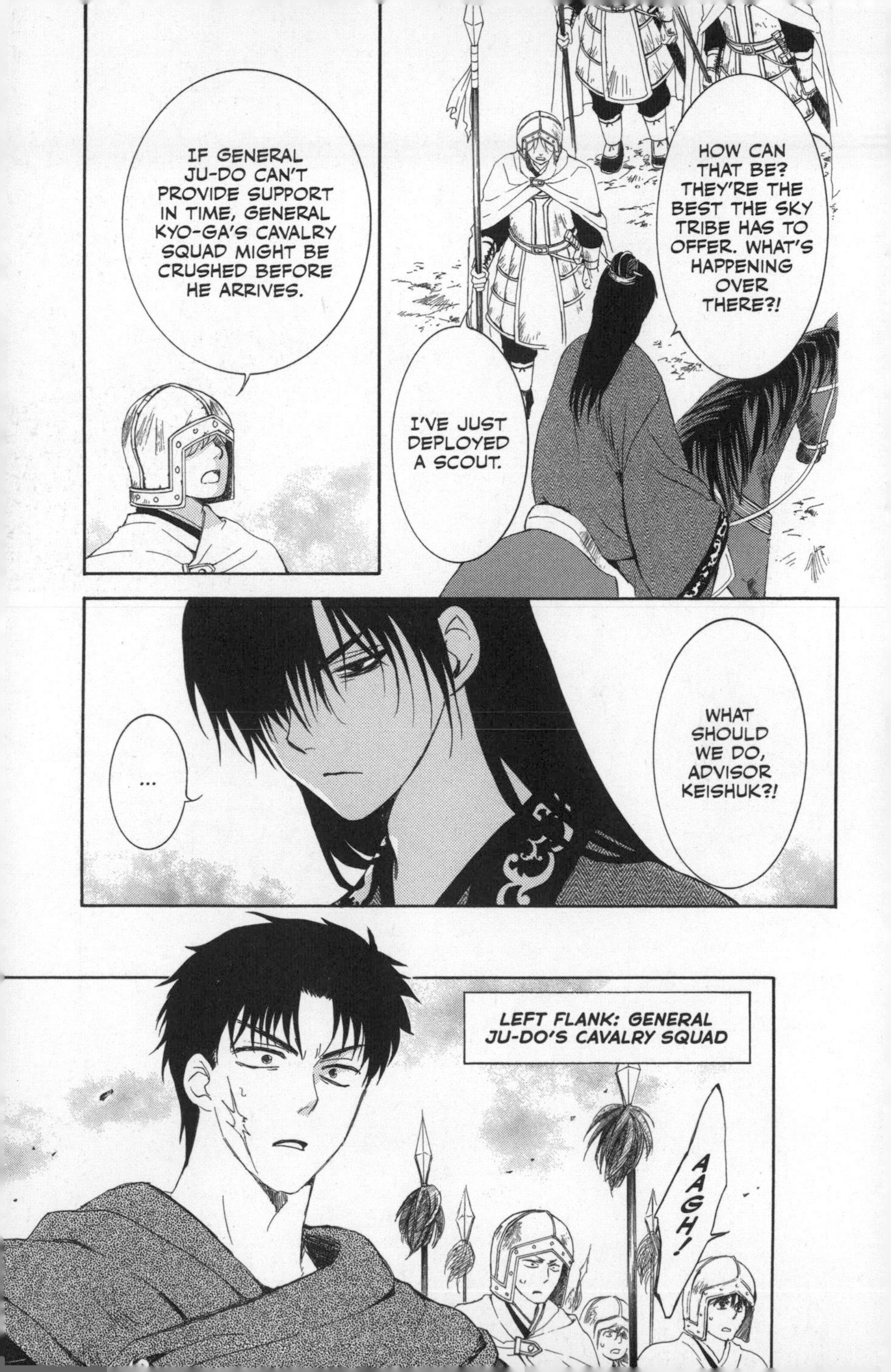
HOW CAN THAT BE? THEY'RE THE BEST THE SKY TRIBE HAS TO OFFER. WHAT'S HAPPENING OVER THERE?!
I'VE JUST DEPLOYED A SCOUT.
IF GENERAL JU-DO CAN'T PROVIDE SUPPORT IN TIME, GENERAL KYO-GA'S CAVALRY SQUAD MIGHT BE CRUSHED BEFORE HE ARRIVES.
WHAT SHOULD WE DO, ADVISOR KEISHUK?!
...
LEFT FLANK: GENERAL JU-DO'S CAVALRY SQUAD
AAGH!

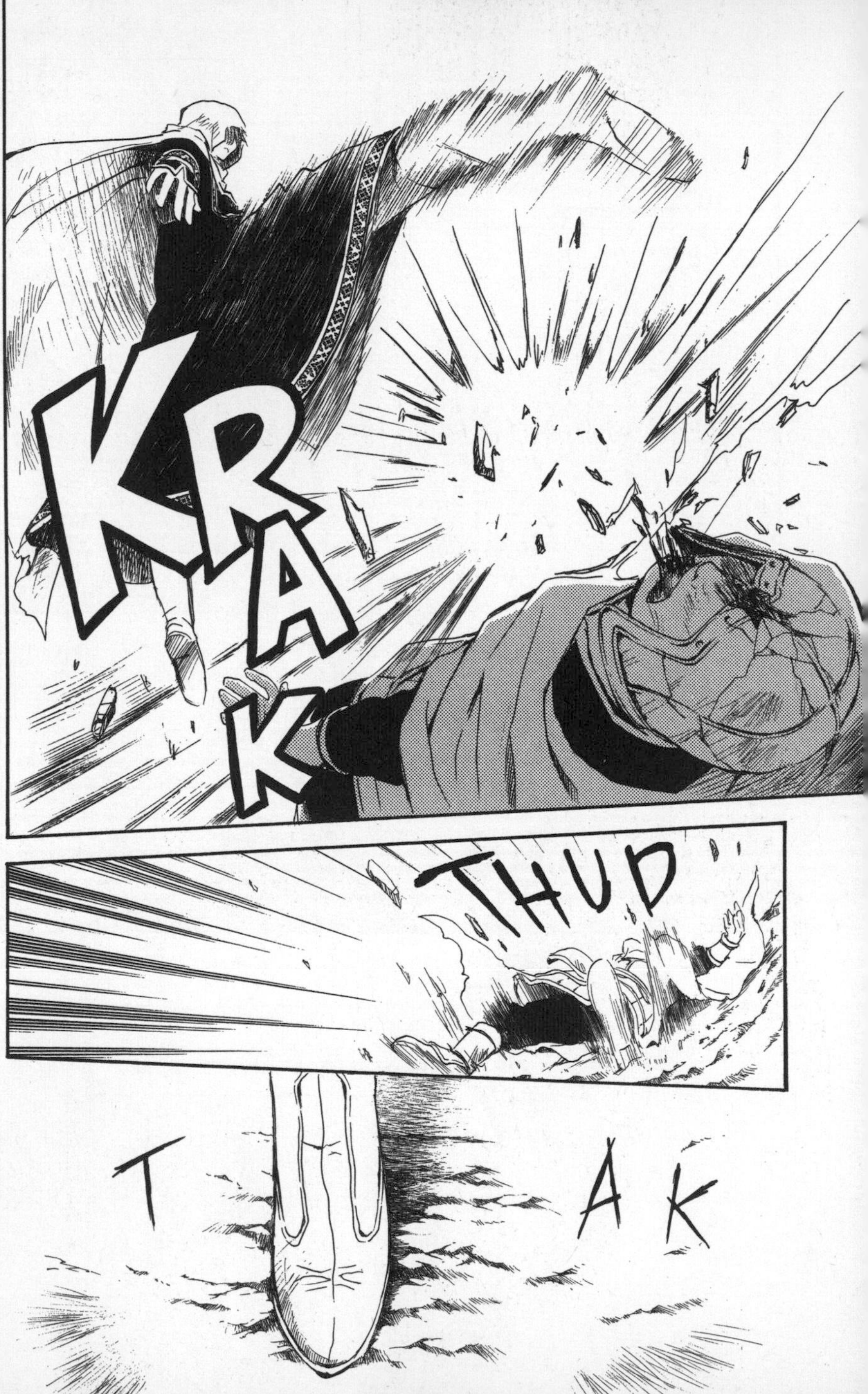
KRAK
THUD
TAK

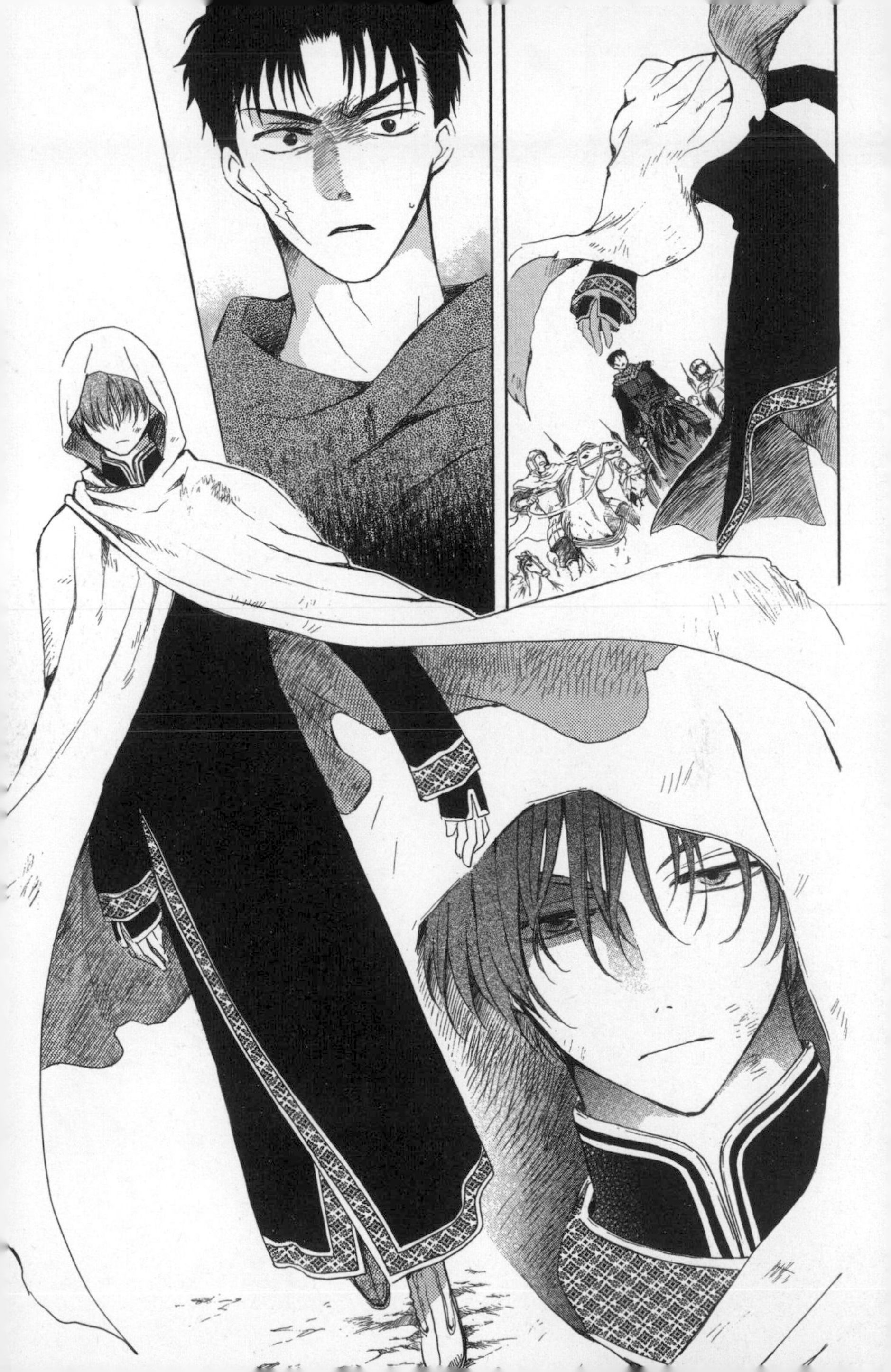

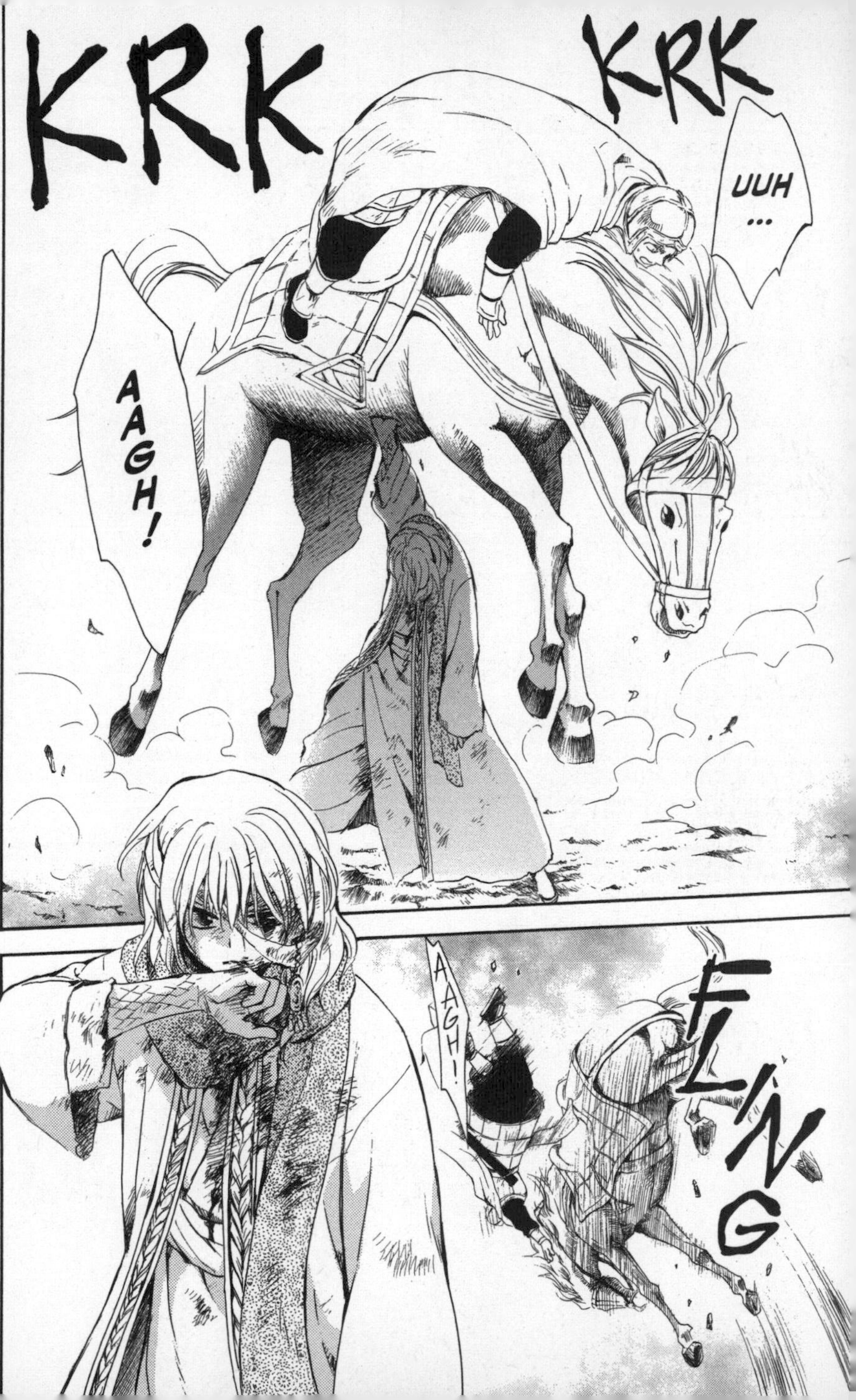
KRK
UUH ...
KRK
AAGH!
FLING
AAGH!

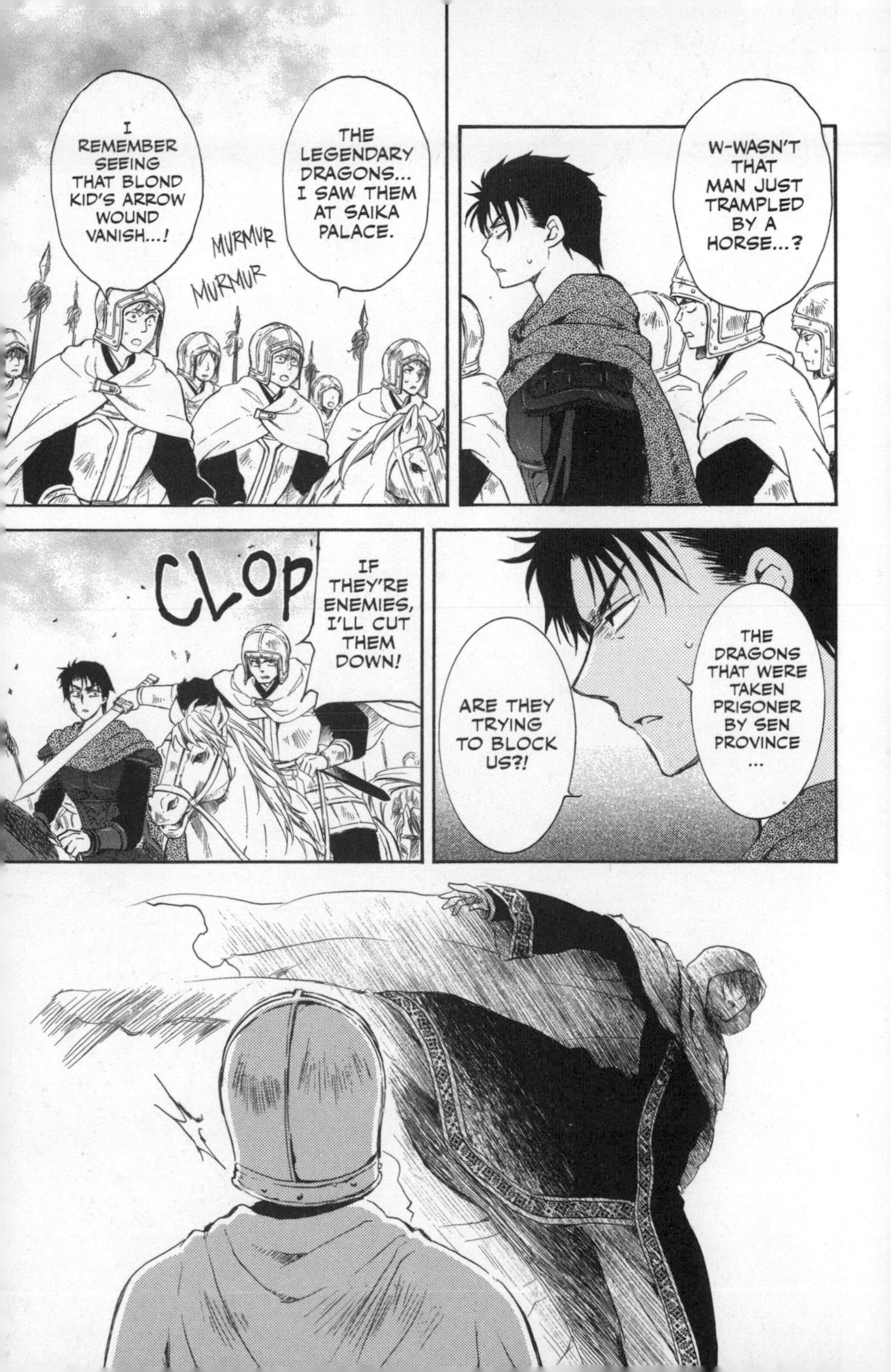
W-WASN'T THAT MAN JUST TRAMPLED BY A HORSE...?
THE LEGENDARY DRAGONS... I SAW THEM AT SAIKA PALACE.
MURMUR
MURMUR
I REMEMBER SEEING THAT BLOND KID'S ARROW WOUND VANISH...!
THE DRAGONS THAT WERE TAKEN PRISONER BY SEN PROVINCE ...
ARE THEY TRYING TO BLOCK US?!
IF THEY'RE ENEMIES, I'LL CUT THEM DOWN!
CLOP

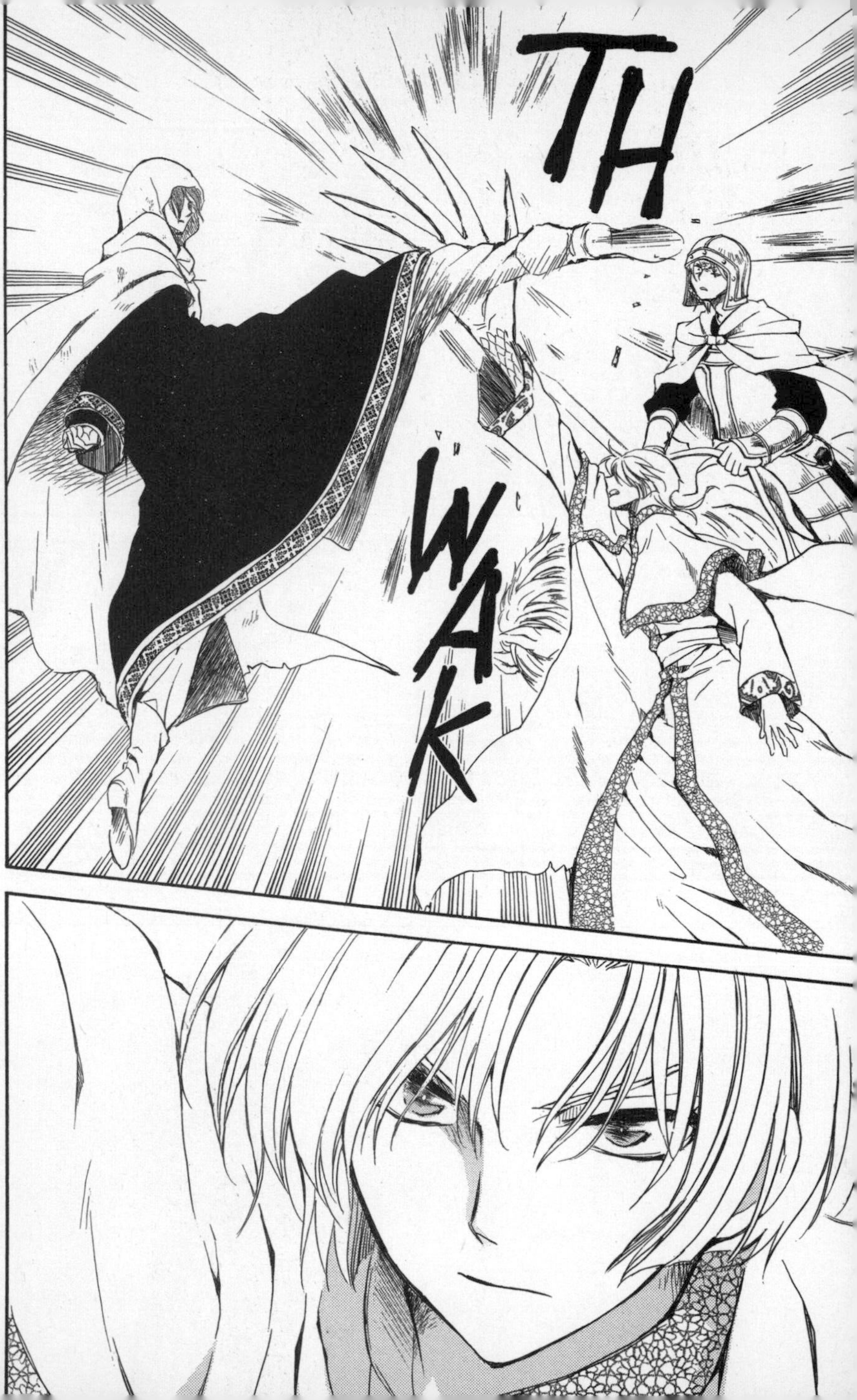
THWAK

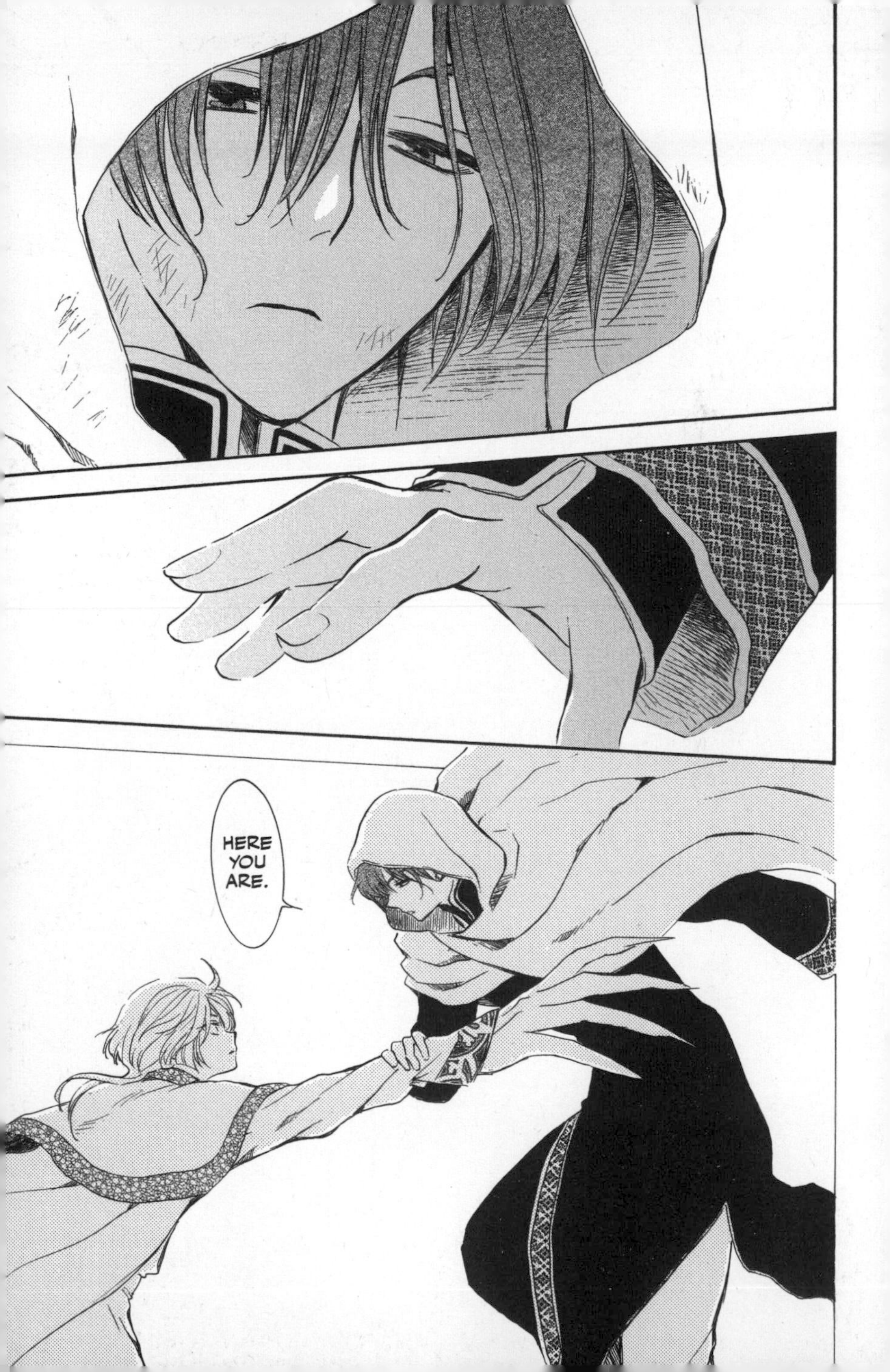
HERE YOU ARE.

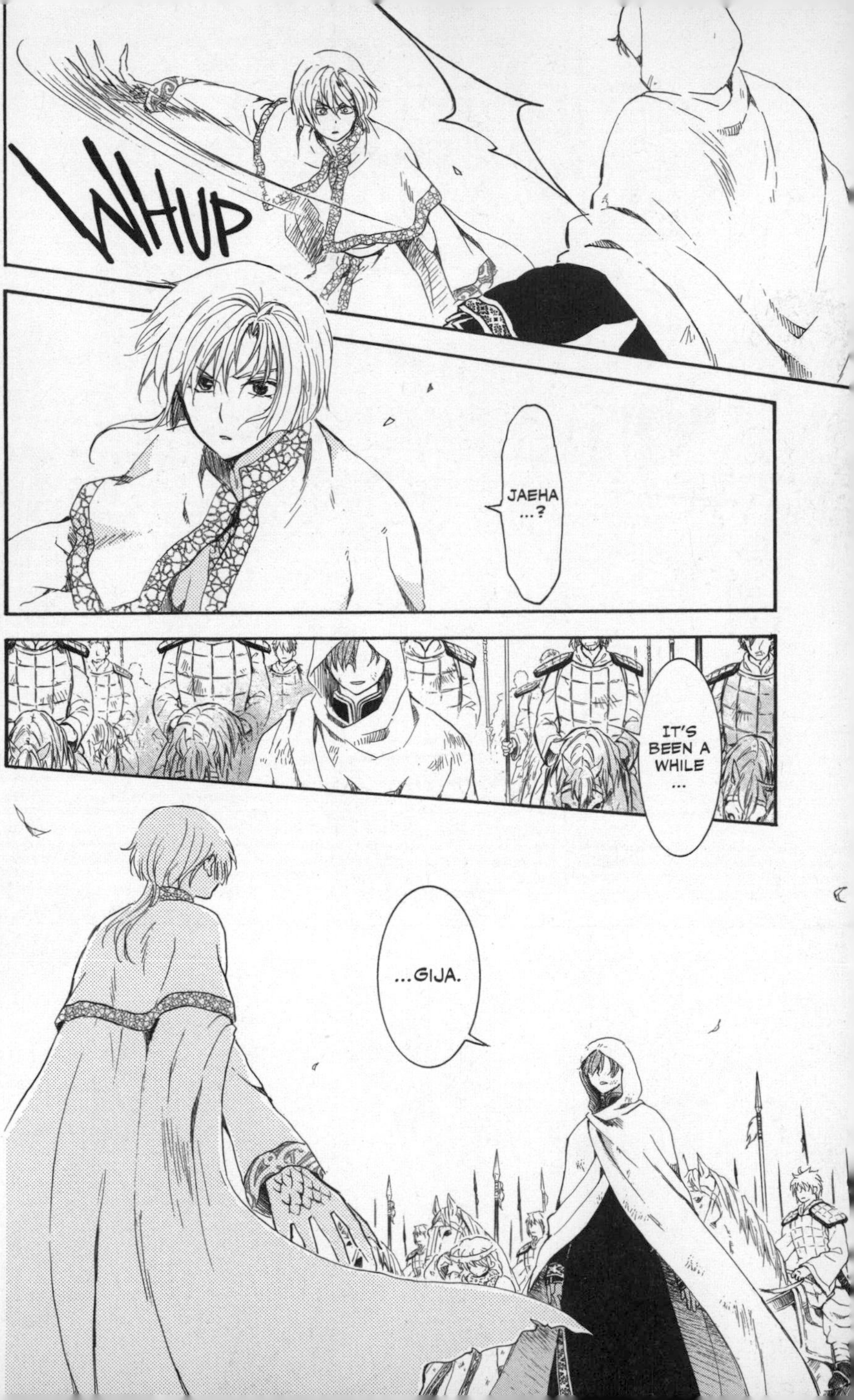
WHUP
JAEHA ...?
IT'S BEEN A WHILE ...
...GIJA.

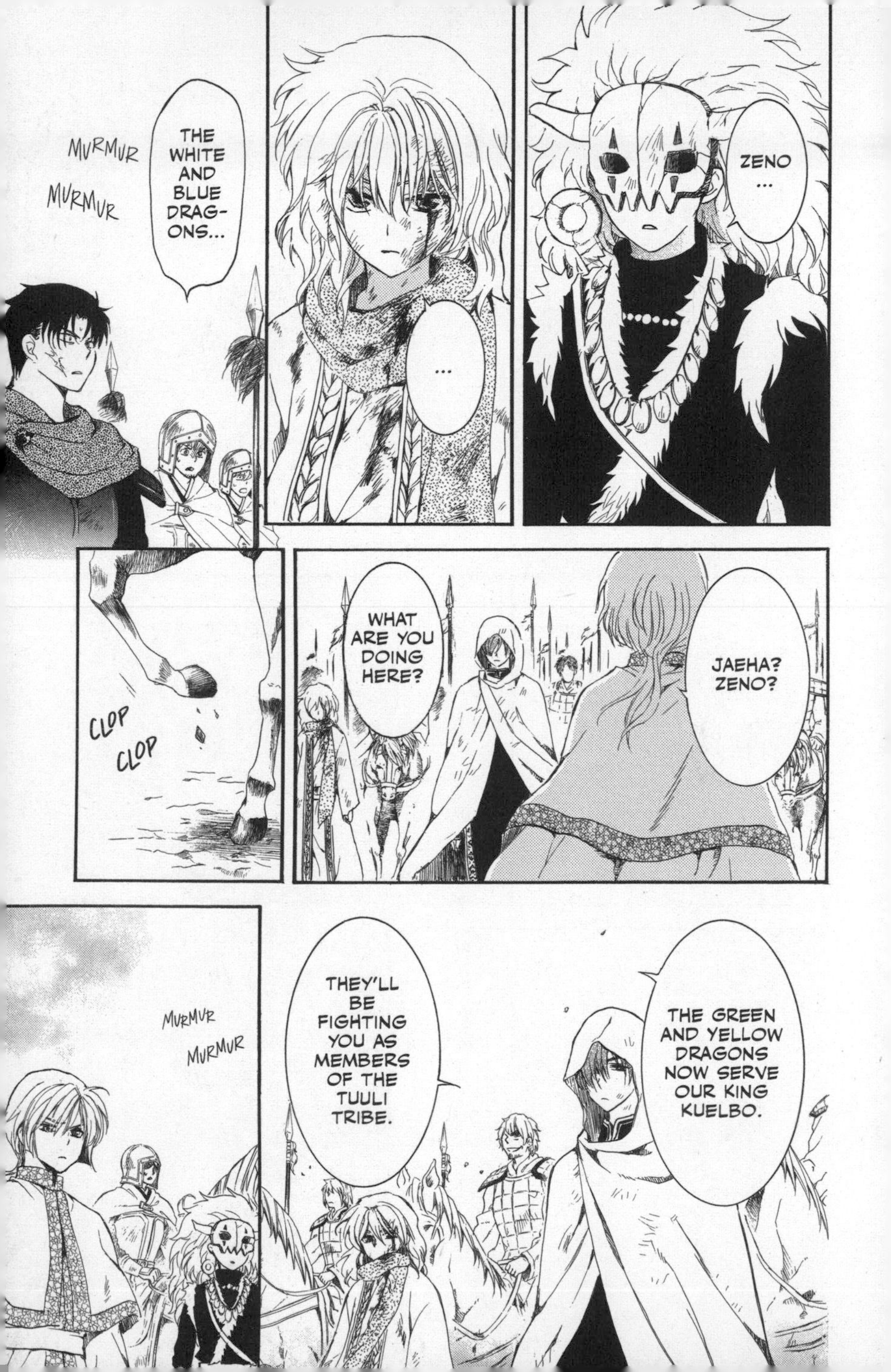
ZENO ...
...
THE WHITE AND BLUE DRAGONS...
MURMUR
MURMUR
JAEHA? ZENO?
WHAT ARE YOU DOING HERE?
CLOP
CLOP
THE GREEN AND YELLOW DRAGONS NOW SERVE OUR KING KUELBO.
THEY'LL BE FIGHTING YOU AS MEMBERS OF THE TUULI TRIBE.
MURMUR
MURMUR

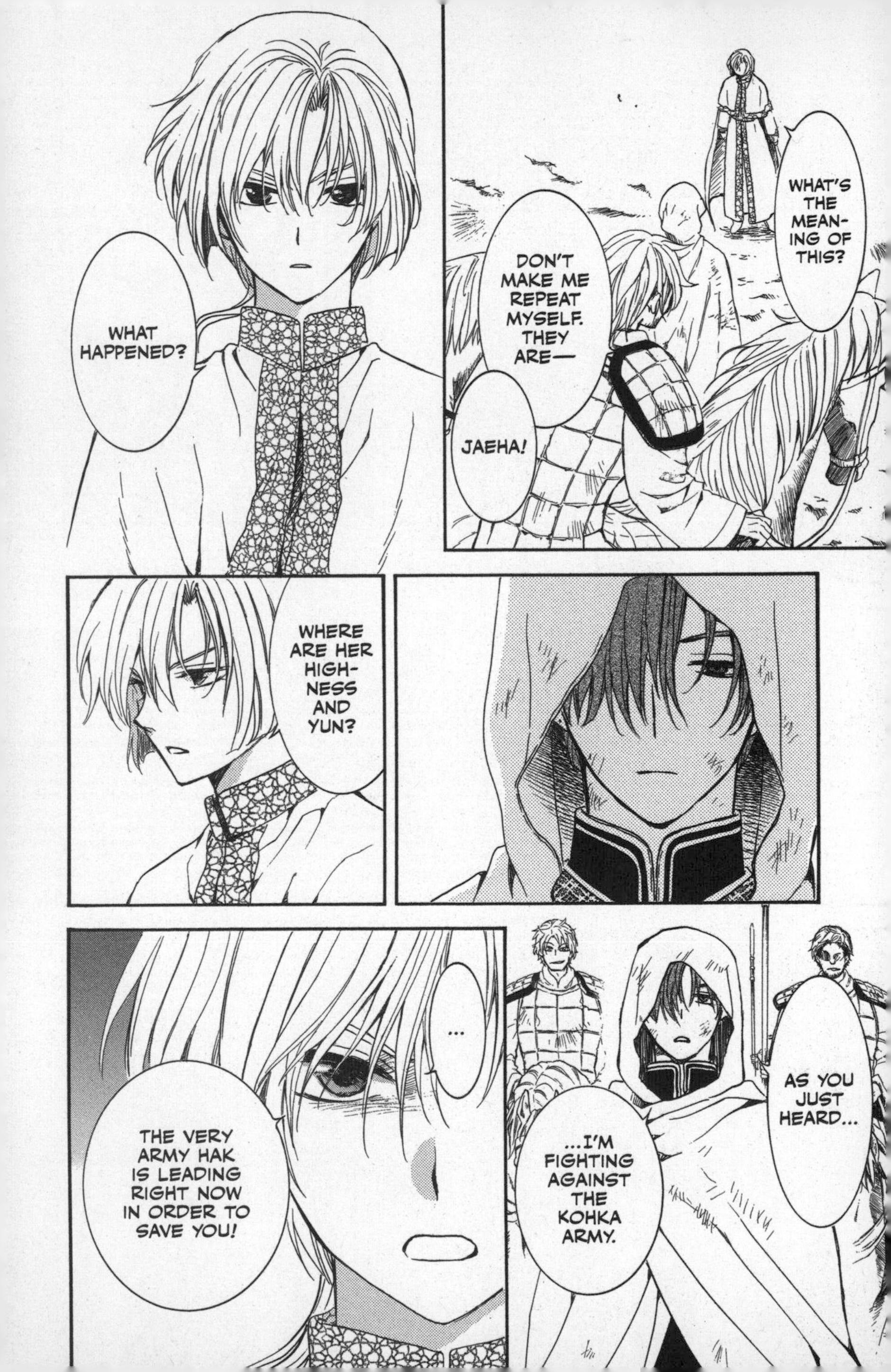
WHAT'S THE MEANING OF THIS?
DON'T MAKE ME REPEAT MYSELF. THEY ARE—
JAEHA!
WHAT HAPPENED?
WHERE ARE HER HIGHNESS AND YUN?
AS YOU JUST HEARD...
...I'M FIGHTING AGAINST THE KOHKA ARMY.
...
THE VERY ARMY HAK IS LEADING RIGHT NOW IN ORDER TO SAVE YOU!

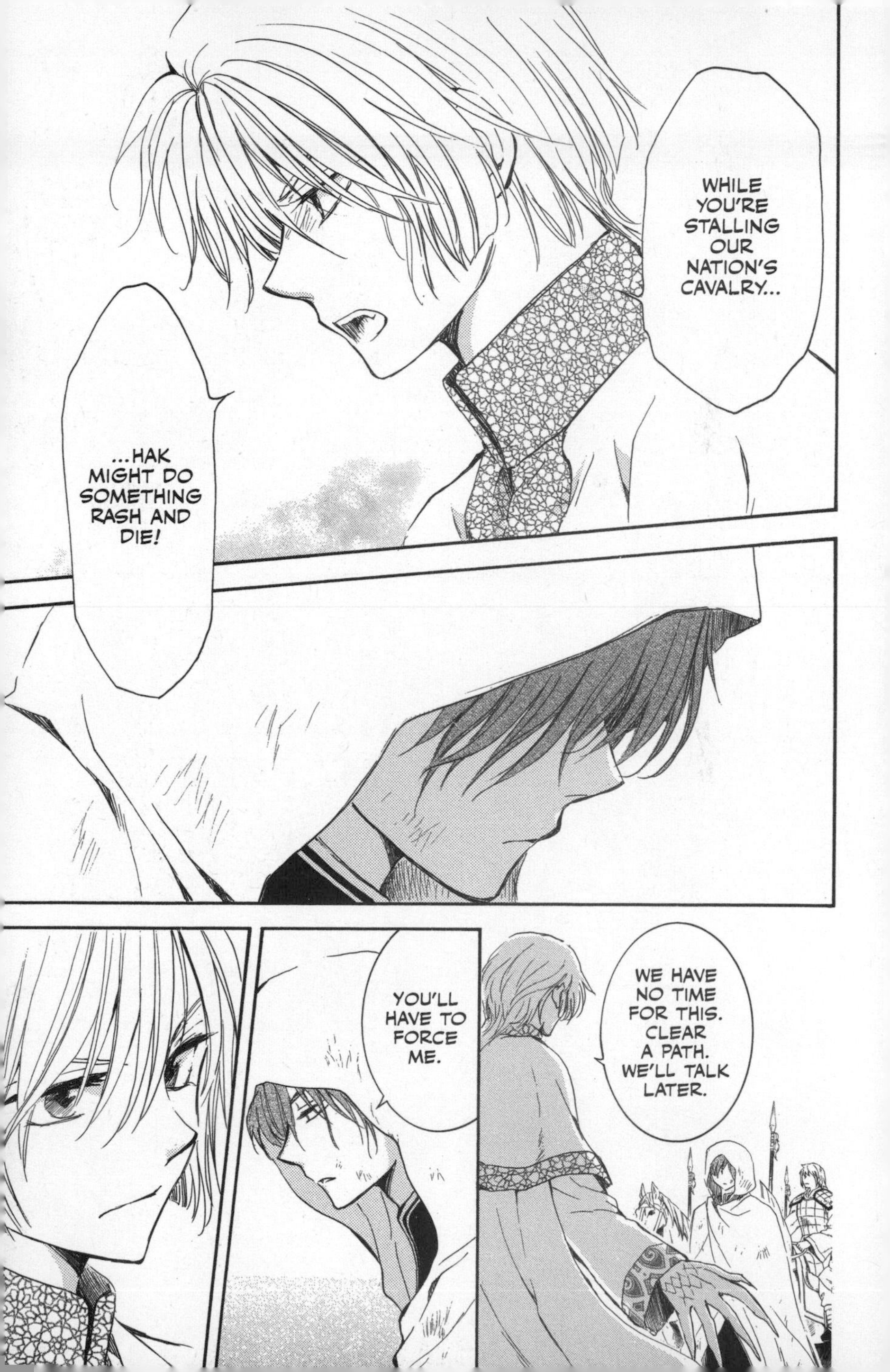
WHILE YOU'RE STALLING OUR NATION'S CAVALRY...
...HAK MIGHT DO SOMETHING RASH AND DIE!
WE HAVE NO TIME FOR THIS. CLEAR A PATH. WE'LL TALK LATER.
YOU'LL HAVE TO FORCE ME.

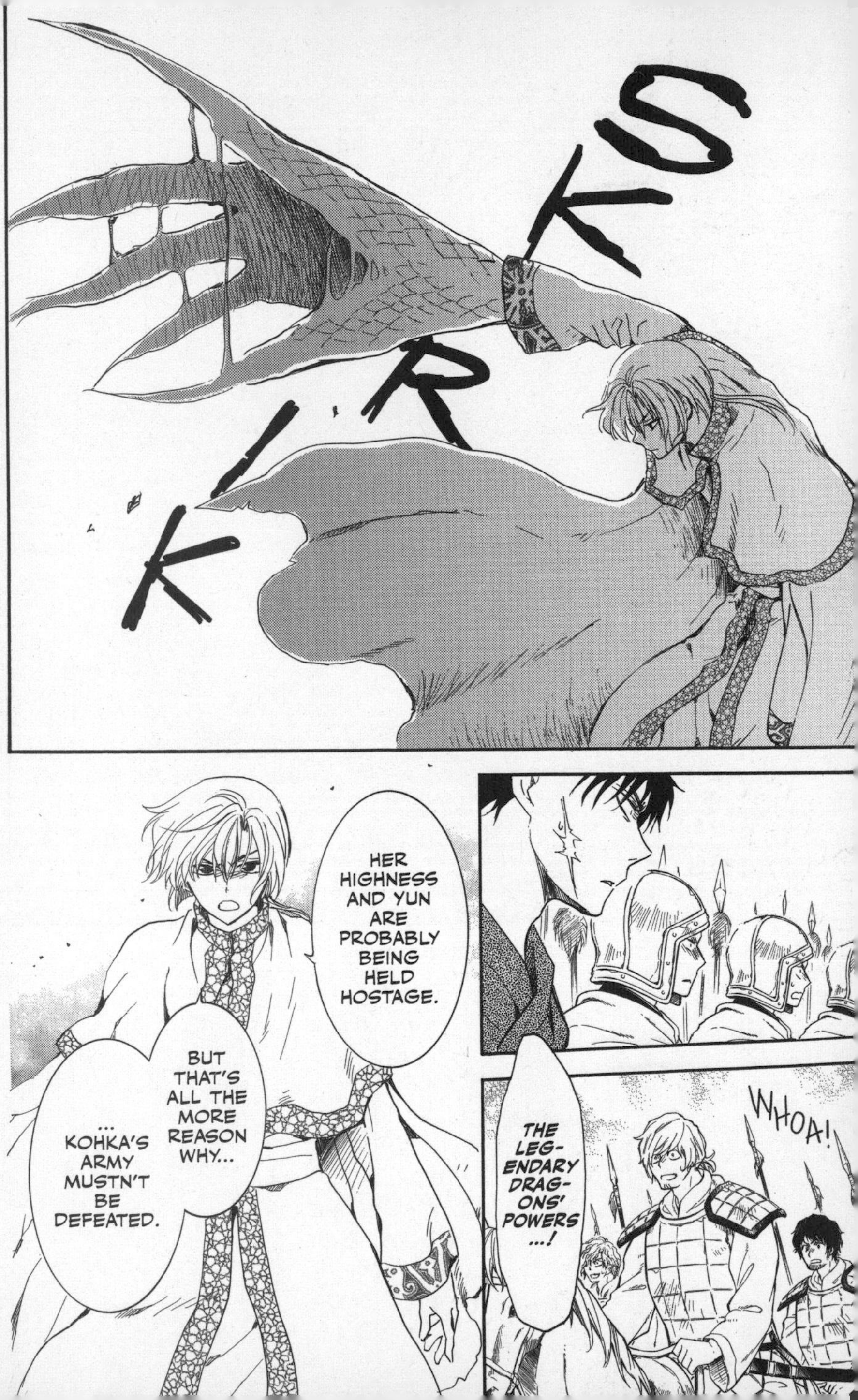
KIRKS
WHOA!
THE LEGENDARY DRAGONS' POWERS...!
HER HIGHNESS AND YUN ARE PROBABLY BEING HELD HOSTAGE.
BUT THAT'S ALL THE MORE REASON WHY...
...KOHKA'S ARMY MUSTN'T BE DEFEATED.

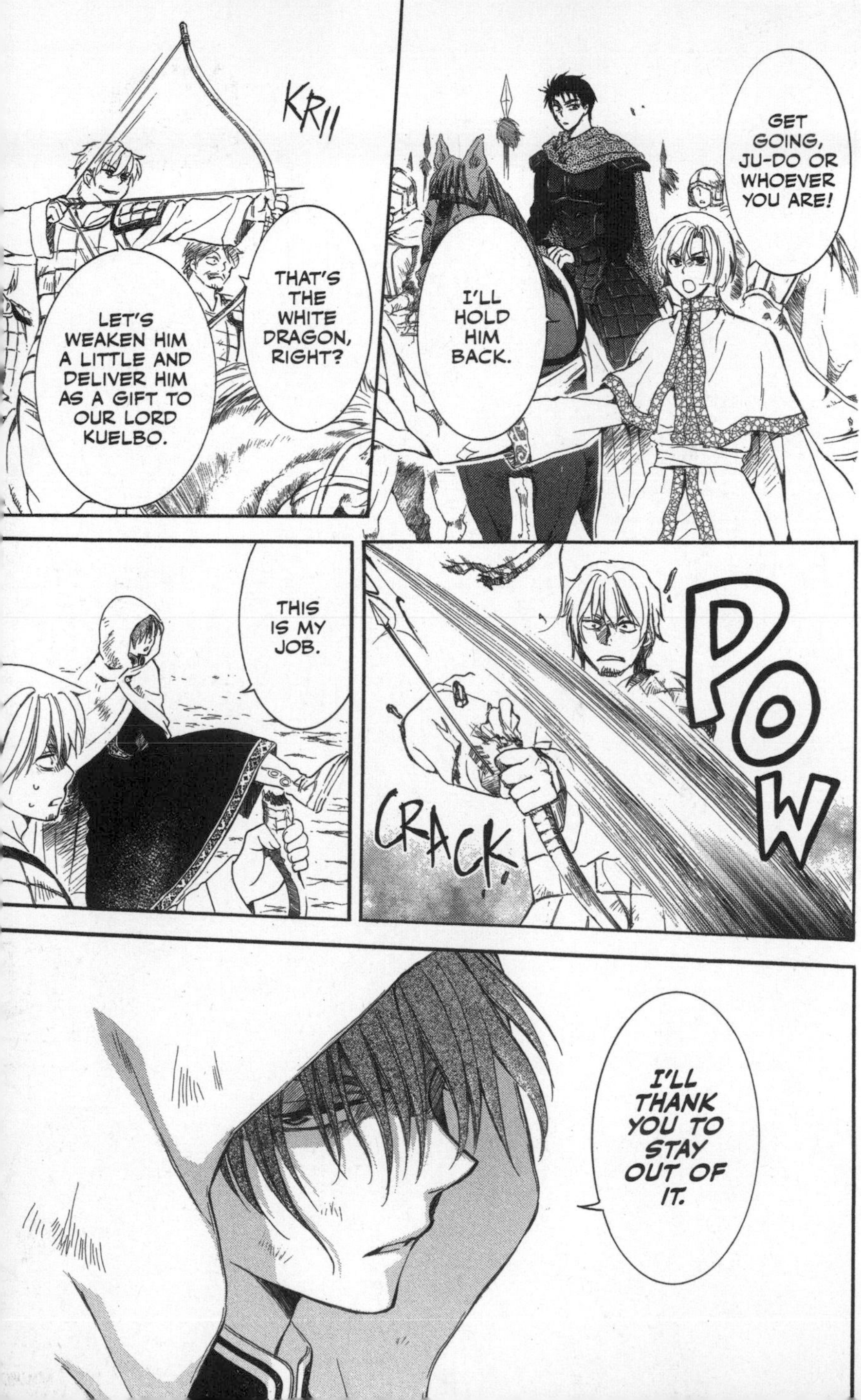
GET GOING, JU-DO OR WHOEVER YOU ARE!
I'LL HOLD HIM BACK.
KRII
THAT'S THE WHITE DRAGON, RIGHT?
LET'S WEAKEN HIM A LITTLE AND DELIVER HIM AS A GIFT TO OUR LORD KUELBO.
POW
CRACK
THIS IS MY JOB.
I'LL THANK YOU TO STAY OUT OF IT.

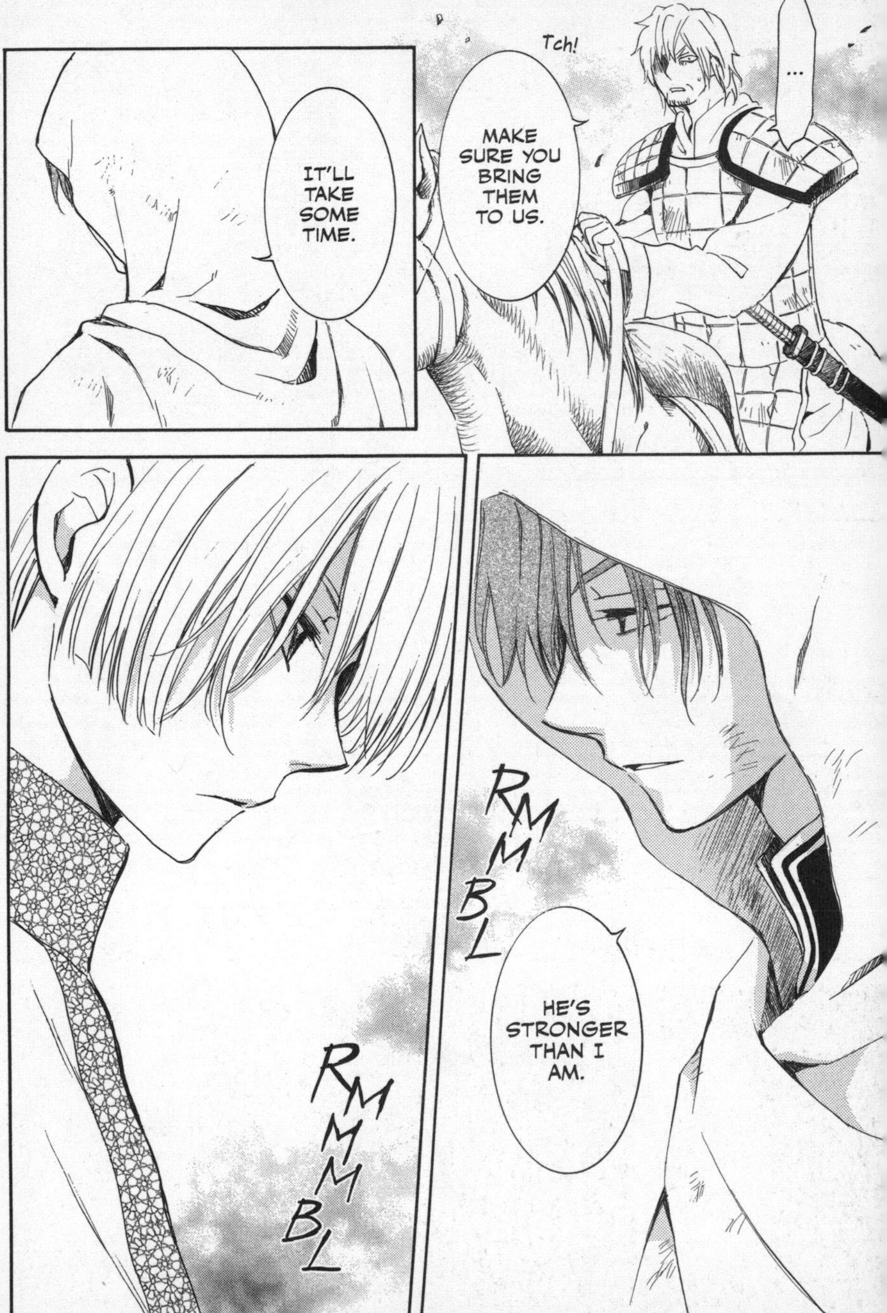
...
Tch!
MAKE SURE YOU BRING THEM TO US.
IT'LL TAKE SOME TIME.
RMMBL
HE'S STRONGER THAN I AM.
RMMMBL

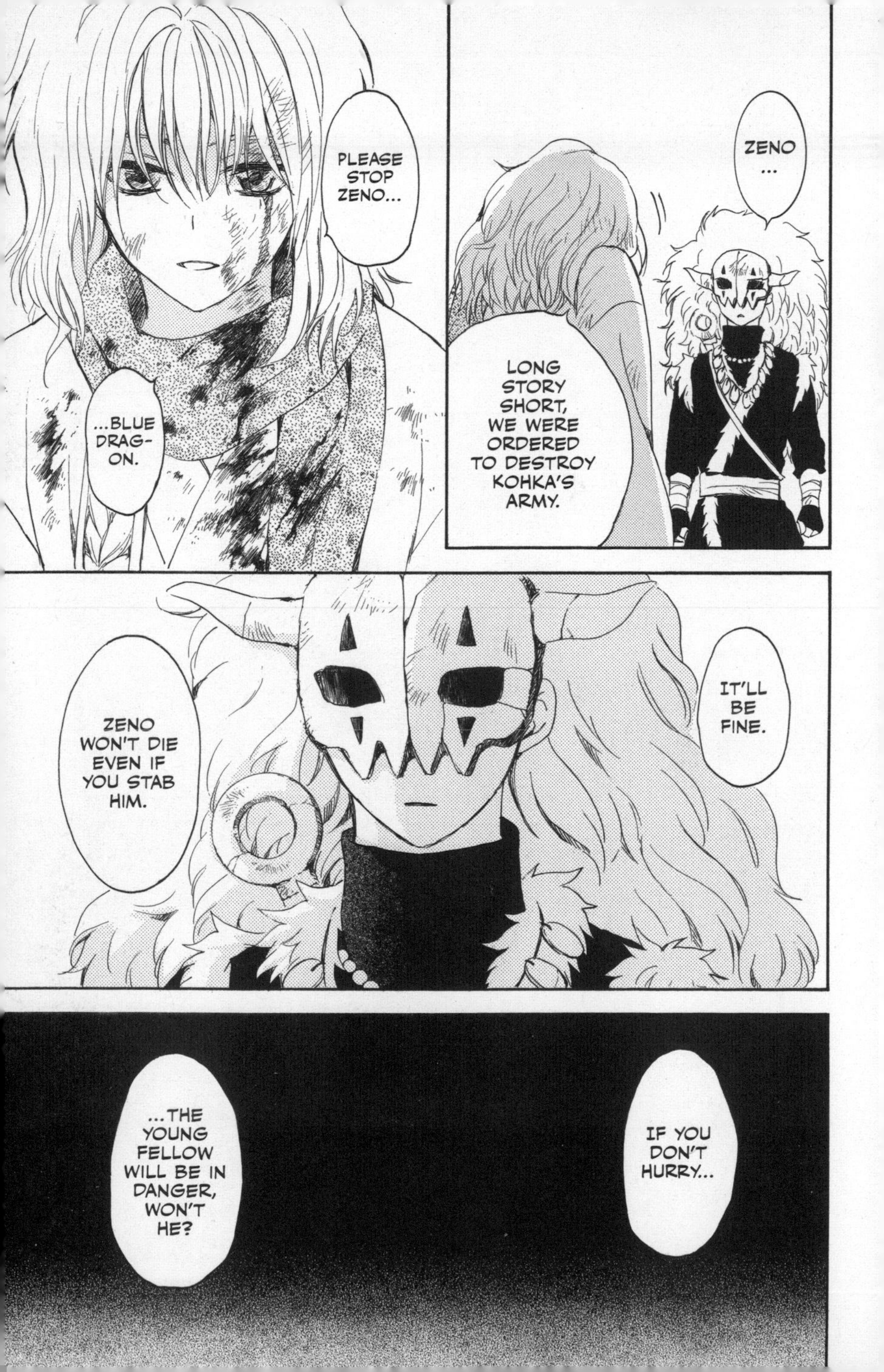
ZENO ...
LONG STORY SHORT, WE WERE ORDERED TO DESTROY KOHKA'S ARMY.
PLEASE STOP ZENO...
...BLUE DRAG-ON.
IT'LL BE FINE.
ZENO WON'T DIE EVEN IF YOU STAB HIM.
IF YOU DON'T HURRY...
...THE YOUNG FELLOW WILL BE IN DANGER, WON'T HE?

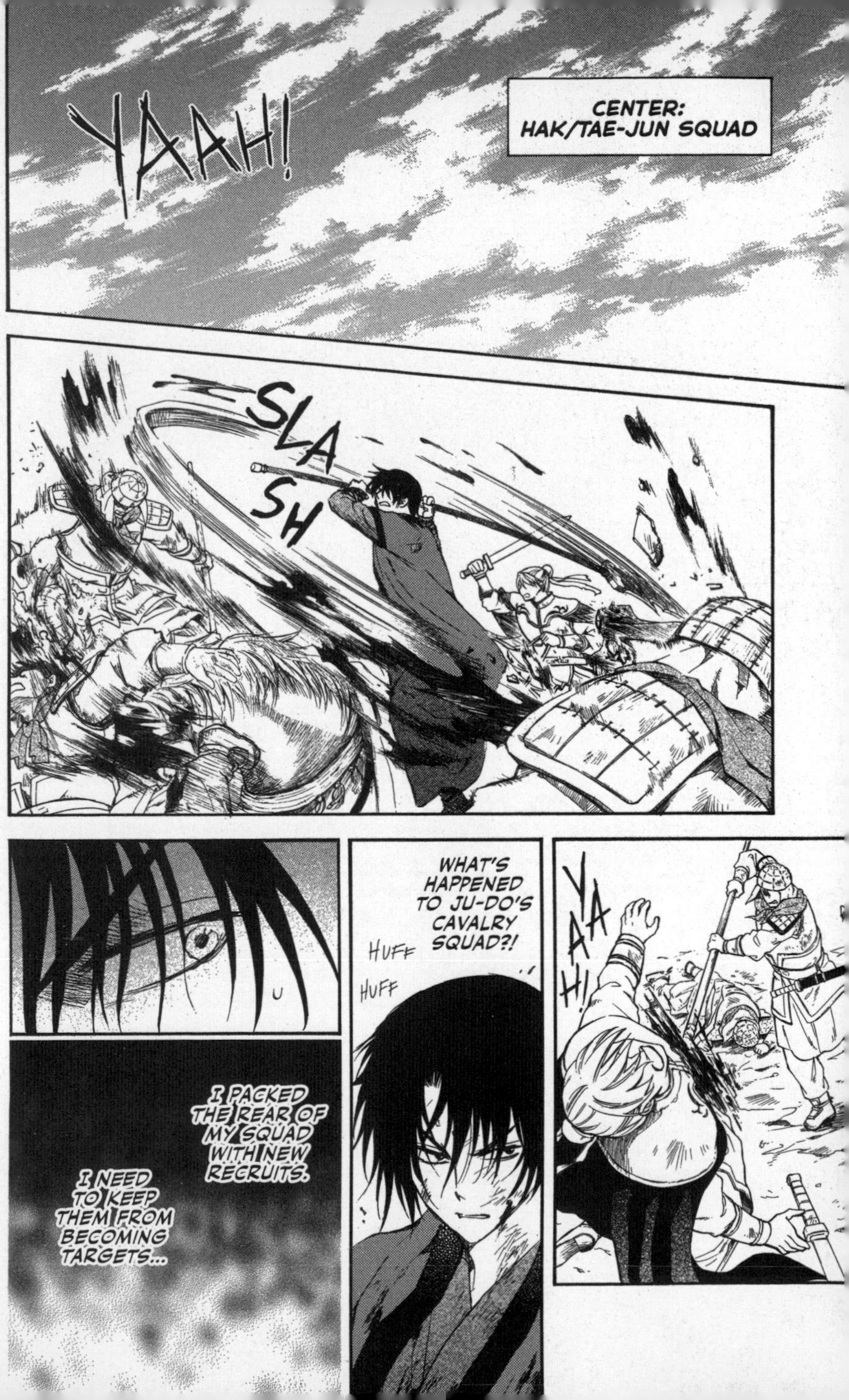
CENTER: HAK/TAE-JUN SQUAD
YAAH!
SLASH
YAAH!
WHAT'S HAPPENED TO JU-DO'S CAVALRY SQUAD?!
HUFF
HUFF
I PACKED THE REAR OF MY SQUAD WITH NEW RECRUITS.
I NEED TO KEEP THEM FROM BECOMING TARGETS...

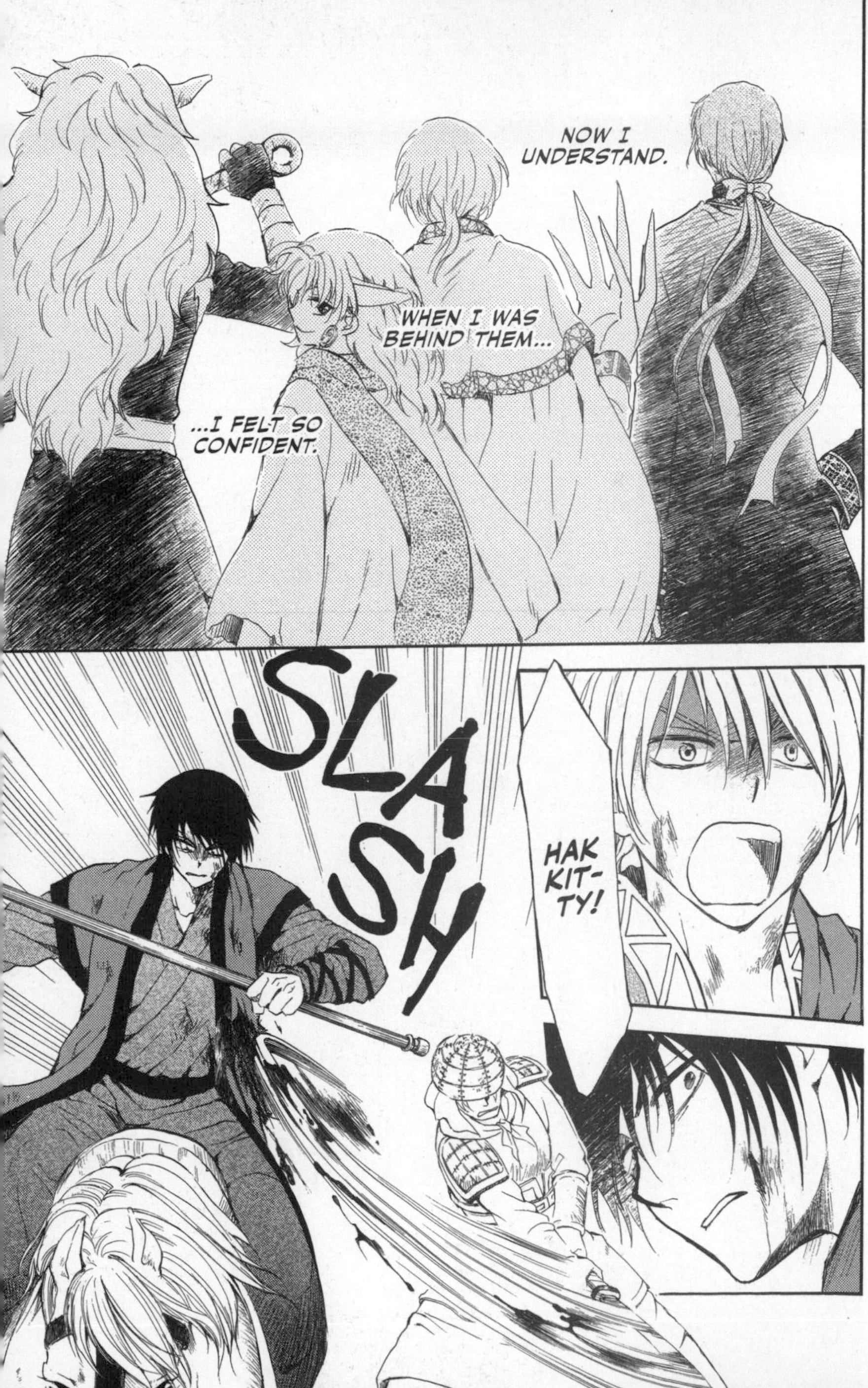
NOW I UNDERSTAND.
WHEN I WAS BEHIND THEM...
...I FELT SO CONFIDENT.
HAK KIT-TY!
SLASH

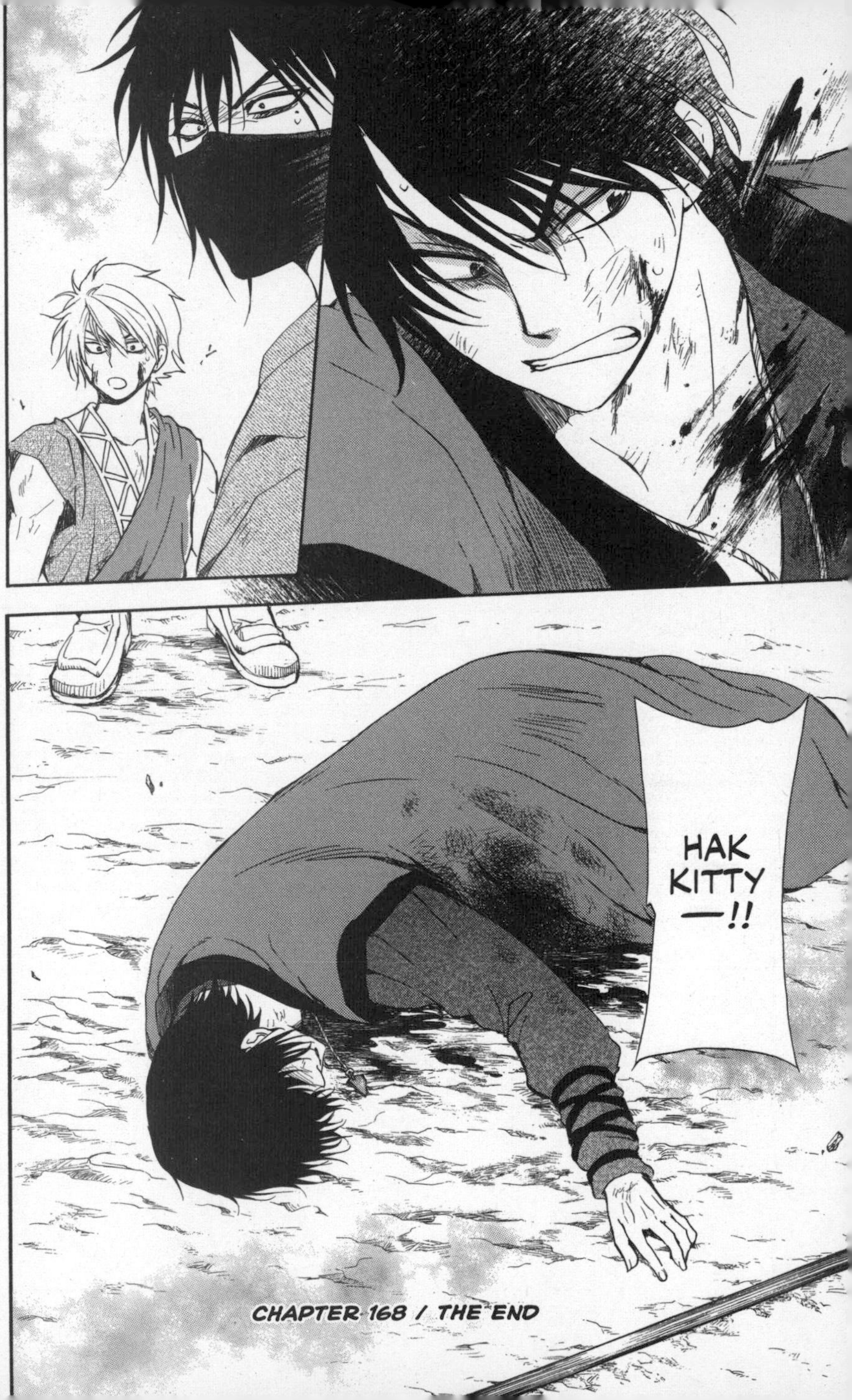
HAK KITTY —!!
CHAPTER 168 / THE END

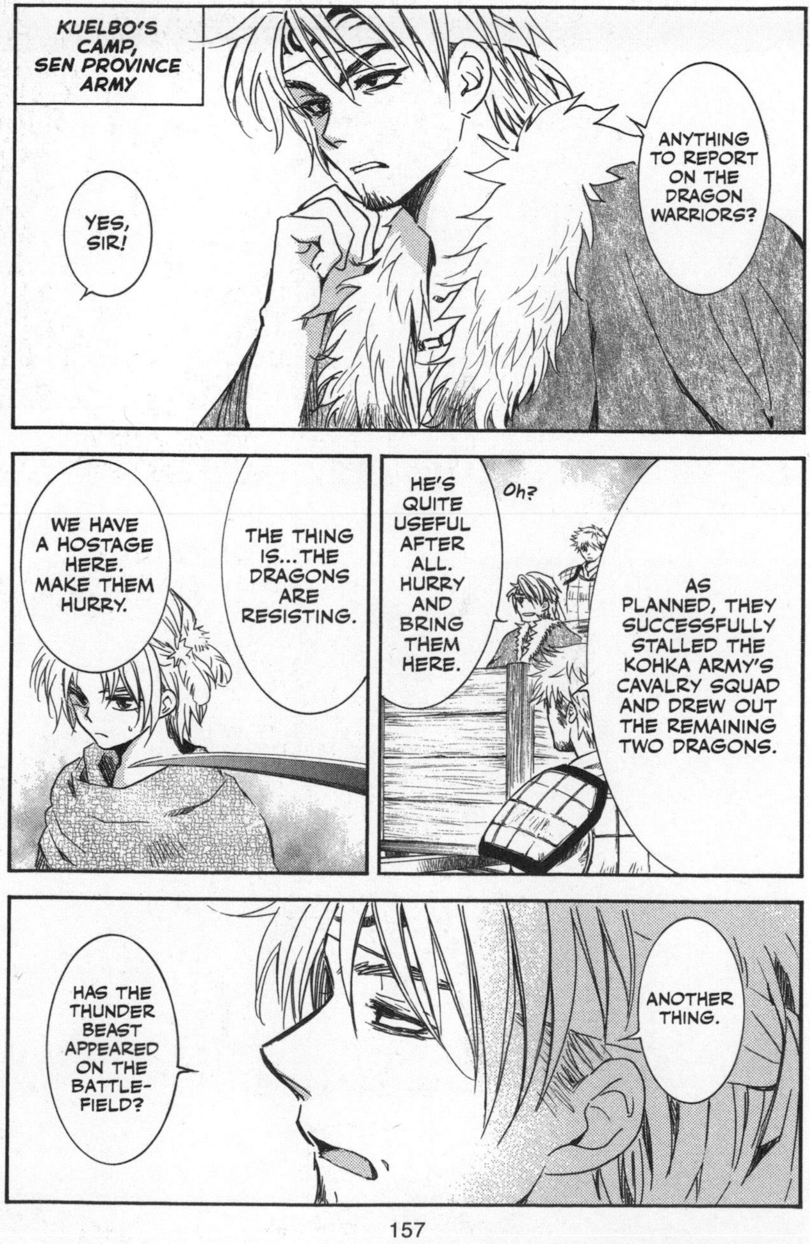
KUELBO'S CAMP, SEN PROVINCE ARMY
ANYTHING TO REPORT ON THE DRAGON WARRIORS?
YES, SIR!
AS PLANNED, THEY SUCCESSFULLY STALLED THE KOHKA ARMY'S CAVALRY SQUAD AND DREW OUT THE REMAINING TWO DRAGONS.
Oh?
HE'S QUITE USEFUL AFTER ALL. HURRY AND BRING THEM HERE.
THE THING IS...THE DRAGONS ARE RESISTING.
WE HAVE A HOSTAGE HERE. MAKE THEM HURRY.
ANOTHER THING.
HAS THE THUNDER BEAST APPEARED ON THE BATTLE-FIELD?

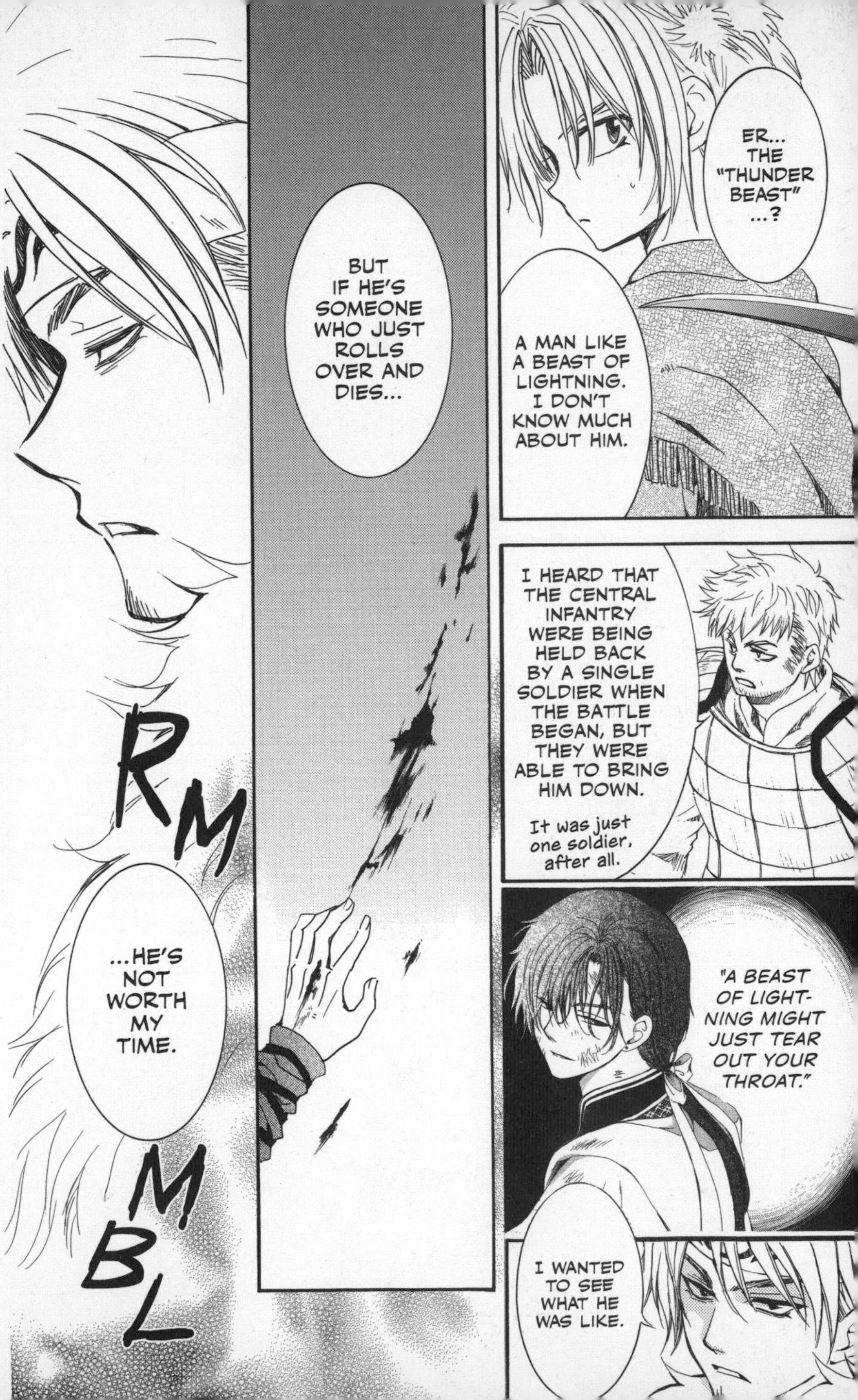
ER... THE "THUNDER BEAST" ...?
A MAN LIKE A BEAST OF LIGHTNING. I DON'T KNOW MUCH ABOUT HIM.
I HEARD THAT THE CENTRAL INFANTRY WERE BEING HELD BACK BY A SINGLE SOLDIER WHEN THE BATTLE BEGAN, BUT THEY WERE ABLE TO BRING HIM DOWN.
It was just one soldier, after all.
"A BEAST OF LIGHTNING MIGHT JUST TEAR OUT YOUR THROAT."
I WANTED TO SEE WHAT HE WAS LIKE.
BUT IF HE'S SOMEONE WHO JUST ROLLS OVER AND DIES...
RMMBL
...HE'S NOT WORTH MY TIME.

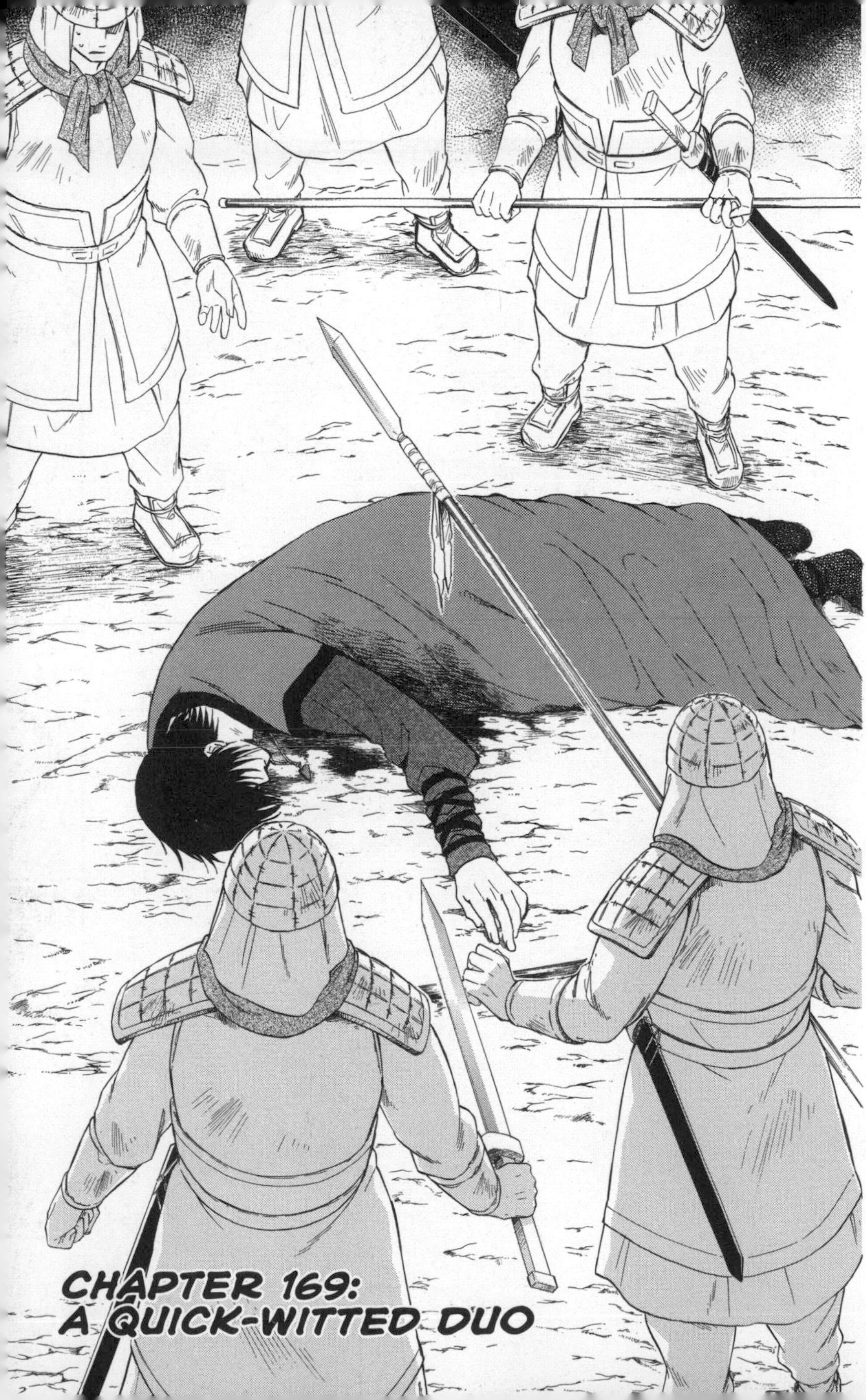
CHAPTER 169:
A QUICK-WITTED DUO

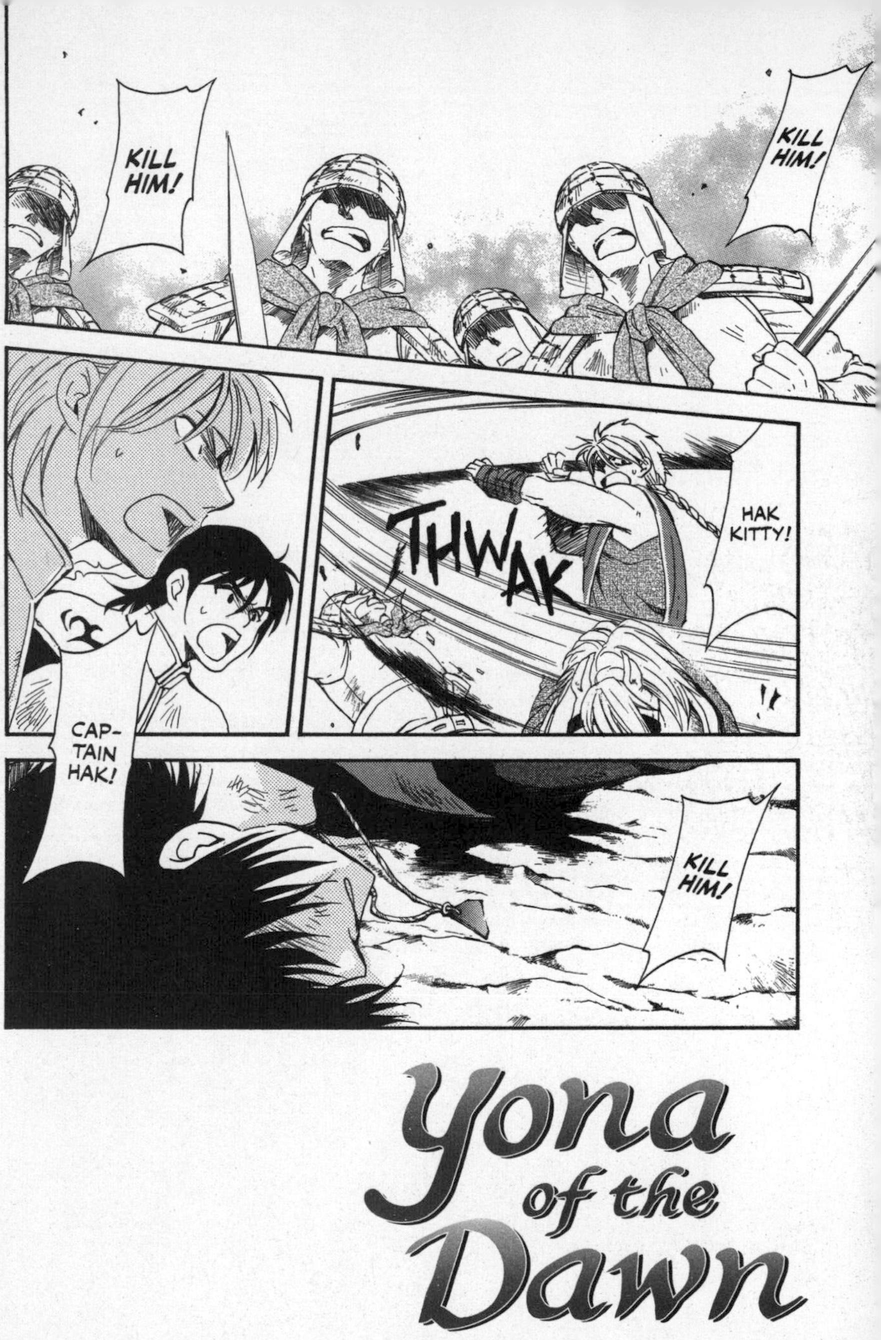
KILL HIM!
KILL HIM!
HAK KITTY!
THWAK
!!
CAP-TAIN HAK!
KILL HIM!

Yona of the Dawn

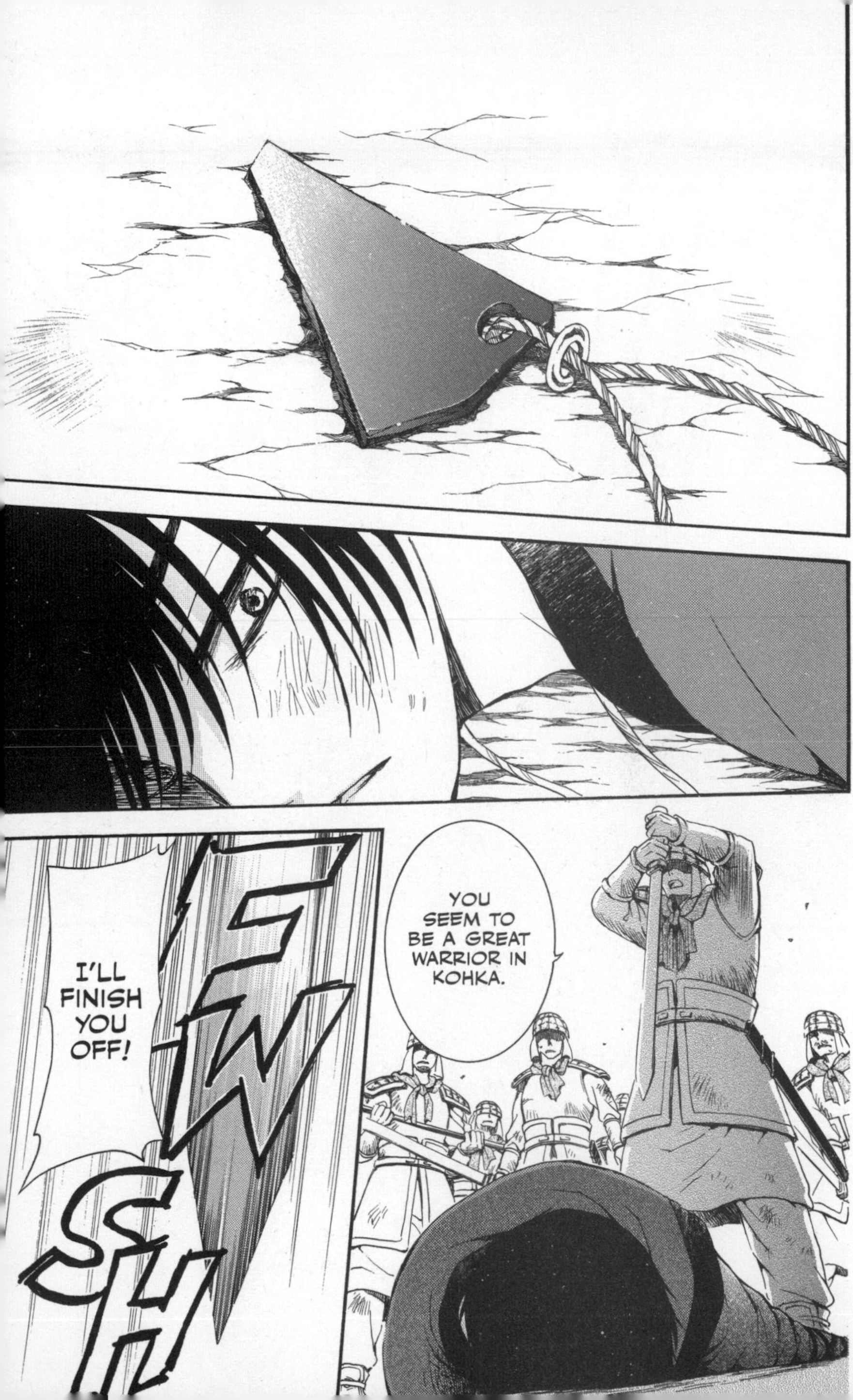
YOU SEEM TO BE A GREAT WARRIOR IN KOHKA.
I'LL FINISH YOU OFF!

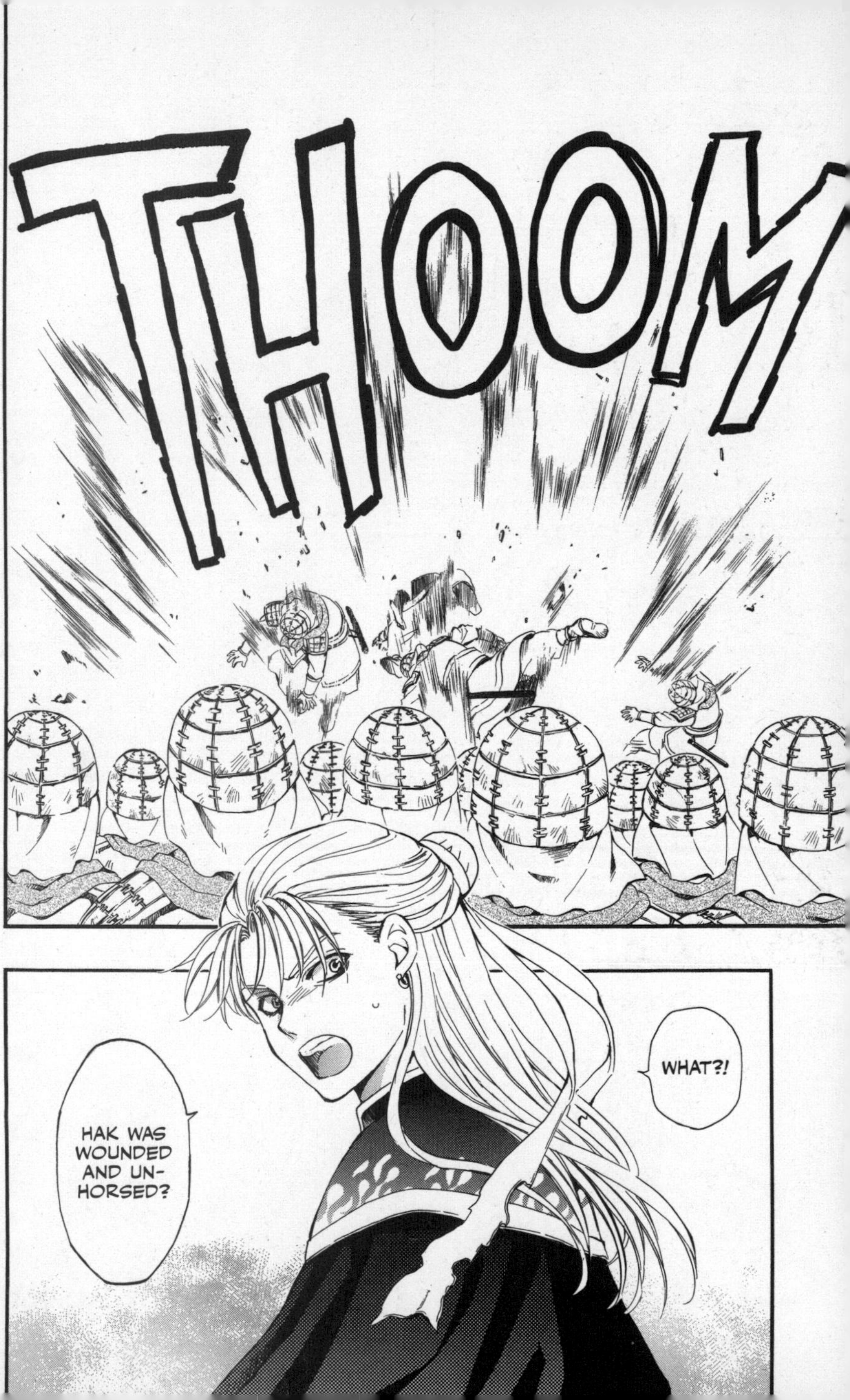
THOOM
WHAT?!
HAK WAS WOUNDED AND UN-HORSED?

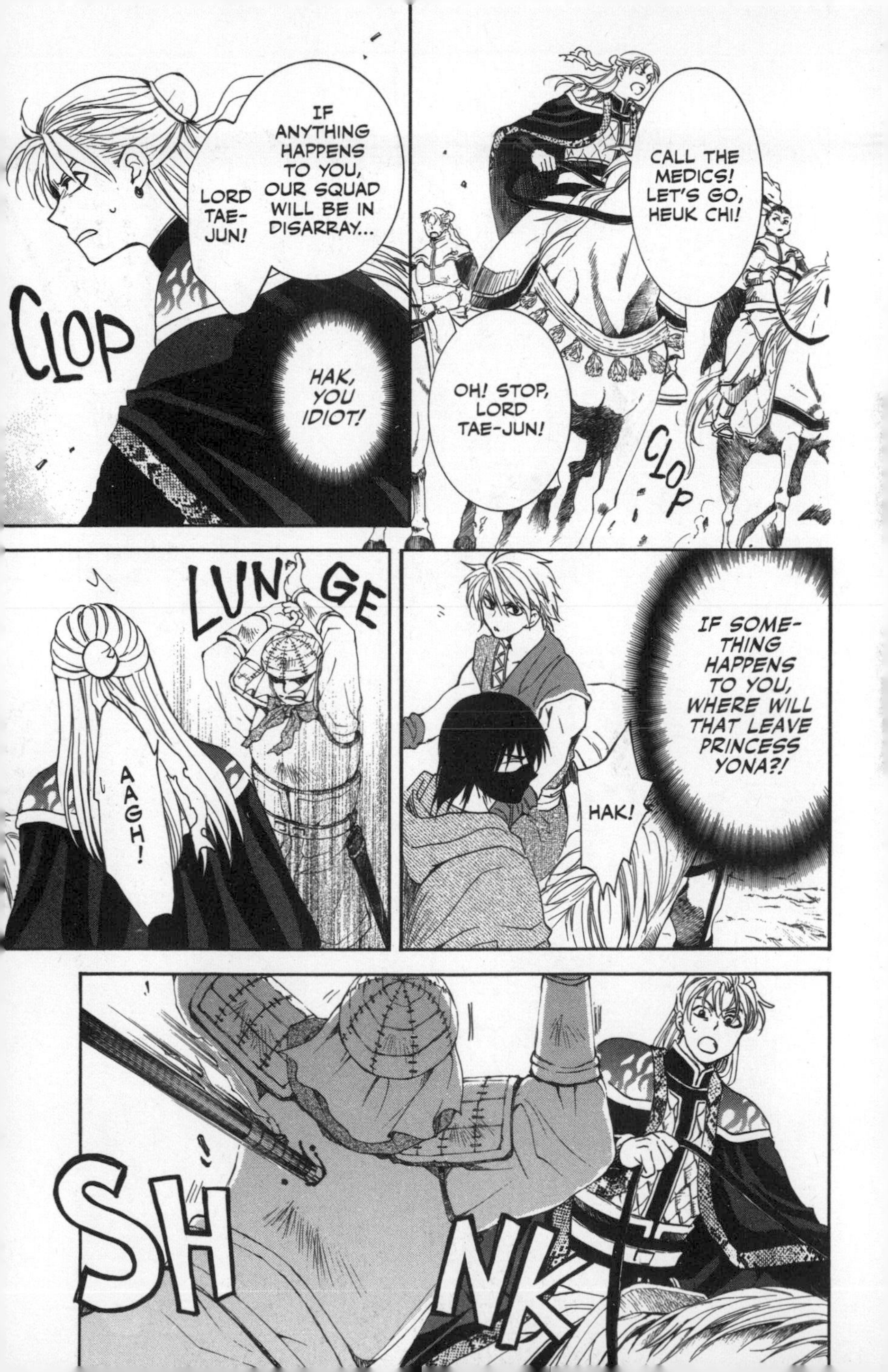
CALL THE MEDICS! LET'S GO, HEUK CHI!
OH! STOP, LORD TAE-JUN!
CLOP
IF ANYTHING HAPPENS TO YOU, OUR SQUAD WILL BE IN DISARRAY...
LORD TAE-JUN!
HAK, YOU IDIOT!
CLOP
IF SOMETHING HAPPENS TO YOU, WHERE WILL THAT LEAVE PRINCESS YONA?!
HAK!
LUNGE
AAGH!
SHNK

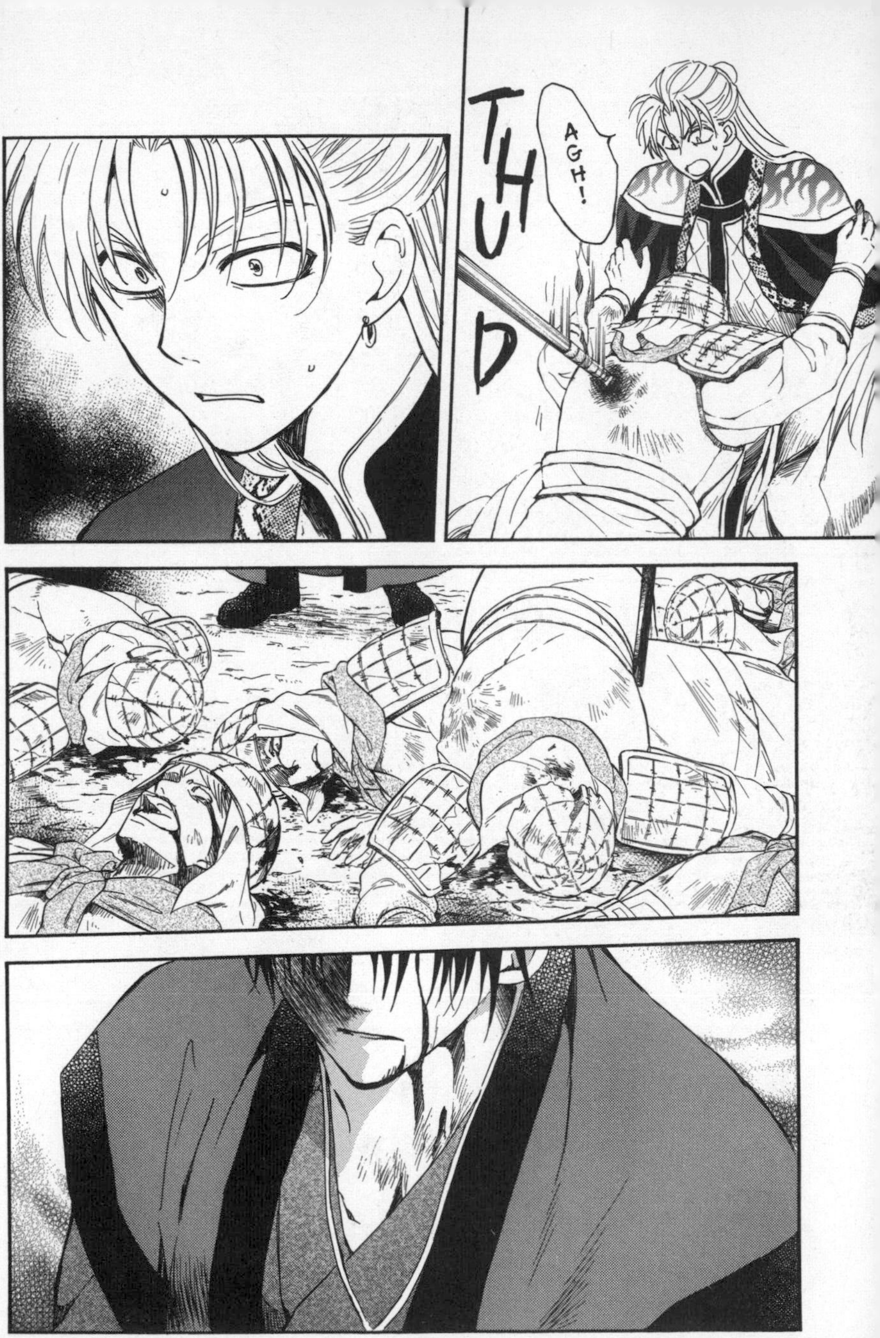
THUD
AGH!

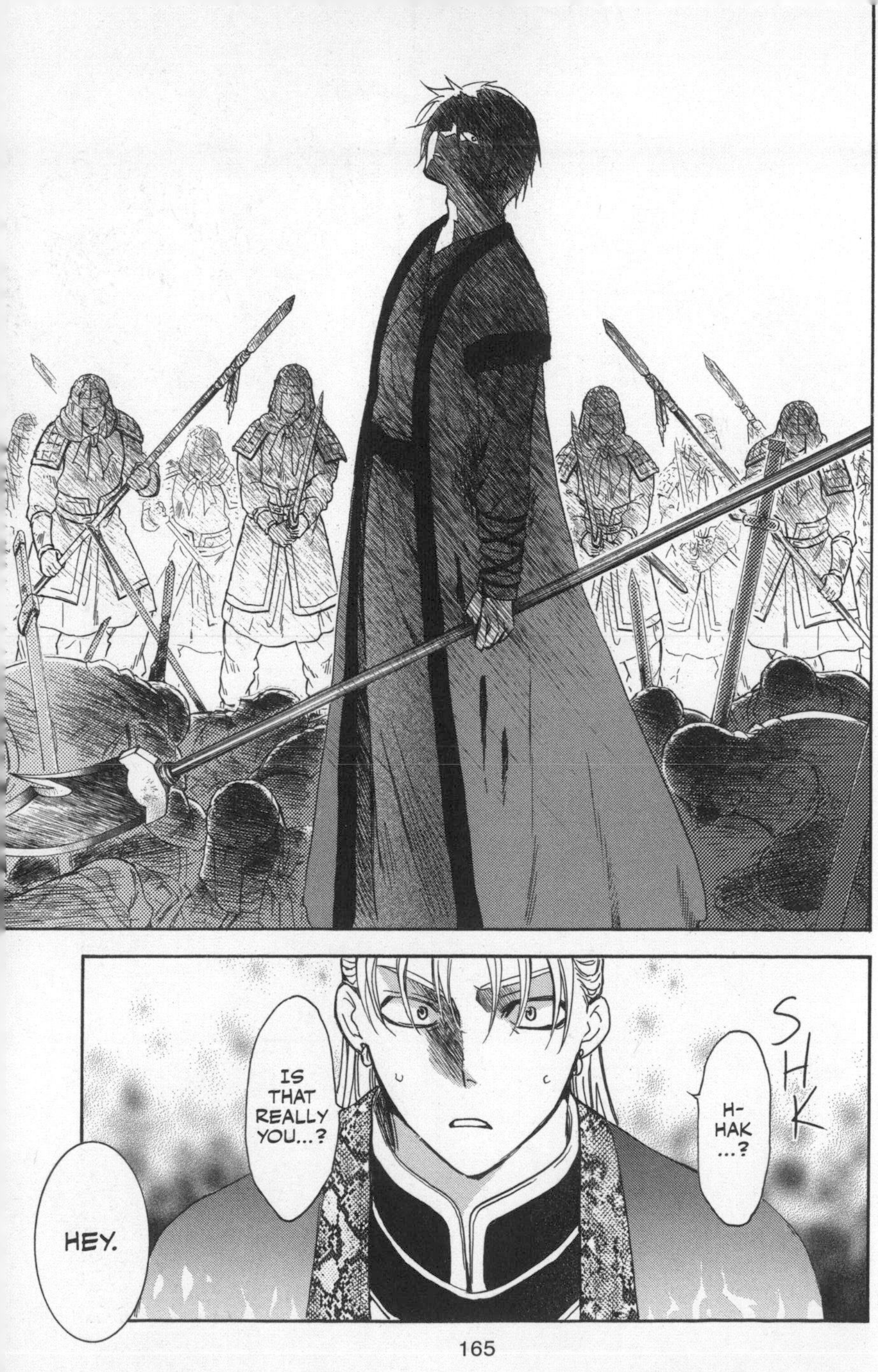
SHK
H-HAK...?
IS THAT REALLY YOU...?
HEY.

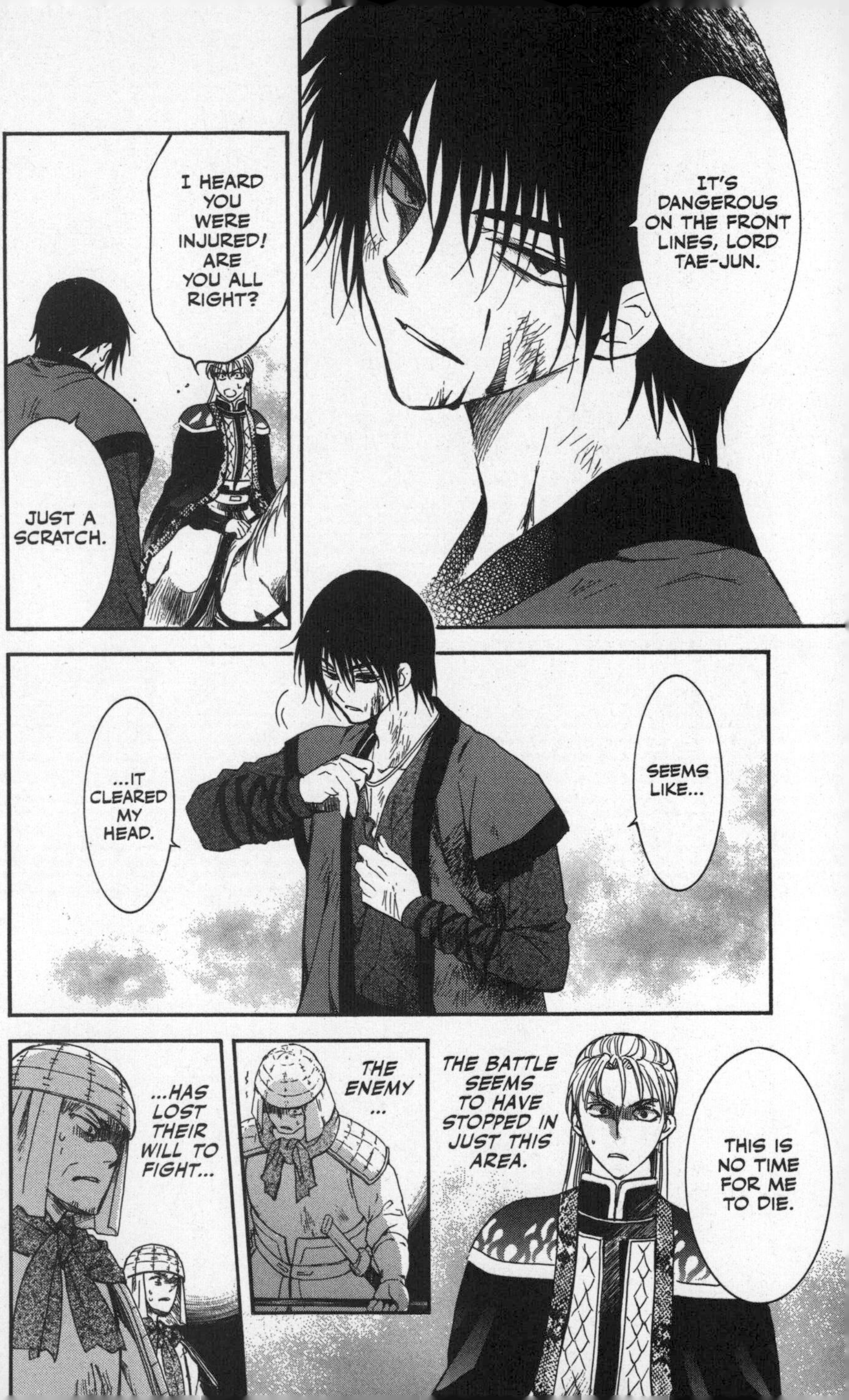
IT'S DANGEROUS ON THE FRONT LINES, LORD TAE-JUN.
I HEARD YOU WERE INJURED! ARE YOU ALL RIGHT?
JUST A SCRATCH.
SEEMS LIKE...
...IT CLEARED MY HEAD.
THIS IS NO TIME FOR ME TO DIE.
THE BATTLE SEEMS TO HAVE STOPPED IN JUST THIS AREA.
THE ENEMY ...
...HAS LOST THEIR WILL TO FIGHT...

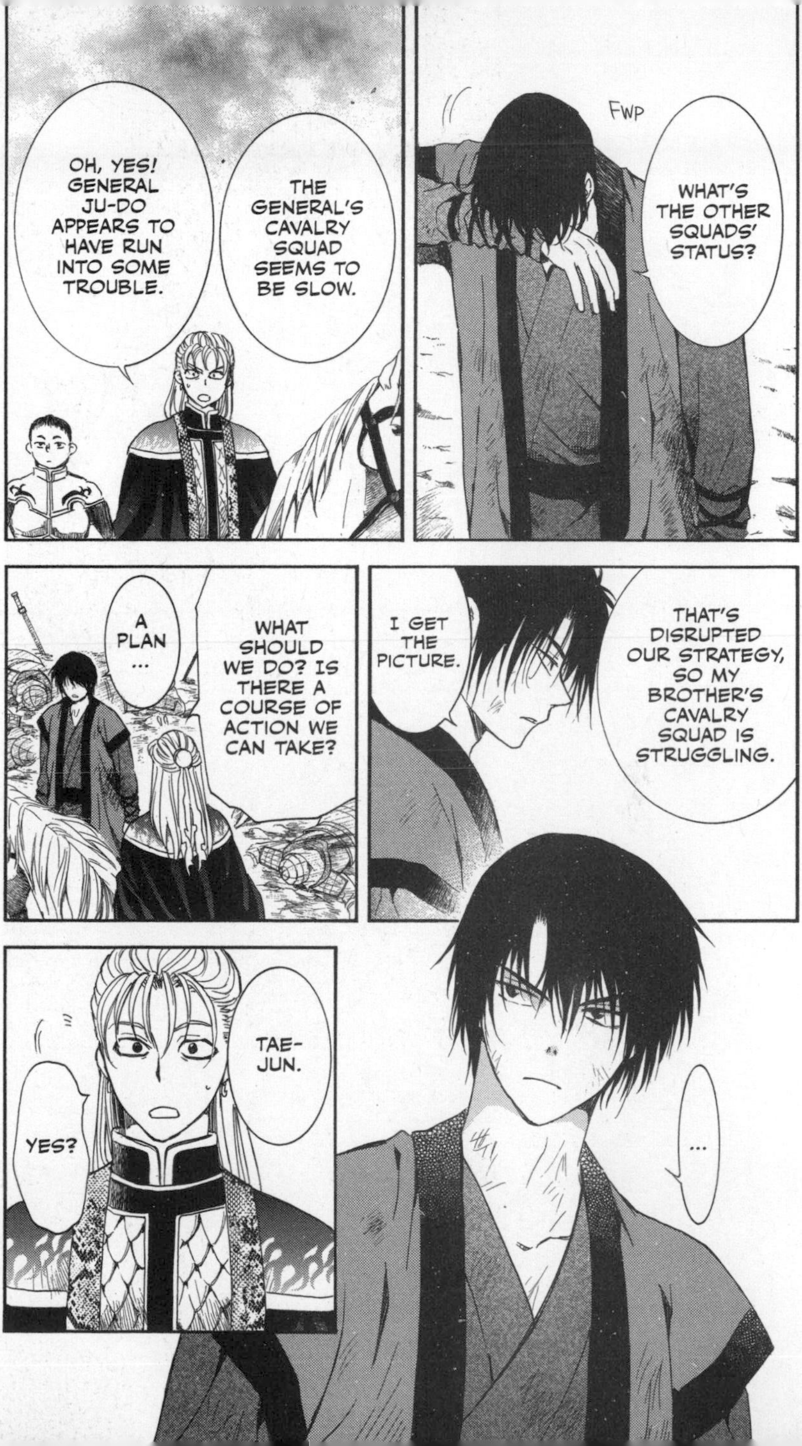
FWP
WHAT'S THE OTHER SQUADS' STATUS?
THE GENERAL'S CAVALRY SQUAD SEEMS TO BE SLOW.
OH, YES! GENERAL JU-DO APPEARS TO HAVE RUN INTO SOME TROUBLE.
THAT'S DISRUPTED OUR STRATEGY, SO MY BROTHER'S CAVALRY SQUAD IS STRUGGLING.
I GET THE PICTURE.
WHAT SHOULD WE DO? IS THERE A COURSE OF ACTION WE CAN TAKE?
A PLAN ...
...
TAE-JUN.
YES?

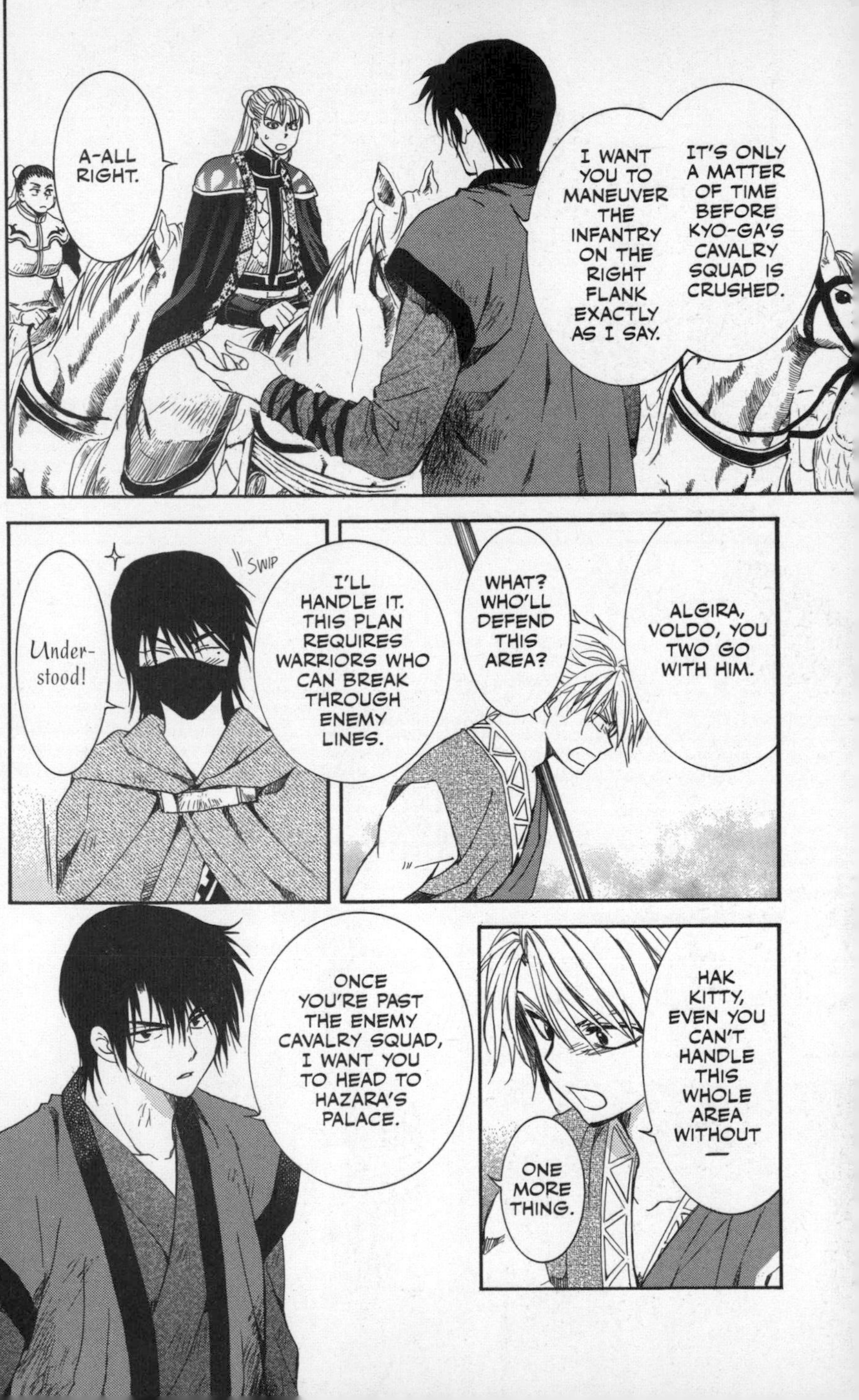
IT'S ONLY A MATTER OF TIME BEFORE KYO-GA'S CAVALRY SQUAD IS CRUSHED.
I WANT YOU TO MANEUVER THE INFANTRY ON THE RIGHT FLANK EXACTLY AS I SAY.
A-ALL RIGHT.
ALGIRA, VOLDO, YOU TWO GO WITH HIM.
WHAT? WHO'LL DEFEND THIS AREA?
SWIP
I'LL HANDLE IT. THIS PLAN REQUIRES WARRIORS WHO CAN BREAK THROUGH ENEMY LINES.
Understood!
HAK KITTY, EVEN YOU CAN'T HANDLE THIS WHOLE AREA WITHOUT—
ONE MORE THING.
ONCE YOU'RE PAST THE ENEMY CAVALRY SQUAD, I WANT YOU TO HEAD TO HAZARA'S PALACE.

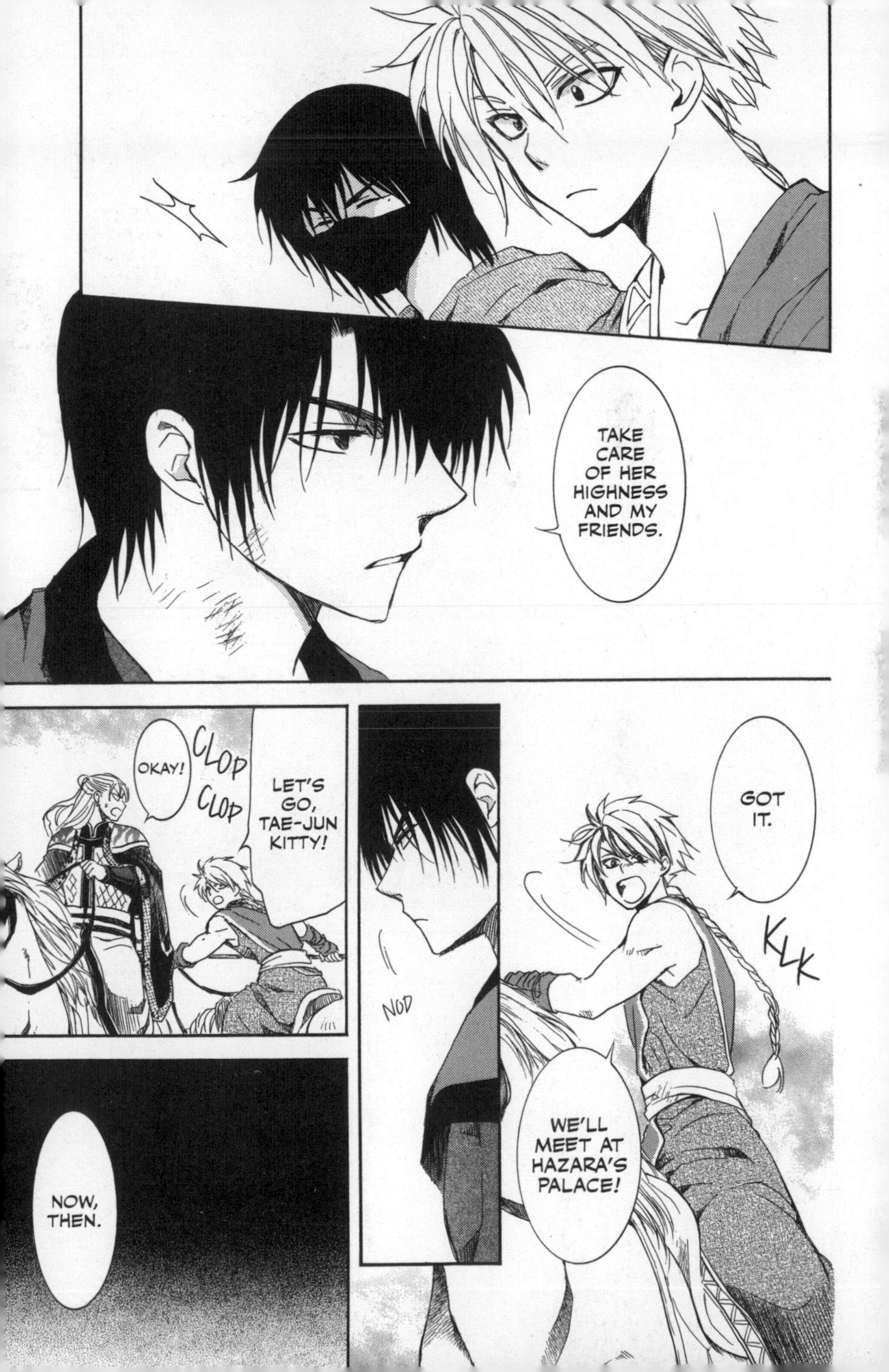
TAKE CARE OF HER HIGHNESS AND MY FRIENDS.
GOT IT.
KLIK
WE'LL MEET AT HAZARA'S PALACE!
NOD
LET'S GO, TAE-JUN KITTY!
CLOP CLOP
OKAY!
NOW, THEN.

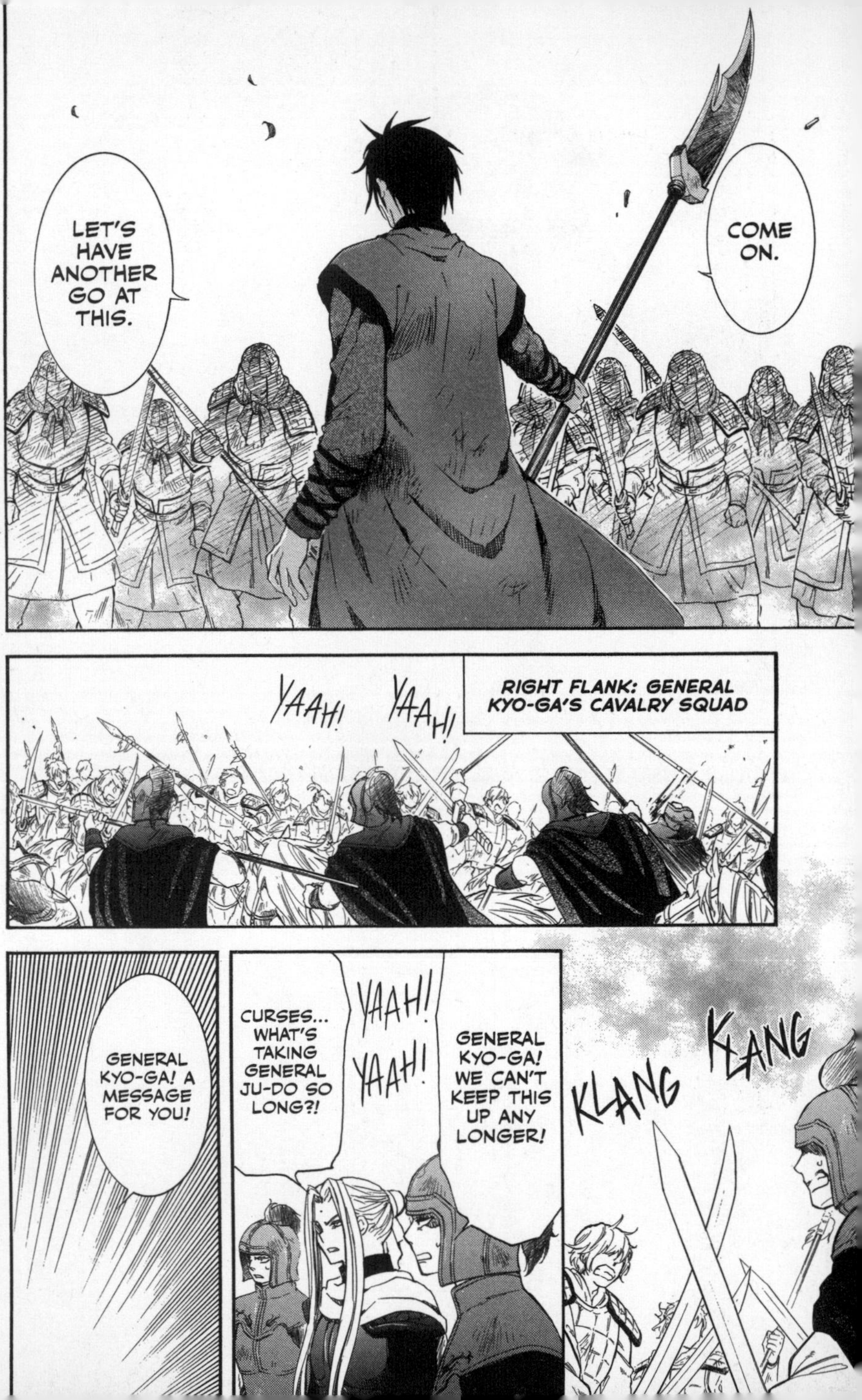
COME ON.
LET'S HAVE ANOTHER GO AT THIS.
RIGHT FLANK: GENERAL KYO-GA'S CAVALRY SQUAD
YAAH!
YAAH!
KLANG
KLANG
GENERAL KYO-GA! WE CAN'T KEEP THIS UP ANY LONGER!
YAAH!
YAAH!
CURSES... WHAT'S TAKING GENERAL JU-DO SO LONG?!
GENERAL KYO-GA! A MESSAGE FOR YOU!

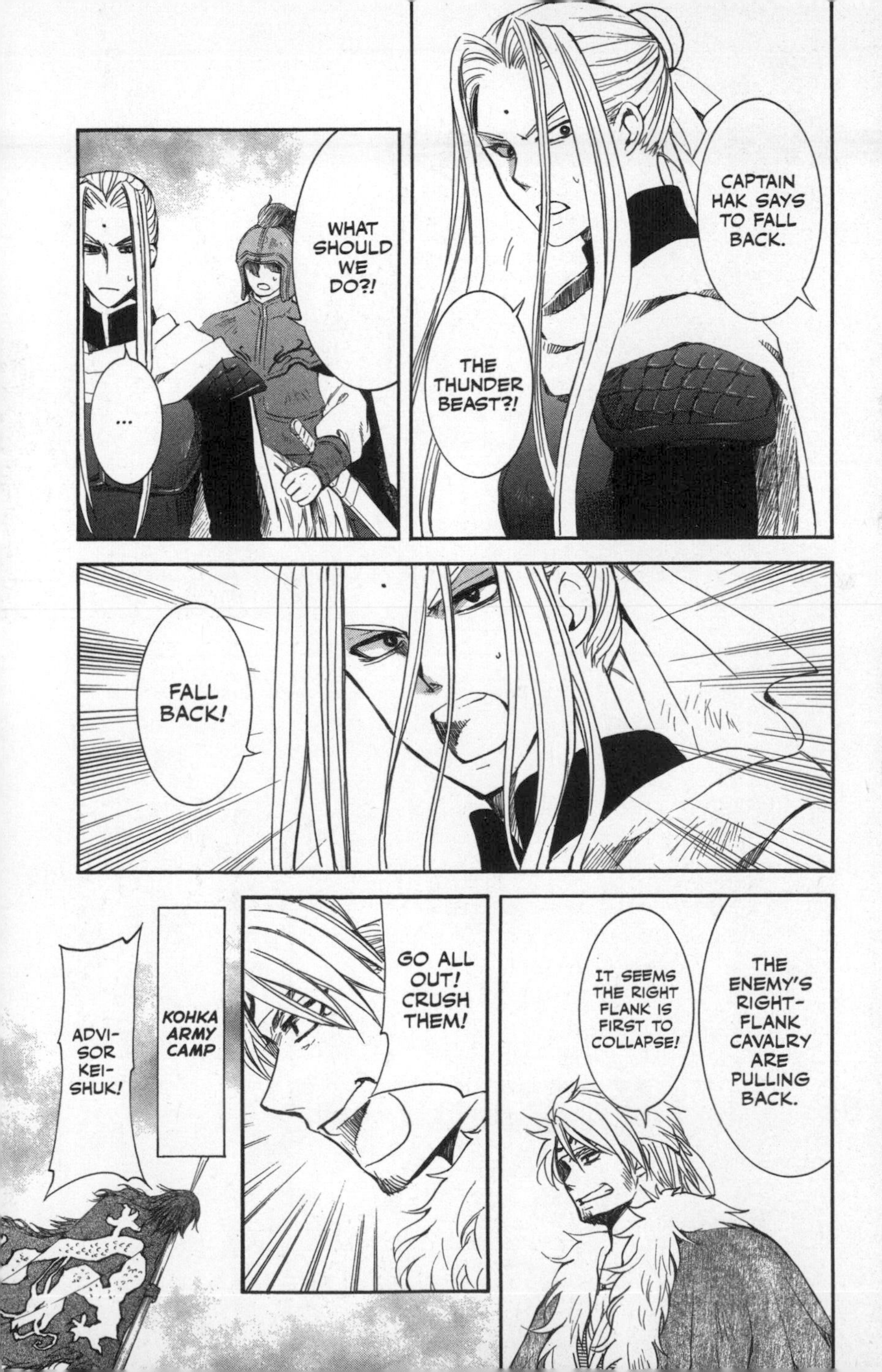

CAPTAIN HAK SAYS TO FALL BACK.
THE THUNDER BEAST?!
WHAT SHOULD WE DO?!
...
FALL BACK!
THE ENEMY'S RIGHT-FLANK CAVALRY ARE PULLING BACK.
IT SEEMS THE RIGHT FLANK IS FIRST TO COLLAPSE!
GO ALL OUT! CRUSH THEM!
KOHKA ARMY CAMP
ADVISOR KEI-SHUK!

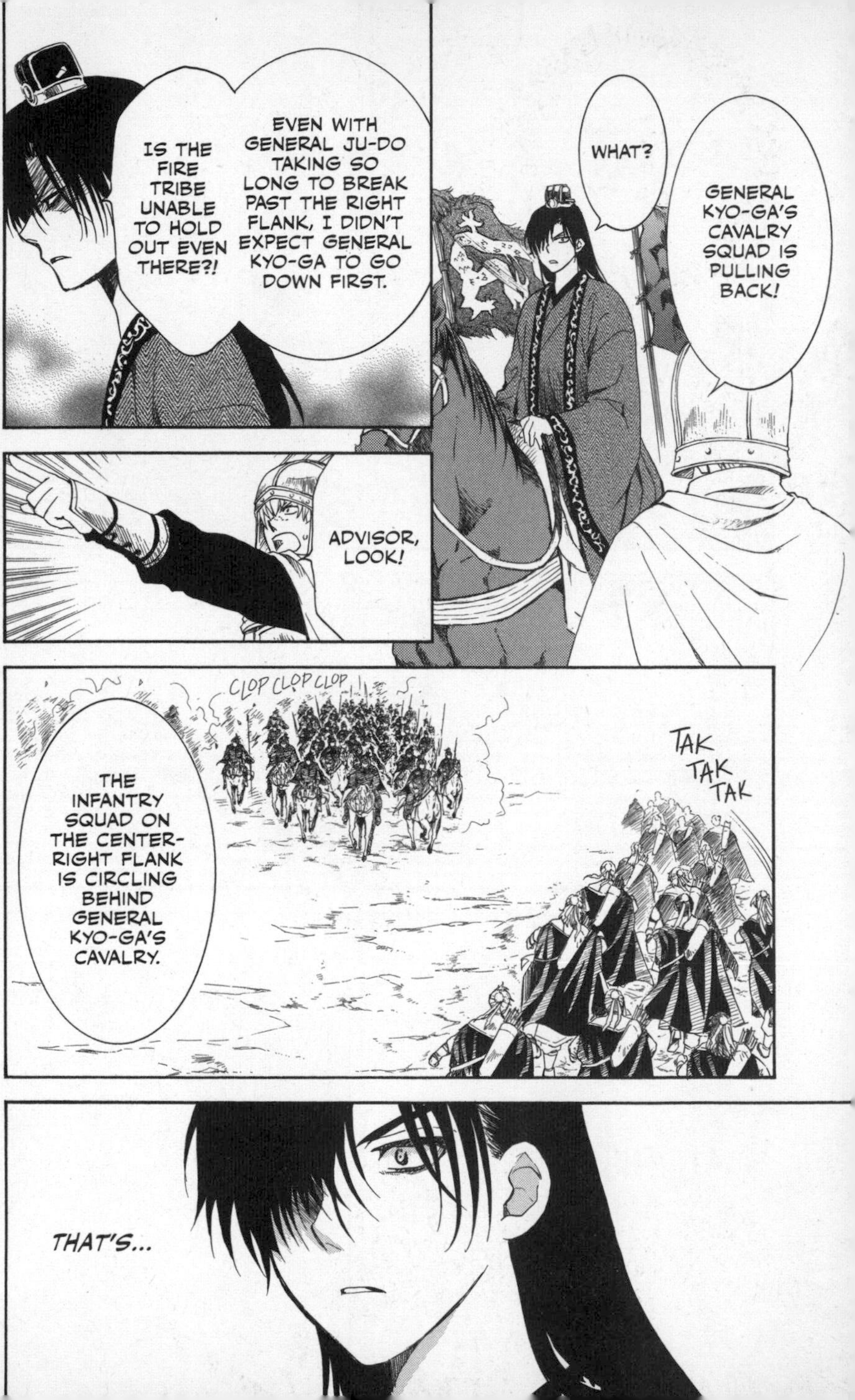
GENERAL KYO-GA'S CAVALRY SQUAD IS PULLING BACK!
WHAT?
EVEN WITH GENERAL JU-DO TAKING SO LONG TO BREAK PAST THE RIGHT FLANK, I DIDN'T EXPECT GENERAL KYO-GA TO GO DOWN FIRST.
IS THE FIRE TRIBE UNABLE TO HOLD OUT EVEN THERE?!
ADVISOR, LOOK!
TAK TAK TAK
CLOP CLOP CLOP
THE INFANTRY SQUAD ON THE CENTER-RIGHT FLANK IS CIRCLING BEHIND GENERAL KYO-GA'S CAVALRY.
THAT'S...

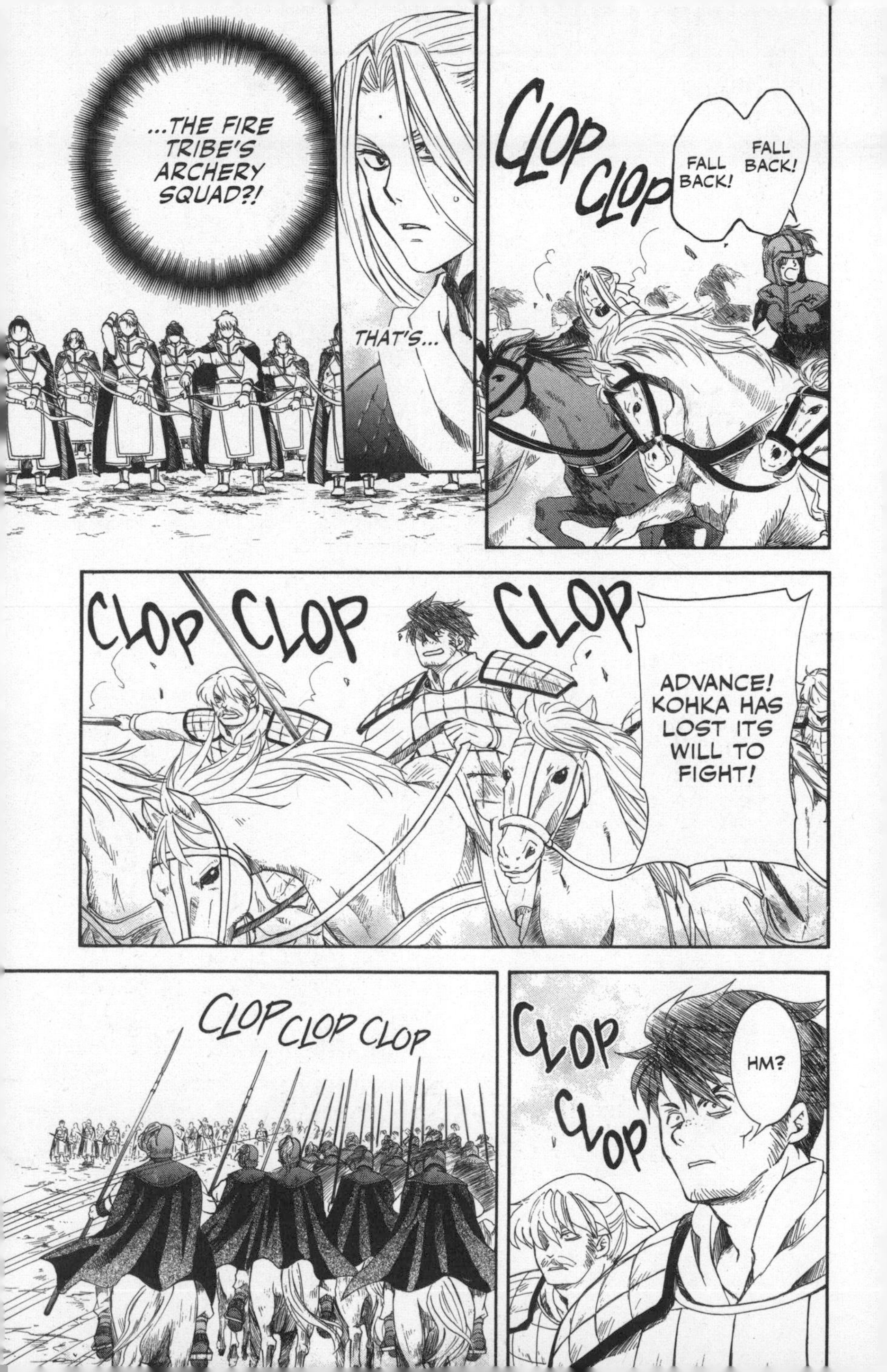
FALL BACK!
FALL BACK!
CLOP CLOP
THAT'S...
...THE FIRE TRIBE'S ARCHERY SQUAD?!
ADVANCE! KOHKA HAS LOST ITS WILL TO FIGHT!
CLOP
CLOP
CLOP
HM?
CLOP CLOP
CLOP CLOP CLOP

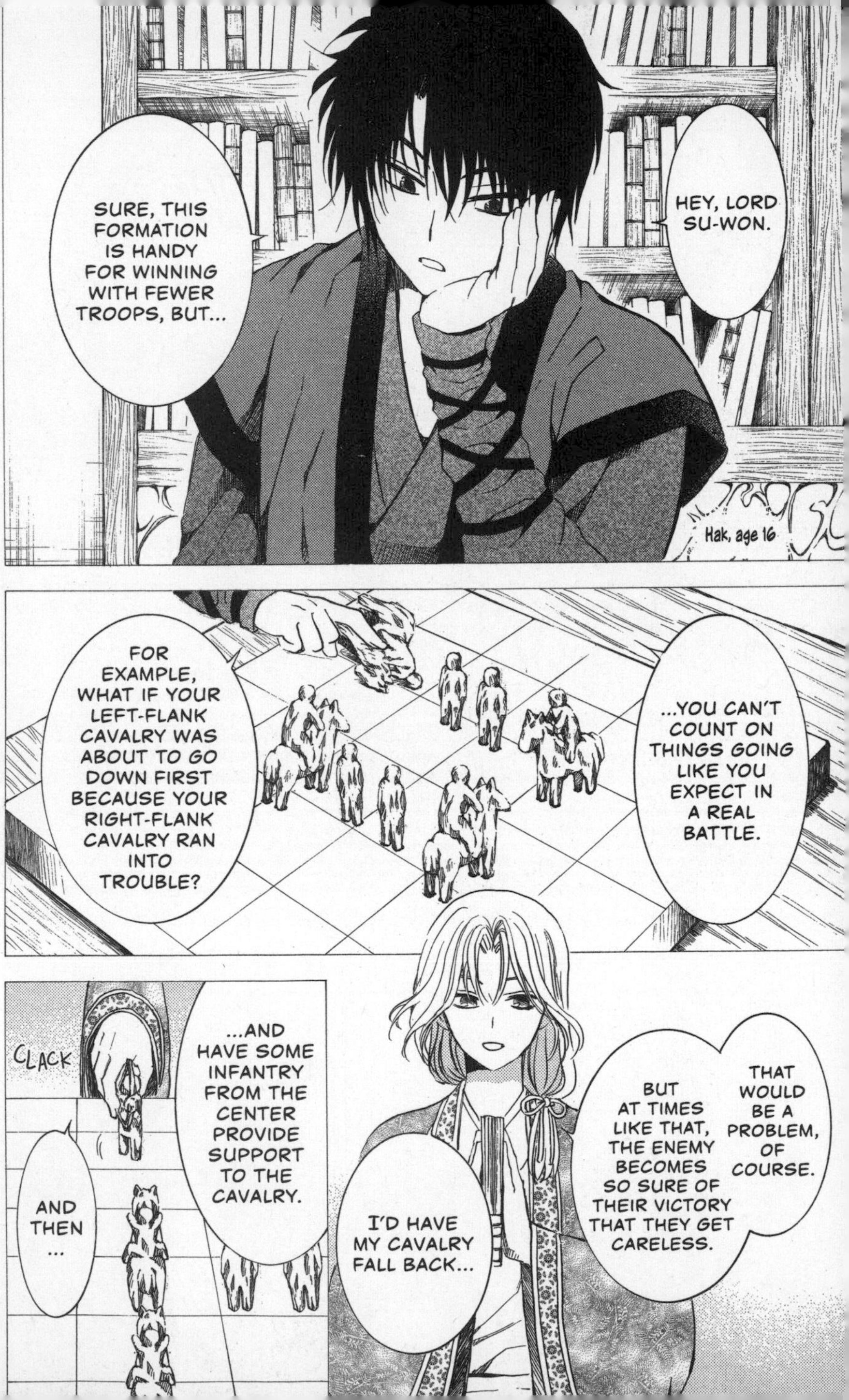
HEY, LORD SU-WON.
SURE, THIS FORMATION IS HANDY FOR WINNING WITH FEWER TROOPS, BUT...
Hak, age 16
...YOU CAN'T COUNT ON THINGS GOING LIKE YOU EXPECT IN A REAL BATTLE.
FOR EXAMPLE, WHAT IF YOUR LEFT-FLANK CAVALRY WAS ABOUT TO GO DOWN FIRST BECAUSE YOUR RIGHT-FLANK CAVALRY RAN INTO TROUBLE?
THAT WOULD BE A PROBLEM, OF COURSE.
BUT AT TIMES LIKE THAT, THE ENEMY BECOMES SO SURE OF THEIR VICTORY THAT THEY GET CARELESS.
I'D HAVE MY CAVALRY FALL BACK...
...AND HAVE SOME INFANTRY FROM THE CENTER PROVIDE SUPPORT TO THE CAVALRY.
CLACK
AND THEN ...

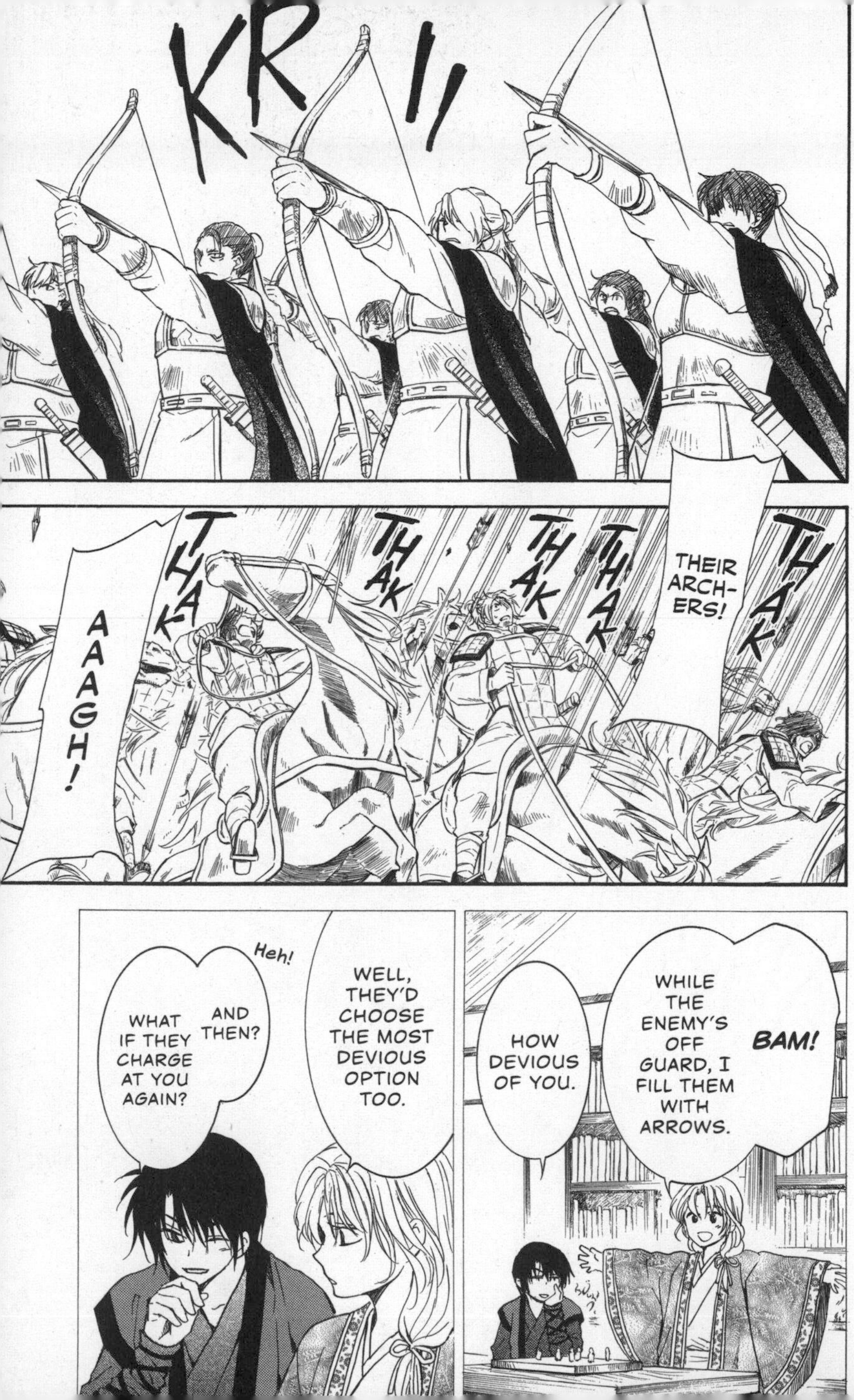
KR
THAK
THEIR ARCHERS!
THAK
THAK
THAK
THAK
AAAGH!
BAM!
WHILE THE ENEMY'S OFF GUARD, I FILL THEM WITH ARROWS.
HOW DEVIOUS OF YOU.
WELL, THEY'D CHOOSE THE MOST DEVIOUS OPTION TOO.
Heh!
AND THEN?
WHAT IF THEY CHARGE AT YOU AGAIN?

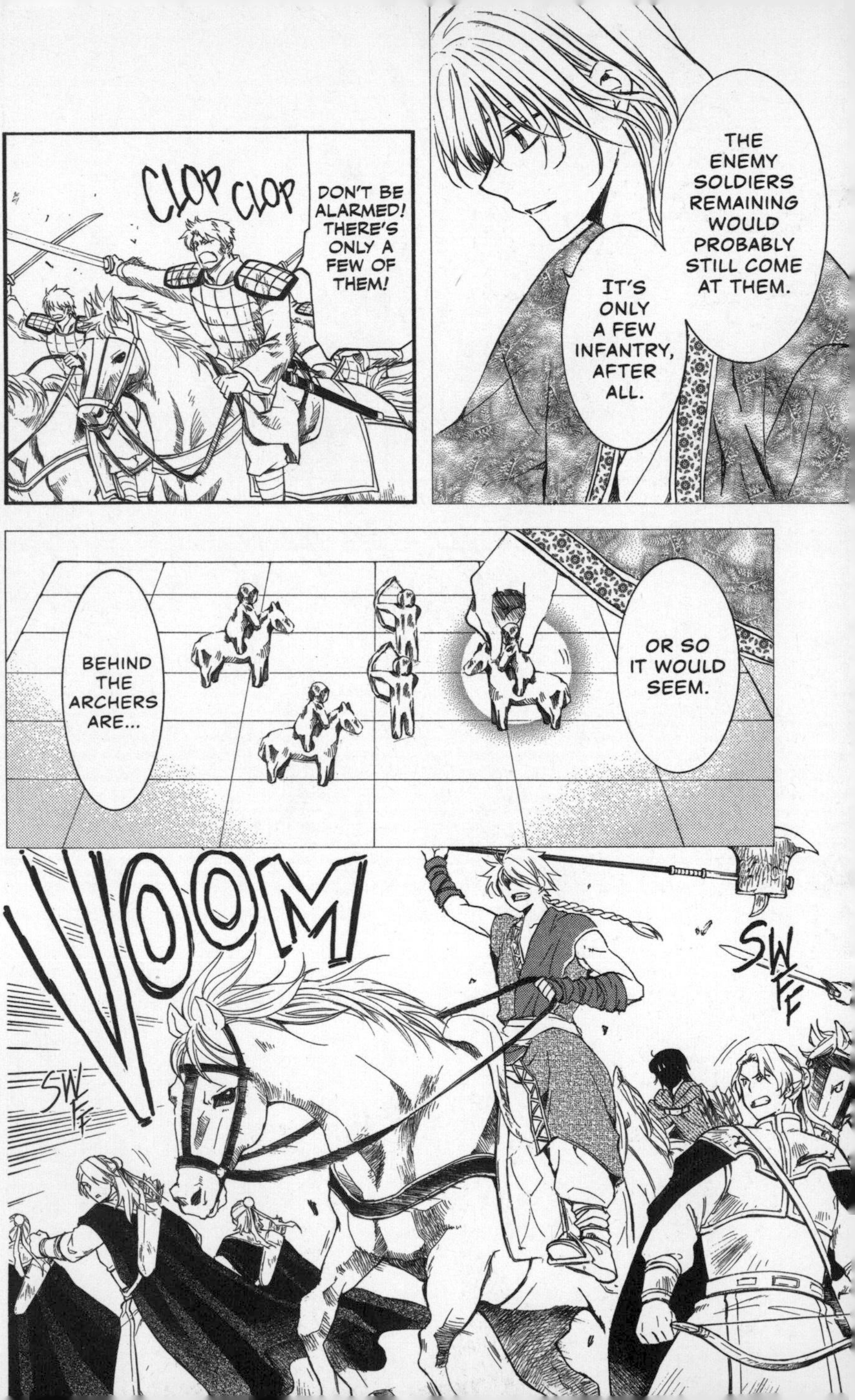
THE ENEMY SOLDIERS REMAINING WOULD PROBABLY STILL COME AT THEM.
IT'S ONLY A FEW INFANTRY, AFTER ALL.
CLOP CLOP
DON'T BE ALARMED! THERE'S ONLY A FEW OF THEM!
OR SO IT WOULD SEEM.
BEHIND THE ARCHERS ARE...
SWFF
VOOM
SWFF

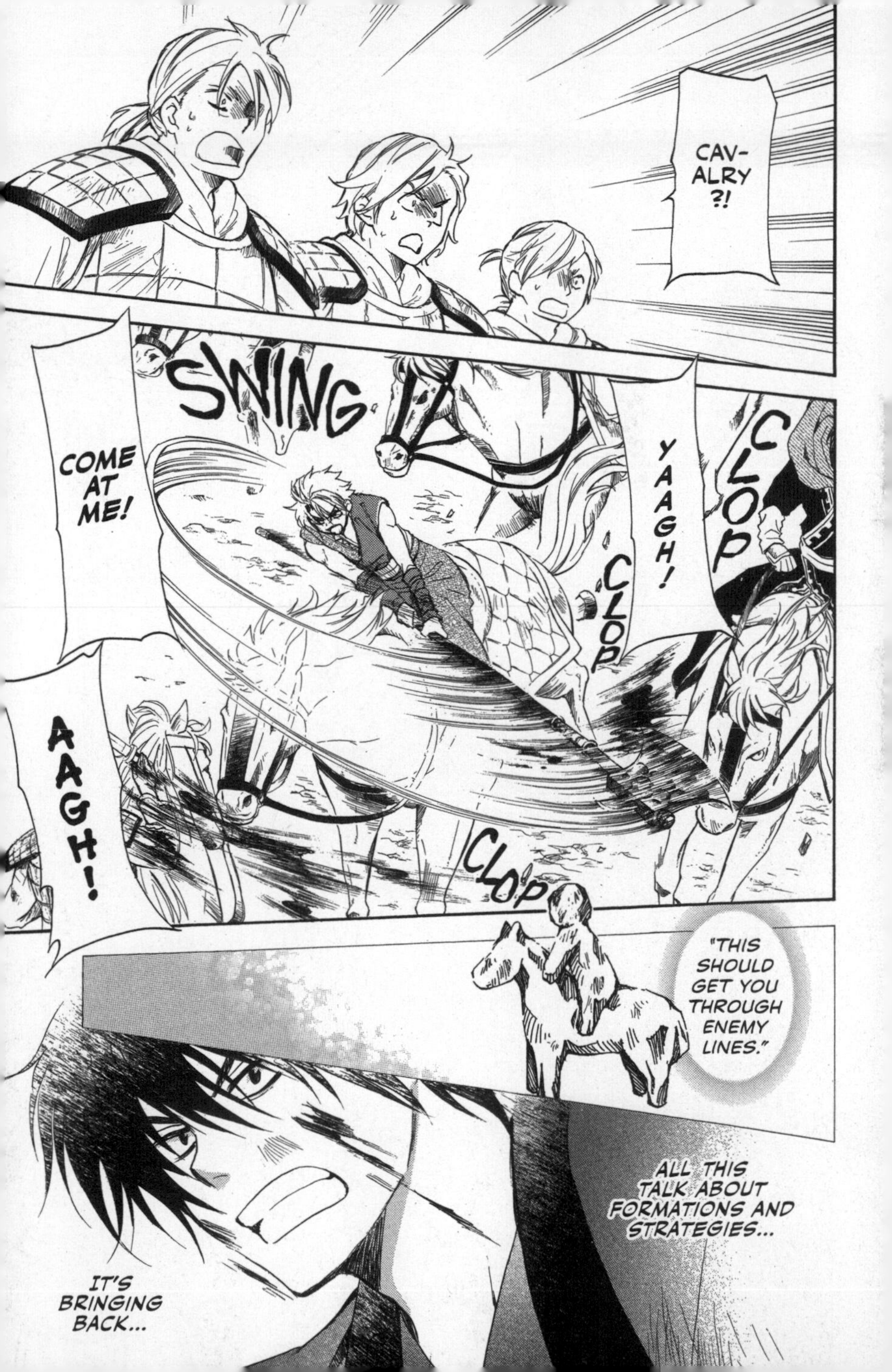
CAV-ALRY?!
CLOP CLOP
YAAGH!
CLOP CLOP
SWING
COME AT ME!
CLOP CLOP
AAGH!
"THIS SHOULD GET YOU THROUGH ENEMY LINES."
ALL THIS TALK ABOUT FORMATIONS AND STRATEGIES...
IT'S BRINGING BACK...

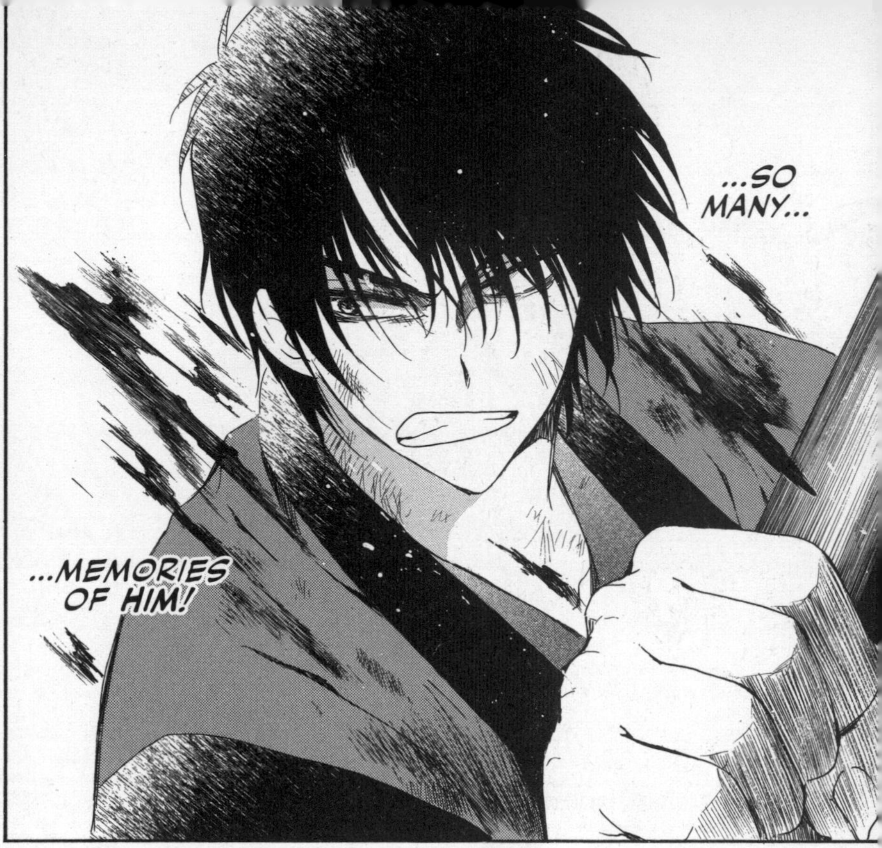
...SO MANY...
...MEMORIES OF HIM!

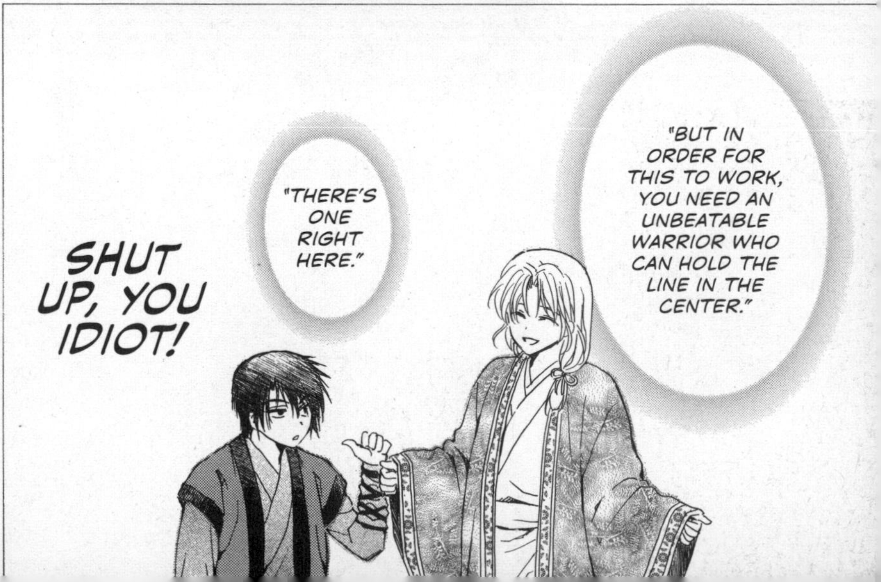
"BUT IN ORDER FOR THIS TO WORK, YOU NEED AN UNBEATABLE WARRIOR WHO CAN HOLD THE LINE IN THE CENTER."
"THERE'S ONE RIGHT HERE."
SHUT UP, YOU IDIOT!

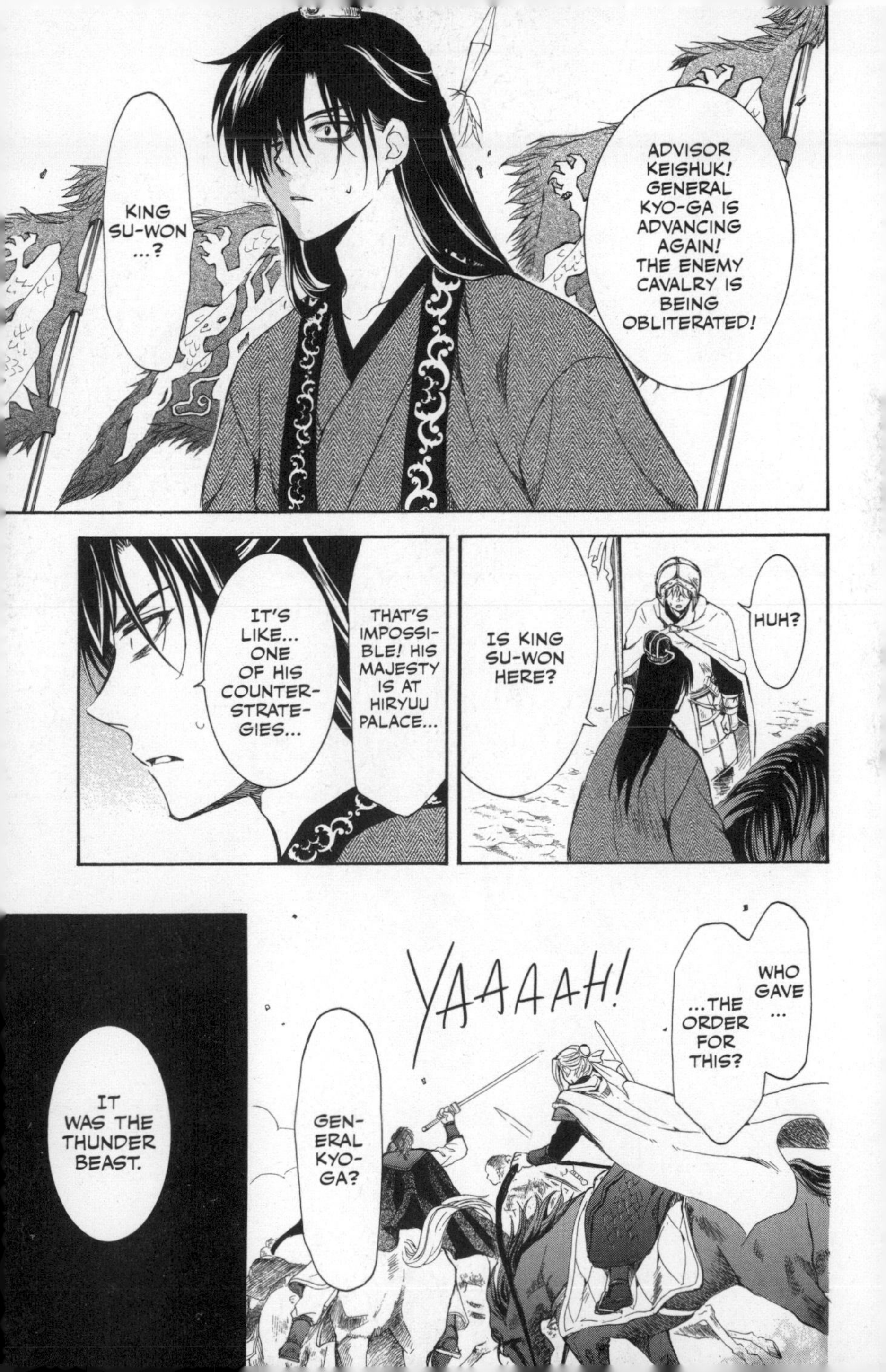
ADVISOR KEISHUK! GENERAL KYO-GA IS ADVANCING AGAIN! THE ENEMY CAVALRY IS BEING OBLITERATED!
KING SU-WON ...?
HUH?
IS KING SU-WON HERE?
THAT'S IMPOSSIBLE! HIS MAJESTY IS AT HIRYUU PALACE...
IT'S LIKE... ONE OF HIS COUNTER-STRATEGIES...
WHO GAVE ...
...THE ORDER FOR THIS?
YAAAAH!
GENERAL KYOGA?
IT WAS THE THUNDER BEAST.

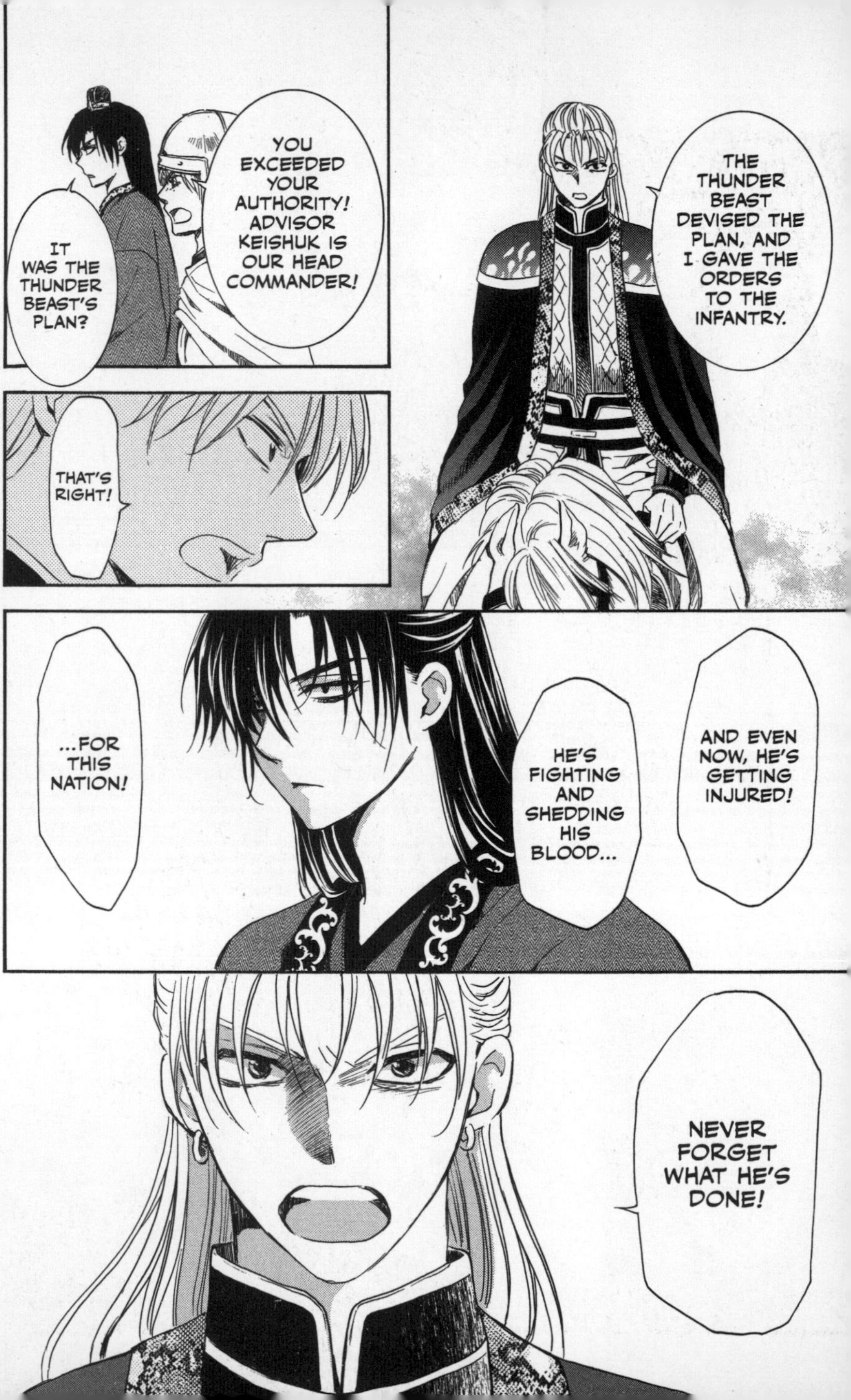
THE THUNDER BEAST DEVISED THE PLAN, AND I GAVE THE ORDERS TO THE INFANTRY.
YOU EXCEEDED YOUR AUTHORITY! ADVISOR KEISHUK IS OUR HEAD COMMANDER!
IT WAS THE THUNDER BEAST'S PLAN?
THAT'S RIGHT!
AND EVEN NOW, HE'S GETTING INJURED!
HE'S FIGHTING AND SHEDDING HIS BLOOD...
...FOR THIS NATION!
NEVER FORGET WHAT HE'S DONE!

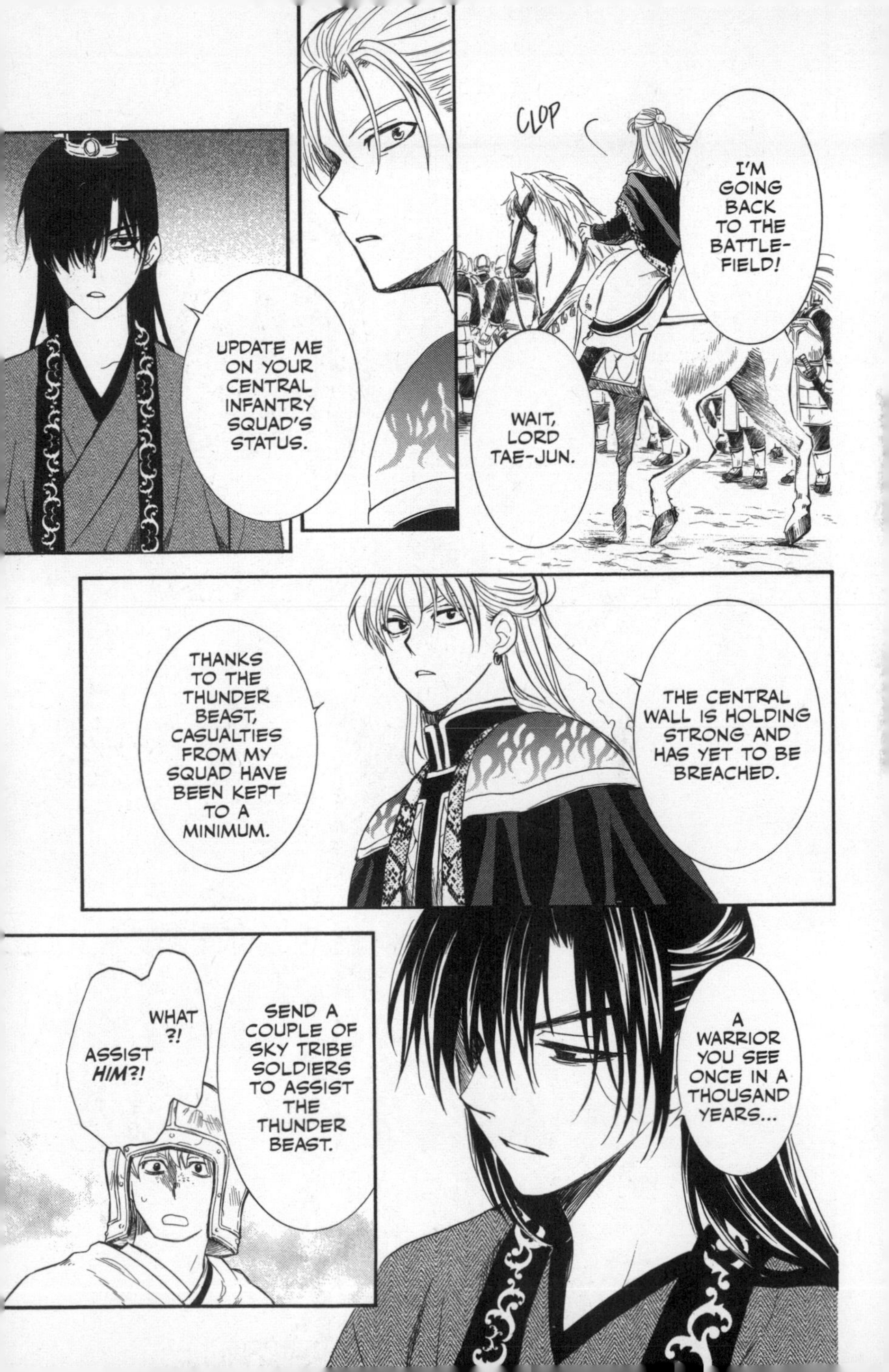
CLOP
I'M GOING BACK TO THE BATTLE-FIELD!
WAIT, LORD TAE-JUN.
UPDATE ME ON YOUR CENTRAL INFANTRY SQUAD'S STATUS.
THE CENTRAL WALL IS HOLDING STRONG AND HAS YET TO BE BREACHED.
THANKS TO THE THUNDER BEAST, CASUALTIES FROM MY SQUAD HAVE BEEN KEPT TO A MINIMUM.
A WARRIOR YOU SEE ONCE IN A THOUSAND YEARS...
SEND A COUPLE OF SKY TRIBE SOLDIERS TO ASSIST THE THUNDER BEAST.
WHAT?! ASSIST *HIM*?!

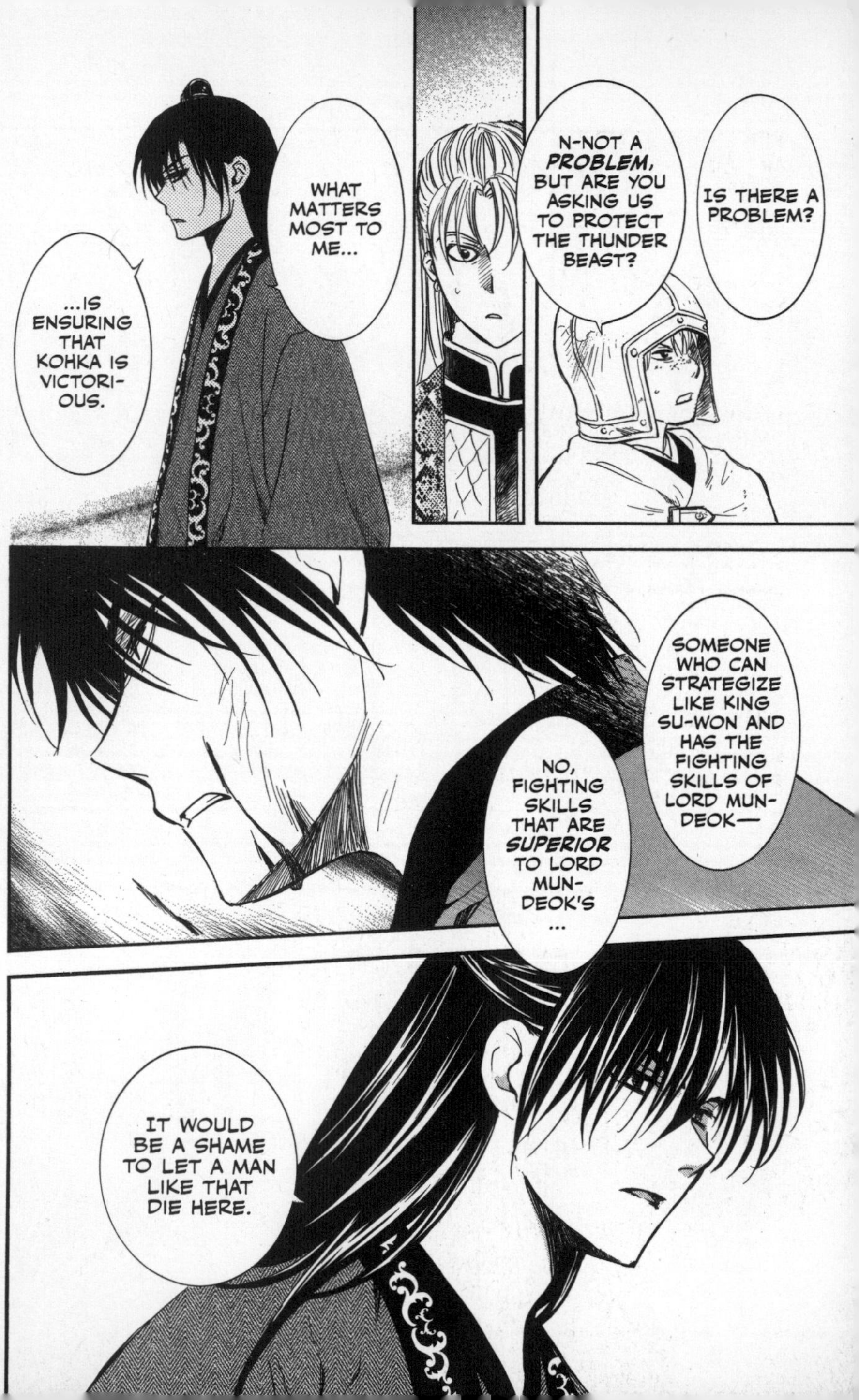
IS THERE A PROBLEM?
N-NOT A *PROBLEM*, BUT ARE YOU ASKING US TO PROTECT THE THUNDER BEAST?
WHAT MATTERS MOST TO ME...
...IS ENSURING THAT KOHKA IS VICTORI-OUS.
SOMEONE WHO CAN STRATEGIZE LIKE KING SU-WON AND HAS THE FIGHTING SKILLS OF LORD MUN-DEOK—
NO, FIGHTING SKILLS THAT ARE *SUPERIOR* TO LORD MUN-DEOK'S ...
IT WOULD BE A SHAME TO LET A MAN LIKE THAT DIE HERE.

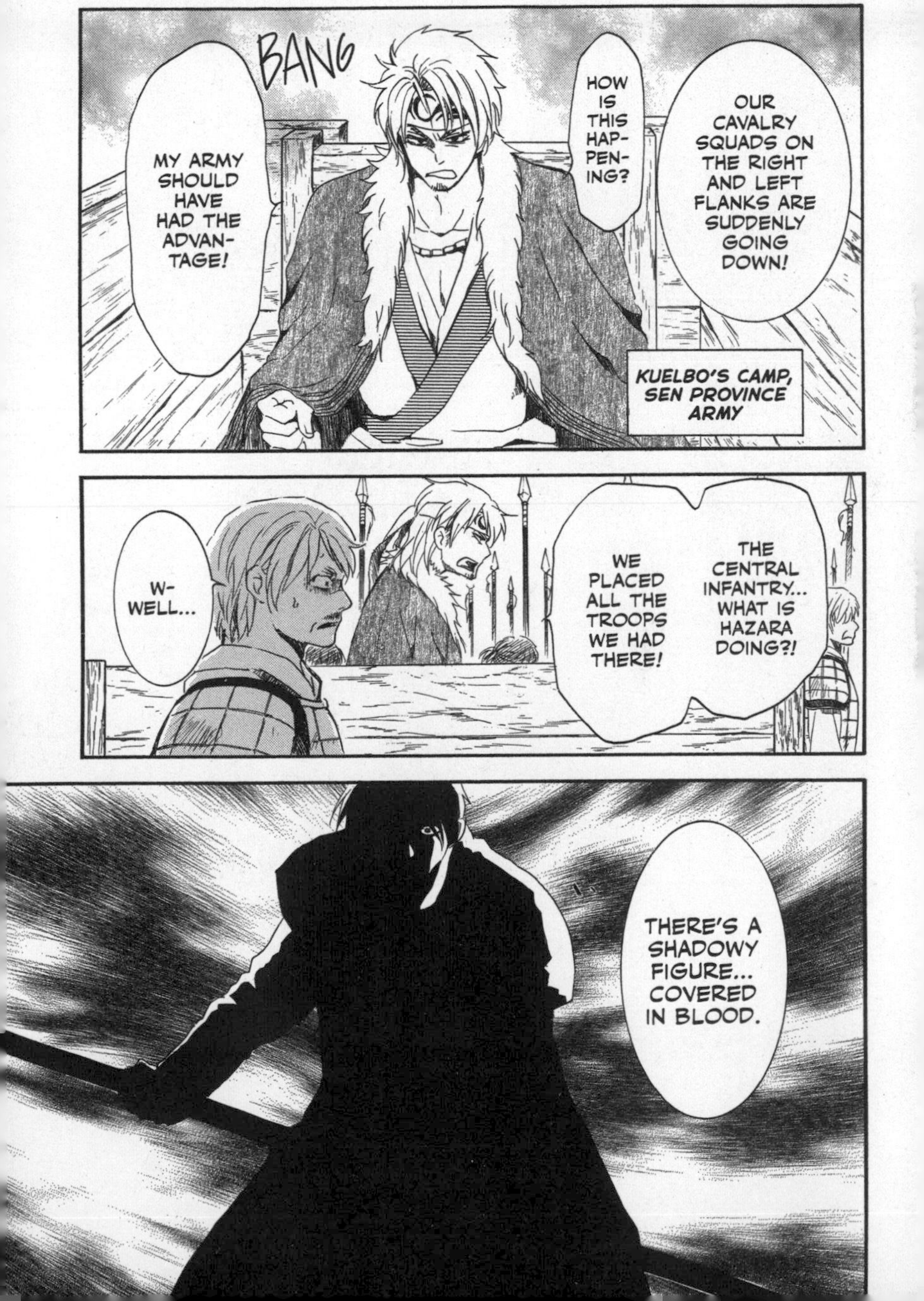
KUELBO'S CAMP, SEN PROVINCE ARMY
OUR CAVALRY SQUADS ON THE RIGHT AND LEFT FLANKS ARE SUDDENLY GOING DOWN!
HOW IS THIS HAP-PEN-ING?
BANG
MY ARMY SHOULD HAVE HAD THE ADVAN-TAGE!
THE CENTRAL INFANTRY... WHAT IS HAZARA DOING?!
WE PLACED ALL THE TROOPS WE HAD THERE!
W-WELL...
THERE'S A SHADOWY FIGURE... COVERED IN BLOOD.

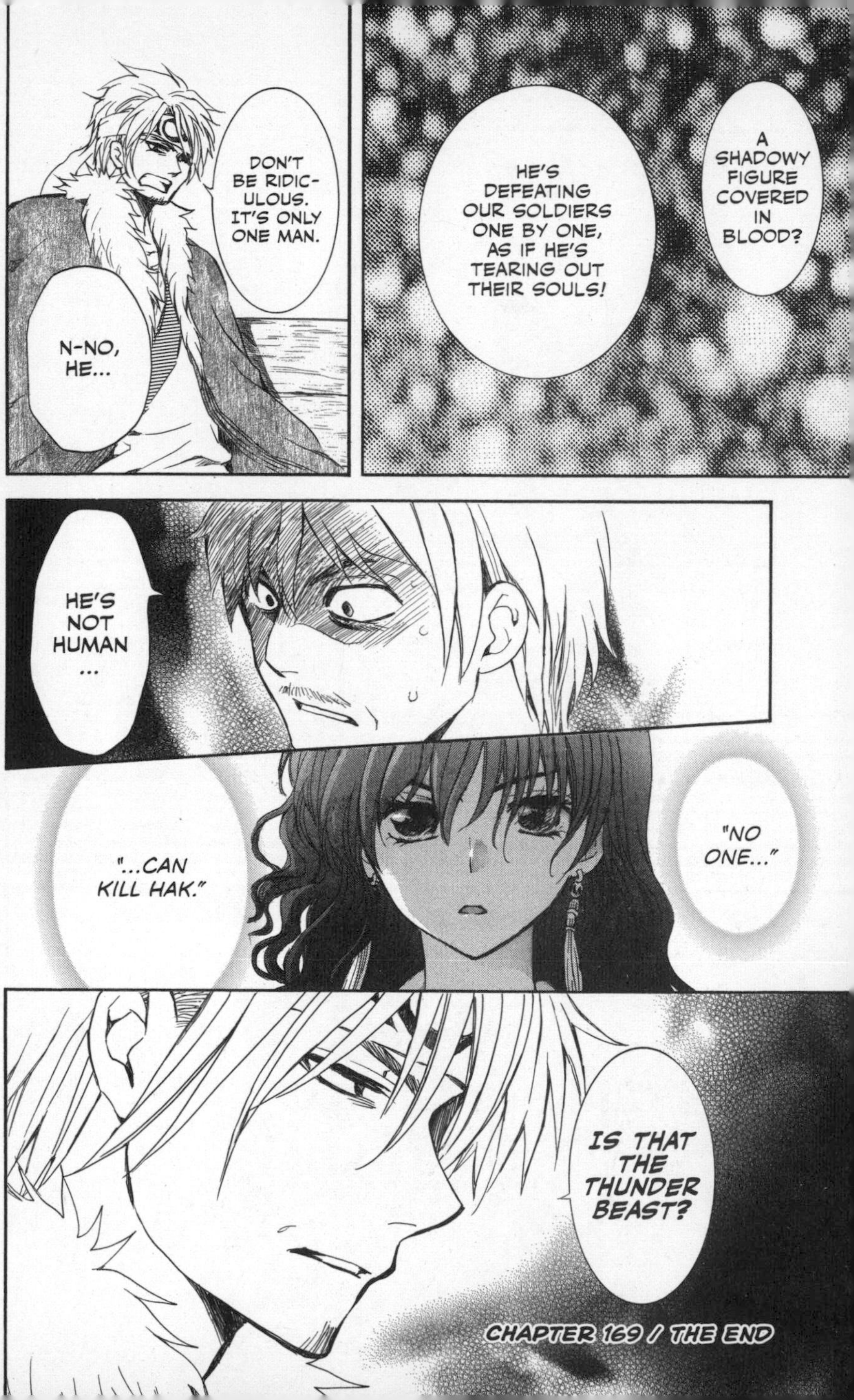
A SHADOWY FIGURE COVERED IN BLOOD?
HE'S DEFEATING OUR SOLDIERS ONE BY ONE, AS IF HE'S TEARING OUT THEIR SOULS!
DON'T BE RIDICULOUS. IT'S ONLY ONE MAN.
N-NO, HE...
HE'S NOT HUMAN ...
"NO ONE..."
"...CAN KILL HAK."
IS THAT THE THUNDER BEAST?
CHAPTER 169 / THE END

Afterword

The picture to the left was something I drew for the *Hana to Yume* Cover Art Request event. It was originally the front page of chapter 164, but we felt it would be confusing to open up the graphic novel and see this. I received many requests during the event. Thank you very much!

It wasn't a two-page spread, so it would have been difficult to draw requests with many characters. I chose one that only included a few characters but that many people would enjoy. The request was "Hak as a vampire and Yona as a nun." My head was full of comical ideas like Yona fighting Hak with a machine gun, or Yona choking Hak with a necklace of garlic. But I figured that wasn't what the person making the request had in mind, so I resisted the urge.

Now then! It's volume 29. The next volume is finally volume 30! That will likely conclude the Kai Empire, Sen Province arc. When I started this series, I never expected it to continue for this long.

To commemorate reaching 30 volumes, there's going to be a deluxe edition in Japan, so please check it out!

A Special Thanks!

My assistants → Mikorun, C.F., Ryo Sakura, Awafuji, Ryo, Eika and my little sister (Thank you for struggling along with me!)

My editor → Tokushige (Thank you for all your help!)

My previous editors and the *Hana to Yume* editorial office...

Everyone who's involved in creating and selling *Yona*-related merchandise...

My beloved family and friends who've always supported me.

And you, for reading this!

Thank you for allowing me to work on *Yona*!

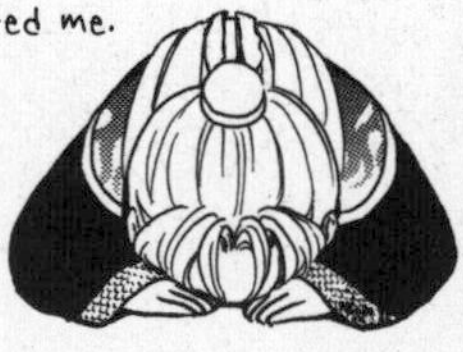

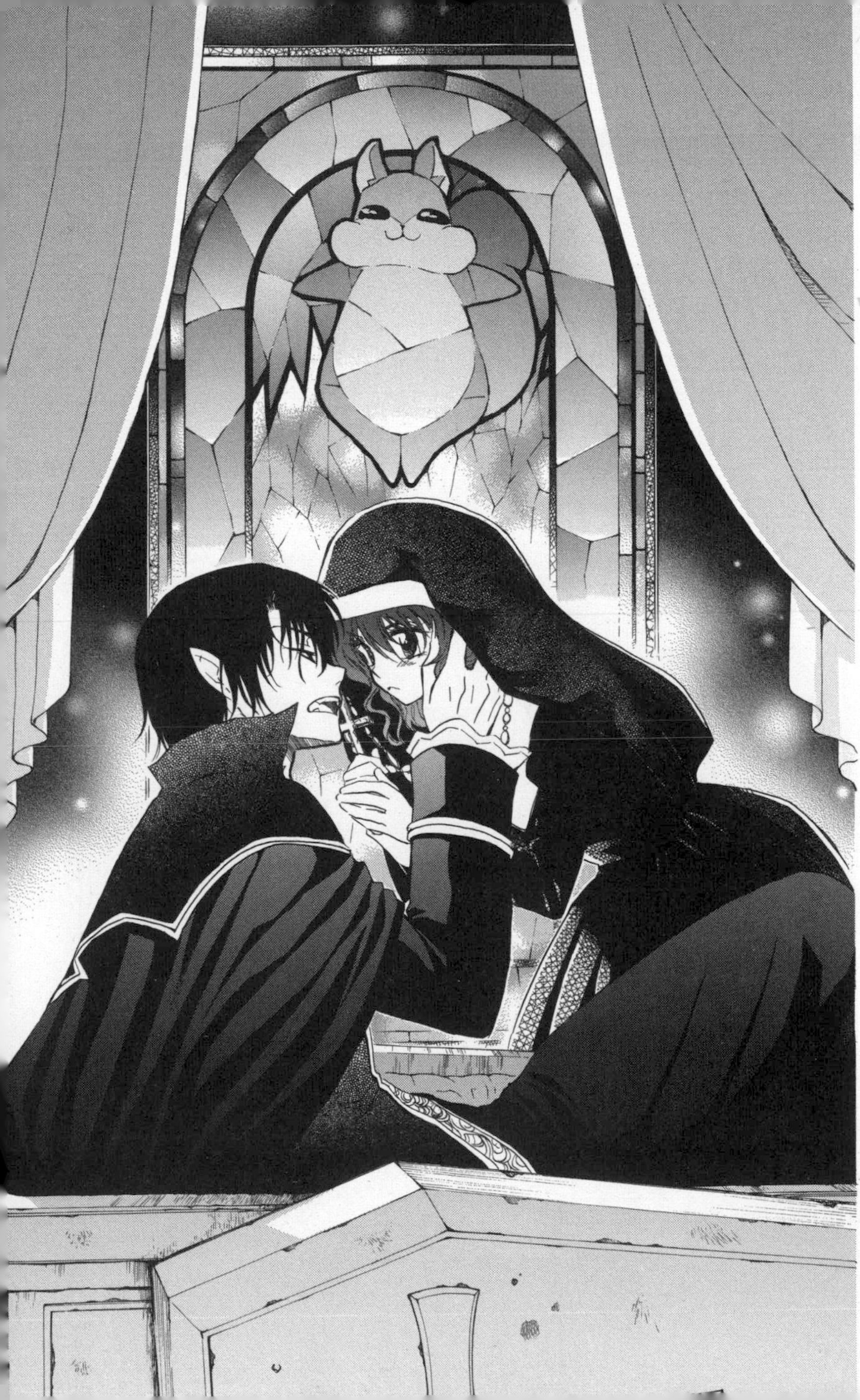

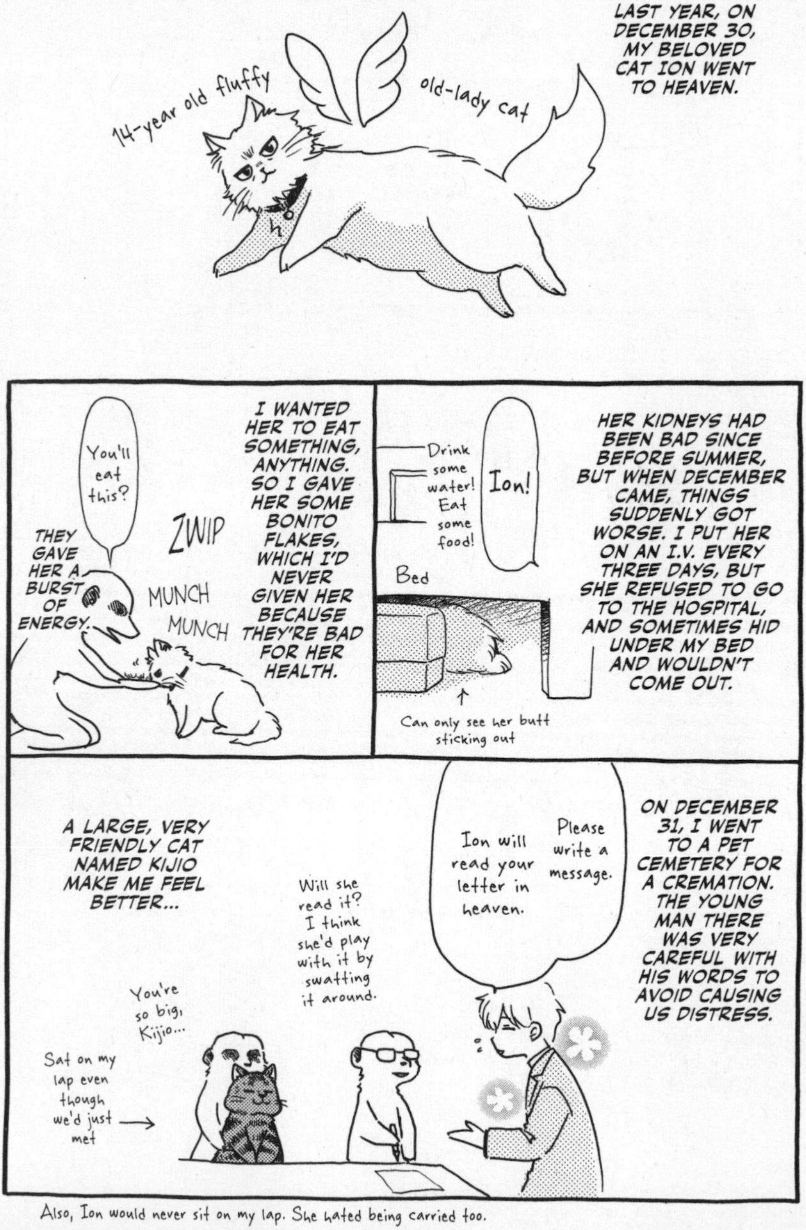
LAST YEAR, ON DECEMBER 30, MY BELOVED CAT ION WENT TO HEAVEN.
14-year old fluffy
old-lady cat
HER KIDNEYS HAD BEEN BAD SINCE BEFORE SUMMER, BUT WHEN DECEMBER CAME, THINGS SUDDENLY GOT WORSE. I PUT HER ON AN I.V. EVERY THREE DAYS, BUT SHE REFUSED TO GO TO THE HOSPITAL, AND SOMETIMES HID UNDER MY BED AND WOULDN'T COME OUT.
Ion!
Drink some water! Eat some food!
Bed
Can only see her butt sticking out
I WANTED HER TO EAT SOMETHING, ANYTHING. SO I GAVE HER SOME BONITO FLAKES, WHICH I'D NEVER GIVEN HER BECAUSE THEY'RE BAD FOR HER HEALTH.
You'll eat this?
ZWIP
THEY GAVE HER A BURST OF ENERGY.
MUNCH
MUNCH
ON DECEMBER 31, I WENT TO A PET CEMETERY FOR A CREMATION. THE YOUNG MAN THERE WAS VERY CAREFUL WITH HIS WORDS TO AVOID CAUSING US DISTRESS.
Please write a message.
Ion will read your letter in heaven.
Will she read it? I think she'd play with it by swatting it around.
A LARGE, VERY FRIENDLY CAT NAMED KIJIO MAKE ME FEEL BETTER...
You're so big, Kijio...
Sat on my lap even though we'd just met

Also, Ion would never sit on my lap. She hated being carried too.

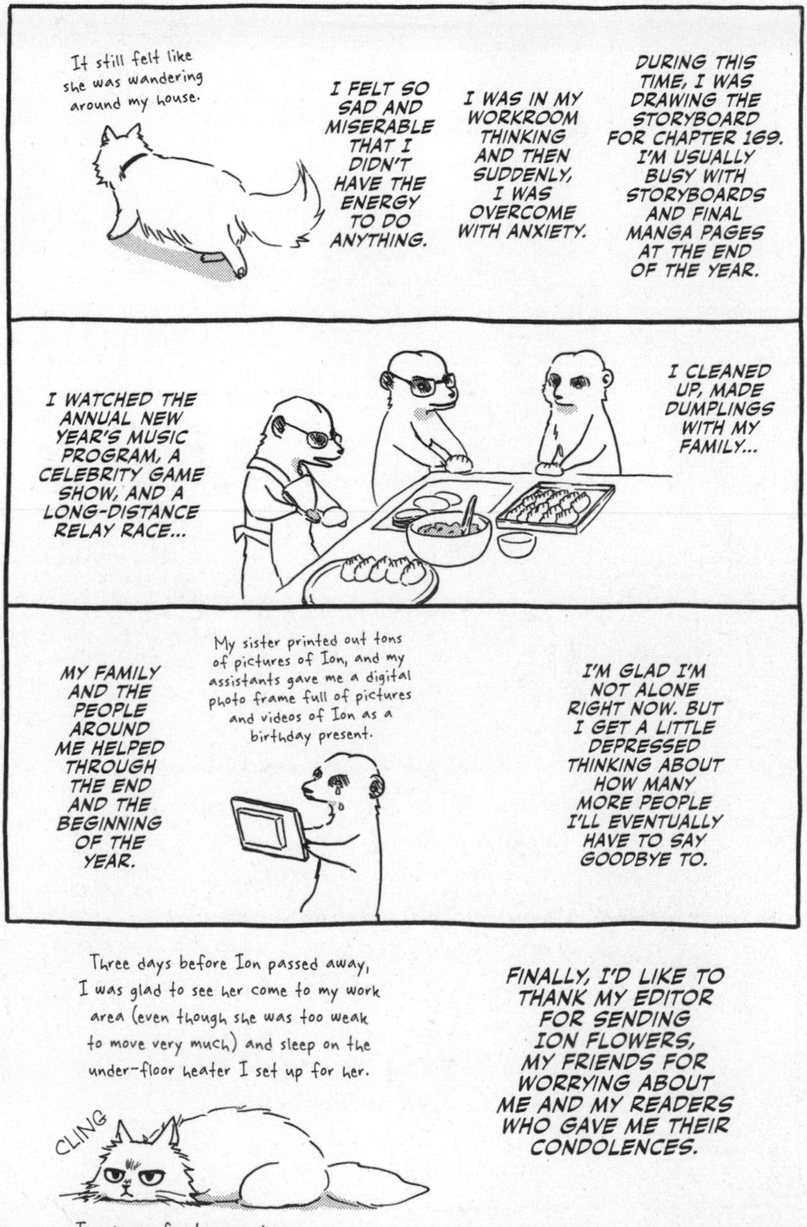
DURING THIS TIME, I WAS DRAWING THE STORYBOARD FOR CHAPTER 169. I'M USUALLY BUSY WITH STORYBOARDS AND FINAL MANGA PAGES AT THE END OF THE YEAR.
I WAS IN MY WORKROOM THINKING AND THEN SUDDENLY, I WAS OVERCOME WITH ANXIETY.
I FELT SO SAD AND MISERABLE THAT I DIDN'T HAVE THE ENERGY TO DO ANYTHING.
It still felt like she was wandering around my house.
I CLEANED UP, MADE DUMPLINGS WITH MY FAMILY...
I WATCHED THE ANNUAL NEW YEAR'S MUSIC PROGRAM, A CELEBRITY GAME SHOW, AND A LONG-DISTANCE RELAY RACE...
I'M GLAD I'M NOT ALONE RIGHT NOW. BUT I GET A LITTLE DEPRESSED THINKING ABOUT HOW MANY MORE PEOPLE I'LL EVENTUALLY HAVE TO SAY GOODBYE TO.
My sister printed out tons of pictures of Ion, and my assistants gave me a digital photo frame full of pictures and videos of Ion as a birthday present.
MY FAMILY AND THE PEOPLE AROUND ME HELPED THROUGH THE END AND THE BEGINNING OF THE YEAR.
FINALLY, I'D LIKE TO THANK MY EDITOR FOR SENDING ION FLOWERS, MY FRIENDS FOR WORRYING ABOUT ME AND MY READERS WHO GAVE ME THEIR CONDOLENCES.
Three days before Ion passed away, I was glad to see her come to my work area (even though she was too weak to move very much) and sleep on the under-floor heater I set up for her.
CLING
Thank you for the happiness you've given me.

Volume 29 is about Hak in battle, so Hak's on the cover. I was planning to draw him with Tae-jun of the Twilight, but it didn't turn out well...

—Mizuho Kusanagi

Born on February 3 in Kumamoto Prefecture in Japan, Mizuho Kusanagi began her professional manga career with *Yoiko no Kokoroe* (The Rules of a Good Child) in 2003. Her other works include *NG Life*, which was serialized in *Hana to Yume* and *The Hana to Yume* magazines and published by Hakusensha in Japan. *Yona of the Dawn* was adapted into an anime in 2014.

YONA OF THE DAWN
VOL.29
Shojo Beat Edition

STORY AND ART BY
MIZUHO KUSANAGI

English Adaptation/Ysabet Reinhardt MacFarlane
Translation/JN Productions
Touch-Up Art & Lettering/Lys Blakeslee
Design/Philana Chen
Editor/Amy Yu

Akatsuki no Yona by Mizuho Kusanagi
© Mizuho Kusanagi 2019
All rights reserved.
First published in Japan in 2019 by HAKUSENSHA, Inc., Tokyo.
English language translation rights arranged with
HAKUSENSHA, Inc., Tokyo.

Printed in the U.S.A.

Published by VIZ Media, LLC
P.O. Box 77010
San Francisco, CA 94107

10 9 8 7 6 5 4 3 2 1
First printing, April 2021

PARENTAL ADVISORY
YONA OF THE DAWN is rated T for Teen and is
recommended for ages 13 and up. This volume
contains violence and suggestive themes.

viz.com

shojobeat.com

This is the last page.

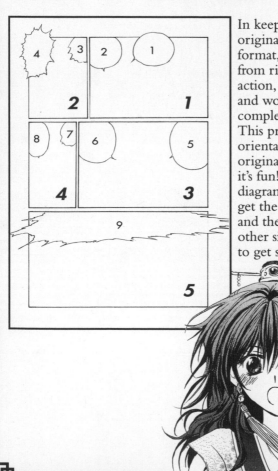

In keeping with the original Japanese comic format, this book reads from right to left—so action, sound effects, and word balloons are completely reversed. This preserves the orientation of the original artwork—plus, it's fun! Check out the diagram shown here to get the hang of things, and then turn to the other side of the book to get started!